W9-DFZ-313

TEACHING NEGOTIATION:
Ideas and Innovations

Michael Wheeler
Editor

PON Books

Program on Negotiation at Harvard Law School

PON Books

Program on Negotiation
at Harvard Law School
500 Pound Hall
Harvard Law School
Cambridge, MA 02138

© 2000 Program on Negotiation at Harvard Law School

All articles from *Negotiation Journal* reprinted with the permission of Plenum Press; "On Teaching Negotiation" Bruce M. Patton; "Using Simulations to Teach Negotiation: Pedagogical Theory and Practice" Lawrence E. Susskind and Jason Corburn reprinted by permission of the authors.

Library of Congress Card Number 00-101840

ISBN 1-880711-17-6

Teaching Negotiation: Ideas and Innovations

Teaching Negotiation

Michael Wheeler

Michael Wheeler is Professor of Management at the Harvard Business School, where he heads the required first-year negotiation course in the MBA program. He also teaches a second-year elective, Negotiating Complex Deals and Disputes, as well as various executive programs. His current research focuses on negotiation systems, that is, regimes to encourage, evaluate, and improve deal-making and dispute resolution on a recurring basis. He also continues to explore new techniques for teaching negotiation, including video and computer–supported materials.

Teaching negotiation is both easy and difficult.

The perils lie with the former. It's not hard for a teacher to win good ratings simply by stringing together some exercises and videos, with a few classic readings from psychology and game theory tossed in for a measure of gravitas. The drama of the cases is enticing: Can the parties snatch agreement from the jaws of impasse; will some unlikely hero end up with the lion's share? Add the pure fun of doing role plays and then of hearing in class tales of personal triumph and disaster, and students are bound to be happy.

The rewards of teaching negotiation, in turn, come from acknowledging its difficulty and being willing to fix something that may not seem broken. Do students really learn something profound or practical from our courses? Specifically, if the goal is to make them more sophisticated analysts, can we be sure that they are able to draw the right parallels and contrasts when they encounter new problems and contexts? Likewise, if we aim to make them more effective negotiators, do we really think that we can change their fundamental behavior?

The implicit answer to such questions is a resounding "yes," at least judging from the proliferation of negotiation courses in recent years. Colleges and universities in the Boston area alone currently list more than 150 courses in the field.[*] Some are general introductions to the topic. Others are specialized by academic discipline or by context—such as labor relations, diplomacy, and entrepreneurship. There are graduate school seminars taught to small groups and required courses taken by hundreds of students each year. And this count does not include university-based executive programs or training in corporations and public agencies. Nor does it reckon initiatives like Workable Peace or the Program for Young Negotiators that are finding their way into secondary schools and lower grades.

---

[*]These courses are identified in the *Dispute Resolution Directory*, published annually by the Program on Negotiation and available through its Clearinghouse.

Expand the domain beyond the Hub to the rest of the United States and beyond, and the number of negotiation-related courses must be measured in the thousands. The teachers who lead these courses have developed curriculums, written cases, and crafted negotiation exercises. In the process of refining their material, they doubtlessly have learned a great deal about the different ways in which negotiation theory and practice can be more effectively taught.

Unfortunately, relatively little of this hard-won learning about pedagogy has been documented. It exists (in unstable form) in the memories of instructors themselves and in teaching notes tucked away some place in their course files. Random bits of knowledge may be passed from colleague to colleague, particularly at institutions where negotiation centers have sprung up or where clearinghouses exist for the sharing of syllabi and materials. Academic and professional groups like the Academy of Management and the Association of American Law Schools also sponsor workshops on pedagogy for their various fields from time to time, though the knowledge shared at such conferences is seldom recorded for outsiders.

That is why the *Negotiation Journal* has always welcomed articles and notes on teaching negotiation. Since its inception in 1985 the *Journal* has typically published two or three pieces a year on pedagogy, each one making a contribution to the evolving state of the art. Many of these pieces have proven to have enduring value, but are available only to people who have easy access to libraries that have archived old issues.

The initial idea of assembling this volume was simply to give deserving material a new life with a wider readership. As it happens, the authors of some of pieces were willing to reanimate them in a real sense by adding commentary on how their ideas and techniques have evolved since their work was originally published. Then the collection from the *Journal* was leavened by the addition of a few selections from other Program on Negotiation publications. When the pieces came together, it became obvious that the value of the collection would be more than the sum of its considerable parts. Taken as a whole, it is testimony to the creativity and dedication negotiation teachers bring to their classrooms—and the obvious delight that they draw from them.

Identifying articles that would be useful to teachers in a wide variety of educational settings was easy. Organizing them was more difficult, as each was originally written to stand on its own. To the various authors' credit, many of the articles have a broad span. A piece may purport to describe a specific case or exercise, for example, but in so doing have much to say more generally about negotiation strategy and learning theory. As a result, it is possible to imagine rather different sequences than the one ultimately chosen here. Readers are encouraged to find their own path through the collection, being alert for useful nuggets hidden away in articles about teaching in domains that might superficially seem foreign to their own.

The book is divided into three sections, the first of which poses the question, "Can negotiation be taught?" This may seem like a disingenuous question, but it was not all that long ago that teachers of negotiation often had to justify the legitimacy of their courses to skeptical deans and curriculum committees. Bruce Patton's lead essay illustrates how a carefully reasoned response to such resistance actually helped illuminate what can be taught in the negotiation classroom. The articles that follow in this section present an array of perspectives that may be used to characterize a course generally and to inform specific class discussion.

The second section, on curriculum design, is led by an article by Roy Lewicki. While he focuses on how the teaching of negotiation has evolved in schools of business, many of the trends and innovations that he notes have echoes in other professional and academic domains. The other articles in this group variously describe curriculums in undergraduate programs, law schools, and institutions outside the United States.

The third section, on specific teaching tools and techniques, is introduced by Lawrence Susskind and Jason Corburn's article, originally published as a PON Working Paper, on the use of simulations. Other selections here variously describe teaching in large classes, advising small groups or even individuals, and using computer technology to support learning.

In the broadest sense, then, the three sections of the book reflect what we teach, who we teach, and how we do it. It is a happy accident that the authors of the articles that keynote the three sections are themselves from different fields. Bruce Patton teaches at a law school; Roy Lewicki at a business school; and Lawrence Susskind at a school of planning. Their insights about negotiation pedagogy, however, transcend academic and professional boundaries. Indeed, cross-disciplinary, cross-contextual work is a hallmark of this entire volume and of the Program on Negotiation itself. Looking ahead, we expect that this cross-fertilization will continue to enrich both the theory and pedagogy of the field. We hope, in particular, that this volume will stimulate other teachers to share their insights and innovations in future pages of the *Negotiation Journal* and in other venues.

We are grateful to the contributors to this collection, some of whom went back to the inkwell to refresh their original work with new perspectives. We are also grateful to several people whose names do not appear as authors but whose influence on this collection has been significant. They include Bill Breslin, editor of the *Negotiation Journal*, whose keen eye sharpened both the form and content of most of what is included here, and Teresa Hill, Director of Publications at the Program on Negotiation, who saw this project through from start to finish. Credit must also go to our late colleague, Jeffrey Rubin, one of the founders of the *Journal* and himself a master teacher. His ideas and example continue to inform our work. Finally, those of us affiliated with the Program on Negotiation have all been privileged to learn from Roger Fisher and Howard Raiffa. Their teaching, research, and practice continue to inspire us.

Cambridge, Massachusetts
January 2000

3

I. Can Negotiation Be Taught?

On Teaching Negotiation

Bruce M. Pattton

Bruce Patton is Deputy Director and co-founder of the Harvard Negotiation Project and Associate Director of the Program on Negotiation at Harvard Law School. From 1985-1999, he was Thaddeus R. Beal Lecturer on Law at Harvard Law School. Patton is also a Director of CMI/Vantage Partners, LLC, a consulting firm that helps organizations build the capacity to manage negotiations and strategic relationships to create value consistently and routinely. His most recent book with Douglas Stone and Sheila Heen is *Difficult Conversations: How to Discuss What Matters Most* (Viking/ Penguin, 1999). Patton's current work focuses on (1) how to create self-sustaining norms that help organi-

On Teaching Negotiation was originally published as a PON Working Paper in January, 1985.

Introduction: The Problem

Most problems with which lawyers deal are resolved through negotiation,[1] and that proportion should increase if the costs of litigation continue to rise. Yet formal training in negotiation has historically been rare and rudimentary, certainly lagging behind the quantity and quality of training offered in litigation skills.[2] The need for effective negotiation training is clear: Although research on how lawyers negotiate has been limited,[3] there is strong evidence to suggest that even respected members of the profession vary enormously in their negotiating proficiency—enough to raise questions about the adequacy of representation being offered.[4] Prominent members of the bar have expressed concern about lawyer competency in basic lawyering skills, including negotiation, and such concerns are reflected in recent proposals to test negotiation and other skills in bar examinations.[5] Law schools and continuing legal education programs need to develop and offer systematic training in the theory and practice of negotiation.

There are a number of obstacles to developing the field of negotiation and effective negotiation training. To begin with, some people still feel that negotiation is an art that cannot be systematically analyzed or taught. Others feel such training is inappropriate in the "academic" law school setting. Aside from these political obstacles, there is a lack of the kind of tested prescriptive theory needed for the most effective and efficient training; neither of the available models—"positional bargaining" or "principled negotiation"—is wholly adequate.

Negotiation training is also challenging because it involves changing people's behavior, not just giving them information. Habits are harder to develop (or change) than facts are to memorize, even with help. Further, the best way to help someone change their behavior is to set a good example, but practicing what you preach is never easy. Effective teachers must monitor their own behavior as well as students'. Finally, to

zations internalize dealing competently with negotiation and conflict (whether with customers, suppliers, or colleagues, in the boardroom or across the matrix), and (2) how to use effective difficult conversation skills to ensure successful implementation of vital initiatives such as strategic planning, TQM, becoming a learning organization, outsourcing, coopetition, alliances, mergers, joint ventures, and so on. He can be reached at tel: 617.495.1617 or tel: 617.354.6090.

make negotiation training widely available, classes need to be large. Unfortunately, large classes encourage fear, distancing, and clique-formation, making it harder to create a supportive atmosphere conducive to self-examination. We need practical ways to overcome these tendencies.

The purpose of this paper is to analyze these obstacles and suggest how they might be overcome in teaching negotiation to law students, although the analysis may apply more broadly. In general, the focus is on the general pedagogical themes of effective teaching rather than the details of syllabus design, although specific approaches are used for illustration and discussed where appropriate. Substantively, while the author is an advocate of "principled negotiation" as developed in *Getting to YES*[6] and elsewhere,[7] this pedagogical analysis is not limited to that theoretical system, except in the section which is explicitly devoted to techniques for teaching principled negotiation.

Ideological and Intellectual Barriers
"It can't be taught"

This appears to be a not uncommon sentiment, even among experienced attorneys, business people, diplomats, and academics. John Dunlop, a consummate academic-practitioner, once concurred, arguing that there was no articulated theory of negotiation, hence no way to learn except by experience.[8] Others argue that negotiation is just "common sense," and you either have it or you don't. Neither argument is borne out by the experience of those who have tried to teach negotiation, nor that of those who teach other skills, such as litigation or writing. Edwards and White, for example, have no trouble listing five useful things their students pick up.[9] Some people may have more innate talent, but everyone can benefit from practice and reflection. Negotiation courses can provide a concentrated input of experience in a context conducive to reflection, analysis, experimentation, and practice. Certainly most graduates of negotiation courses believe their course experiences have had a substantial impact on their skills and confidence;[10] the latter perception can be self-fulfilling.

More concrete evidence for the efficacy of negotiation training comes from Israel Unterman of San Diego

8

State University Business School. He arranges near the end of his negotiation course to have his students negotiate with local business people. According to Professor Unterman, the students' results for whichever side they represent are, in the aggregate, significantly better than those of the experienced business people who represented that side.[11] While Professor Unterman's experiment should be replicated elsewhere and with lawyers, I think his results will not be surprising to negotiation teachers and will not prove anomalous. After all, mastery of most skills depends as much on critical analysis and review as on practice—both are necessary, neither alone is sufficient.

Why do sensible people argue that negotiation cannot be taught? I can think of two possibilities. First, some people may feel threatened. A successful training program must have standards of competence with which to judge its graduates and some systematic theory about the process being taught. Not knowing how they would measure up to such standards, and perhaps doubting the organization of their own decision-making processes, insecure people might well feel uneasy with the concept that training was possible and might make others "better" negotiators than them.

Other people, like John Dunlop, may simply be unfamiliar with how useful prescriptive theory can be extracted from their accumulated experience. Most good practitioners are quite predictably systematic in action, but they may not be consciously aware of their system.[12] Careful observers can articulate the operating principles of such a system for explicit consideration, testing, and training of others. Some people may think that there can be no theory of negotiation because there are no single "right" answers to indeterminate questions such as, "Who should make the first offer?" But rigorous analysis of experience can illuminate a range of factors to weigh in thinking about such questions. These factors can be taught, and considering them results in an increased probability of successful decision-making.

"Skills courses are inappropriate for a scholarly institution"
There has long been a scholarly prejudice against "practical" or "skills" courses allegedly appropriate only for "trade schools," but the basis of the prejudice is illusive. It is argued, for ex-

Reflections

In returning to this paper after 15 years, it is interesting to note both how much has changed, and what has not. I was a little surprised to find how much I still agree with what is here. Time, experience, and growth in the field have added to our understanding and repertoire of what to do and made some choices more complex, but basic principles endure. So this comment aims mostly at supplementing and updating the original paper.

Substantive Negotiation Theory

Dealing with a growing body of material. One change in the field, recently accelerating, is the growth in academic knowledge and study of negotiation. This is mostly in the form of empirical correlations and descriptive typologies; there has been relatively less work on the prescriptive side.[1] With more

9

stuff in the literature to "know" about negotiation, teachers face more of a choice in course design between focusing on knowledge transfer or skill building, and/or in what order. No single course can do both as thoroughly as in the past.

I would argue for a balance, but with the initial focus weighted toward skill building and learning by doing. The reasons are as stated in the paper: knowledge is most deeply and usefully understood in the context of doing, so learning "about" negotiation will be better appreciated by a more experienced and sophisticated negotiator. Also, someone with a frame of experience will be better able to consider the prescriptive implications of largely descriptive information. While this ordering may run counter to the natural inclination of teachers who are more comfort-

ample, that such courses teach only basic skills, while traditional courses teach substantive knowledge and theory.[13] Yet almost every law professor will cite teaching students "to think like a lawyer" as a major purpose of the "substantive" first year curriculum. Indeed, the traditional curriculum incorporates writing assignments to develop skills of clear exposition, oral assignments to develop skills of advocacy, and in all respects puts a premium on skills of logical analysis, syllogistic reasoning, precision, issue-spotting, and moving from particular facts to general propositions and back flexibly and creatively. Not only are these all skills, they are all vital to a good negotiator and should be central to any negotiation training.

Alternately, it is sometimes argued that "skills" courses merely provide practice in particular lawyering tasks that can be learned (perhaps better) on the job after graduation. This confuses "can" with "should." In the eighteenth century all legal training was on the job. The justification for law schools is that systematic analysis, organization, and presentation of "the law" is a more efficient and reliable way to train lawyers. Beyond that, there has developed a sense that a broader perspective on the profession is desirable and should be pursued through legal scholarship. Thus we have the academic discipline as well as the profession of law. There is certainly no inherent reason why such an important lawyer's skill as negotiation should not be studied and taught as systematically as contracts and the adjudication process.

There is a third charge, however: that negotiation training (and other skills courses) are without serious intellectual content. Though on its face this assertion is puzzling, since any field dealing with human decision-making is bound to be more complex than one focused on a formalistic system of rules,[14] nevertheless it begins to explain the prejudice: Negotiation may be seen as so complex and so little understood in rigorous fashion as to make impossible any course of intellectual rigor commensurate with traditional courses. Also, negotiation focuses on the human dimension in lawyering, on the confusing and "irrational" instead of the clean and logical. Psychology is traditionally not the forte of most law professors. Perhaps the human dimension should be more a part of the traditional curriculum as well ("critical" legal scholars would certainly say so), but there the lack is less central.[15]

10

In fact, a fair amount is known about how people, including lawyers, think about and act in negotiations, and how they are likely to respond to particular approaches. Stages of negotiation have been observed, and tactics catalogued. Case studies are available.[16] More broadly, the field of psychology may be less advanced than that of physics, but much is known. We are a long way from the pioneering courses of Robert Mathews that consisted exclusively of exercises negotiated by students in front of the class and discussion of those negotiations.[17] Much information remains ungathered, but at least the roots of a discipline of negotiation exist now.

Yet either because there is so much more to learn or because negotiation seems such an active topic, a purely *descriptive* approach to teaching negotiation (akin, for example, to the teaching of property) seems inadequate.[18] Certainly practitioners are more interested in *prescriptive* theory—guidelines that relate their actions with desired outcomes. It is more useful. Any tendency to prescription, however, reinforces suspicions of inadequate rigor: It is much harder to document causal hypotheses than facts. Most social science research is descriptive for just this reason (looking, for example, to determine when people are most likely to make the first offer, as opposed to developing a hypothesis about when a negotiator *should* make the first offer, and when not). It is assumed that eventually the incremental collection of valid information will lead to causal understanding, but that speculation before then would be unscientific.

There are two potential problems with this assumption. First, describing a system may not be the best way to produce prescriptive theory about operating in that system, and second, it may not produce any prescriptive theory at all, no matter how long you work at it. If human nature is changing over time, then no conclusions will be possible from our collected observations, because they will not be descriptions of the same thing. Even if human nature is basically unchanging, it is still complex. We can never be sure that our passive observation will encompass the full range of possible behaviors, nor will it be easy to support any conclusions about how to bring about particular patterns of behavior. For that, experimental evidence is needed.

The goals of description and prescription also create different incentives. If your goal is description, the incentive is

able with the traditional knowledge transfer model, that tension is not new.

Including affect. My original paper does not focus much on the role of feelings in negotiation, although the role of relationship is certainly noted. Yet clearly feelings play an important part in real-world negotiation decision making and in building or harming relationships. To the extent it is important and useful for a negotiator to be able to get in synch with (or at least recognize and understand) the communication and thinking styles of their counterpart, then the realm of affect is important to know. While many people prefer to interact in the realm of meaning, others prefer affect, just as others orient to the perspective of power. Sensitivity to such differences can avoid much misunderstanding. Even for those primarily focused

11

on meaning, feelings can play an important role, if they interpret proposals or arguments as hostile or unfair. Social psychological and communications theory is now more accessible to negotiation teachers, and deserves some attention.

Learning and Learning Facilitation Theory

Generalization takes practice. Recent work by Leigh Thompson and others suggests that people need practice in drawing process lessons from negotiation experience and applying such lessons in a different substantive context. Asking students explicitly to reflect on what general guidelines might be drawn from an exercise and how they might be applied in specific alternative contexts helps make this more of a habit.[2] Experience in the Negotiation Workshop at Harvard Law School likewise

to focus attention on the most enduring and stable characteristics of the human system you are describing. ("More powerful negotiators tend to get better deals.") In contrast, if your goal is to develop prescriptive hypotheses about how to control change in a system, the incentive is to concentrate on the effects of perturbing the most manipulable characteristics of the system. ("Taking a negotiator's material resources as fixed, that negotiator can still increase the chances of a favorable outcome by emphasizing legitimacy, demonstrating trustworthiness, preparing with great care, ...") The goal of describing tends to produce deterministic-sounding explanations; individual actors are constrained to operate on the assumption of free will.

Finally, the goal of description is too easily satisfied: the product need only be "true". ("Women live longer than men.") Prescriptive theory is judged by a sterner standard—it must be useful. ("To increase your life expectancy by seven years, don't smoke.") Indeed, some propositions may be useful that are known to be false or only partially true. Many rules of thumb are in that category. The subway map is an example of a helpful distortion; if it were more accurate, it would be less understandable. Description is easier and less risky, and it fits with the academic preference for originality over synthesis, but in the real world not all truths are equally useful or interesting.

If the prejudice against "skills" courses is rooted in a fear of sloppy reasoning and irrational prejudice, it fails to distinguish between slick, Aristotelian platitudes and a serious effort to produce dis-confirmable hypotheses which may yet take further time and testing to achieve wide acceptance. In a world of scarce intellectual resources with mounting social and political tension, it is imperative that the social ethic of academe not only tolerate but encourage efforts to improve our ability to deal with our problems. There is a balance to be struck between objectivity and social responsibility, but it is a balance. With careful attention to the presentation of evidence, the avoidance of intolerant bias, and encouragement of independent critical assessment, courses that encompass prescriptive inquiry as well as descriptive presentation should, at the least, be richer.

Imperfect Theory
Assuming that teaching negotiation in a rigorous academic

setting is desirable, there is next the question of content. The field of negotiation is far from a clean slate theoretically, but the available material is neither consistent, fully developed, or of uniform quality or usefulness. Commercial courses have largely been limited to vast menus of poorly developed rules and anecdotal material. Few have a serious practice component.[19] On the other hand, most academic work done to date has been in the realm of game theory. Much of this work is fascinating, but its implications for practice are not at all obvious.[20] The problem is that game theoreticians take as fixed precisely those variables that in the real world are the most complex, hard to predict or understand, and perhaps most significantly manipulable.

A variety of relevant psychological work also exists, but those studies tend to suffer from the caveat that propositions about human behavior drawn from carefully controlled studies are likely to apply only in situations where conditions are carefully controlled.[21] Anecdotal case material is available, but without some analytic framework its value for training is greatly reduced. Likewise, some descriptive empirical work has been done,[22] but its implications for practice are also limited (unless you take an imitative approach). Almost no effort has been made to test prescriptive hypotheses systematically in a realistic setting, not least because the research techniques needed are not fully developed.

What prescriptive theory does exist can be seen as comprising two competing and often inconsistent models, both of which are flawed. Undoubtedly there is valid information in both awaiting theoretical synthesis. The traditional model can be called positional bargaining. It views negotiation as essentially a process of manipulation focused on getting the best possible deal from the other side.[23] Issues can be divided between distributive, zero-sum issues and integrative issues where joint gains and mutually beneficial trade-offs are possible and desirable. Bargaining involves taking and justifying concrete positions and resisting concessions. The available theory focuses on choosing initial positions, on concession-making strategies, and on the desirability and techniques of "strategic misrepresentation."

suggests the importance of sharing and reviewing the logical quality of those generalizations and applications. With practice, people get better at recognizing untested assumptions and alternative explanations and holding them as hypotheses, greatly increasing the quality of their theory-building and learning.

Practice components skills as well as "putting it all together." Professor Chris Argyris of the Harvard Business and Education Schools advised the Negotiation Workshop teaching team to specify as exactly as possible what we would want participants to say or do under given conditions, and then to have them practice exactly those responses. This facilitated a very helpful advance in our work.

At the time, exercises in the Workshop were almost all full-scale negotiations. We had gone through a phase where many of these exercises were tailored to the "point of the day," such as being creative about options or soliciting interests. However, this encouraged participants to focus on "guessing the trick," rather than analyzing each context on its merits, so we moved to using more robust exercises, while giving extra focus in review to themes of current interest.

The problem was our lack of confidence in participants' awareness of and ability to reflect on their performance. Observation and video review are helpful, yet hard to offer more than periodically. Fishbowl "laboratories" can be quite helpful in clarifying exactly what various approaches might look like in practice and where they might lead, but still do not bridge the gap between recognition of the behavior in others and ability to produce it yourself.

Positional bargaining is the model most people seem to associate with negotiation, often with distaste. It is the model of the bazaar, the classic association of the word "negotiation," despite the more familiar and less adversarial ways each of us negotiates every day. In some cases positional bargaining does produce efficient transactions, and sometimes wise results.[24] Trading on the floor of the stock market is the best example of an activity where pure positional bargaining is effective and useful. In other cases, however, positional bargaining can produce disastrous results, and it seldom describes accurately what people actually do in negotiation. For example, as in traditional economics, positional theories assume that people are aiming to maximize their tangible rewards. There is considerable evidence, however, that most people most of the time are more interested in satisficing—in not getting taken or, where it is possible to tell, in not doing noticeably worse than others.[25]

The most serious flaw of the positional model is that it ignores the potential effects of the process itself on the options invented, considered, and chosen by the parties, on how those options are valued by the parties, and on the parties relationship. An emphasis on positions and maximization promotes stubbornness, ill will, and distrust, and discourages creative inventing or the communication of interests needed for inventing Pareto-efficient options. The model tends to ignore the interest people may have in appearing legitimate and in establishing or maintaining a good relationship with the people on the other side. Either of these interests can turn any seemingly distributive situation into an integrative one. In fact, in many negotiations the parties' relationship is far more important than the substantive outcome, as in most negotiations within a marriage or successful joint venture. Likewise, efforts to appear legitimate are one of the most universally observable characteristics of negotiation. The map of issues is thus potentially dynamic, not rigidly static. As a result, whether a negotiation is handled adversarially or as a shared problem is likely to have observable effects on the parties' satisfaction with the outcome.

The competing prescriptive theoretical model is called "principled negotiation,"[26] The theory of principled negotiation is that rather than sacrificing the relationship to the pursuit of substantive gain, or vice versa (through positional bargaining focused on what the parties say they will or won't do), the parties should recognize their goal as dealing with both the relationship and the substance on their respective merits. Instead of positions, commitments, threats, and justifications, they should talk, side by side, about interests, principles, options, and objective criteria that help define those merits and make them concrete.

While not suggesting that there are determinate answers to questions of fairness, the theory of principled negotiation is that arguing about criteria and interests, rather than determination and positions, will encourage clearer communication, greater understanding, more inventing, and better reality-testing of options, and avoid much negative feedback to the relationship and the creation of needs for face-saving. In addition, if one assumes that the parties' primary goal is in not getting taken, in satisfying, then the ultimate indeterminacy of fairness will probably not be much of a bar to agreement. Once people feel that they understand the important aspects of the situation (that there are no hidden surprises), they can usually find an amicable way to split the difference between the limits of a range of reasonable fairness whose general limits are more or less mutually acknowledged.

Principled negotiation as formulated to date still has its problems, however. Intended at least primarily as a functional, not an ethical theory, its handling of traditional elements of negotiation power, especially lock-in tactics, and in general the question of trade-offs between legitimacy and efficacy, re-

Argyris's suggestion led us to create focused "mini-exercises" to practice specific, helpful component habits of thought and language from which repertoire a skilled negotiator will build and refine approaches to a complex and dynamic problem. For example, we might give participants a single "positional" statement and ask them to reframe it first as a statement about interests, then in the alternative as an invitation to brainstorm options, then as a move to discuss legitimate standards, then as a reflection on the state of the relationship, etc.

Here's an example to illustrate what this might look like:

Stimulus:	"We'll offer you $10,000."
Reframe to Interests:	"So money is a key interest of yours?"
Reframe to Options:	"That's one option. Another might be..."
Reframe to Standards:	"Where does the number $10,000 come from?"
Reframe to Relationship:	"You know, you can say $10,000 and I could demand $100,000 and we can haggle from there. But that seems pretty uncreative. I'm wondering if we couldn't come up with something that would make both our clients' happy. What do you think?"

These kinds of focused exercises have proven quite effective in increasing the quality of participants' negotiating performance. They have led us to a standard design of going back and forth between short, focused exercises and full-scale "put it all together" negotiations.

Levels of learning. Work with the organizational theorist and interventionist Diana McLain Smith has led me to think in terms of three "levels" or kinds of learning that call for three different kinds of "teaching." The first level is when you are offering someone a new skill or insight that addresses a felt need for which they do not already have a construct. Once they see the value, skill-building is simply a matter of practice. For example, you suggest to someone that differences of belief about what will happen in the future can be dealt with by making contingent

mains murky. The admonition in *Getting to YES* to "separate the people from the problem,"[27] though an important principle for one class of problems, seems to ignore and encourage overlooking the vital links between the relationship and the process used to deal with the substance. The theory of looking for "wise" outcomes is never explained.[28]

The theoretical justification and procedural guidelines for simple joint-gain trade-offs where the outcome differs from what objective criteria would lead to are also passed over lightly. The entire relationship between talking and acting, and the theory of acting consistent with the goals and principles of the model have yet to be elaborated. There is also work to be done in clarifying the analysis of transaction costs associated with changing the negotiating game to principled negotiation from a traditional model. When is it worth making the effort, and when not? Overall, this model avoids many of the problems of positional bargaining, but it is not yet complete, and as yet does not provide answers for all the questions addressed by the traditional model.

Given this unsettled theoretical base, a prescriptively-oriented course in negotiation will need to be built around the theory-building capabilities of students and professor in analyzing their own collective experience. One compensation of such an active and open-ended structure, however, is the potential for greater participant engagement in the learning process. How to use what students know on their own, their experience in organized exercises, and research and theory developed by others to help students become better negotiators is the subject of the rest of this paper.

The Teaching Challenge

Useful negotiation training should increase a student's confidence, competence, and satisfaction in dealing with a broad range of negotiation contexts and roles. In addition, good training should help student slearn how to keep learning from future experience—analyzing, generalizing, and testing on their own.[29] These goals aim at changes in behavior and attitudes, not the accumulation of factual knowledge, although knowledge may be an agent of change. Changes achieved should be long-lasting. A student's learning curve should continue to rise after the course, instead of slowly falling back toward its starting point (as it would tend to do with courses oriented toward learning facts). Good training should be more like a launch than a climax, as illustrated in Figure 1.

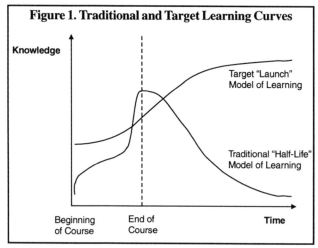

Figure 1. Traditional and Target Learning Curves

This section explores how negotiation training can be designed to achieve these goals. It looks first at basic theory about learning skills, turns to a discussion of obstacles that lie in the way of teaching good negotiation skills, then finally develops some approaches for overcoming these obstacles.

To Understand is to Invent
The need for theory. Mastering a skill requires theory and practice, whether it is the skill of letting out the clutch on a car or the skill of captivating an audience with rhetoric. A skill is mastered when you can recognize all appropriate times to apply the skill and are able then to apply it effectively. Theory, an understanding of how to apply the skill and why it works, is needed to insure confidence and continued success under varied conditions. Without some theory, you cannot adapt a skill to changing conditions. The deeper, more accurate, and more clearly articulated the theory, the greater the potential power of the actor. Thus between two effective rural preachers, the one whose theory is the more general—"use the metaphors people are used to" versus "use the farming metaphor"—will be more successful with broader audiences.

contracts. At this level the teaching metaphor is explaining.

The second level is needed when the person already has an unconscious, automatic way of dealing with such situations, one whose limits are leading to unsatisfying results. Change at this level first requires the person to become aware of their current approach, to slow it down and analyze it, then to modify it as appropriate and practice the new approach until it slowly becomes as automatic as was the original. This is a kind of learning that Professors Argyris and Donald Schön of M.I.T. have written about extensively. A simple example might be changing how someone responds to advocacy from more of the same to some form of inquiry, or at least a balance of advocacy and inquiry. Teaching at this level

17

is more intense and interactive. It involves much use and careful review of video or audio tapes of performance over a period of time.

The third level comes into play when work at the second level seems to fail. Despite diligent efforts at awareness building and practicing new approaches, key patterns of behavior and interaction recur and prove intractable. The hypothesis is that this happens when the new behaviors are inconsistent with deeply held images of how relationships work in general and of this individual's role in such relationships, images rooted in the individual's formative family and work experiences. These ideas of relationship are also largely unconscious, and they provide the structure for much of a person's life. This kind of learning is associated with family systems therapy, where Dr.

The need for practice. Practice is needed in developing a skill both to understnad theory about it and to develop competence in its application. Practice is also required to develop habits. In other words, to teach skills it is not enough to explain them. Lecturing someone on the theory and techniques of riding a bicycle will not prepare them to go peddling down the street on their own. Roger Fisher tells a delightful story about a friend's young son who insisted on learning "how to drive the jeep" one rainy Saturday. After carefully memorizing the explanation, he rushed to his father and declared, "Daddy, I've learned how to drive a jeep. Listen."

The need for practice to understand theory. The need for practice to master a skill is seldom forgotten. The need to try to do something before you can begin to understand it, however, while a truism in everyday life ("Let the clutch out slowly" just doesn't mean anything until you try it), has often been forgotten in formal education. Math, for example, is usually "explained" long before students have figured out for what, concretely, it is useful. The result for many is unnecessary confusion and discouragement.[30] More than forty years ago, Piaget commented on his conclusions from studying the learning process (especially of math and sciences): "Abstraction is only a sort of trickery and deflection of the mind if it doesn't constitute the crowning stage of a series of previously uninterrupted concrete actions."[31] Thirty years later, he listed as a fundamental condition of successful intellectual training the use of methods that "require that every new truth to be learned be rediscovered or at least reconstructed by the student."[32] In other words, to understand theory you have to invent it for yourself out of your own experience.[33]

There are several reasons why this is so. Any human experience is extremely complex in terms of the amount and relationship of information involved. Language is too imprecise and too inefficient to convey all that information conveniently, even if we could identify everything we needed to say. On the receiving end, our ability to pay attention and to relate words to precise feelings is also imperfect. Further, the amount of information we can process consciously is limited, and far less than the total sensory input the brain routinely deals with unconsciously. The creation of nerve pathways associated with skilled action and particular thoughts or experiences is also not under conscious control.

While we can with hard work imagine what a particular situation will be like, and that preparation will be helpful when the time comes, our fantasy will never be the same as the real thing. Likewise, the greater our engagement in an actual situation, the more impact it is likely to have on us. Observing something will be more affective than listening to a description of it, and doing something ourselves more affective than watching someone else do it.[34] Good training should therefore be as active as possible.

Practicing negotiation skills. For students to learn by doing, negotiation training should be structured around actual negotiations and negotiation exercises that allow participants to develop and practice skills and theory. "Real" negotiations will have the greatest impact, so teachers should look for opportunities to negotiate or examples of negotiation that occur in the classroom or participants' daily lives to experience, observe, and analyze. Simulations are the next best choice, and they are easier to plan around. Real or simulated, these negotiations should be as varied and broad in scope as possible, so that students can get a feel for the entire "forest," not just a few paths. The broader one's experience, the easier and more useful it is to develop more general theory. This is because the comparative frame brings to light variables that might be taken as givens in any one context.

Exercises can vary in factual context (from negotiating with a mechanic to negotiating with Albania), role and authority of the negotiator, number of parties, size of teams, time frame, scope of task (including the number, complexity, and tangibility of the issues, and the clarity of the goals), formality of agreement, degree of conflict or overlap of interests, sharpness of ethical choices, presence of third parties and/or clients, and so on.

Exercises with a strong emotional impact will spur more vigorous thought and create more salient and affective memories. Emotional impact is usually the product of surprise, of assumptions put into stark relief and challenged. A good example of an exercise with emotional impact is the

David Kantor has been a seminal theorist and practitioner. An example might be helping someone who has a strong tendency to try (and to feel responsible) to "fix" any problem in their environment to broaden their repertoire to include merely "surviving" some upsets with equanimity. Teaching at this level is more therapeutic, it involves inquiry into a person's meaning and value systems, and helping them "rewrite" their personal story by engaging in "frame-breaking" activity experiments. While such work often extends over months or years, shorter interventions can also be helpful.

Work at the first and second of these levels is reasonably normal and expected in a classroom environment. Work at the third level is possible, especially with the help of psychological professionals, but calls for more explicit negotiation with a

19

participant and some form of "informed consent" before going far. Yet if a participant or consulting client has clearly articulated goals, I find it helpful to realize that work at all three levels may be required to achieve those goals. The three levels form essentially a hierarchy of interventions of increasing difficulty and corresponding scope and power. The Negotiation Workshop at Harvard Law School now includes some work at each level, with most of that at the third level carried out in collaboration with family therapists in a single, five-hour, voluntary exercise done in groups of three students.[3]

Stages of learning. Another concept I now find helpful is that of a stage theory of learning. This is the notion that people are likely to go through certain recognizable cognitive or behavioral phases as their sophistication and understanding of certain ideas develop. Know-

Pepulator Pricing Exercise.[35] A modified prisoner's dilemma, the exercise involves two giants of the Pepulator industry who together control and supply the entire market. Independently and without communication, each company has to set the price ($10, $20, or $30) at which it will sell pepulators on a monthly basis. A company's profits for that month are then a function of (1) how high (or low) the price is, but mostly of (2) what price the other company sets. The company setting the lower price has higher profits. If the prices set are equal, the companies have equal profits, but the actual amount of profits will be higher the higher the price. The profit schedule is shown in Figure 2 (at right).

Pepulator is played over at least eight months. Each company is represented by a 4- to 6-person board of directors. Before months 3 and 7, one representative from each company is allowed to meet with their counterpart and, if they wish, reach an agreement about future pricing decisions (under a suspension of the anti-trust laws). Profits for month 4 are doubled, and for months 7 and 8 are quadrupled for the company with the higher profit for that month. A running record of the cumulative profits of each team is kept in each board room.

The central issues in this game are trust and competition. Considerable psychological research has been done on games of this type, and the results of Pepulator are consistent with other findings.[36] Those teams that are cooperative and mutually trusting enough so that both price consistently at $30 achieve cumulative profits higher (often far higher) than other teams (including "winning" teams), with only rare exceptions. The average of trusting teams' profits far outstrips that of noncooperative teams' profits. Teams that reach a 30-30 outcome early in the game tend to stay there, but these teams are in the minority. Teams that do not achieve 30-30 by the end of month 4 often never get there. Although teams are typically instructed that the objective of the exercise is solely to maximize one's own firm's profits, a majority of teams seem to be strongly influenced by comparisons with the other side even in situations where competitive behavior will predictably lower long-run profits.[37]

Substantively, Pepulator emphasizes both the power of cooperation (and the pitfalls of competition) in many circumstances and the fact that some people will compete no matter what. The emotional impact comes from the fact that some teams double-cross the other side and others do not. Double-crosses often involve outright face-to-face lying and misleading without making any flatly incorrect statements, and sometimes involve going back on handshakes or overruling the agreement reached (on instructions) by a team's negotiator. This behavior is seen by some people as "just business; it has nothing to do with my personal word," and by others as violently repulsive and completely irremediable. Some people from cooperative teams tend to feel righteous about their performance, others that "There but for the grace of God go I." The fact that such differences of perception not only exist but, as here, are common is another important lesson from the exercise. It is fair to say that no one who plays this game ever forgets it.[38]

Exercises can also be used to help participants expand their repertoire of interpersonal skills by allowing them to experiment with roles they would be unlikely to assume on their own. For example, people who usually feel hurt instead of angry when taken advantage of by a friend can practice displaying and using their anger. People who would never ordinarily act as a leader can practice taking control of a meeting. Experience indicates that most people are quite capable of assuming uncharacteristic roles, apparently relying on some empathetic understanding of similar behavior that they have observed or can imagine, but that they are

ing these can aid a teacher in coaching that development. As an example, we know that many people learning to deal respectfully with someone with whom they disagree go through a phase of not raising any conflictual concerns at all. Likewise, some people grab onto the idea of fairness and standards and begin to accept any deal that can be justified, rather than pushing for the best or most appropriate deal they can make.

The challenge of openness and transparency. While a stage

Figure 2. Pepulator Pricing Exercise Payoff Schedule

		Pulsar Pepulator's Price		
		\$30	**\$20**	**\$10**
Consolidated Pepulator's Price	*\$30*	*\$110* \$110	*\$20* \$180	*\$20* \$150
	\$20	*\$180* \$20	*\$80* \$80	*\$30* \$150
	\$10	*\$150* \$20	*\$150* \$30	*\$50* \$50

Monthly Profits in \$millions

theory of learning is helpful, it also raises a challenge for the teacher — how to remain open to the possibility that a participant is seeing something you are missing. This challenge appears in my original paper as well, and is not directly addressed. For example, John Holt's story of not explicitly correcting a young girl's pronunciation assumes that this is a level one learning situation and that the teacher knows the correct pronunciation. We can imagine a scenario, unlikely but possible, where neither of these is true. Likewise, we can imagine a teacher who sees a participant struggling with a level two learning situation and crafts some kind of unfreezing "a-ha!" experience to help the participant see the contours and limits of their current behavioral pattern. The success of the experience depends on hiding its true

often unprepared for the results. They generally avoid certain behaviors because they imagine that they would be unproductive and uncomfortable. In fact, they often discover that others can readily adapt to their change and often turn it to productive advantage. With this insight and further encouragement, people can practice this new skill and add it to their personal repertoire, or at least retain a new sense of choice.[39]

The need for review. As important as getting experience is reviewing and analyzing it. What worked well? Why? What did not? Why? How could things have been done better? Looking out for surprises and patterns is especially important. Surprises mark where events don't comport with our expectations. We learn something by figuring out why they didn't. Patterns point to hypotheses that can be clarified and tested, and then become part of our repertoire. Did or do our perceptions differ from others'? If so, what do they see that we don't and vice versa, and how did that come to be? Do our assumptions make sense? Have they been tested? What new approaches seem worth trying? Videotape can be quite helpful in review, reducing the need to rely on memory and providing a way to test perceptions.

A good review process should be iterative, reinforcing and building on insights developed previously. Likewise the exercises providing grist for review should grow incrementally more complex over time as student perceptions grow more subtle with experience. In this way skill and confidence can develop gradually and comprehensively.

The teacher as mentor. Through review and analysis of experience a careful and dedicated thinker might develop great confidence, effectiveness, and understanding as a negotiator. Yet it could take a great deal of time, and in fact, few people have the analytic skill and creative genius to reach on their own the level of clarity and understanding reached by thinkers who have gone before. Clearly something can be learned from others, and their steps can be retraced efficiently. Since the hardest part of solving many problems is figuring out the right question to ask, or the right way to frame the question, one way to reduce the burden facing students is to start them off pointed in the right direction, by carefully structuring the exercises they undertake. Likewise, they can be helped to look ahead and recognize dead ends onto which they may stumble. Piaget saw a teacher's roles as just these: as an organizer, pointing the way toward the central problems and arranging opportunities for exploration, and as a source of questions and counter examples to stimulate further thought about over-hasty conclusions.[40]

A teacher can also be an efficient source of factual information. Further, once students have developed a sufficient base of experience and understanding on their own, a teacher can provide precision, elegance, and a unifying coherence that relates particular events and observations to a bigger picture, or a larger framework. Finally, with enough initial learning by doing, students can sometimes progress rapidly merely by following an explanation. Readings as well as the teacher can become quite stimulating at this point. Practice is still needed to cement and fill out such understanding, of course, and to develop proficiency in related skills.

The need for patience and restraint. Success for a teacher in these roles requires restraint and a fine balance of many factors. Sometimes mistaken conclusions are a necessary step to further progress; the student, if not diverted, will correct them after a little further work. Too intrusive a presence too quick to criticize risks derailing the effort to have students think it through themselves. John Holt, for example, has written about a young girl who was mispronouncing a word she had recently learned; her usage was otherwise perfect. Rather than point out her "error," he found unostentatious ways to pronounce the word correctly in the next few minutes. The girl soon picked up the correct pronunciation in passing without self-consciousness.[41] Criticism here would only have caused an unpleasant and distracting defensiveness. As a metaphor, we can think of the professor's role as "learning facilitation" (student-centered) instead of teaching (instructor-centered). The learning facilitator prefers demonstration to criticism, questioning to preaching.

Being too ready to criticize or explain may encourage students just to wait until the teacher provides "the answer." Too authoritative a voice invites ridicule and resistance, or, worse, imitation. Most people are sensitive judges of exaggeration, and tend to find it pompous in authority figures. Negotiation

purpose. And what happens if the experience does *not* unfreeze the participant's view? Is the participant "stuck," or is it the *teacher's* view that is too limited?

To some extent this is a dilemma requiring judgment, because there is no clean solution. In general, the kind of on-the-merits relationship I advocate in the paper calls for a bias toward transparency in teaching, letting participants know at least generally what you are proposing to do and why. Yet in some situations transparency would get in the way of potential learning. In these situations, the teacher needs to assess the strength of their conviction of what's needed and the data on which it's based, and then decide how much effort it is reasonable to invest based on those assumptions. At some point, the balance may shift and call for coming clean with the participant. Yet a participant's self-report is not necessarily a good test of a teacher's insight. The participant may report, for example, "No, I wasn't upset at all," and yet continue to exhibit behavior it would be hard to interpret as anything else.

Whatever balance a teacher strikes in the face of such dilemmas, I think the overriding principle should be that the teacher's approach should be open at least in theory to review and reflection by someone at some point, whether the participant or a fellow teacher or supervisor. Even if there is no supervision in fact, as a teacher I try to behave *as if* there will be, using that constructed expectation to guide and limit my discretion. And as I move from level one learning to interventions aimed at level two and especially level three learning, my sense of a need for transparency with the participant increases proportionately.

remains an inexact discipline, and students know it. A teacher given to absolute assertions will lose respect. Alternatively, the example may lead some students to imitate the facade of pretending to know more than they do. Learning facilitation does not mean giving no feedback; humility is needed, however, about one's mastery of the "answers."

How then should a teacher provide guidance? In Piaget's words, "What is desired is that the teacher cease being a lecturer, satisfied with transmitting ready-made solutions; his role should rather be that of a mentor stimulating initiative and research."[42] This requires openness to new ideas and a state of mutual respect. There is a major difference between a rigid, "cookbook" approach to "learning by doing," and a true commitment to student self-discovery. In the former, the teacher is in control, in the latter, the students. It is a matter of the teacher's attitude and flexibility, and students can always sense the difference. For students to take their own thoughts seriously, it helps for the teacher to do so. That requires an open mind receptive to new ideas, and respect for the students' potential to produce them.[43] Students, of course, should also have a teacher they respect as worth listening to. We conclude, with Piaget, that the goal of learning by inventing is most likely to be achieved where there is a relationship of mutual respect between students and teacher.[44]

In the area of negotiation, however, an active, experiential course built around exercises and review, with easy access to the best available prescriptive theory, and a relationship of mutual respect between teacher and students may still not regularly achieve our goal of increased competence. If the classroom is run on more traditional, authoritarian lines, the chances of success are even less. The reasons why are the subject of the next section.

Barriers to Success

The major obstacles to success in negotiation training stem from the fact that students are not learning negotiation skills de novo. Rather, progress requires them to change habits long developed and deeply ingrained. Many habits are so deeply internalized as to be unconscious, and they often rest on equally ingrained assumptions that may bias an individual's entire world view. Change may require slowing down the reasoning behind an individual's standard behaviors until the underlying assump-

24

tions can be identified and tested, and then slowly developing skill in operating under new assumptions. The skills and motivation for such self-analysis are rare, and even when basic assumptions are identified, it is often hard to evaluate them in the absence of persuasively articulated alternatives. Further, the very prospect of change can seem threatening, and it is often met consciously and unconsciously with resistance.

.**No clean slate.** Children begin learning skills of negotiation almost as soon as they are born. The first time a correlation is made between crying and increased attention, a child has begun learning to negotiate. Children learn by trial and error, by imitation, by analogy, and by accident. This learning is mostly unconscious (or preconscious,) since it begins before the development of self-awareness and verbal ability.[45] It reflects only the most rudimentary logic—simple correlation, perhaps not even repeated, and such correlations have to be extremely short-term. Combined with uncritical imitation, especially of parents, the result is often a series of disconnected, inconsistent tactics with nothing in common except perhaps a common goal, such as getting attention.

Some of the more recognizable behaviors that many people learn in some form in early childhood include:

Making a lot of noise when balked (the squeaky wheel);
Making others feel responsible for your problems;
Bullying;
Treating others as if they are the problem;
Giving up to avoid conflict;
Reacting reflexively to what others do, but assuming their actions are all coldly calculated;
Assuming that if you are right, others must be wrong;
Assuming that others want what you want;
Hiding what you really want; demanding more than you need or expect to get;
Never admitting mistakes (even to yourself);
Listening only to find out whether the other person agrees with you (otherwise planning your rebuttal);
Acting on your own assumptions as though they were incontrovertible facts, and avoiding any testing of those assumptions;

teacher and participant awareness that no learning is value neutral. Consider, for example, a recent report which found that studying economics caused students' behavior to become more selfish.[4] The implication is that the emphasis in the material on individual value maximization increased the salience of such a world view for the students.

Teaching Large Groups

At the time of my original paper, our experiments with enlarging the Negotiation Workshop were just beginning and, as reported, not wholly successful. Since then, things have improved dramatically, and the Workshop is routinely taught to groups of 144. One key in these classes is to conduct much of the work in Working Groups of no more than 24 participants. Large "plenary" sessions are reserved for lectures and demonstrations.[5] (This also assumes a time-intensive course model. The Negotiation Workshop is taught either on a 9-5 model for three straight weeks, or from 2-6:30 p.m. on two afternoons a week during fourteen weeks of a regular semester.)

Two models for the supervision of Working Groups have been used. One relies entirely on student Teaching Assistants. The other uses one Lecturer and one Teaching Assistant. Both assume there will be two facilitators in the Working Group, both for effective facilitation and to help participants separate the substantive material from the person presenting it. In student-led Working Groups, senior faculty participate periodically as "guests."

The all-student TA model has been extremely effective. It has the notable advantage of participants feeling freer to

Reacting defensively to any questioning of your assumptions and arguments;

Always faulting others motives, never your expectations.

To some extent, of course, these behaviors may be effective. They may help a child satisfy basic needs for attention, comfort, and security, including the security of not feeling guilty. Yet they are not behaviors that we would in general recommend. They do not promote clear communication, valid analysis, or emotional control; indeed, they impede all three. If both sides use the same tactic, the result is worse. On the whole, these strategies tend to reflect untested assumptions, over generalizations, and major errors of deduction.

These drawbacks, however, are not apparent to the child, because they are the product of more sophisticated analysis than that of which most preadolescent are capable.[46] Never consciously adopted and reinforced by apparent success, such behaviors can become deeply embedded skills, perhaps even defining a significant aspect of an individual's personality. By the time a person has developed skills of logic sufficient to evaluate them effectively, these behaviors are so skilled and automatic that it takes a particularly dramatic surprise or setback to bring them into conscious awareness. Nor do they stand out as abnormal behaviors, because they are in fact quite common. While many people come to see the logical problems in others' behavior, and even in particular examples of their own, few ever bring the bulk of their own interpersonal behavior into alignment with their insights. Hence there are few examples of more rational actors available either to children or adults. Bad habits are normal, and, through imitation and socialization, replicating.

Untested assumptions. Certain negotiation-related assumptions and behaviors are especially common and troublesome.[47] The first is a tendency to look at all conflict as a win/lose situation where everyone is out for themselves. An associated action strategy is to try to maintain unilateral control of all important factors in a negotiation. Such an approach discourages the sharing of information that can lead to creative joint gains, discourages the building of trust and cooperation that can make possible powerful options not available to the parties alone or working separately, and deprives the parties of the potential pleasures and rewards of interdependence. Further, win/lose thinking and behavior tends to be contagious. It implies a threat, and people react to protect themselves. The most obvious reaction is to try and win yourself; it takes a thoughtful person to stop and consider other options for "changing the game." Even then it is hard to discuss win/lose assumptions: If a person is out to "win," their best strategy is not to let the other side know it. (In fact, the other side usually does know it, but they try to hide that fact for the same reason.) Again, as with all these behaviors, win/lose thinking is sometimes functional, but it is not always so. A broader view would be more generally applicable without sacrificing anything.

Related to the effort to keep control of the negotiation process is a strategy of advocating one's views and positions without encouraging any critical inquiry or testing of them. Why give the other side an opening when our views are correct anyway? Not testing one's own views, however, is an error. The brain is an information processor—it sorts, filters, categorizes, labels, and stores the body's sensory experience. Thus there is a long chain of filtering and abstraction—distortion—between any event and our thoughts or memories of it. There is a wealth of formal evidence for the everyday truism that no two people perceive the same event in the same way. Reasoning that ignores the probable difference between perception and reality—by failing to frame those perceptions as hypotheses subject to disconfirmation or revision—is faulty reasoning. Indeed, general semanticists have defined sanity as a matter of degree proportional to one's awareness of the distinctions between reality, one's experience of reality, one's memory of experience, and one's abstraction from that memory.[48]

A simple exercise is often used to illustrate this point. The exercise is based on a well-known sketch, "My Wife and my Mother -in-Law" by W. E. Hill (*Puck*, 1915), that can be seen either as a beautiful young woman or as a much older and less attractive woman. Almost everyone seeing the picture for the first time sees only one of these two possibilities, and quickly locks into that perception. Such lock-in is enhanced if they are asked to write down their private estimate of the woman's age, if they are invited to form a group consensus on her age in a group of others who see that possibility, and if they choose a spokesperson to negotiate the issue with the other camp. In the end,

think out loud in the Working Group than they often feel with a grading faculty member present (TAs are not responsible for grading). Student TAs are trained not as lecturers or content providers, but as facilitators. Their job is to ensure the rigor of discussions and reflections (they are called the "rigor police"). They are trained carefully for this purpose in daily and advance sessions. TAs are chosen from among the best students in prior classes and informally progress through a hierarchy from "second" to "lead" TA. Most teach more than once between summer executive education programs and regular semester courses. They are usually paid, but on occasion have received credit as an advanced seminar, for which their reflections were written up in a journal. All TAs agree that they learn even more from the teaching experience than their initial participant experience.

The TA model has the advantage of being self-sustaining. Each class generates new TAs who join a rolling community. The best of the best often pursue a career in the area, and find this work invaluable training. This model does, however, require a senior faculty resource to spend significant time in each class training and supervising the TA pool.

The Lecturer model has been a more recent experiment, and results have also been good. The obvious advantage is having more senior faculty resource in contact with participants at all times. The disadvantages are that the senior faculty tends to fill more of the "air time" in the Working Group and their presence tends to inhibit participation by some. There are also three more subtle disadvantages: (1) a diminution

many people cannot see the other woman for quite some time, even, when it is pointed out.

Recently, another interesting sidelight has developed in this exercise. In one version of the exercise small pictures are passed out in advance of the ambiguous picture that are drawn in such a way as to show only one or the other of the women. Astonishingly, some people, who have previously seen the two-women picture and recognize the exercise, look at the similar but entirely one-woman cards and insist that they show two women, directly contrary to the evidence of their senses. This is a powerful demonstration of the distorting power of memory and abstraction.[49]

A third troublesome and related behavior can be called self-censorship and unilateral face-saving (for both sides). When people sense that someone else does not see things the way they do, they often hesitate to say so directly for fear of a defensive reaction that would be distracting and produce bad feeling. Imagine a supervisory relationship, for example. No boss wants to provoke a "work-to-rule" rebellion; no subordinate ordinarily wants to annoy the boss. Instead of a direct approach, people often ask leading questions to help the other party figure things out for themselves. Usually, however, the other person has their own differing perception of what is going on, and the leading questions produce unexpected responses. If at this point neither party questions their own perceptions or opens them up to challenge by stating them explicitly (that might produce a defensive reaction), it is unlikely that either party will really hear what the other is trying to say. The very assumptions that should be discussed are hidden by self-censorship and unilateral efforts at face-saving.

Reacting. The tendency for people to react to events without regard to consequences, instead of acting purposively to further their interests, is nearly universal and especially unconstructive. This is the tendency of people to act in ways that produce reasonably foreseeable, yet unexpected, undesirable, and unnecessary consequences—to decide how to respond to the acts of others without giving careful consideration to what we would like to have happen next and what behavior of ours would be most likely to bring that about. We consider our own choice, but not those that will be faced by others as a result of our actions. And we ignore the likelihood that others are similarly ignoring how we will see our choices.

Let me give an example from family mediation.[50] A mother was concerned that her daughter had begun to lie to her. The daughter had found that her mother tended to get angry and unhappy when the daughter told her that she was going to see her boyfriend, whom the mother disapproved of for some reasonable and some rather arbitrary reasons. The daughter began to avoid telling her mother where she was going, and later, lying about her plans. The mother, sensing her daughter's evasions and lying, associated this unprecedented behavior with her daughter's boyfriend and concluded that he was the cause, a bad influence. The daughter, feeling that her mother's attitude toward her boyfriend was unreasonable and unfair, and becoming more so, began to feel more and more justified in lying about her activities, and did so increasingly. Angry, hurt, and seriously concerned, the mother finally forbade her daughter to see the boy again. Outraged at this injustice, the daughter said she was going to work, then spent the night with her boyfriend in the park and refused to call her mother for almost 24 hours, despite encouragement to do so from the boyfriend. Frantic and despairing, the mother called the police and sought a restraining order against the boyfriend. The police referred the matter to mediation.

The experienced are not immune. In the spring of 1979 an outraged U.S. Senate passed a resolution condemning the more than 200 executions that had taken place in Iran in the months after the Shah's departure and Ayatollah Khomeini's return. Convicted by decentralized "people's courts" that had sprung up throughout a disorganized Iran, the condemned were mostly accused of committing crimes as part of the Shah's regime. Some had been members of his secret police, which had a dismal human rights record; others were bureaucrats. At least a few were persecuted for other reasons, including religious prejudice. From the U.S. perspective, this summary, almost vigilante justice seemed cruel and uncivilized. Most Iranians, however, knowing that at least some of those executed were notorious torturers, found the U.S. position disingenuous after 25 years of relative silence while the torture continued. The Senate's resolu-

in the attraction of the somewhat diminished TA role; (2) a smaller and less-experienced TA pool (only half as many are needed); (3) less, and less formal TA training. This latter is an advantage in that it saves considerable senior faculty time and effort. However, as current Lecturers have been drawn mostly from the pool of TAs trained under the old system, the longer-term viability of this approach is uncertain. Finally, the Lecturer model does seem to reduce overall course cohesion, as there is greater divergence in what each Working Group covers and how.

Thoughts for the Future

There remain many unmet challenges and opportunities in teaching negotiation. Perhaps foremost among them would be the creation of a good assessment tool that could efficiently and persuasively assess a participant's skills before, during, and after a course. A tool for assessing teachers would also be useful. Beyond that, there remains much work to be done in building substantive theory; translating theory into corresponding concrete, operational skills; and designing efficient and effective learning activities for building such skills. I hope these ideas will stimulate others to share their progress and ideas.

Notes on *Reflections*
1. Additional prescriptive material on principled negotiation can be found in "Ten Questions People Ask About *Getting to YES*," added to the second edition of *Getting to YES* (1991); in William Ury, *Getting Past No: Negotiating your Way from Confrontation to Cooperation* (Bantam, 1991, revised edition, 1993); and in Douglas Stone, Bruce Patton, and Sheila Heen, *Difficult Conversations: How to Discuss What Matters Most* (Viking/

tion was roundly applauded domestically and in some international fora. Yet far from being shaken, the Iranians' belief in their own righteousness, and U.S. perfidy, visibly—and rather predictably—increased.[51]

To some extent, reactive, nonpurposive behavior may reflect less a bad habit than an undeveloped skill. Being purposive often requires insight, self-restraint, and a broader, somewhat detached perspective. In that case, negotiation training is faced not only with the need to overcome entrenched bad habits, but also with the need to stimulate basic emotional and intellectual growth and control. Both kinds of change, however, are often difficult to bring about.

The difficulty of changing. In real life there is no time to consciously analyze and plan the majority of our actions. Instead we rely on unconscious reasoning processes that are generally fast and highly automatic. As we have discussed, these processes are first learned early and implicitly, mostly by unconscious imitation, and often with less than ideal results. These processes adjust and improve somewhat with experience, but for the most part they are relatively stable.

To change such automatic reasoning processes you have to slow them down and make them conscious, analyze and revise each step of the syllogism, and then slowly practice the revised approach until it is back up to speed and once again an automatic skill. Each of these steps can be extremely difficult. For most people most of the time, the gap between their conscious thought about action and their unconscious reasoning for action is startlingly large. Chris Argyris, for example, has studied people's reactions to a partial transcript of a conversation between a superior and a subordinate whose work had recently become unsatisfactory. Asked to describe how they might respond to a request from the superior, Y, such as, "How do you think I did with X [the subordinate]?" responses such as the following were typical over thousands of respondents:[52]

"Y, your statement ['X, you seem to be carrying a chip on your shoulder'] is projective and interpretive."

"Y, your statement ['Our teachers cannot have those characteristics'] is a putdown for X."

The first statement says that Y should not be interpretive with X, yet the writer is being interpretive in just this way with Y. The second statement, that Y should not put down X, may be experienced by Y as a putdown.

Such unconscious contradictions are extraordinary and often apparent to listeners, yet go unnoticed by the perpetrator. Argyris reports that even once people become aware of these contradictions they are often unable to eliminate them, because they are not under conscious control.[53] Further, the process of unilateral face-saving reduces the chance that such contradictions will ever be brought successfully to the actor's attention, and the tendency to avoid inquiry may make action unlikely if they are.

Assuming someone wants to change an unconscious reasoning for action process, they need first to slow down that process to identify and understand its steps. Slowing down action decisions in that way is not something that occurs naturally. It requires a deliberate decision for which there is seldom much (recognized) incentive. An unconscious process can also be complex and responsive to a wide variety of factors. Dealing with all these factors consciously and systematically can be difficult and also takes time.

Once a process is identified, the process of evaluation is even more difficult. It involves finding and questioning the assumptions underlying and involved in the process. It is difficult to recognize assumptions of which you are not aware. It requires highly precise logic and insight to spot one's own non sequiturs, especially when a set of assumptions form a consistent, self-reinforcing system or "paradigm." Alternative assumptions may not be at all obvious, and it may well be impossible for most people to invent them on their own. Consider again the example of the young lady/old lady picture. Teachers can help, clarifying logic, suggesting alternative assumptions, and serving as alternative role models, but the prevalence of the unsatisfactory approaches discussed above may make suitable teachers hard to find.

Finally, bringing revised approaches up to speed requires not only practice but extreme concentration to avoid slipping back into the old familiar mode under the press of events. Each unanticipated context or related behavior is a potential opportunity for backsliding. The old approaches are skilled and familiar. Bridging the gap between conscious reasoning about action and unconscious reasoning for action

Penguin, 1999). Some broader ideas are offered in David Lax and James Sebenius, *The Manager as Negotiator* (Free Press, 1986) and Roy J. Lewicki, David M. Saunders, and John W. Minton, *Essentials of Negotiation*, third edition (McGraw-Hill, 1999).

2. James J. Gillespie, Leigh L. Thompson, Jeffrey Loewenstein, and Dedre Gentner, "Lessons from Analogical Reasoning in the Teaching of Negotiation" (reprinted in this volume).

3. See John Richardson, "Teaching Interpersonal Skills in Negotiation" (unpublished, 1992), and Scott Peppet, "A Guide to Leading the Interpersonal Skills (IPS) Exercise" (unpublished, 1995).

4. See, for example, Robert H. Frank, Thomas Gilovich, and Dennis T. Regan, "Does Studying Economics Inhibit Cooperation?" 7 *J. Econ. Perspectives* 159 (1993).

5. Plenaries can also be highly interactive and even involve high-energy in-place exercises. For some ideas on how to do this, see my paper, *Some Techniques for Teaching Negotiation in Large Groups*, 11 Neg.J. 403 (1995) (reprinted in this volume.)

requires a high degree of skilled self-awareness. Such awareness should be one focus of negotiation training. A psychologist or psychiatrist may be a useful adjunct in pursuing this goal.

Not only is change difficult to accomplish, people often resist it, especially if they feel it is being forced on them. Why and how that is accomplished is the subject of the next section.

Resistance to change. Psychologists and common sense tell us that human behavior is motivated, not random. We act to satisfy needs developed in response to stimuli and remembered stimuli.[54] Food, shelter, and other aspects of bodily security and comfort are perhaps the most basic human needs, but psychological needs are also important motivators. A sense of control over one's environment, companionship, a sense of belonging, approval, recognition, and love have all been suggested as basic components of emotional security and satisfaction. It is thought that more complex and specific goals are all ultimately rooted in these most basic needs.[55]

From this perspective, learning is a behavior that can help us satisfy our needs. Understanding, for example, gives a sense of and is a means to control of one's environment. Similarly, we can learn behaviors to avoid pain, find pleasure, save energy, gain recognition (internal or external), and generally enhance our physical and emotional security in myriad ways. Not surprisingly, children, intensely aware of their vulnerability and dependence on adults (no matter how benevolent), are voracious and powerful learners[56] (though, as we have discussed, they are not the most discriminating learners). Dependence, like many other things, is desirable only in moderation.[57]

At any given time, some needs may seem more important than others. A starving person, for example, will be more concerned about finding food than about getting uncomfortably wet in the rain. Since, as studies have shown, we can only think about a limited number of things at a time,[58] we naturally focus our attention on those needs that seem most urgent and important. Depending on the degree of concentration required, this may mean at times that we ignore less important needs entirely. This has been demonstrated in various ways experimentally.

In one experiment an electrode was implanted in a cat's brain to monitor incoming signals from the cat's auditory nerves. A loudspeaker was placed near the cat that emitted a regular, distracting click. The receiving electrode in the cat's brain recorded a regular incoming signal until a mouse crossed the cat's field of vision. At that instant, the monitored area of the cat's cortex ceased to receive any signals from the ear, although the speaker continued to click. Concerned with more important needs, the cat's brain apparently found a way to block unwanted information from the ear.[59] Another study showed that the electrical signal generated in a cat's ear decreased over time if the click remained constant, but registered any novel sounds normally.[60] A third experiment studied what people could remember when different messages were played into different ears at the same time and they were told to repeat one of them aloud as they heard it. Afterward, no one could remember that the unattended message had changed from English to German.[61]

Avoiding cognitive dissonance. The fact that some needs are more important than others leads to several hypotheses about what and how people learn that are supported by considerable evidence. The first hypothesis is that learning is not inevitable—where it might be upsetting in some way, we may avoid it. This conclusion is based on the assumption "that people have a strong need for consistency (consonance) among their beliefs and actions,"[62] related presumably to a sense of control, belonging, and identity. If conflicting information comes to light, an individual may satisfy this need by changing his or her beliefs. However, the greater an individual's commitment to a given belief or course of action, the more likely it is that conflicting, "dissonant" information will be experienced as threatening. Being "wrong" can reduce public status and self-esteem and increase one's sense of vulnerability (lack of control). Hence people may well prefer to avoid admitting error. In that case, they must find another way to maintain the consistency of their beliefs or, as it is usually put, to avoid cognitive dissonance.

One alternative approach may be not to notice the dissonant information or to give it little weight ("a fluke"). This is called seeing what you want to see or "selective perception." Even scientists are not immune from this phenomenon when the conclusions drawn from data have important personal or political consequences.[63] Stereotypes are often maintained this way, with personal direct experience considered an exception to a general unquestioned rule absorbed from others. John Holt has described teachers who unconsciously give students subtle verbal and gestural clues to indicate correct answers in math. He explains this as a way to avoid recognizing that these students lack any real understanding of the subject and would mostly fail without such help. Such a conclusion would not only be politically dangerous for the teacher, but also conflict with the teacher's self-image as a good teacher.[64] In general, whether dissonant information leads to changed beliefs or selective perception is likely to depend on how deeply, publicly, and socially committed someone is to the original belief—that is, how psychologically expensive it would be to change.

Another way to reduce dissonance is to interpret ambiguous information in a supportive way. The result can be called "partisan perceptions." Thus a vigorous new Russian initiative on arms control could be seen as an opening offer indicating increased concern about superpower tensions or as bassly self-serving and utterly disingenuous propaganda. Partisan perceptions are often self-fulfilling assumptions. Treating an action as hostile and responding accordingly, for example, is highly likely to result in a truly hostile counterreaction that not only seems to verify oyour origininal unsupported assumption, but makes it true (and difficult to show that it might not have been originally). Roger Fisher's classic example of self-fulfilling partisan perceptions about the Golan Heights is shown in Figure 3. Selective perception and partisan interpretation often go together and can be called "evidence gathering," as opposed to unbiased information gathering.

Evidence collecting is easiest when there is some "partial validity" to the partisan perception you are trying to "prove." It is natural and—in this context—functional to reason that if you are right (as you have "proved" to yourself), then any differing views must be wrong. A more precise and unbiased thinker, however, would also consider the possibility (even probability if it is known that the other person feels strongly on the subject after much thought) that they are working with different and perhaps some additional information. The precise thinker would then attempt to test this possibility by trying to find places where the two parties' assumptions differed and then examining the reasons for the differences.

A third way cognitive dissonance can be avoided is by reinterpreting or elaborating your own beliefs, instead of abandoning them. If this effort falls afoul of Occam's razor,[65] however, the costs of admitting error may be less than the ridicule associated with not changing. This is likely to be so unless you can find group support for your reinterpretation. Group support may not be hard to find if you are part of a group all of whom share the same problem. Indeed, the very threat of dissonance may spur greater commitment to the group's challenged beliefs and efforts to persuade new converts. The ability to gain converts is powerfully legitimating.

These theories help explain some of the most bizarre episodes of human (and inhuman) behavior including, for example, flat earth societies, racial supremacy groups, end–of–the–world religions, the Jonestown mass suicide, and Nazi genocide.[66] When the psychological stakes are high, the evidence suggests that the dispassionate accumulation, evaluation, and incorporation of valid information is the exception rather than the rule.

There are perhaps two basic approaches to combating evidence collecting and other change-resisting dissonance-reduction strategies. The first is to increase the difficulty of subsequent reinterpretation by reaching an explicit prior agreement on the identity of disputed assumptions and what would be a fair test of them. The second is to surround targets with a social context encouraging change. This would imply isolating the target from other members of a potential reinforcing group and placing them in a group that takes the dissonant information at face value and actively resists efforts to ignore or distort it.[67] In addition, the cost of change can be reduced by providing a group that, while disagreeing with the target's original beliefs, nevertheless appears unlikely to use the target's change of views as a psychological club and is personally accepting of the target, so that the target's sense of security and belonging is protected.

The desire to avoid cognitive dissonance can also be used to promote change. One way, similar to the approach above but useful where the students commitment to a particular view or behavior is less formal and public, is simply to demonstrate the alternative clearly and persuasively while appearing to assume that the student is fully in accord with it. Adopting the new behavior does not then require of the student any "official" change at all, while refusing to go along may precipitate a confrontation. John Holt's approach to the young girl mispronouncing a word followed this pattern. A second technique is to help the student redefine their original stance so that the new information or behavior is accommodated in a constructive way without having to admit that the previous stance was wrong. Asking a too talkative student to help the teacher make sure that everyone has a chance to participate, and approaches like, "You and I, of course, are mature enough to recognize when it is best to . . . ," are examples of this second approach.

Fear of the unknown. Even when people accept that their current beliefs or habits are not ideal, people may resist change. One reason is that there is always uncertainty about the benefits of change. As discussed previously, nothing can be truly known and understood until it is experienced, but uncertainty tends to decrease one's sense of security and control. Second, the process of change is risky—it involves vulnerability, even if the end product will not. A lobster, for example, is better off discarding an old shell and growing a larger and stronger one, but the price is enduring an interval with no shell at all. Finally, the benefits of change may not be immediate. Thus the desire to avoid the risks of changing may outweigh the present value of uncertain long-term benefits.

This is not a problem of dissonance, but fear, and the fear is at least partially valid. Dissonance may become a factor, if being afraid is inconsistent with your self-image. Then, instead of admitting fear, you may construct alternative explanations and justifications for your refusal to change and collect evidence to support those stories. In that case, you may need help from others to recognize and face your fear. Facing your fear may not be sufficient to overcome it, however. For that, you will probably have to be persuaded that the benefits of change are greater or more certain than you think, that the risks of not changing are greater than you think, or that your fear of the process of change is less justified (or less seemly) than you think.

Those who have already made the change or who were always otherwise are the most credible sources of information about the relative benefits of changing or not. Examples of people who wasted resources by waiting too long to change are helpful in explaining the risks of non-action. Generals, for example, should consider the fate of the magnificent Polish cavalry in the face of German armor at the beginning of the Second World War to help them avoid always preparing for the last war instead of the next. As to fear of the process of change, others with more experience can help persuade you that your ability to handle the unknown is greater than you may think, and your own experience over

---

Figure 3. Partisan Perceptions (Examples as prepared by a third party)

Some Syrian Perceptions

Syria is an under-developed country that wants and needs peace.

The Golan is part of Syria and must be returned; if Israel wants us to respect its sovereignty, it must respect ours.

Israel's building civilian settlements on the Golan demonstrates that Israel's true goal is expansion.

Recently there has been a great change in Syrian thinking towards peace and towards acceptance of Israel.

If the United States did not give military aid to Israel it would have to withdraw from Arab land and make peace with the Arabs.

Our interest in peace is demonstrated by our acceptance of the disengagement agreement, the U.N. resolutions, and Kissinger as mediator. and by our resuming diplomatic relations with Israel's strongest ally, the United States. The next move toward peace is up to Israel.

In exchange for the Golan (and something for the Palestinians) we could live in peace with Israel.

Israel has no real interest in peace as demonstrated by its massive military preparations.

We will fight, if necessary, to regain the Golan which is part of our country.

Israel is keeping the Golan, and therefore we must prepare for war.

Some Israeli Perceptions

Syria is a military dictatorship within the Soviet orbit.

The Golan is not the problem; Syria shelled Israel when Syria held the Golan before 1967.

Syria's insistence on the so-called rights of the Palestinians demonstrates that Syria's true goal is to destroy Israel.

Syrians did not accept Israel in 1948 and we have been fighting ever since; we know them well based on years of bitter experience.

If the Soviet Union did not give military aid to Syria it would have to accept the existence of Israel and make peace with it.

Our interest in peace is well known, and is further demonstrated by the one-sided disengagement agreement where in exchange for a few words we withdrew from substantial Syrian territory, including Kuneitra. The next move toward peace is up to Syria.

In exchange for real peace we could return to Syria all or most of the Golan.

Syria has no real interest in peace as demonstrated by its massive military preparations.

It would be absurd for us to give up the Golan without real peace.

Syria is preparing for war, and therefore we must keep the Golan.

© 1979 Roger Fisher

time can confirm it. This is essentially a process of creating and then exploiting cognitive dissonance (using a history of successful adaptation to defeat a self-image of incompetence).

Since the need to change (including learning, change in what you know) is one of the few certain things in life, it is important to develop a balanced perception of the merits and drawbacks of change, and confidence in your ability to effect a successful change. With confidence, the willingness to face change (even revel in it) can be greatly empowering, especially in dealing with those who fear change. There are important limits, however, to what others can do to help you in this development.

The counter productivity of coercion. Starting from the premises that people act to satisfy needs, that some needs are more important to us than others, and that learning is one strategy for satisfying needs, we have discussed how people sometimes ignore or distort upsetting information, and how, even if they process the information, they may choose not to act wisely on it. A third important hypothesis is that people will concentrate on learning what they think will help them satisfy those of their needs that seem most pressing at any given time. A starving person, for example, is more likely to practice archery than playing the flute, no matter how much the person enjoys hearing the latter.

An important part of teaching is thus creating a situation where learning about the intended subject is high on each student's list of priorities. This goal is not so easy to achieve, and it requires careful attention to the logic of the underlying premise to avoid unintended consequences. Indeed, the difficulty of the task is illustrated by the fact that both the structure of traditional education and the most powerful critiques of that structure rest on the same premise—that students will learn to satisfy their most pressing needs.

The theory of traditional education is that what students need to know in the long term may not seem to them the most relevant or interesting things to think about in the short term, so additional incentives and aids to learning (beyond the material's intrinsic interest) are required to keep students' attention and insure diligent effort. These incentives take the form of tests, grades, oral praise and criticism, honor rolls, detentions, and so on. In terms of basic needs, however, coping with such incentives can become more urgently important to students than learning the intended material.

These measures attack students' sense of security. They identify performance with love and self-worth. They set students at competitive odds with one another. This implicitly makes satisfaction of students' most vital needs—for approval, recognition, appreciation, power, and other elements of physical and emotional security—into a potentially scarce commodity. At the same time it attacks students' sense of group identity and thus their ability to counter withdrawal of adult protection with mutual psychological support. The net effect is to encourage a powerful fear of failure, and also a legitimate concern that the price of success will be envy, distancing, and alienation from one's peers.[68] In addition, giving in or even cooperating with coercion can threaten a student's sense of control, independence, and corresponding self-respect. Domination is degrading, at least to the extent that it is seen as illegitimate.[69]

Essentially as intended, these measures are often experienced as dangerous and immediate threats that rivet all attention on the problem of finding means to neutralize or protect against their potentially devastating psychological effects. It takes an unusually secure and independent-minded person not to feel so threatened, and most people are risk-averse about their emotional security. Learning the intended material, however, is not the only solution to this problem, and without more it is not a sufficient counter to all aspects of the problem. Nor, for many students is it the easiest approach. One common solution is figuring out a strategy for getting the best grade with the least effort, thereby protecting oneself from the opprobrium of bad grades while still protecting one's self-respect in the face of coercion. Another possibility is finding some reason for refusing to try, such as, "I can't do math," or "School is a crock." Some students find alternative bases for self and peer respect, such as athletics, popularity, or even fantasy.[70] All such strategies avoid the psychological risk of failure and frustrate the teacher's attempt at coercion.

It is perhaps not impossible to keep grades and other incentives from becoming ends instead of means, but the danger is great, and especially so for younger students. Once established, a non-learning strategy for coping with incentives is likely to become a habit, an entrenched self-fulfilling part of a student's self-image well-defended by evidence collecting and partial validity. In that event the incentives exercise was a disaster. Further, the aftertaste of coercion may keep some students from ever acquiring a taste for learning in its own right, and may teach others to use coercion to pursue their ends.

Ironically, while coercion elicits a strong reaction in accord with the basic desire for autonomy, the equally basic desire for competence can produce a powerful motivation to emulate a competent, attractive, and confident role model. There is strong evidence to suggest that the goals of traditional educators can be achieved more easily, effectively, and comprehensively by finding in yourself and letting students see the satisfaction and functionality you experience in what you hope they will learn, and more importantly, giving them the freedom and responsibility to learn by doing.[71] (Being a good role model does not mean showing off. That is merely another way to put down students to feed your own ego, and it is counterproductive.[72]) Certainly there will still be some resistance: after all, being an active participant in the learning process involves more work, engagement, and personal risk—it requires taking responsibility for the outcome, but this too can be overcome in time.

Teachers face the same problems. Teachers, unfortunately, face the same obstacles to change as students. They develop the same flawed negotiation strategies as a child, and find it as difficult as others to identify or challenge these behaviors. It is extremely difficult to admit that one's entire system of operation, a system fully supported by your brethren, is largely and disastrously counterproductive. The dissonance is enormous. How much easier to collect evidence for self-fulfilling assumptions that students are lazy, unmotivated, rebellious, and stupid; that grades are necessary to let others know how students rank against each other; that you are doing the best you can under the circumstances; and so on.

It is, however, the task and challenge of teaching to overcome such obstacles. For it is in the success of the teacher as a role model that we can hope to overcome the barriers to success in negotiation training discussed in this section: unsatisfactory, but ingrained and unconscious operating assumptions; avoidance of inquiry; self-fulfilling assumptions; evidence collecting; fear of change; and reliance on coercion. Why that is and how it can be done is the subject of the next section.

Teaching by Example

There are, as we have discussed, essentially two ways of learning behavior: implicitly, by unconscious imitation (or reaction), and explicitly, by consciously analyzing and generalizing from concrete experience. On the level of implicit learning, much can be taught by setting a good example, that is, by negotiating in the view of students as best you can in the way you would like them to learn to negotiate. Actions can speak louder than words, though seldom as unambiguously. As we have seen, however, if students already have well-developed unconscious negotiating behaviors, changing those behaviors (if change is desirable) may require making them the subject of explicit learning.

Explicit learning, we have argued, should be rooted in learning by doing, in inventing from concrete experience, with the teacher organizing the experience and then serving as a resource and coach. Again as we have seen, however, there may be various psychological impediments in the way of drawing accurate conclusions from such experience and acting on them by making appropriate behavioral modifications. In that event, the teacher's role should be to safeguard the process of change in thinking and behavior by facilitating clear reasoning, appropriate paradigm shifts, and the decision to change. Since the success of this effort ultimately depends on the decision of students to cooperate, the effort to teach negotiation can properly be seen as itself a negotiation—one whose process will inevitably serve as a powerful example for students.

The need for congruence between content and process. It is important that the negotiation process used in the teaching effort be the same as that the teacher would like students to learn. Otherwise, the implicit and the explicit messages will be dissonant. If students think the teacher is unaware of the dissonance, they may lose respect. If they think the dissonance is conscious, they will consider it an attempt at deception and hence coercion, and it will spawn resistance. In either case, one possible outcome is that they themselves learn to do one thing and say another. Yet that is unlikely to be any more effective a strategy for the students than for the teacher.

Unfortunately, the traditional approach to teaching reflects many of the common negotiating behaviors we have discussed. It envisions a one-way knowledge transfer controlled by the teacher, whether the particular conception is closer to "pouring knowledge from an ever-bounteous pitcher into leaky, every-needy vessels,"[73] or to an aggressive "massage parlor" for working participants over and molding them into some better state. There are right and wrong answers, and they and the process are nonnegotiable, coercive, and adversarial. The way to "win points" in the traditional classroom is to put down someone. This approach is more likely to reinforce existing habits than to stimulate careful reevaluation of them. It is especially incompatible with those visions of negotiation that emphasize treating the problem are shared, the other side as people, and the goal as a mutually acceptable solution justifiable by objective standards, principles of fairness, or mutually beneficial trade-offs.

Needed is an overall approach to training structured around inventing that both exemplifies and promotes clear reasoning. Within this broad approach, particular ideas about and approaches to negotiation can be raised by exercises and associated discussion and exemplified by the teacher. Our analysis of the barriers to change and learning suggests the elements of such an approach: motivate by attraction instead of coercion; demonstrate competence, confidence, congruence, and openness; and combat evidence collecting and other departures from clear reasoning by confronting them and advocating inquiry.

Attract, don't push. As a metaphor, it may be helpful to frame the goal in this alternative approach to teaching not as "pushing" participants from where they are to where you would like them to be, but rather as standing where you would like them to end up and attracting them in that direction. As we have discussed, people do not like to feel pushed, even in directions in which they want to go (unless they have specifically asked for or agreed to it), but they will volunteer tremendous efforts doing things they decide to do on their own. This approach requires respecting students enough to acknowledge their responsibility for deciding to learn, or, more precisely, to collaborate in the learning process. As with John Holt's little girl, it also helps to avoid criticism and even praise, if it would cause uncomfortable self-consciousness.

What then does it take to be attractive? First, confidence and competence. Everybody normal wants to be like that. Congruence between thought and action, and self-awareness of it, is an important part of competence; it is a source of personal power, partly because it represents clear communication. Like an actor, the effective teacher projects his or her vision of how people should deal with one another, using every transaction as an opportunity to reinforce their point and build a more complete picture. Though this should be done clearly, it should not be done ostentatiously. Too perfect and advanced a model may seem too daunting. Most people compare themselves with people of just slightly greater ability.[74] (Likewise, children imitate best other children who are just slightly more advanced.[75]) Praise should also be well-considered. Too often effusive praise is really an effort to take the credit yourself.[76]

The need for openness. Second, being attractive takes a certain openness. The best teachers are open to challenge and to new ideas, accepting them without defensiveness and proposing ways to test the issue. To some extent, openness is a part of competence. It is a fact that no one knows everything, and anyone who seems to think otherwise is wrong. Mistakes that are not admitted cause us to lose a little bit of respect and some of our desire to be like our role model, and we are led to wonder what else they might be wrong about. A lack of openness is also arrogant—it shows a lack of respect for us, suggesting that the actor couldn't possibly have anything to learn from us. That too is almost certainly a mistake, and it is an attack on our self-esteem. Such attacks often lead to unconstructive defensive reactions, rather than clear communication. Conversely, openness is a mark of respect, a gesture of warmth and expectation inviting the recipient to live up to it and not to jeopardize it.

Openness represents vulnerability. Many people, operating on win/lose assumptions, fear vulnerability, but vulnerability is a necessary precondition to closeness and affection.[77] More often it precipitates reciprocity than predation.[78] Finally, openness is the hallmark of a learner, and we would like to teach people to be learners. Openness in a teacher sells the idea that there is nothing wrong with having something to learn, that it is nothing of which to be ashamed. It is a counter to the common feeling of shame about ignorance that motivates an attitude of, "You can't teach me anything." The combination of confidence and competence with openness and vulnerability can be irresistible.

An example of what demonstrating openness might mean in practice concerns theory. Treating other people's theory as always open to challenge is not uncommon. Treating one's own hard-won ideas as merely "works in progress" subject to change can be much harder. Yet this approach is likely to be good for the theory and can have major effects on student motivation. Collaborating in the active development of theory, no matter how peripherally, is a major change of pace from most law school classes. It is "real," and fun, and side by side. This kind of excitement can produce as much engagement in a class as almost any other technique.[79]

Probably the hardest part of being open is admitting mistakes. At least as much as everyone else, teachers don't like to be wrong, and they like people knowing they blew it even less. Yet a readiness to admit error when called for, without undue shame or meekness, actually sends a powerful message of self-confidence. If effective training requires that the professor set a good example, and not admitting mistakes is counterproductive, a straightforward recognition that nobody's perfect is the out that keeps teaching from being limited to perfect teachers. In fact, a good counter to student evidence collecting might be to say right up front that you as professor are sure to make some mistakes in the class and have discrepancies between what you are saying and what you are doing. You can make it the students' responsibility to call you on it when it happens.

Confront disagreements with inquiry. The last component of our general approach to training involves actively confronting possible departures from clear reasoning and advocating inquiry on the issue. Misunderstandings or disagreements may and likely will arise between participants, and between one or more participants and the professor. Only if confronted can such misunderstandings be clarified; otherwise they may become fodder for evidence collecting. Clarification may mean additional precision, mutual education, or recognition of the need for additional information or theory (what Roger Fisher calls "second-order agreement"[80]).

There are two approaches to confrontation. One is a side-by-side coaching approach. The professor (or student) steps figuratively or actually beside the actor either as a coach or double and demonstrates an alternative behavior. This is especially appropriate when the actor has indicated a desire to achieve consistent behavior, but is having trouble doing it. Direct confrontation is the second approach. "It seems to me if I am hearing you correctly that you are assuming X. Do I hear you correctly? I am not sure X is valid. To me it seems inconsistent with Y and Z. How do you see it?"

Such confrontation must itself be consistent, or "congruent," with clear reasoning. Congruent confrontation and inquiry means first, treating your own views as perceptions that may be incomplete or in error and should be tested; second, looking for and acknowledging partial validity in the perceptions of others; third, clarifying and advocating inquiry in all disputes; and fourth, holding yourself open to and ready to act on the results of such inquiry.

Take responsibility for your own perceptions. Taking responsibility for your own perceptions is a form of openness. Operationally, it generally means phrasing your statements as conclusions or opinions rather than facts, and offering your evidence and reasoning for scrutiny: "When you did that, I felt like you did not give a damn about how I would be affected," instead of, "You're a bastard." It recognizes the possibility that you may be, at least partially, in error, or that you may lack crucial information. Stating your views in this way makes it harder to dismiss them. "You're a bastard," is an attributory conclusion that the listener can deny—after all, they should know better than you. In contrast, "I felt like you did not give a damn," is an attribution about you. If you say you felt that way, the listener can't deny it (except by calling you a liar); they can only argue that you were wrong. At that point we have a foundation for inquiry where before there were only partisan perceptions. A corollary of taking responsibility for your own perceptions is helping others to do the same. The process is recursive: If they say, "You're a bastard," you might reply, "What I hear you saying is that when I did X, you felt like... Did I hear you correctly?"

Acknowledge partial validity. As we have discussed, most people who feel strongly about their views on some issue tend to react to those who disagree by concluding either that the dissenters have thought less deeply about the issue or that they are looking out for narrow self-interest of some kind. Thinking that, these people tend to collect evidence to support their position and to ignore or explain away conflicting information. It is usually more accurate and more educational to assume that people with strongly held, but opposing, views are seeing things about the situation that you do not, things that you would probably think significant if you saw them too. You still might not, and quite likely would not, agree with the other side's reasoning, but in part that will probably be because you see some things that they do not. Understanding both sides may lead you to adopt a third, improved view.

Looking for and recognizing partial validity in the other side's views will educate you. Acknowledging your understanding may help educate them. Indeed, to express others' arguments as well or better than they can themselves, and then to explain precisely how and why you disagree, is one of the most powerful persuasive techniques known. Once you have demonstrated your understanding of their views, they can no longer dismiss your disagreement as lack of understanding. Instead they must recognize and deal with your competing arguments. (In fact, this kind of "active listening" tends to be a necessary precondition for getting an opposing party to listen to you.) Again, the result is to lay a foundation for inquiry where before there were only partisan perceptions.

The need for a psychological component. We have already discussed the importance of confronting disputes and the how and why of being open to change. The complexity and central place of psychological considerations in both the subject matter and the process of teaching negotiation suggests that consideration of these issues be an explicit part of any negotiation training. As with other course components, this can be accomplished both by using some exercises that emphasize such issues, and by maintaining the psychological perspective as a continuing theme throughout the training . Again, a psychological professional may be desirable: Not only will they have the knowledge and training to explain and confront crucial behaviors, a good professional can also serve as an example of better behavioral approaches.

The preceding considerations apply no matter what approach to negotiation a teacher advocates, except perhaps a strictly coercive approach that might be classified as something other than negotiation. The general rule for more specific themes is simply: Be congruent. In dealing with students, in operating in front of them, and in designing the structure and rules of the training, follow the dictates of the themes you wish to espouse. As an example, the next section explores how this might be done in teaching the theory of principled negotiation.

Principled Negotiation in the Classroom
Principled negotiation is a systematic approach emphasizing that within the limits defined by the parties' best alternatives to negotiated agreement the problem of reaching agreement is shared, and will be better solved by clarifying interests, inventing options, and referring to objective standards and principles of fairness in discussing what an agreement ought to be than by a contest of will focused on what each side says they will or won't do. Attention is focused on satisfying underlying interests instead of arguing blindly over rigid, one-sided positions, on inventing options that make the most of possible joint gains, and on treating the other side with courtesy and respect independent of the discussion of the merits. A principled negotiator is committed to being open to reason, but not movable by threats.

Formulate and adhere to standards. A teacher committed to principled negotiation should have reasons for all aspects of a course and their own behavior. Further, they should be prepared (within the reasonable constraints of time, energy, and equitable distribution of attention) to discuss these reasons, and, if persuaded, to change. This does not necessarily require complete rationality." It is perfectly reasonable to say that something "just feels right (or wrong)", if that is true, but there would seem to be an obligation in fairness to cooperate in any effort to articulate what underlies such a feeling. If students are to be officially (or even unofficially) evaluated as part of the training, traditional principles of fairness would call for the standards of judgment to be announced in advance and applied uniformly and impartially (or for it to be announced in advance that one or both of these things would not be done). The standards themselves should also be justified.

There are many aspects of a course to consider, including the scheduling and length of classes, the choice of and time devoted to exercises, the agenda for discussions, the themes of the course, due dates for any required work, and the process of the course. Process encompasses how much of the course direction is generally under student and how much under the professor's control, and the structure of various activities. Negotiation being a group activity, and a professor's time being somewhat limited, negotiation training cannot proceed wholly at any individual's convenience. A course's institutional setting may also impose constraints of time and structure on a course. Finally, a professor is entitled to some prerogatives of choice in what they are interested in working on and how they would like to share it. The point is to be prepared to explain and, if reasonable, negotiate.

Feedback, evaluation, and grades. Naturally the area in which students will be most interested in knowing and discussing a professor's standards is in the area of grading. Grading per se is certainly not inconsistent with the idea of principled negotiation to the extent the standards applied are perceived as legitimate (by the students, the professor, and/or the institution). To the extent that grades are relied on as incentives, however, they may become ends in themselves distorting student priorities. Further, applying standards is difficult, and defending their application is a particularly rigorous test of one's skill in separating the merits of the problem from the relationship while still dealing effectively with both. It is important to have a well-considered theory of evaluation.

Grading can be based on any number or combination of things. One option is to have students keep a daily journal of their thinking about negotiation (their reflections on their experience, not just a catalog of events). A journal gives a rich insight into a student's effort, depth, and quality of thinking, and experience suggests it is not especially difficult to sort journals into categories for grading.[81] Having to keep a journal may also stimulate more reflection, although the requirement can also breed resentment or efforts to "polish the apple." Providing samples of exemplary journals may discourage the latter, as they would be formidable to fake and it would certainly require a lot of thought. Samples can also be illuminating and stimulating to students, especially those having little experience with diaries or self-examination. The disadvantages of a journal requirement include the time taken away from preparation or additional exercises, and the fact that a journal emphasizes writing and analysis over results in actual negotiation. Any kind of paper requirement shares more or less the same advantages and disadvantages.

The most contested question in negotiation training is whether or not to base part of a student's grade on their outcomes in negotiation.[82] Exercises are likely to be taken seriously whether the outcomes are formally evaluated or not—pride and simple curiosity seem to be perfectly adequate incentives for most people. The argument for evaluating outcomes is that better outcomes are the central goal of training, and that outcomes are the most objective, and therefore fairest, measure of skill. The question arises, however, of how to evaluate outcomes. Should factors such as likely durability of an agreement, degree of exploitation of joint gains, post-negotiation relationship of the parties, or even recognition of larger community interests play a part? And how do you go about ranking intangible against tangible benefits?

One approach is to give students a fixed point scale for various factors. Such an approach is significantly artificial. Exact weighting of factors are not available in the real world, and furthermore, how various factors are weighed is in fact subject to change in response to the process of negotiation itself, as discussed in previous section of this paper. Inventing options that have not previously been considered is also an important and powerful real world skill, yet it cannot be built in to a rigid point scale announced in advance. This would not be a problem if no points were announced and outcomes were evaluated after the fact. In either case, however, students may object that evaluation of their outcomes involves value choices with which they may not agree. Should their grades depend on playing a game according to rules of which they do not approve?

Perhaps the most serious argument against evaluating students on the basis of the outcomes of their negotiations is that the pressure of evaluation will discourage experimentation and learning. This is exactly the reverse of our goal. The point of a negotiation training course is to give students the opportunity to learn by experimenting with and evaluating different approaches. Increasing the stakes is most likely to make them more risk averse. Perhaps this effect could be avoided by grading the outcomes of only one or a few final exercises, and not the bulk of exercises around which a course is designed.[83]

One final evaluation option is the traditional written examination. As with grades in general, there is nothing intrinsically wrong with examinations. As an evaluation mechanism for negotiation training, it is vulnerable to the charge that it cannot test anything of central importance to the course. A student's ability to talk about the process of negotiation does not necessarily bear any resemblance to their skills as a negotiator, except to the extent that the test can be designed as a negotiation with the grader.

Share control. Students with years of experience in traditional classrooms may be slow to recognize or acknowledge an "open" principled classroom. There is a need to develop some trust that you really are open to negotiation and legitimate challenge. It may be worth keeping a special watch for opportunities to conduct a "real" negotiation with or among the participants. Likewise, when a challenge does come it must be treated seriously and with a real openness to persuasion. Carrying through this commitment may well impose some cost, at least in terms of inconvenience. Indeed, students may quite naturally, if perhaps unfairly, look at what sharing control is actually costing the professor in deciding whether they really believe in it.

As an example, there is no reason that the syllabus of a course should not be open to reasonable negotiation. If careful thought went into its development, then sharing that thought should be more persuasive than embarrassing. If it was not well thought out then it might well be improved. In any event, no advance plan can anticipate actual events, and it is questionable whether there is any one "best" way to organize a course. Every group of people is different, and the very request for a change is likely to make it functional at least to discuss the issue.

There is another area where it may be important to stress student choice. As we have discussed, exercises with high emotional impact are especially powerful. That impact often results from students being surprised. For example, consider an engaging and diverting exercise where the best solution is actually to reach no agreement. The problem is that surprising people can be risky; they sometimes get upset when their expectations are balked without warning, and they can feel used.[84] By explaining in a low-key way at the beginning of a course why you think such surprises are valuable and then asking permission to undertake this kind of manipulation of student' s experience, these risks can be avoided. Even if a student's only alternative to agreement is to withdraw from the course, giving this permission is experienced as a binding commitment not to complain.

Humanize the process. If one's goal were to control students in a hierarchical interaction, as is traditional, then personal distancing of the authority figure seems to help. In negotiation, however, distancing tends to produce distrust and resentment, despite the common aspiration to inscrutability. To test this, try negotiating with someone while wearing mirrored sunglasses. (This makes a good class demonstration.) Distancing denies equality, of power and vulnerability. Principled negotiation calls for dealing with other negotiators (in this context students) as people, apart from status, performance, or power relationship.

Students and teacher need not like one another, although that can help, but we have argued that they do need mutual respect. This too may require a special effort to break down stereotypes and barriers to communication built up from past experience. At Harvard Law School, for example, Professors Fisher and Sander often exploit the more relaxed social conventions of dining for this purpose by inviting their students to their homes for dinner early in a negotiation workshop. They also spend the first hour or two of a workshop having each participant tell a three-minute story about a negotiation they have been in that meant something to them and what they learned from it.[85] Immediately, other students become unique individuals instead of generic bodies in the crowd.

Making personal contact with students does not, for a principled negotiator, mean lowering substantive standards—not one whit. The point of principled negotiation is to permit a dialogue focused on objective standards that does not involve or promote implicit attributions about the other party's motives or character. One can be supportive of the person on the other side, open to reason, and yet firmly committed to demanding substantive standards. The only requirement for congruence in this process is that you make yourself accountable for your choice of standards and for your application of them.

The principle of reciprocity. One general test for congruence between the theory and practice of principled negotiation is to ask whether you would feel fairly treated standing in the other side's shoes, and if not, whether you would feel that was the fault of the other negotiator or the broader context of the negotiation. This is an especially sensitive test for people in as unequal a power relationship as graduate teachers and students often feel themselves to be.

Enlarging the Course

Most academic negotiation courses have been taught to groups of under thirty students.[86] Most are structured around a variety of negotiation exercises with various kinds of feedback (discussion with the other party, discussion with the professor, videotape, comparison of outcomes with other groups, and so on) and group review and discussion. Efficiency demands, if possible, that ways be found to increase the student to professor ratio without making a major sacrifice in the quality of each student's experience. The main difficulties lie in structuring review and discussion, although the administrative undertaking is daunting. Large groups promote disengagement, depersonalization, and passivism. Countering these tendencies requires considerable skill and sensitivity running a large class, massive and precise preparation, and if at all possible, the use of teaching assistants to replace large with small group discussions. With adequate human and material resources the result should be satisfactory.

The Individual in a Large Group

Loss of engagement. It is a simple fact of division that there is less "air time" per person available in a larger group than a smaller. The opportunities to participate and to some extent control the activity of the group are similarly less. This may not be a problem if the activity is a lecture or demonstration, but those approaches do not represent the kind of learning by doing necessary for effective negotiation training. There is also a tendency for a larger group to be a more demanding and critical audience. Perhaps a better performance is felt to be a quid pro quo for less participation, or perhaps it is merely reflects recognition that the cost of the performance—in terms of other people's time—is higher. Alternatively, it may be that in a small group people are more accommodating as a personal favor, but in a large group they do not experience the same level of intimacy.

The Socratic case method is an attempt to compensate for loss of actual activity with vicarious engagement. By motivating interest in a topic, focusing discussion on one narrowly-defined question at a time, and making everyone liable to take over actual participation at any given moment, the technique aims to have everyone thinking along as if they were the person speaking. In addition, the use of case studies is an efficient way to sensitize people to major themes, contexts, and possible mistakes. The traditional Socratic method, however, can only deal with explicit learning. Because participants are limited to talking about action instead of acting, their ingrained operating habits remain unexamined and unchanged.

One obvious approach for overcoming this drawback would be to invite participants not merely to talk about what should be done but to proceed as an actor doing what they recommend, with the professor or another participant playing the other party. However, this approach immediately takes away the focus of the discussion. Instead of extended focus on a single narrow question, there is now no discussion of a rapid series of questions—stop action is replaced with full forward. The result is to replace Socratic discussion with a demonstration. Demonstrations, like all examples, are powerful teaching tools, but they are essentially passive. They need to be regularly and rapidly paired with opportunities to experiment with any insights picked up.

Threats to self-worth and security. It is difficult for many people in a large homogenous group (especially those who base self-esteem on comparisons with others) to maintain their sense of specialness and self-worth. Asserting oneself in such a context involves an implicit statement that you are more worth listening to than others. That is a high-risk act, removing you somewhat from the security of being a regular member of the group, and setting yourself up for criticism from any who themselves feel threatened by your initiative. Large groups also emphasize the unequal power relationship between students and the professor, another potential threat to self-esteem.

In response to such feelings, which create cognitive dissonance, people are prone to fall back on their usual repertoire of dissonance-reduction strategies. They may disengage from the experience, saying to themselves, "It's not my bag," or "This is just obvious common sense," or "This is baloney," and collecting evidence to support those views. Or they may just withdraw into passivism without any conscious rationale. They may feel alienated and alone, and they may become hostile and even aggressive toward the professor and perhaps other participants. These feelings may lead people to play point-scoring and "gotcha" games, looking for mistakes or grievances to harp on.[87] Avoiding such reactions requires an energetic effort of inclusion, and if that doesn't work, confrontation. Developing a sense of inclusion may require a fairly high rate of participant activity, preferably doing things they feel are relevant and as part of a group of people they feel are like them.[88]

Depersonalization. One effect of a large group can be to make people feel unimportant. At times, this can become a complete loss of individual identity (and responsibility), replacing it with a group identity ruled by emotions. At the extreme the group becomes a mindless mob.[89] Loss of individuality is accompanied by loosening of the usual social restraints on our behavior; people will do things as part of a group that they would never consider on their own. Further, freeing the beast in this way can be extremely satisfying, although it may produce guilt later on.[90]

Not only do crowds reduce one's own sense of individuality, they promote the depersonalization and abstraction of others. Other people become objects. Perhaps this is because of an information overflow. What makes people unique individuals like ourselves are their particularized idiosyncracies and differences. In a large group, however, it is impossible to hold such detailed information in mind about everyone—it is simply too much information to think about at once. Instead we retreat to broader, simpler, and more abstract concepts—people become ideas, abstractions, things. In this level of unreality we can contemplate many things at a far remove from their particularized human consequences and have no ready reality check on our conclusions.[91] Like stereotypes, for example, such abstractions cannot be disproven by single instances of nonconformity. Indeed such nonconformity may increase commitment to an abstract belief in conformance with cognitive dissonance theory.[92]

Mobs are unlikely to occur in the classroom, but lesser group effects may. People may enjoy cruel fun at the expense or discomfort of others.[93] They may elevate relatively minor complaints to major proportions.[94] The variety of their perceptions and opinions may diminish and converge to avoid nonconformity.[95] This may occur even when a person's expressed views remain unchanged![96] Courtesy, patience, empathy, and rationality may all decline.[97] Teachers too may be affected in this way. They will face a tendency to think of students as undifferentiated, to react to the sins of a few with vengeance on the whole, and to ignore individuals for the benefit of the larger group. Each of these behaviors is likely to produce a negative reaction from students, and can easily reinforce any negative student perceptions. To combat such effects we need ways to reinforce and maintain a perceptual mode rooted at the level of individuals.

Maintaining the "Level of Individuals"
Setting an example. As with other unconscious behavior patterns, one of the most persuasive techniques a teacher can use to bring about change is to exemplify the alternative. Beyond the strictures of clear reasoning discussed in the third part ("The Teaching Challenge") of this paper, this involves several behaviors specifically intended to combat depersonalization. One of the simplest, though it may not be easy, is to memorize and use student's names, preferably their first names, since those imply greater intimacy. It is important to do this early on, and to be conscientious and comprehensive, to have the maximum initial impact on student expectations and perceptions of the class. Students know that memorizing names for most people requires a major effort; it is a powerful message that the teacher is strongly engaged in the course and caring about individuals.[98] This effort may give rise to a feeling of obligation to return a personal favor. It also makes it easier for the professor to confront nonoptimal behaviors in class on a personal level as a friend, instead of as an authority figure dispensing judgment.

A second behavior concerns how student comments and questions are dealt with in a large class. Because time is scarce and questions are seldom framed or timed in the way a professor would prefer to cover the themes she or he thinks important, professors tend to answer somewhat different questions than those that are asked, and then often to go on from there. Naturally enough, this approach tends to leave the questioner unsatisfied. The professor may reason, in essence, that this is a price that has to be paid to communicate efficiently with the class as a whole. In fact, however, the cost is much greater, because this discourtesy to one student tends to be seen and felt by all as insulting, and often as deceptive as well. On top of their primary effect, these feelings may well distract students from hearing what the professor was working at such cost to say.

To avoid this effect, questions either have to be answered to the questioner's satisfaction or the professor has to explain and perhaps negotiate not doing so. The simple techniques of repeating the student's question before beginning to answer, and asking before going on, "Does that answer your question?" or "Is that responsive?" can help ensure compliance. Once the question is dealt with as asked, the professor can of course move on to the question they think should be considered. More than just avoiding resentment, focusing on questions students actually ask sends several other important messages. First, it reemphasizes that it is what is going on in students' heads that counts. The point is not for the professor to think clearly about the subject. Second, it reinforces the importance of each individual. Finally, it puts responsibility on the student to think. (This message, though, can be somewhat diluted if the professor makes a habit of answering questions students could think through on their own. Seeing that the questioner ultimately feels answered—and that the professor communicates awareness of and concern for that end—does not mean that the professor has to answer every question directly or themselves. They can quite consistently respond with questions of their own, as long as the last question is, "Does that answer your question?" and the answer is "Yes" or "I need to think about it," or the like.)

A third behavior professors should monitor closely is their tendency to categorize and label students and their comments. Labels de-emphasize uniqueness. Categorizing student responses, even to oneself, tends to make them seem boring. If students pick up on such a feeling, as they well may, it may remind them of how many other students have gone before, which is also depersonalizing. It may also make them resentful, since it can be taken as an attack on their self-esteem. Finally, categorizing responses tends to stimulate canned responses instead of individually tailored ones. Since no two students ever follow precisely the same paths of reasoning, a canned response will seldom be ideal. On top of that, it may be less persuasive merely because it is less personal.

Confronting depersonalizing behavior. In addition to carefully molding their own behavior as an example, teachers can help students to change depersonalizing behavior by confronting it. Confrontation can be direct, with analysis and explanation, side-by-side, suggesting alternative language and having the student try it out, or a combination of both, with side-by-side followed by explanation. As always, teachers in confronting should be careful to take responsibility for their perceptions and encourage testing of all assumptions including their own.

Increasing Engagement

Students in a large class can, subject to the availability of working space, be given the same program of exercises as a smaller workshop. Much of the worth of exercises, however, comes from the review and coaching of a student's performance, individually and in group discussion. Here is where the logistics of a large class threaten the quality of student experience. Given a finite amount of professorial time, the larger the class the less of that time is available for any given student. One approach to the large class problem is simply to accept a diminution in training effectiveness and weigh that against the benefits of spreading training over a larger number of people. Indeed, to some extent such a diminution seems inevitable. The question, however, is how to minimize the loss of quality.

Optimize the match of purpose and process. One way to maximize the impact of a large class is to choose with care the class structure or process best suited to the instructor's purpose at any given time. If the task is one of explicit review, analysis, or theory-building, the best approach may be a focused Socratic dialog. A rough rule of thumb is that the degree of focus of the discussion should be proportional to the number of participants, to take account of the decreased access to air time. If the task is to challenge paradigms, examine implicit behavior, or explain possible behaviors, the best route may be a demonstration. Demonstrations can be offered as exemplary, probably performed by the instructor, or as illustrative, to provide a concrete basis for focused discussion. Finally, the most efficient approach to simple information transfer (for which mere memorization is a sufficient initial response) remains the lecture.

Another mechanism that can be useful is small group meetings among participants without an instructor. These can take advantage of the desire for the respect of others to generate a more reliable and intensive effort by participants. This is perhaps especially suited to preparation exercises, and probably works best if students are to have prepared a written product in advance that they are to share with each other.[99] Co-participants in an exercise can also fruitfully be asked to review the process and outcome of the exercise together. Conceivably, if expectations were carefully set in advance, more ambitious use might be made of small group discussion. Students could, for example, be expected to form official study groups to review and synthesize their experience in the course and to formulate thematic questions for large group discussion. Many students do arrange and participate in such groups on their own in law schools. It is not inconceivable that the practice could be sponsored more systematically.

Use student teaching assistants. One traditional way to spread a senior instructor thinner is to transfer some of the professor's functions to more junior teaching assistants. These can be especially impressive former graduates of the course or of more advanced courses. Teaching assistants can facilitate small group discussions of the exercises and larger themes. They can also greatly increase the amount of individual feedback available to students.

The drawback is in the uncertain quality of that feedback. Few teaching assistants have the skills or experience to rival the professor. Regular meetings of the assistants with the professor are important to promote consistency of outlook and approach, although as in other contexts what people say and what they do will be at variance. A more meaningful interaction with the professor would be to have the teaching assistants themselves form a more advanced class also working to understand negotiation better and to build better theory. This increases the assistant's engagement and understanding of the material and helps give them the excitement of current work in progress to share with students.

Radical options. Two more unusual options can be suggested for increasing student engagement. They are applicable to any course, but their benefits, if achieved, might be of greater marginal utility in a large class. The first is to empower students themselves to administer the course. The second is to incorporate students into the grading process, not necessarily for themselves, but for their fellow students. Putting students in charge of the course certainly risks chaos, but it guarantees a rich lode of fully "real" negotiation experience to analyze, review, and with which to experiment further. An instructor with the necessary skill to take advantage of this material in real time, and while themselves being a party to the negotiations might produce an astonishingly powerful learning experience.

Having students evaluate one another also introduces an element of real negotiation into the classroom, and it provides a legitimate incentive for closer scrutiny of the elements and practice of effective negotiation. Presumably students would be asked to justify their evaluations and to do so on the basis of criteria against which they themselves are prepared to be measured. No doubt other radical options are available. Students might undertake to write short monographs on narrow themes in small groups, for example. Perhaps these groups could correspond to their teaching assistant working groups. Students themselves might be asked to invent a radical option. Their own proposal would carry special legitimacy.

Conclusion: Uncertain
At this point experience with training large groups in negotiation in a serious academic setting is too limited for final conclusions about its ultimate feasibility and effectiveness. More experimentation in a variety of contexts, with a greater variety of instructors, and using different course structures is needed. There is no known reason in theory why considerable success should not be possible.

Conclusion
We have argued, from evidence, that there is a pressing need for professional education in negotiation, and that such education is eminently possible. Providing that training most effectively, however, requires considerable pedagogical skill and expertise. It is in many ways a more challenging undertaking than any course aimed at information transfer, and even, because of the overlap of content and process, more challenging than courses aimed at the develop-

ment of familiarity and understanding of established theory. Success is possible, however, and demands honesty, integrity, curiosity, and security more than perfection in a professor.

The potential rewards of widespread effective negotiation training are correspondingly large. The increasing cost, complexity, and delays in litigation are rapidly increasing the demand for effective alternatives. Legislative, executive, and regulatory processes are all bogging down in inefficient negotiation and litigation approaches. Improvement in the international negotiating framework is increasingly basic to our physical security. Improvement in each of these areas will be more likely to the extent that systematic, sophisticated, and effective training in negotiation becomes more widely available. Indeed, the effect of comprehensive negotiation training could, given the quality of interpersonal assumptions and behavior now common, revolutionize our society, potentially narrowing the gap between the theory and the reality of democracy farther than ever before. It is worth the effort to make such training widely available.

Notes

1. The figure most often given is 90%. Gerald Williams in *Legal Negotiation and Settlement* (West, 1983), at 1, cites statistics for U.S. District Courts and some aspects of state and local court experience suggesting that fewer than 10% of the cases actually filed go to trial, and fewer still go on to a verdict. Given that litigation is only a subset of the things lawyers do, and the wide range of activities that can be thought of as negotiation or preparation for negotiation, 90% seems a reasonable, and perhaps even a conservative, figure.

2. At Harvard Law School, for example, there are currently seven litigation-related courses with a total of twelve sections. In contrast, there are now only four courses related to negotiation and mediation (one of which has no experiential component), with a total of five sections. There have of course been scattered negotiation courses for some time, but Harry T. Edwards' and James J. White's pioneering textbook, *Problems, Readings and Materials on The Lawyer As a Negotiator* (West), did not appear until 1977, and widespread attention to the subject dates from about that time. Whereas trial advocacy and litigation training for new litigation associates of large firms is now well-established, and the National Institute for Trial Advocacy has experienced concern, law firm interest in negotiation training is just beginning, and there is no centralized and reputable supplier.

3. Williams, supra note 1, at v-vii. Williams' work is perhaps the first systematic, empirical analysis of how lawyers negotiate.

4. Williams, supra note 1, at 6-7. Williams had forty experienced attorneys negotiate one-on-one the same simulated personal injury case. Fourteen of the twenty pairs were willing to submit a written record of their results. These settlements ranged from $15,000 to $95,000 in an almost even distribution.

5. See, e.g., Slonim, Bar Exam Experiment Could Blaze New Path, 66 *ABA J.* 139 (1980), reporting an experiment in California aimed at testing bar applicants in areas such as legal research and negotiation. Slonim's quotes of Armando Menocal III, Chairman of the

California Committee of Bar Examiners, are quite startling: "'We all agree that if it is appropriate to screen people for the practice of law, the only valid test is one that determines who is competent to practice, so the public is protected.'... 'No bar examination has ever been validated as related to fitness to practice law.'... 'We all know many incompetent practitioners who have passed bar exams.'...Menocal adds: 'Many people strongly suspect that law school graduates who would be competent to practice are failing exams.'" See also, *Lawyer Competency: The Role of the Law Schools* (1979) by the American Bar Association Section of Legal Education and Admissions to the Bar, which recommends that courses in negotiation and other practical skills be offered in all law schools.

6. Roger Fisher and William Ury, with Bruce Patton, Editor, *Getting to YES: Negotiating Agreement Without Giving In,* Houghton Mifflin, 1991 (2nd edition).

7. See especially, Roger Fisher with the help of William Ury, *International Mediation: A Working Guide; Ideas for the Practitioner* (Harvard Negotiation Project, 1978); Fisher and Ury, *Principled Negotiation*, December 1980 Draft Edition (unpublished); Bruce Patton, *Reassessing Getting to YES and Principled Negotiation* (PON Working Paper 85-6, 1985); and Fisher, Negotiating Power: Getting and Using Influence, 27 *American Behavioral Scientist* 149 (1983).

8. Conversation reported by Professor Roger Fisher of Harvard Law School.

9. Edwards and White, supra note 2, at 52-6.

10. Students in courses taught by Professors Roger Fisher and Frank Sander at Harvard Law School have been nearly unanimous in such comments, even several years after the course. Further, most feel that the course gave them the skills to keep learning from their post-course experience. Professor Gerald Williams (Brigham Young University School of Law), Henry Edwards (Harvard University), Stephen Goldberg (University of Chicago), and many other reports similar feeling among their students. Conference on Teaching Negotiation in Law Schools sponsored by the Harvard Law School Program on Dispute Resolution and the Association of American Law Schools, October 1982.

11. Professor Unterman discussed his experience in a presentation to the Foreign Service Institute's June 9-10, 1983 Conference on International Negotiation in Washington, D.C. Reported to the author by Roger Fisher and Lawrence Susskind.

12. See the works of John Grinder, Richard Bandler, and Robert Dilts related to neurolinguistic programming and genius, for example, Bandler and Grinder, *Frogs Into Princes* (Real People Press, 1979); Dilts, *Strategies of Genius* (Meta Publications, 1995); or Grinder and Judith Delozier, *Turtles All the Way Down: Prerequisites to Personal Genius* (Metamorphosis Press, 1995).

13. Edwards and White, supra note 2, at 1.

14. There is a story, possibly apocryphal but in character, that Einstein was asked, shortly after the Second World War, why, when the nearly incomprehensible secrets of the invisible atom had been unlocked, we had still not solved the familiar problem of war. His alleged reply: "Politics is more complicated than physics."

15. Derek Bok in *The President's Report, 1981-82* (Harvard University) made this argument among other criticisms of the legal profession. Even medicine has suffered from a similar oversight. See, e.g., Derek Bok, *The President's Report, 1982-83* (Harvard University) or Martha Weinman Lear's much more personal account, *Heartsounds* (Pocket Books, 1980).

16. See, e.g., Howard Raiffa, *The Art and Science of Negotiation* (Harvard University Press, 1982); Jeffrey Z. Rubin and Bert R. Brown, *The Social Psychology of Bargaining and Negotiation* (Academic Press, 1975); Williams, supra note 1; Richard E. Walton and Robert B. McKersie, *A Behavioral Theory of Labor Negotiations* (McGraw Hill, 1965); and case studies such as John C. Campbell, ed., *Successful Negotiation: Trieste 1954* (Princeton University Press, 1976); Jeffrey Z. Rubin, ed., *Dynamics of Third Party Intervention: Kissinger In the Middle East* (Praeger, 1981); and I. William Zartman, *The 50% Solution* (Anchor Books, 1976).

17. Robert E. Mathews, Negotiation: A Pedagogical Challenge, 6 *Journal Legal Education.* 93 (1953).

18. The objection may be raised that the Socratic method is often used to teach subjects such as property precisely to develop real understanding of the subject instead of mindless memorization. Yet the goal remains mere understanding. There is no practice in drafting and few real application exercises at all.

19. Perhaps the most popular commercial course is Gerald Nierenberg's Negotiation Institute in New York. Typically this is a one- or two-day seminar for more than a hundred people. Advertisements received in my mail offer participants four books and other materials and promise information on more than 2.5 million variables in negotiation (according to a *Wall Street Journal* article excerpted in the latest [March 1984]) brochure.

20. Howard Raiffa, supra note 15, at 2-5, an eminent game theoretian among many other accomplishments, makes an eloquent autobiographical comment on this problem in the prologue to his book.

21. Essentially the same problem as with game theory.

22. Williams, supra note 1, is the most extensive empirical work done with lawyers.

23. See Fisher, Ury, and Patton, supra note 6, Introduction and Chapter 1.

24. See David Gold, Zero-Sum Bargaining (unpublished) or Roger Fisher, Toward Second-Order Agreement, 34 *J. Legal Ed.* 1 (1984).

25. See, e.g., R. M. Chert and J. G. March, *A Behavioral Theory of the Firm* (Prentice-Hall, 1963). People's behavior is also strongly influence by their degree of risk aversion. Fewer people will risk their life savings on a 10 to 1 chance of a tenfold return than will risk one-tenth of their savings on a 5 to 1 chance of a fivefold return.

26. The term is from Fisher, Ury, and Patton, supra note 6.

27. Fisher, Ury, and Patton, supra note 6, Chapter 2.

28. Fisher, Ury, and Patton, supra note 6, at 4.

29. This refers to conscious, systematic learning. Unconscious or implicit learning, including conditioning, is continuous, but seldom systematic and often illogical. See infra.

30. See John Holt, *How Children Fail* (Pitman, 1964), at 91-101, 121-123. See also note 32.

31. Jean Piaget, The Right to Education in the Present World (1984), in *To Understand Is to Invent; The Future of Education* (English language translation: Viking, 1973), at 103.

32. Piaget, A Foundation for Tomorrow's Education (1972), in *To Understand Is to Invent*, supra note 30, at 15.

33. Thus the title of Piaget's book, supra note 30. John Holt gives a dramatic illustration of this principle in *How Children Learn* (Pitman, 1969), at 180-81. He describes a group of children who, given a piece of paper and shown a finished product, had no trouble making a folded paper fan. Their teacher then carefully read them the instructions in their textbook for the task. They were good instructions and the teacher read them slowly and clearly. At the end, not one student could make another fan, even with their original lying in front of them. He argues that these children might well have been able to turn their own reality into symbols, if asked, but were not able to turn another's symbols into their reality.

34. This hierarchy may not hold if something we observe triggers a pre-existing fear or becomes the basis for a fantasy.

35. Created for the Harvard Negotiation Project by Mark Drooks and revised by Mark N. Gordon. copyright Harvard Law School 1982, 1985, 1987, and 1990 by the President and Fellows of Harvard College. All rights reserved. Available from the PON Clearinghouse, Program on Negotiation, Harvard Law School, Cambridge, MA 02138, tel. 495-1684.

36. See, e.g., Bertram H. Raven and Jeffrey Z. Rubin, *Social Psychology,* second edition (John Wiley & Sons, 1983), at 360-90; Douglas R. Hofstadter, "Metamagical Themes: Computer Tournaments of the Prisoner's Dilemma Suggest How Cooperation Evolves," 248 *Scientific American* 16 (1983); Rubin and Brown, supra note 15, at 20-25.

37. The game has been used with approximately 340 Harvard Law students over three years who have taken one of the Negotiation Workshops taught by Professors Fisher and Sander, and by more than two hundred experienced lawyers in corporate seminars taught by Professor Fisher. The results have not been formally tabulated, but are largely consistent across both groups.

38. More than a year after playing Pepulator, one student astonished the author by describing precisely which members of her class had been on what teams, where they had met, and salient features of each of the two games that were played.

39. This technique was brought to the author's attention by Dr. Richard Chasin of the Harvard Medical School, who used it in the January 1984 Negotiation Workshops, supra note 36, at Harvard Law School.

40. Piaget (1972), supra note 31, at 16. Piaget worked mostly with children, but the thrust of his argument applies to anyone learning theory, and is widely accepted as such.

41. Holt (1969), supra note 32, at 72.

42. Piaget (1972), supra note 31, at 16.

43. Piaget defines respect with some precision as a mixture of affection and fear. In this context, the fear would be of losing prestige in the other's eyes. Piaget (1948), supra note 30, at 113, 116.

44. Id., at 107, 118.

45. Most children have a sense of the separateness of their bodies by the age of two. Most children's first words come at around twelve months, although sounds are perceived categorically very early. Their verbal ability increases dramatically over the next two years, more slowly thereafter. See Howard Gardner, *Developmental Psychology*, second edition (Little, Brown, 1982), at 132, 161.

46. The capacity for systematic formal logical analysis is a primary characteristic of adolescence. Id., at 514-21.

47. Chris Argyris, *Reasoning, Learning, and Action: Individual and Organizational* (Jossey-Bass, 1982), at 85-101.

48. Alfred Rorzybski, *Science and Sanity: An Introduction to Non-Aristotelian Systems and General Semantics*, fourth edition (Institute of General Semantics, 1958).

49. Some related experimental data are described in Raven and Rubin, supra note 35, at 86-98, 562-65.

50. The author was one of two co-mediators working for the Children's Hearings Project in Cambridge, Massachusetts.

51. It can be argued that in fact the primary purpose of the Senate's action was to garner domestic approval, but the record shows strongly emotional language on the merits.

52. Chris Argyris, supra note 46, at 29, 32, 43.

53. Id., at 37-38.

54. See Harold J. Leavitt, *Managerial Psychology; An Introduction to Individuals, Pairs, and Groups in Organizations*, fourth edition (U. Chicago Press, 1964), at 7-10.

55. See E. Mavis Hetherington and Ross D. Parke, *Child Psychology: A Contemporary Viewpoint* (McGraw-Hill, 1975), at 174-178; Raven and Rubin, supra note 35, at 67-68; Leavitt, supra note 53. at 12-20.

56. See Holt (1969), supra note 32, at 8.

57. See Leavitt, supra note 53, at 13-18. See also Carol Gilligan, *In a Different Voice; Psychological Theory and Women's Development* (Harvard University Press, 1982), Chapters 1 and 2. Whether the child experiences dependence as mostly satisfying or frustrating is thought by many personality theorists to be a major determinant of security or insecurity, and also to affect a person's ability to form successful adult relationships. In general, people feel ambivalent about dependence. They may dislike their lack of power, on the one hand, but appreciate their lack of responsibility on the other.

58. See G. A. Miller, The Magical Number Seven, Plus or Minus Two: Some Limits on Our Capacity for Processing Information, 63 *Psych. Rev.* 81 (1956). Miller's hypothesis, widely accepted, is that we can keep in mind no more than seven (plus or minus two) "meaningful chunks" of information at any given time.

59. David H. Hubel, Calvin O. Henson, Rupert Allen, and Robert Gallambos, Attention Units in the Auditory Cortex, 129 *Science* 1279 (1959). See also G. Horn, Electrical Activity of the Cerebral Cortex of the Unanaethetized Cat During Attentive Behavior, 83 *Brain* 57 (1960).

60. Raul Hernandez-Peon, Harold Scherer, and Michel Jouvet, Modification of Electric Activity in Cochlear Nucleus During "Attention" in Unanaesthetized Cats, 123 *Science* 331 (1956). A later experiment showed that the reduction in cochlear activity was probably the result of muscular contractions associated generally with arousal, rather than of a direct signal from the reticular formation in the brain. The signals were only reduced, however; they never actually ceased as in the Hubel experiment, supra note 58.

61. E. C. Cherry, Some Experiments on the Recognition of Speech with One and Two Ears, 25 J. *Acoustical Society of America* 975 (1953).

62. Raven and Rubin, supra note 35, at 7. The theory of cognitive dissonance was proposed by Leon Festinger in *A Theory of Cognitive Dissonance* (Stanford University Press, 1957).

63. See Thomas Kuhn, *The Structure of Scientific Revolutions*, second edition, enlarged (University Chicago Press, 1970), Chapter VIII, at 77.

64. Holt (1964), supra note 29, at 80; Holt (1969), supra note 32, at 79-80, 135.

65. A rule of science and logic favoring the theory with the fewest unsupported assumptions that fits the known facts. Most adults are sensitive to the concept, whether or not they have heard of the rule.

66. Most of these examples are suggested in Raven and Rubin, supra note 35, at 2-15. On the Holocaust, see Raul Bilberg, The Nature of the Process, at 24ff, and John P. Sabini and Maury Silver, Destroying the Innocent with a Clear Conscience: A Sociopsychology of the Holocaust, at 346ff, in Joel E. Dimsdale, *Survivors, Victims, and Perpetrators: Essays on the Nazi Holocaust* (HemisPhere, 1980).

67. The theory of cognitive dissonance was first tested in an experiment by Leon Festinger, Henry W. Riecken, and Stanley Schachter reported in *When Prophecy Fails* (University Minnesota Press, 1956). They observed the members of an end-of-the-world group as their prophecy failed. Those members who spent the time together "found" new information explaining the discrepancy, reinterpreted their beliefs, and went out to find new converts, as predicted. Also as predicted, those members of the group who awaited the prophecy elsewhere, surrounded by nonbelievers, experienced disillusionment and embarrassment.

68. See Holt (1964), supra note 29, at 38ff; Matina Horner, Toward an Understanding of Achievement-Related Conflicts in Women. 28 J. *Social Issues* 157 (1972).

69. See Piaget (1948), supra note 30, at 124.

70. See Holt (1964), supra note 29, at 38-49, 57-59.

71. See, e.g., Piaget (1948), supra note 30, at 122-26; Neil Postman and Charles Weingartner, *Teaching as a Subversive Activity* (Dell, 1969), Chapter XI.

72. See Holt (1969), supra note 32, at 86-93.

73. Roger Fisher, Some Notes on Pedagogical Theory, from the General Memorandum for Negotiation, a course taught at Harvard Law School by Professor Fisher in the spring of 1984, at 3. The "massage parlor" metaphor is also from Professor Fisher. Raven and Rubin, supra note 35, at 74-77.

74. Holt (1969), supra note 32, at 88-89.

75. Holt (1969), supra note 32, at 88-89.

76. See Bolt (1964), supra note 29, at 42-45.

77. Raven and Rubin, supra note 35, at 118.

78. Id., at 119. See also A. L. Chaikin and V. J. Derlega, *Sharing Intimacy: What We Reveal to Others* (Prentice-Hall/ Spectrum, 1975).

79. In the Negotiation Workshops, supra note 36, student evaluations have been highest in those semesters when new theory was most actively under development. The same classes have led to the most productive and long-lasting relationships with former students.

80. First-order agreement would refer to a settlement of the primary issues. Second-order agreement means reaching a consensus on what the precise differences between the parties are.

81. Journals have been used to grade students taking the Negotiation Workshop, supra note 36, and Negotiation, supra note 72, since the winter term in 1979. Both the author and Professor Fisher have found it relatively easy to sort journals into quality categories. Deciding on the grades to assign to these categories has been for more difficult.

82. Another approach is to offer detailed evaluation and ranking of outcomes for all possible exercises in a course, without tying this information to grades. This can be a lot of work, but may be worth it. It was tried once, full scale, in a Harvard Law School Negotiation Workshop in the early 1990s with good results. More recently the Harvard Business School's mandatory first-year negotiation course has made use of automated reports generated through on-line reporting.

83. The classic approach to an outcome-based evaluation scheme is described by Edwards and White in their text, supra note 2, at 2-3. It is a duplicate bridge model.

84. Several years ago a new undergraduate introductory biology course was offered at Harvard. Suitable as a medical school prerequisite, it looked to be easier than the regular course. More than 250 people signed up. The instructors had expected no more than 100; facilities and their enthusiasm were limited. It was announced, several days before the first class, that there would be a lottery for admission. At that point a line of angry students formed outside the course office, each demanding to be let in for one reason or another. Tempers flared and complaints were bitter. "I planned my whole schedule around this course," was a common plaint. Yet the fact is that more than 50% of the courses in the Harvard catalog are restricted in enrollment, many of the largest and most popular require a lottery for admission (including the pre-med staple, organic chemistry), no one has ever protested (though several have pleaded), and students are not required to file a final study card until two weeks into the semester. This brouhaha was entirely a product of unexpected changed expectations.

85. Negotiation Workshops, supra note 36.

86. Roger Fisher has now taught two courses, supra note 72, to groups of around 80 students in the spring of 1983 and 1984 at Harvard Law School. Results are not as satisfactory as in the smaller Negotiation Workshops. Williams, supra note 1, reports in his accompanying *Teacher's Manual with Course Materials and Problems for Negotiation* (West, 1983), at 1, that he has taught up to 85 students at a time.

87. See Eric Berne, *Games People Play: The Psychology of Human Relationships* (Grove, 1964), at 85-87, for a description of the "gotcha" game.

88. Raven and Rubin, supra note 35, at 553, 569-70.

89. Id., at 546.

90. Id., at 546-50.

91. Thinking about "the enemy" in wartime is a good example of this phenomenon. Lyndon Johnson is said always to have referred to the host of forces on the other side in Vietnam as "He." Compare Mark Twain, The War Prayer.

92. Festinger, supra note 66.

93. In the Negotiation Workshops, supra note 36, a psychologist has often been used to review videotapes of class members in front of the rest of the class. In groups of 24, this produces a strongly supportive and cohesive group affect. When something similar was tried with a group of 88 students, supra note 72, bizarre swings of behavior were observed in members of the audience. Watching someone they knew, they demonstrated behavior similar to that of participants in the small group. But watching people they did not know, they amused themselves and others by a variety of derogatory and insensitive comments.

94. In Negotiation, supra note 72, students have several times complained bitterly about administrative incompetence when told an extra trip to the course office (centrally located) would be necessary to incorporate some last-minute innovation or scheduling. Many of the same students, after continuing in this vein for five minutes or more, will then say, when asked, that the course was without question one of the best courses they had taken at the law school. In contrast, students in the smaller Workshops, supra note 36, often complain about the extremely intensive schedule, but almost always explicitly in the frame of, "This is great, but just too much."

95. Raven and Rubin, supra note 35, at 562-76.

96. Id., at 584-85.

97. Observations by the author, Professor Fisher, and teaching assistants of students in Negotiation, supra note 72.

98. Roger Fisher tells a story about an extraordinary demonstration of this approach involving Professor Ernest Brown, a former colleague. Professor Brown was in the habit of studying the pictures of his future students (which they were required to provide as part of the school's admissions process) before they arrived, and memorizing names and faces. Thus it happened that a new first-year student, fresh from the armed forces after World War II and his home in the Midwest, and never having been on the east coast before, arrived in Boston and took the subway to Harvard Square. As he emerged from the subway stairs, baggage in hand, a distinguished looking passerby looked directly at him and said, "Good morning, Mr. Scott. Welcome to Cambridge."

99. This technique has proven extremely effective in two large continuing legal education courses taught at Harvard Law School by Roger Fisher in the summers of 1981 and 1983. Paired off on the first day of class, participants met and reviewed written exercises each morning before class. Though the class was devoted to lecture, engagement was high. Not a single seat was empty in either of the last two classes even though the first was at 8:30 on Saturday morning.

An Interview
With Mary Parker Follett

Albie M. Davis

"I was an accidental bureaucrat, since my roots are in community organizing," says **Albie Davis** of her 16 years as director of mediation for the 69 district courts in Massachusetts. During those 16 years, she did all that she could within the system to promote a productive, respectful relationship between community-based mediation programs and the Trial Court. There were successes and disappointments. By 1999 it was time to move on. For Davis, moving on has meant moving to Maine, learning to live on less, and freeing up time to think, write, and

This article first appeared in *Negotiation Journal*, July 1989: Volume 5, Number 3, pages 223-235.

In the early 1900s, long before contemporary authors on the subject, Mary Parker Follett was an advocate for creative and constructive approaches toward conflict resolution. Yet today, few of us know her name or have read her work. Why did Follett fade from our view? One reason, given by an admirer of hers, Elliot M. Fox, appeared in a 1968 publication honoring what would have been her 100th birthday: "She almost always expressed herself in simple, fairly commonplace terms. Perhaps she would be more carefully studied if she had developed a jargon that invited periodic efforts at interpretation. As it is, her phraseology was so ordinary that few feel the need to explain it" (Fox 1968). Undoubtedly there are additional explanations why she did not maintain her reputation as a pioneer, and it would be interesting to explore them. For the time being, however, the most important task is to bring Follett's ideas back, into our line of vision. We have much to learn and she has much to teach us. I have designed this article to encourage that process.

Far ahead of her times, Follett moved easily between the worlds of theory and practice, between interpersonal examples and international ones, between speculation and assurance. Her writing remains fresh, nondogmatic, experimental, and inspiring. To paraphrase her would be to do her a disservice. For this reason, I use the device of an imaginary interview. The questions are mine and, I hope, yours. Follett's responses are entirely in her own words as recorded in three books: *The New State* (1918) and *The Creative Experience* (1924), which she authored, and *Dynamic Administration* (1942), a collection of her papers. Citations are provided at the end of each answer and will appear as follows: *The New State* (NS); *The Creative Experience*, (CE); and *Dynamic Administration*, (DA). Full information on each citation is available in the accompanying reference section.

The brief second section of the article begins to answer the question, "who was Mary Parker Follett?" and to explore the significance of her ideas and possible reasons why her

redirect her energy. She plans to gather the research she has done on Mary Parker Follett into a book highlighting Follett's life and unique philosophy. Davis can be reached at: 13 Knox Street, Thomaston, ME 04861. Telephone: (207) 354-8562. Email: albiedavis@aol.com.

work has not received wider recognition from the conflict resolution movement.

I regret that after a decade of activity in this field, I did not become acquainted with Follett until early this year. Now that I am familiar with her writing, I see Follett as must reading. Therefore, I have included a list of her works and publications about her as an appendix. Ideally, some day soon, all of her books will be reprinted and widely distributed. At present, however, many of these publications are out of print, so some dectective work will be necessary on the part of readers. Enjoy the search. You will be rewarded!

THE INTERVIEW

Davis: *Thank you for agreeing to this interview. I find your ideas so stimulating and significant, it is difficult to know where to begin. As a starting point, however, could you share your thoughts on the nature of conflict?*

Follett: As conflict—difference—is here in the world, as we cannot avoid it, we should, I think, use it. Instead of condemning it, we should set it to work for us. Why not? What does the mechanical engineer do with friction? Of course his chief job is to eliminate friction, but it is true that he also capitalizes friction. The transmission of power by belts depends on friction between the belt and the pulley. The friction between the driving wheel of the locomotive and the track is necessary to haul the train. All polishing is done by friction. The music of the violin we get by friction. We left the savage state when we discovered fire by friction. We talk of the friction of mind on mind as a good thing. So in business, too, we have to know when to try to eliminate friction and when to try to capitalize it, when to see what work we can make it do. (DA, p. 30-31)

Davis: *What method of dealing with conflict do you recommend?*

Follett: There are three main ways of dealing with conflict: domination, compromise, and integration. Domination, obviously, is a victory of one side over the other. This is the easiest way of dealing with conflict, the easiest for the moment but not usually successful in the long run...

The second way of dealing with conflict, that of compromise, we understand well, for it is the way we settle most of our controversies; each side gives up a little in order to have peace, or, to speak more accurately, in order that the activity which has been interrupted by the conflict may go on. Compromise is the basis of trade union tactics. In collective bargaining, the trade unionist asks for more than he expects to get, allows for what is going to be lopped off in the conference. Thus we often do not know what he really thinks he should have, and this ignorance is a great barrier to dealing with conflict fruitfully.

But I certainly ought not to imply that compromise is peculiarly a trade union method. It is the accepted, the approved, way of ending controversy. Yet no one really wants to compromise, because that means a giving up of something. Is there, then, any other method of ending conflict?

There is a way beginning now to be recognized at least, and even occasionally followed: when two desires are *integrated*, that means that a solution has been found in which both desires have found a place, that neither side has had to sacrifice anything.

Let us take a very simple illustration. In the Harvard Library one day in one of the smaller rooms, someone wanted the window open, I wanted it shut. We opened the window in the next room, where no one was sitting. This was not a compromise, because there was no curtailing of desire; we both got what we really wanted. For I did not want a closed room, I simply did not want the north wind to blow directly on me: likewise the other occupant did not want that particular window open, he merely wanted more air in the room.

I have already given this illustration in print. I repeat it here because this instance, from its lack of any complications, shows my point at once I think. (DA, p. 32)

Davis: *I agree. Its simplicity is its virtue. You'll be pleased to know the story has lasted over time. Fisher and Ury use it in* Getting to YES *(1981, p. 41) to illustrate the concept of focusing on interests, not positions. They mention your name in their foreword. What advice do you give to the person wishing to try your integrative approach toward negotiation?*

Reflections

One of my favorite Follett concepts is circular response, or, as she expresses it, "I never react to you, but to you-plus-me;" or to be more accurate, it is "I-plus-you reacting to you-plus-me." By the very process of meeting, we both become something different. (CE 62) My relationship with Follett follows such a path. When I first met Follett some ten years ago, I knew immediately that I must write about her, but only by letting her speak in her own voice. After all, how do you paraphrase someone who says of the potential in conflict, "All polishing is done by friction." The idea of an interview seemed natural. To my delight, Jeff Rubin, then editor of the *Negotiation Journal*, became my greatest supporter in this endeavor and William Breslin, as the journal's superb managing editor, provided invaluable moral and technical support.

The reverse process of selecting concepts, then constructing questions to bring them alive led to a sense of intimacy with Follett and a desire to bring her to life once again. I asked my good friend and colleague, Janet Rifkin, professor at the University of Massachusetts Amherst, if she knew anyone who might become Follett the way actors have taken on the persona of Mark Twain. Eileen Stewart is a great actor, she said of our mutual friend and then president of the Massachusetts Association of Mediation programs. Eileen, in response to my initial request replied, "Who's Mary Parker Follett! Never heard of her. Not interested!" She did agree, however, to consider the notion and I sent her some of Follett's writing. She called back within minutes of receiving the mailing saying, "I must do this!"

So, Eileen, as Follett, gave a talk and took questions at the 1989 conference of the

Follett: If we do not think that differing necessarily means fighting, even when two desires both claim right of way, if we think that integration is more profitable than conquering or compromising, the first step toward this consummation is to bring the differences into the open. We cannot hope to integrate our differences unless we know what they are. The first rule, then, for obtaining integration is to put your cards on the table, face the real issue, uncover the conflict, bring the whole thing into the open. (DA, p. 36)

Davis: *"The whole thing?" What do you mean by that?*

Follett: The highest lights in a situation are not always those which are most indicative of the real issues involved. Many situations are decidedly complex, involve numerous and varied activities, overlapping activities. There is too great a tendency (perhaps encouraged by popular journalism) to deal with the dramatic moments, forgetting that these are not always the most significant moments...To *find the significant rather than the dramatic features* of industrial controversy, of a disagreement in regard to policy on boards of directors or between managers, is essential to integrative business policies. (DA, p. 7E0)

Davis: *After determining the significant rather than the dramatic geatures of a controversy, what next?*

Follett: Take the demands of both sides and break them up into their constituent parts. Contemporary psychology shows how fatal it is to try to deal with conglomerates. I know a boy who wanted a college education. His father died and he had to go to work at once to support his mother. Had he then to give up his desire? No, for on analysis he found that what he wanted was not a college education, but an education, and there were still ways of getting that. You remember the southern girl who said, "Why, I always thought 'damned Yankee' was one word until I came north." (DA, p. 7E0)

Davis: *Can you further illustrate this concept of breaking up demands into their constituent parts?*

Follett: You will notice that to break up a problem into its various parts involves the examination of symbols, involves, that is, the careful scrutiny of the language used to see what it really means. A friend of mine wanted to go to Europe, but also she did not want to spend the money it would cost. Was there any integration? Yes, she found one. In order to understand it, let us use the method I am advocating; let us ask what did "going to Europe" symbolize to her? In order to do that, we have to break up this whole, "going to Europe." What does "going to Europe" stand for to different people? A sea voyage, seeing beautiful places, meeting new people, a rest or change from daily duties, a dozen other things. Now, this woman had taught for a few years after leaving college and then had gone away and led a somewhat secluded life for a good many years. "Going to Europe" was to her a symbol not of snow mountains, or cathedrals, or pictures, but of meeting people—that was what she wanted. When she was asked to teach in a summer school of young men and women where she would meet a rather interesting staff of teachers and a rather interesting group of students, she immediately accepted. This was her integration. This was not a substitution for her wish, it was her real wish fulfilled. (DA, p. 43)

Davis: *What do you see as the obstacles to the integrative approach to conflict?*

Follett: It requires a high order of intelligence, keen perception and discrimination, more than all, a brilliant inventiveness; it is easier for the trade union to fight than to suggest a better way of running the factory.

Another obstacle to integration is that our way of life has habituated many of us to enjoy domination. Integration seems to many a tamer affair; it leaves no "thrills" of conquest.

Another obstacle to integration is that the matter in dispute is often *theorized* over instead of being taken up as a proposed activity. I have been interested to watch how

Society of Professionals in Dispute Resolution (SPIDR) in Washington, D.C. I enlisted Wally Warfield, Margaret Shaw, and Fred Ferris to serve as a respondents to Follett's talk, and in that process, it was Follett responding to Warfield responding to Shaw, responding to the audience, and so on. I shall never forget Follett's response to Wally when he suggested during his introduction that, since times were more informal than when she was last on this earth, perhaps we might call her Mary. Why of course, Mr. Warfield, she graciously replied to the delight of the audience who thereafter directed their questions to Miss Follett.

In 1992 SPIDR created a Follett award to recognize those who show passion, risk-taking and innovation in their approach to conflict resolution. The first award was presented to Roberta Jamison, Ombuds of Ontario. The most recent (1999) was given to two activist judges from Argentina—Gladys Stella Alvarez and Elena

Ines Highton. During her acceptance speech, Judge Alvarez recalled that she was present at the original Follett performance and was deeply touched by her philosophy.

I was lucky enough to be in South Africa to present the 1995 Follett award to the Community Dispute Resolution Trust (winner that year along with Independent Mediation Service of South Africa and Richard Salem's Conflict Management Initiatives for their work developing conflict resolution in South Africa). I was a bit nervous wondering whether the words of Follett, in some respects a quintessential Yankee, would resonate in the post-apartheid New South Africa. I made my talk very short, less than a minute, concluding with Follett's observation that "As long as we think of difference as that which divides us,

often disagreement disappears when theorizing ends and the question is of some definite activity to be undertaken.

A serious obstacle to integration...is the language used...I think that the "grievance committees" which exist in most factories are a mistake. I do not like the "trouble specialists" of the Ford plant. I wish it were not so often stated that shop or department committees were formed to "settle disputes."

I have left untouched one of the chief obstacles to integration—namely, the undue influence of leaders—the manipulation of the unscrupulous on the one hand, and the suggestibility of the crowd on the other. Moreover, even when the power of suggestion is not used deliberately, it exists in all meetings between people; the whole emotional field of human intercourse has to be taken fully into account in dealing with methods of reconciliation. (DA, p. 45-48)

Davis: *I find myself attracted to your notion of solving problems by working together to solve them, rather than theorizing about how they might be solved. Could you expand on this idea?*

Follett: Through our observation of human relations, through the teachings of psychology, we learn that from our concrete activities spring both the power and the guide for those activities. Experience is the dynamo station; here are generated will and purpose. Further, and of the utmost importance, here too arise the standard with which to judge that same will and purpose. Men used to say that they relied on their wives' intuitions, but wives today are more apt to be out viewing facts for themselves than staying at home intuiting. (CE, p. 85)

Davis: *How do you incorporate your activity-oriented approach toward problem solving into your ideas about integrative negotiations?*

Follett: To put this still another way: integration, the resolution of conflict, the harmonizing of difference, must take place on the motor level, not on the intellectual level. We cannot get genuine agreement by mere discussion in conference. As our responses are governed by past habits, by what has been incorporated in the organism, the only way of getting other responses is by getting other things incorporated in the organism.

We have not understood this: A man goes home from an international conference and wonders why he cannot carry his people with him in regard to what has there been agreed on. We assign a number of reasons for this; the real reason is that agreement has to come from and through what is going on every day in that nation. To persuade his people into verbal acceptance means only a pseudoagreement, and the underlying dissent will only crop up again in some other form...Genuine integration occurs in the sphere of activities, and not of ideas or wills. Hence the present aim of our international conferences is wrong; the aim should be not intellectual agreement alone, but to provide opportunities for actual agreement through the activities of the nations involved. (CE, p. 150)

Davis: *So, you see your ideas having application to both interpersonal and international affairs!*

Follett: The only thing that will help toward any genuine solution of our world problems today are methods which will open the way for those responses which will help to create a different situation. Concepts can never be presented to me merely, they must be knitted into the structure of my being, and this can be done only through my own activity. (CE, p. 151)

Davis: *But, don't your concepts for constructive conflict require a world where people share the same values?*

Follett: What people often mean by getting rid of conflict is getting rid of diversity, and it is of the utmost importance that these should not be considered the same. We may wish to abolish conflict, but we cannot get rid of diversity. We must face life as it is and understand that diversity is its most essential feature...Fear of difference is dread of life itself. It is possible to conceive conflict as not necessarily a wasteful outbreak of incompatibilities, but a normal process by which socially valuable differences register themselves for the enrichment of all concerned. (CE, p. 300)

Davis: *What would you recommend we do to increase the use of the integrative approach?*

we shall surely dislike it; when we think of it as that which unites us, we shall cherish it." (NS, 39) The applause for the recipients and Follett was resounding and several African participants came up at the end of the ceremony to copy down the exact wording of the quote. The living nature of Follett's philosophy seems to transcend cultural boundaries and continues to energize me some ten years after our original meeting.

Follett: Perhaps the greatest of all obstacles to intention is our lack of training for it. In our college debates we try always to beat the other side. In the circular announcing the courses to be given at the Bryn Mawr Summer School for Workers, I find: "English Composition and Public Speaking: to develop the art of oral and written expression." I think that in addition to this, there should be classes in discussion which should aim to teach the "art" of cooperative thinking. (DA, p. 48)

Davis: *The integrative approach toward conflict that you recommend—some critics totally would say it is naive, wishful thinking. An integrative negotiator won't stand a chance against a combative one. How would you respond to them?*

Follett: Some people tell me that they like what I have written on integration, but say that I am talking of what ought to be instead of what is. But indeed I am not; I am talking neither of what is, to any great extent, or of what ought to be merely, but of what perhaps may be. This we can discover only by experiment. That is all I am urging, that we try experiments in methods of resolving differences; differences on the board of directors, with fellow managers or heads of departments, with employees. or in other relations. If we do this, we may take a different attitude toward conflict. (DA. p. 34)

Davis: *By seeking to understand the desires of the other person, doesn't the integrative negotiator risk giving in to those who would dominate?*

Follett: A friend of mine said to me, "Open-mindedness is the whole thing, isn't it?" No, it isn't; it (negotiation) needs just as great a respect for your own view as for that of others, and a firm upholding of it until you are convinced. Mushy people are no more good at this than stubborn people. (DA, p. 48)

Davis: *Thomas Colosi teaches that "the creation and maintenance of doubts about the consequences of nonagreement (or one decision versus another) is central to inducing skeptics to settle" (Colosi, 1985, p. 934). What do you see as central to settlement?*

Follett: One of the most important reasons for bringing the desire of each side to a place where they can be clearly examined and valued is that evaluation often leads to revaluation. We progress by a revaluation of desire, but usually we do not stop to examine a desire until another is disputing right of way with it. Watch the evolution of your desires from childhood through youth, etc. The baby has many infantile desires which are not compatible with his wish for approbation; therefore he revalues his desires. We see this all through our life. We want to do so-and-so, but we do not estimate how much this really means to us until it comes into conflict with another desire. Revaluation is the flower of comparison. This conception of the revaluation of desire is necessary to keep in the foreground of our thinking in dealing with conflict, for neither side ever "gives in" really, it is hopeless to expect it, but there often comes a moment when there is a simultaneous revaluation of interests on both sides and unity precipitates itself...Integration is often more a spontaneous flowing together of desire than one might think; from what I have said; the revaluing of interests on both sides may lead the interests to fit into each other, so that all find some place in the final solution. (DA, p. 39-40)

Davis: *In* Getting to YES *(1981, p. 118) ,Fisher and Ury recommend the "one- text procedure," that is, drawing out the interests of both sides and using that combined information to build a solution. What are your thoughts on this concept?*

Follett: The *field of desire* is an important psychological and sociological conception; many conflicts could, I believe, be prevented from ending disastrously by getting the desires of each side into one field of vision where they could be viewed together and compared. We all believe to a certain extent in Freud's "sublimation," but I believe still more that various desires get orientated toward one another and take on different values in the process of orientation. (DA, p. 39)

Davis: *In* Disputes and Negotiations: A Cross-Cultural Perspective *(1979), Philip H. Gulliver speaks of the two principal general processes in negotiation—the cyclical and the developmental. He describes various phases which move toward agreement while shifting between moods of antagonism or coordination. Do you see conflict as having a cyclical nature?*

Follett: The conception of circular behavior throws much light on conflict, for I now realize that I can never fight you, I am always fighting you plus me. I have put it this way: that response is always to a relation. I respond, not only to you, but to the relation between you and me. Employees do not respond only to their employers, but to the relation between themselves and their employers...Circular behavior as the basis of integration gives us the key to constructive conflict. (DA, p. 45)

Davis: *I am reminded of the challenge to the orthodox scientific method presented by James Gleick in* Chaos: Making a New Science *(1987). He notes that "tiny differences in input could quickly become overwhelming differences in output," thus leading to the notion of the "butterfly effect," that is, a "butterfly stirring the air today in Peking can transform storm systems next month in New York." You seem to have anticipated the butterfly effect in relation to problem-solving.*

Follett: We can never understand the total situation without taking into account the evolving situation. And when a situation changes, we have not a new variation under the old fact, but a new fact...A professor of philosophy told me that it made him dizzy to talk with me because, he says, he wishes always to compare varying things with something stationary. (CE, p. 69)

Davis: *I'd like to shift to another topic. Today experiments with mediation, arbitration and various dispute resolution hybrids are taking place in every nook and cranny of society. Arbitration and conciliation or mediation are undoubtedly the most commonly used processes; in fact, the two words are often used interchangably. What do you see as the primary features of each process?*

Follett: In regard to the difference between conciliation and arbitration, while in practice it is often difficult to draw the line, in theory the two are wholly different. The principle of arbitration is that of an adjudicated dispute; the arbitrator... hears both sides and gives the decision. In cases of conciliation, an attempt is made to bring the two sides to agreement. It is encouraging that conciliation is pretty generally recognized to be a more satisfactory way of settling industrial disputes than arbitration. In many cases arbitration is resorted to only when conciliation fails. (DA, p. 230)

Davis: *Do you favor one process over the other?*

Follett: In pure arbitration the only task recognized is that of deciding between, not of bringing the two parties *together*. The conciliator or mediator, on the other hand, tries to energize the two parties to the controversy to reach their own decision. Unless both sides are satisfied, the struggle will go on, underneath if not openly.

 If I have seemed to speak against arbitration as a method of settling industrial disputes, it must be understood that I believe in it unless a better way can be made to work, as I am entirely in favor of it for international disputes—until we find a better way. (DA, p. 238)

Davis: *You use the expression "pure arbitration." What do you mean by that?*

Follett: I had to do that because we have so many different methods followed in arbitration...I think we may say that the most successful arbitrator is one who does not "arbitrate," but who gets the parties in the controversy face to face and helps them to work out the decision for themselves, helps them to larger understandings, to reciprocal modifyings and adjustments. (DA, p. 237-238)

Davis: *"Make the forum fit the fuss!" That's a contemporary expression in the dispute resolution field to capture the notion that the process used to settle a conflict should be in some way tailored to the particular situation. Do you have any recommendations about appropriateness?*

Follett: The search in the settling of disputes should always be for the best future activities of the parties concerned. This very fundamental psychological principle is accepted by most conciliators. An impartial chairman in the clothing industry said to me, "The courts are concerned with what has happened; our problem is always what is going to happen afterwards." Another man said to me, "Arbitration looks to the past, conciliation to the future." (DA, p. 238)

Davis: *Let's look to the future of the world as a whole. Are you hopeful? Will those of us who seek a path to peace find a way?*

Follett: In making a plea for some experiment in international cooperation, I remember, with humiliation, that we have fought because it is the easy way. Fighting solves no problems. The problems which brought on...war will all be there to be settled when the war ends. But we have war as the line of least resistance. We have war when the mind gives up its job of agreeing as too difficult. It is often stated that conflict is a necessity of the human soul, and that if conflict should ever disappear from among us, individuals would deteriorate and society collapse. But the effort of agreeing is so much more strenuous than the comparatively easy stunt of fighting that we can harden our spiritual muscles much more effectively on the former than the latter.

Suppose I disagree with you in a discussion and we make no effort to join our ideas, but "fight it out." I hammer away with my idea, I try to find all the weakest parts of yours, I refuse to see anything good in what you think. That is not nearly so difficult as trying to recognize all the possible subtle interweavings of thought, how one part of your thought, or even one aspect of one part, may unite with one part or one aspect of one part of mine. Likewise with cooperation and competition in business: cooperation is going to prove so much more difficult than competition that there is not the slightest danger of any one getting soft under it. (NS, p. 3S7)

Davis: *Are you saying, then, that facing conflict constructively is hard work, but it must be done?*

Follett: We have thought of peace as the passive and war as the active way of living. The opposite is true. War is not the most strenuous life. It is a kind of rest-cure compared to the task of reconciling our differences....From war to peace is not from the strenuous to the easy existence; it is from the futile to the effective, from the stagnant to the active, from the destructive to the creative way of life... We may be angry and fight, we may feel kindly and want peace—it is all about the same. The world will be regenerated by the people who rise above both these passive ways and heroically seek, by whatever hardship, by whatever toil, the methods by which people can agree. (NS, p. 358-359)

Davis: *Thank you! You've given me much to think about and a new respect for the value of my own experience.*

Follett: Experience may be hard but we claim its gifts because they are real, even though our feet bleed on its stones. (CE, p. 302)

ABOUT MARY PARKER FOLLETT

To read Mary Parker Follett's fresh and original work, knowing it was written or spoken so many years ago, is to wonder: Who was she? How did she develop her visionary ideas? And, why haven't I heard of her earlier?

To the extent that she is known today, it is usually in the field of business administration, for that is where she focused much of her thought during the last ten years of her life. After her death, the talks she gave to business administrators were collected together into *Dynamic Administration* (1942), which, for a time, was highly influential in the field of business management. Today, there is a movement in the business world to revive and revisit Follett. Her work is popular in Japan, where her ideas about leadership and management are highly valued, and in Britain, where she lived and lectured during the last years of her life. Yet, to call her "the first management consultant" or an "organizational consultant," as is often done, is equivalent to describing Leonardo da Vinci as a "graphic artist." Her interests are much deeper and broader.

For a time, Follett was acknowledged for her contributions to the field of integrative negotiation. In one of the most frequently cited books in our field, *A Behavioral Theory of Labor Negotiation: An Analysis of a Social Interaction System* (Walton and McKersie 1965), the authors investigate the concepts of integrative and distributive bargaining. They duly credit Follett several times, noting that "in a pioneering and impressionistic statement about administration, Mary Parker Follett discusses the concept of integrative bargaining." Walton and McKersie's 1965 credits seem to be Follett's Waterloo in the field of negotiation and conflict resolution. From that time on, with few exceptions, when integrative bargaining is discussed, it is generally they who are cited. Follett falls through the cracks, so to speak, to resurface some 15 years later in the acknowledgment section of Fisher and Ury's bestseller, *Getting to YES*. A very few of the older members of our field are familiar with her work, but she is unknown to the great majority.

No full biography of Follett exists and the available information about her is both skimpy and contradictory. The good news, however, is that since 1981 Joan C. Tonn, a professor at the University of Massachusetts/Boston, has been working on a biography. The book, which a small but growing number of Follett's fans eagerly await, will be published by Oxford University Press late in 1990 or early in 1991.

When I told Tonn that I was writing an article about Follett's ideas and wanted to include background information, she cautioned me, noting, "Much of what is written is wrong, including what Follett said about herself." Rather than a complete chronological accounting, then, I will paint a more impressionistic picture of Follett. While many facets of her life remain a mystery, one thing is clear: she evoked a passionate response in those who knew her personally, and she continues to do so in those who meet her for the first time through the written word.

Tonn agrees it is safe to say that Follett was born in Quincy, Massachusetts, a suburb of Boston, in 1868 and that she died in 1933 at the age of 65 in Boston.

Follett displayed her quick mind at an early age, graduated from lower school early and entered the prestigious Thayer Academy in South Braintree, a suburb adjacent to Quincy, when she was 11 or 12. Anne Boynton Thompson, herself a brilliant scholar, taught Follett during her teenage years at Thayer, and remained a friend and strong influence throughout her life. In 1885, both Follett's father and her maternal grandfather died, leaving her an inheritance of sufficient size to permit her to live independently for the remainder of her life. Follett's freedom from financial pressures undoubtedly allowed her to follow her fertile mind wherever it took her, and it took her many places.

In 1888, at the age of 20, she enrolled in the Society for the Collegiate Instruction of Women by Professors and Other Instructors at Harvard, or "The Annexe," which had been organized about ten years earlier to allow women to enjoy the benefits of Harvard College. During Follett's student days, the Annexe became Radcliffe College. The impressive faculty at Harvard included George Santayana and William James, the latter of whom appeared to have a strong influence upon Follett's thinking. The person at Radcliffe who had the greatest influence, however, was Professor Albert Bushnell Hart, from whom she took the equivalent of ten semesters of history. Hart pushed his students to produce original research and to draw original conclusions.

A major clue to Follett's unique abilities is found in her first book, *The Speaker of the House*, which was started originally in 1889-90 as a required thesis for a two-semester history course with Professor Hart. Follett was a tireless researcher of the past, and was fearless about obtaining first-hand information. She examined every possible historical document available and conducted interviews with current and retired speakers as well as other members of Congress. At 23, while studying at Newnham College in England, she presented a paper on the topic before the Historical Society. She continued her research when she returned to Radcliffe, and the book was published in 1896, when she was but 28. *The Speaker* was immediately recognized as a significant contribution to the field of political science and brought Follett a degree of prominence unusual for someone her age and even more unusual for one of her gender. Teddy Roosevelt gave the book high marks and indicated that he thought Follett "understood the operation of Congress a great deal better than Woodrow Wilson," whose *Congressional Government* had appeared the previous y ear (Roosevelt, p. 177).

When *The Speaker* so clearly demonstrated Follett's scholarly talents, friends expected her to pursue an academic career. She surprised them by plunging into what then was called social work, but which might more appropriately be called community organizing today. These activities provided her with direct experience in managing hundreds of people and in balancing the interests of many groups.

The most notable of her achievements centered around the public schools, an interest which she shared with Isobel Briggs, her companion of 30 years and Ella Cabot Lyman, a best friend who remained a devoted supporter of Follett throughout her life. Follett saw that school buildings were empty in the afternoon and evenings, and that neighborhoods needed community centers to provide recreation and services such as job placement. She started the community schools program in Boston and helped it become a national movement, working hand-in-hand with people from all backgrounds. All the while, she kept detailed notes about her activities and the consequences of them. After a dozen or more years of effective work at the community level, she began to write the story of the extended school movement. In time, she realized that her interests went far beyond one successful community-based enterprise to the whole notion of the role of groups in assuring democracy. Her second book, *The New State: Group Organization The Solution of Popular Government*, was published in 1918 and, once again, she received positive reviews. In a prophetic convergence of the thinking of two people who would ultimately have great impact of the field of dispute resolution, Follett asked Roscoe Pound, Dean of Harvard Law School, to review her manuscript. (*The New State*, p. 15).

By now Follett had become both a public figure in Massachusetts and a nationally-known author. She was invited to sit on boards that set minimum wages, on arbitration panels, and on various committees which further convinced her that adversarial notions of conflict interfered with the ability of groups to come up with creative solutions. These experiences led her to write her third successful book, *The Creative Experience* (1926).

Ever the learner, the analyst, the synthesizer, the philosopher, she moved boldly into the world of business while in her fifties. "I have been asked several times why I am studying business management," Follett wrote. "I will try to tell you. Free to choose between different paths of study, I have chosen this for a number of reasons. First of all, it is among business men (not all, but a few) that I find the greatest vitality of thinking today, and I like to do my thinking where it is most alive...Here the ideal and the practical have joined hands. That is why I am working at business management, because, while I care for the ideal, it is only because I want to help bring it into our everyday affairs" (*Dynamic Administration*, p. 17).

She liked the willingness of business people to experiment. She talked of the contrast between economists and politicians, whose discussions seemed to go nowhere, and of businessmen who "were not theorizing or dogmatizing," but "were thinking of what they had actually done and...were willing to try new ways the next morning, so to speak." Business responded with equal enthusiasm to Follett. From 1924 on, she became a featured speaker at the most important business conferences held in the United States and in England. In the last years of her life, she made her home with Dame Katherine Furse in Chelsea, England, and lectured at various British institutions, including the London School of Economics.

In the fall of 1933, Follett took a trip to Boston to ascertain the impact of the Depression upon her investments and to check into her health which had been a cause of concern. She underwent an operation, perhaps for a goiter, and it was found that she had invasive cancer. She died two days after the operation at the Deaconess Hospital in Boston, on December 18, 1933. Shortly after Follett's death, Dame Furse summed up her special skill of communication in a letter to their mutual friend, Ella Lyman Cabot: "what I miss most now is Mary's power of expression" wrote Furse, "She knew how to find words for all that is finest and best, never elaborate tiresome words, but the right words every time" (Furse 1934).

Conclusion

There are several reasons why it is important for the field of dispute resolution to become reacquainted with Mary Parker Follett. First of all, her ideas remain fresh and visionary—she is still ahead of her times. We need her creative flexible thinking to help us dust the cobwebs from our theory and practice. Secondly, her ideas deserve to be read in full. When her concepts are taken out of context, something essential is lost, for her thinking is holistic. As Pauline Graham observes in the introduction to *Dynamic Managing: The Follett Way*, "Some of the spokes of her wheel have been reinvented since then...but not all." (Graham 1987: 4).

Lastly, both women and men in the profession should take pride in the fact that a woman originally articulated the integrative approach to negotiation. Our field, which is increasingly being stratified by gender, with women at the lower-paid and less prestigious end of the evolving hierarchy, is at risk. We must do everything we can to encourage the original and invaluable contributions of women. Follett provides us with a strong role model.

Note

I am indebted to the following people for inspiration and assistance on this article: John Chandler, Margaret Shaw, Carol Davis Pino, Janet Rifkin and Matthew Davis, for sharing my obsession to learn more about Follett and for helping me find sources of information; Linda L. Putnam, Department of Communication, Purdue University, for sending me her own and other contemporary articles on or about Follett; Claudia Morner, friend, neighbor and Boston College librarian for her imaginative investigation; Jane Knowles, archivist, and the many staff members of the Schlesinger Library at Radcliffe College who gave so freely of their expertise and resources; and J. William Breslin, Managing Editor of *Negotiation Journal* for editorial assistance "above and beyond the call of duty."

References

Colosi, T. 1983. Negotiation in the public and private sectors: A core model. *American Behavioral Scientist*, 27:229-253.

Fisher, R. and Ury, W. L. 1981. *Getting to YES: Negotiating agreement without giving in*. Boston: Houghton Mifflin.

Follett, M. P. 1896. *The Speaker of the House of Representatives*. Cambridge. Mass.: Radcliffe College Monographs No. 5.

———. 1918. *The new state: Group organization the solution of popular government*. New York: Longmans, Green and Co.

———. 1924. *Creative experience*. New York: Longmans, Green and Co.

———. 1942. *Dynamic administration: The collected papers of Mary Parker Follett*, ed. H. C. Metcalf and L. Urwick. New York: Harper.

Fox, E. M. 1968. Mary Parker Follett: The enduring contribution. *Public Administration Review* 28 (reprint).

Furse, R. 1934. Letter to Ella Cabot Lyman. Schlesinger Library. Radcliffe
  College: Cambridge, Mass.
Gleick. J. 1987. *Chaos: The making of a new science* New York: Penguin Books.
Graham, P. 1987. *Dynamic managing: The Follett way.* London: Professional
  Publishing Lirnited.
Gulliver, P. H. 1979. *Disputes and negotiations: A cross-cultural perspective.* New
  York: Academic Press.
Roosevelt, T. 1896. *American Historical Review* 2: 177.
Walton, R. E. and McKersie, R. B. 1965. *A behavioral theory of labor negotiation.*
  New York: McGraw-Hill.

Appendix I: A Brief Bibliography of Books and Articles about Mary Parker Follett

Cabot, R. C. 1934. Mary Parker Follett: An appreciation. *Radcliffe Quarterly*
  p. 80-82.
Follett, M. P. 1896. *The Speaker of the House of Representatives.* Cambridge, Mass.:
  Radcliffe College Monographs. No. 5.
———. 1918 *The New State: Group organization the solution of popular government.*
  New
  York: Longmans, Green and Co.
———. 1924. *Creative experience.* New York: Longrnans, Green.
———. 1924 *Creative experience.* Reprint. New York: Peter Smith. 1951.
———. 1942. *Dynamic administration: The collected papers of Mary Parker Follett,* ed.
  H. C. Metcalf and L. Urwick. New York: Harper.
———. 1978. The giving of orders. *Classics of Organization Theory,* ed. J. M.
  Shatritz and R H. Whirbeck. Oak Park. Ill.: Moore Publishing.
———. 1987. *Freedom and Co-ordination: Lectures in business organization.*
  Reprint. New York Garland Publishing, Ink
Fox, E. M. 1968. Mary Parker Follett: The enduring contribution. *Public Adminis-tration
  Review* 28 (reprint).
Graham, P. 1987. *Dynamic managing: The Follett way.* London: Professional
  Publishing Limited.
Hata, S. 1983. Mary Parker Follett: The Boston environrnent and other influences.
  Presented at 43rd Annual Meeting, Academy ot Management. Dallas. Texas.
  August 16.
Lindeman, E. C. 1934. Outline of Mary Follett's contributions to modern thought.
  Survey Graphic 73: 86.
Lyons, N. 1988. Negotiating conflict: Rediscovering the art of Mary Parker
  Follett. *Institute for the Management of Lifelong Education Bulletin* 1: 8-9.
Parker, L. E. 1984. Control in organization life: The contribution of Mary Parker Follett.
  Academy of Management Review 9: 736-745.

Putnam, L. L. 1987. *Reframing integrative and distributive bargaining: An interaction perspective.* Presented at the Conference on Research on Negotiation in Organizations. Mt. Sterling, Ohio. April 24-26.

Stever, J. A. 1986. Mary Parker Follett and the quest for pragmatic administration. *Administration and Society* 18: 159-177.

Urwick, L. 1935. The problem of organization: A study of the work of Mary Parker Follett. *Bulletin of the Taylor Society* 1: 163-169.

Wood, A. E. 1926. The social philosophy of Mary Parker Follett. *Social Forces* 759-769.

In 1995, Pauline Graham published an edited volume, *Mary Parker Follett, Prophet of Management: a Celebration of her Writings from the 1920s*, with an introduction by Peter F. Drucker and a preface by Rosabeth Moss Kanter, as a Harvard Business School Press Classic.

The Love for Three Oranges
Or: What Did We Miss About Ms. Follett in the Library?

Deborah M. Kolb

Deborah M. Kolb is professor of management at the Simmons College Graduate School of Management, 409 Commonwealth Ave., Boston, Mass. 02215. She is a senior fellow and former executive director of the Program on Negotiation at Harvard Law School.

Prologue: I was recently asked to write a paper based on the reissuing of Mary Parker Follett's writings on conflict, management, and a variety of other topics. While rereading Follett, I was reminded of discussions Jeff Rubin and I had over the years about the proverbial orange and the two sisters who were negotiating its use: Would they suboptimize by cutting the orange in half or figure out that one wants juice and the other rind? Jeff argued that the story originated with Fisher and Ury in *Getting to YES* (1981). Having run the *Ugli Orange Exercise* for years, I knew that this story predated GTY. I attributed it to Ms. Follett, and would tease Jeff that this was but another example of a good idea from a woman coopted by a man. We were both wrong. The story, as best I can determine, originates with Robert House (1982:130-133) in *Experiences in Management and Organizational Behavior.* My use of oranges in the title comes from these bantering sessions and Jeff's love of music.

* * *

The work of Mary Parker Follett is enthusiastically being revived in negotiation and dispute resolution (Davis 1991), where Follett is becoming known as the mother of the contemporary field. In part, we can trace this resurgence of interest in Follett to societal changes regarding the value of negotiations as a means to deal with differences. Not so long ago, negotiation was viewed as a rather sordid affair, associated with haggling, dickering, bartering, swapping, and back-room deal making. Nowadays, negotiation is recognized as a serious social activity for solving problems of grand and modest scale alike (Adler 1993), a process that pervades every level of human interaction.

As perceptions of negotiation have changed, curiosity about how to do it—and do it effectively—has been piqued. It is here that Mary Parker Follett's ideas are particularly illuminating. Her notions about how to deal with conflict—by domination, compromise, or preferably, integration—prefigure much of the most popular thinking about negotiation. Although it appears

This article first appeared in *Negotiation Journal*, October 1995: Volume 11, Number 4, pages 339-348.

81

that there is a close correlation between Follett's ideas about integration and more recent treatments of mutual gains, integrative, or "win-win" negotiations (see Davis 1991), a closer reading suggests that her views of negotiators and the process of integration have qualities that those who have followed have overlooked.

Ms. Follett in the Library

Conflict, according to Follett, is avoided or suppressed because we fear its divisiveness and lack the skills to deal with it constructively. In a talk before the Bureau of Personnel Administrators in 1925, entitled "Constructive Conflict," she outlines three primary ways to deal with differences—domination, compromise, and integration. Integration is the preferred way, and Follett's story of her experience in the library is used to illustrate it:

> ...when two desires are integrated, that means that a solution has been found in which both desires have found a place that neither has had to sacrifice anything. Let us take some very simple illustration. In the Harvard Library one day, in one of the smaller rooms, someone wanted the window open, I wanted it shut. We opened the window in the next room, where no one was sitting. This was not a compromise because there was no curtailing of desire; we both got what we really wanted. For I did not want a closed room, I simply did not want the north wind to blow directly on me; likewise the other occupant did not want that particular window open, he merely wanted more air in the room (Graham 1995:69).[1]

Compromise and integration are still very much with us in negotiation theory and practice. Compromise is the prominent solution to what is variously labeled as zero-sum, distributive, or positional negotiations. Integration involves invention, what Follett (Graham 1995:189) calls the finding of a third way: "...the clever thing to do is to recognize this and not to let one's thinking stay within the boundaries of two alternatives which are mutually exclusive." To arrive at integrative solutions, parties must bring their differences out into the open and distinguish the real demand from those put forward (Graham 1995:75) or, more popularly, separate interests from positions (Fisher, Ury, and Patton 1991). Success in integrative negotiation is achieved when parties can identify their respective interests, then revalue them in light of the other's response so that both can see where their interests fit together and that all may find some place in the final solution (Graham 1995:75). Rather than simple compromises, exchange in integrative bargaining means that negotiators make trades based on differences in preferences and utilities (Lax and Sebenius 1986). In that way, higher joint benefit is possible than through compromise. In other words, I am willing to let you have the window open as long as you do it in such a way that it does not disturb my papers.

As Follett's ideas are credited in current thinking about mutual gains, it is this notion of working from the interests of the different parties that are emphasized. Her talk on constructive conflict is filled with examples of how, by understanding the true interests of the parties, one can find solutions that meet those interests. There is the story of the Dairymen's Cooperative League and the uphill and downhill loaders' fight over priority in unloading cans of milk; the solution to their dispute is to change the position of the unloading platform. This framework—that parties come to the table with interests and that integration is a process of discovery of those interests, through which new agreements can be reached—is basic to contemporary thinking about negotiations. Although the examples she uses conform closely to this conclusion, in the words she uses, Follett seems to be implying something more about relationships and what true integration implies. A closer look at her notions about relationships and the integration process suggest that we may have missed some key insights about what happened in the library.

Relating and Revaluing

The dominant discourse in negotiation frames the mutual gains process as one primarily of exchange among self-interested but enlightened negotiators (Kolb and Putnam, in press; Putnam 1994). Mary Parker Follett would surely applaud the prominence given to these methods as a preferred approach to deal with difference. But she would probably be surprised at how the focus on achieving integrative outcomes has made the integrative processes she envisioned all but invisible. In particular, she might question the individualistic focus of theory and research, the prominence given to self-interest, and the rather static notions about what constitute mutual gains (see Gray 1994; Putnam 1994; Kolb and Putnam, in press). She might wonder what happened to the importance of relationships, the value of interaction as the place where interests are given meaning and revalued so that integration becomes an opportunity for innovation and learning.

Recent theory and research frame negotiations as an individualistic undertaking where autonomous, self-interested negotiators make strategic choices to realize their goals (see Rubin and Brown 1976; Neale and Bazerman 1991; Thompson 1990; and Putnam 1994 for a critique). Self-interest is an assumption that is deeply embedded in negotiation theory and practice (Deutsch 1960). In distributive models, the negotiator uses all means at her disposal—threats, commitments, bluffs—to satisfy those interests (Schelling 1960). In the integrative, the other's concerns are also to be taken into account (Fisher, Ury, and Patton 1991; Walton and McKersie 1965). The dual concern model explicitly connects the self and other as two independent considerations; achieving win-win outcomes crucially depends on both parties having both concerns (Carnevale and Pruitt 1993).

Although theories (like the dual concern model) might suggest that something more about relationships is intended than self-interest, that is not generally the case. Concern for the other is an outgrowth of self-interest. The concept of "enlightened self-interest" captures how self and others' interests are connected. The added word "enlightened" refers to the acknowledgment by each side that the other is also likely to be pursuing a path of self-interest—and that it may be possible for both to do well in the exchange (Rubin 1991:4).[2] In other words, relationship is defined instrumentally (Northrup 1991; Putnam 1994).

Empirical research focuses almost exclusively on individuals and how they can achieve their enlightened self-interest. Influenced significantly by the work of Howard Raiffa (1982), recent approaches embrace the goal of asymmetric prescription/description (Lax and Sebenius 1986; Neale and Bazerman 1991). These works draw from empirical research to offer advice to a negotiator on the likely behaviors of the other party. Underlying this body of knowledge is a view that negotiators have interests (as distinct from positions) that they seek to advance. The goal of negotiation is to improve upon available alternatives to agreement, and to do so in ways that push toward efficient, pie-expanding deals. Abilities to achieve these goals are marred by nonrational assumptions about the process—overconfidence, anchoring, framing, reactive devaluation, misconstrual, and traps, among others (Neale and Bazerman 1991; Kahneman and Tversky 1979; Robinson, Keltner, and Ross 1994; Ross and Stillinger 1991; Rubin, Pruitt, and Kim 1993).

The negotiation process itself is generally understood as an exchange between self-interested individuals.[3] Given its roots in economic theory where the market is seen as the preeminent institutional allocator of goods, services, and most everything else in social life, it is not surprising that negotiations are rooted in this exchange model (Hartsock 1985; Sebenius 1992). In distributive negotiations, the exchange is framed as a compromise.

In integrative negotiations, exchange is modeled as tradeoffs in the form of package agreements (Lax and Sebenius 1986; Susskind and Cruikshank 1987). Pruitt (1981) identifies several different kinds of trades common in negotiation: trade on low-priority issues in return for ones that have higher priority; pay in different kinds of compensation; cost cutting where one party gets what it wants and the other party gets its costs cut; and bridging, where different interests become the basis of an agreement. Among the factors that become resources for these bridging trades are differences in risk, beliefs about the future, the value of time, money, and relationship, and need for control (Lax and Sebenius 1986; Susskind and Cruikshank 1987). The negotiator's language of if, then—if I make this concession, then what will you do?—and reciprocity suggests the depth of our belief about negotiations being a matter of trades (Putnam and Roloff 1992).[4]

Follett's story about what happened in the library can be read as generally consistent with these ideas. She would recognize some of her method in dicta such as inventing options for mutual gain (Fisher, Ury, and Patton 1991), or packaging agreements based on difference (Susskind and Cruikshank 1987), or creating value based on adding new issues (Lax and Sebenius 1986). But Follett seemed to have something else in mind when she wrote about relationships and integration. In *Creative Experience* (1924), in an intriguing chapter on what she calls the circular experience, she begins to develop a relational conception of individual action that locates interests in interaction and not primarily as a product of individual choice. Indeed, one might read some of her writings and see in them an explicit rejection of self-interest, even of the enlightened variety. What Follett says (Graham 1995:117) in regard to collective bargaining is that "...my reason for my very strong advocacy of employee association is not chiefly to bring about equal power, but because this helps us to approach functional unity. I should want to make a 'side,' not for a fair fight, not for fighting at all, but in order that it should enrich the whole."

84

Follett's method of integration is based on notions about connected and mutually influencing relationships between parties and the interaction as the site for learning and development. "I never react to you," wrote Follett (Graham 1995: 42), "but to you-plus-me; or to be more accurate, it is I-plus-you reacting to you-plus-me...That is in the very process of meeting, we both become something different." In intriguing parallel with some of the work of feminist psychologists (Miller 1976; Chodorow 1978; Jordan et al. 1992), who criticize the limitations of individualistic, autonomous, self-contained notions of action, Follett (Graham 1995:41) emphasizes the ways individuals grow in connection and in relationship with each other: "Through circular response we are creating each other all the time."

When integration is seen primarily as an interactive activity, the notion of the self-interested negotiator and how those interests are realized changes the focus from individuals to relationships. In contemporary theory, individual preparation as to one's own interests and anticipating the other's interests is reinforced in most practical methods. A variety of techniques exists to assist the negotiator in analyzing how an opponent will respond (on the bases of rational analysis) to particular proposals a party might make (Fisher, Ury and Patton 1991). Follett, too, discusses anticipating response as a necessary condition for integration. But her development of the notion of revaluing positions actually challenges how much negotiators can accomplish in the absence of face-to-face activity.

Follett implies that one cannot assess the true value of one's interests in the absence of the other. She suggests (Graham 1995:75) that negotiators do not really understand the meaning and value of an issue until that priority comes into conflict with another's interests: "...we do not stop to examine a desire until another is disputing right of way with it." Indeed, the very goals we seek are not established in isolation. "Activity," Follett wrote (Graham 1995:56), "always does more than embody purpose, it evolves purpose." The notion that the meanings of interests and priorities are emergent, the result more of interaction than preplanned activity, fits the conclusions of researchers who have analyzed negotiations in situ (see Friedman 1994; Kolb 1983; Putnam 1990) and recent work on feminist theorizing about negotiations (Gray 1994; Kolb and Putnam, in press). When the meanings of issues, interests, and outcomes are seen not as preplanned but as emerging from the interactive process, then notions about what planning around self-interest actually entails take on different meanings. Negotiators use planning around self-interests as a means to establish position or standing in a negotiation, to manage impressions of credibility and legitimacy (Friedman 1994; Kolb 1985). From such positions, connections between and among negotiators are built so that co-construction of meanings about issues, interests, and outcomes are possible (Putnam 1985).

When individual self-interest dominates thinking about the negotiation encounter, then the elements that comprise relationship building and the construction of mutuality diminish in importance and-or are cast primarily in instrumental terms (Kolb and Putnam, in press; Northrup 1991). Recent research, however, based on feminist readings of negotiation theory, research, and practice suggest that a significant component of the negotiation process is the creation of a frame of connectedness within which negotiations can take place (Kolb and Putnam, in press). Believing that there is some sense of shared fate, negotiators who emphasize connectedness and interdependence strive to develop a trusting, comfortable, and compatible basis upon which to deal, even over the most difficult issues (Kolb 1995).

Framing a connected context involves establishing trust and feelings of interdependence. Negotiators engage in rituals of trust establishment whose function is, in part, to develop connections, establish and reaffirm good working relationships, and maintain some sense of shared fate even in the face of potentially difficult problems (Forester 1993; Friedman 1994). Creating a connected context is about the invisible work of negotiations (Kolb 1992). Invisible work entails trying to establish relationships on a more personal basis at and away from the bargaining table. It means learning about others outside their official roles and finding ways to strengthen the ties (Granovetter 1973).

In the world of the self-interested negotiator, the task is to figure out the interests of both parties. Good deals are ones that meet these respective separate interests. An alternative to the self-interested negotiator is the connected negotiator. These are negotiators who see the process as one based on mutuality, connectedness, and interdependence. To act in a connected fashion requires finding ways to reframe what appears as self-interest into connected interests.

The process of integration looks rather different under a connected model. In the place of strategic and tactical moves, a connected approach leads to new understandings and definitions of issues and problems. Indeed, a close examination of how plans surface in negotiation, how bargaining interests are revealed and understood and how positions change reveals that outcomes are rarely the result of strategic intent (Putnam 1994). When goals and interests are seen as unstable rather than fixed, then arguments and counterarguments become forms of reflection in which the very goals and interests come to be redefined and revalued.

Rather than persuasion or brainstorming tactics, the negotiation dialogue can be seen as a form of storytelling or narrative (Cobb 1993; Conley and O'Barr 1990; Putnam 1990). Issues, interests, and options are not really discrete matters; rather, they are nested in conversations that give them meaning. They are not separate from the arguments that are used to support them. Negotiators narrate their version of events in cohesive fashion and under a moral order that frames what is possible. In other words, negotiators tell different stories to each other in which their interests, their issues, their positions, and the possibilities they envision are located. By concentrating on these stories and how they are told, negotiators invent new stories and new understandings that become the bases for their agreements (Cobb 1993; Keough 1987; Putnam 1985; Putnam, Wilson, and Turner 1990; Roloff and Jordan 1992). The positioning of parties in the discourse facilitates different kinds of stories, some of which open up the possibilities for innovation and learning (Cobb 1993). From this perspective, the very process of working together in new ways is as important as the potential outcomes. Or, in the words of Follett (Graham 1991:35): "The heart of the truth about integration is the connection between the relating of two activities, their interactive influence, and the values thereby created."

What we missed about Ms. Follett in the library was the connection she had with her colleague and the dialogue that ensued. All that has come down is what they did with the windows.

* * *

Epilogue: Several years ago, Jeff Rubin and I began a dialogue about relationships in negotiation. Dissatisfied with the concept of asymmetric prescription/description (Raiffa 1982), where one gives advice to the individual negotiator, we began to think about the relationship as the locus of inquiry. We did not see relationships in instrumental terms. Rather, like a play, where actors have roles that make them dependent upon each other's performance of their part, we talked about the kind of advice we could give to all the actors as a holistic entity. If we hadn't been so preoccupied with the oranges, a closer reading of Follett's work might have helped our enterprise.

Notes

This article is adapted from a longer article by the author, Lisa Jensen, and Vonda Shannon, to appear in a forthcoming issue of the journal *Organization*. The title of the Kolb-Jensen-Shannon article is: "She Said It All Before: Or, What Did We Miss About Ms. Follett in the Library?"

1. Here and throughout this article, all references to the work of Mary Parker Follett are from the newly published book, *Mary Parker Follett: Prophet of Management*, edited by Pauline Graham (1995).
2. Self-interest is so basic to the psychological research that it is built into study designs. First, the laboratory study with its ubiquitous role play builds into its structure a self-interested model of the negotiator. Role players are provided with legitimate interests as a preliminary to their efforts to negotiate their differences. Second, the definition of optimal outcome that is built into the role play is also based on the notions of enlightened self-interest. When negotiators put the concern of others before themselves, they make more rapid concessions and fail to reach win-win solutions (Carnevale and Pruitt 1993). Similarly, recent research on friends, dating couples, and people who identify with each other suggests that when these identity ties are salient, negotiators operate less out of self-interest (Halpern 1992; Smith 1993). Under these circumstances, achieving fair outcomes overrides self-interest. Yet, when laboratory negotiators do this, they fail to reach win-win agreements (again as defined by the experiment).
3. Nancy Hartsock (1985) criticizes exchange theory as rooted fundamentally in the experience of one gender. It obscures, she claims, relations of domination and power by insisting that, at least initially, each individual is equal to every other, and that interactions can be understood as transactions that are unstructured by institutions. Further, she suggests that exchange is based on a model of individual gain where the fundamental relationship between people is instrumental or extrinsic.

4. The assumption that mutual gains come primarily from making advantageous trades is embedded in the research paradigm. Using scoreable games that place differential values on outcomes, laboratory researchers structure their experiments as ones of trade. Buyers and sellers in the marketplace negotiate over a series of issues, such as delivery time, discount terms, and financing terms or salary, office location, and geographical location. Value-maximizing agreements come from making trades on issues of different priority to the buyer and the seller as opposed to split-the-difference compromises (Pruitt and Carnevale 1993; Bazerman and Neale 1992; Kramer 1995).

References
Adler, P. 1993. The future of alternative dispute resolution: Reflections on ADR as a social movement. In *The possibility of popular justice: A case study of community mediation in the United States*, edited by S.E. Merry and N. Milner. Ann Arbor: University of Michigan Press.
Bazerman, M. and M. Neale. 1991. *Negotiating rationally*. New York: Free Press.
Chodorow, N. 1978. *The reproduction of mothering*. Berkeley: University of California Press.
Cobb, S. 1993. Empowerment and mediation: A narrative perspective. *Negotiation Journal* 9(3): 245-261.
Conley, J. and W. O'Barr. 1990. *Rules v. Relationships*. Chicago: University of Chicago Press.
Davis, A. 1991. An interview with Mary Parker Follett. *In Negotiation theory and practice*, edited by J. W. Breslin and J.Z. Rubin. Cambridge, Mass.: PON Books (The Program on Negotiation at Harvard Law School).
Deutsch, M. 1960. The effect of motivational orientation upon trust and suspicion. *Human Relations* 13: 123-139.
Fisher, R. and W. Ury. 1981. *Getting to YES: Negotiating agreement without giving in*. Boston: Houghton Mifflin.
Fisher, R. W. Ury, and B. Patton. 1991. *Getting to YES: Negotiating agreement without giving in*. 2nd edition. New York: Penguin Books.
Follett, M.P. 1924. *Creative experience*. New York: Longmans, Green.
Forester, J. 1993. *Beyond dialogue to transformative learning: How deliberative rituals encourage political judgment in community planning processes*. Working Papers on Planning, Dept. of City and Regional Planning, Cornell University, Ithaca, N.Y.
Friedman, R.A. 1994. *Front stage, backstage: The dramatic structure of labor negotiations*. Cambridge, Mass.: MIT Press.
Graham, P., editor. 1995. *Mary Parker Follett: Prophet of management*. Boston: Harvard Business School Press.

Granovetter, M. 1973. The strength of weak ties. *American Journal of Sociology* 78: 1360-1380.

Gray, B. 1994. The gender-based foundations of negotiation theory. In *Research on negotiation in organizations*, vol. 4, edited by R. Lewicki, B. Sheppard and R. Bies. Greenwich, Conn.: JAI Press

Halpern, J. 1992. *Friendship's effects on the buyer-seller relationship,* Paper presented at the annual meeting of the Academy of Management, Las Vegas, Nev., August.

Hartsock, N. 1985. Exchange theory: Critique from a feminist standpoint. *Current perspectives in social theory,* vol. 6 Greenwich, Conn.: JAI Press.

House, R. 1982. The ugli orange exercise. In *Experiences in Management and Organizational Behavior,* edited by D.T. Hall, D.D. Bowen, R.J. Lewicki; and F.S. Hall. 2nd ed. New York: John Wiley & Sons.

Jordan, J., A. Kaplan, J.B. Miller, I.P. Stiver, and J.L. Surrey. 1991. *Women's growth in connection.* New York: Guilford Press.

Kahneman, D. and A. Tversky. 1979. Prospect theory: An analysis of decisions under risk. *Econometrica* 47: 263-291.

Keough, C.M. 1987. The nature and function of argument in organizational bargaining research. *Southern Speech Communication Journal* 50: 1-17.

Kolb, D.M. 1995. *Shifting ground: Digging at negotiation theory from a gender perspective.* Paper presented at the Seminar in Feminist Practice, University of Michigan, March 1995.

———. 1992. Women's work: Peacemaking behind the scenes. In *Hidden conflict in organizations: Uncovering behind-the-scenes disputes,* edited by D.M. Kolb and J. Bartunek. Newbury Park, Calif.: Sage.

———. 1985. To be a mediator: Expressive tactics in mediation. *Journal of Social Issues* 41: 11-27.

———. 1983. *The mediators.* Cambridge, Mass.: MIT Press.

Kolb, D.M. and L.L. Putnam. In press. Through the looking glass: Negotiation theory refracted through the lens of gender. In *Frontiers in dispute resolution in labor relations and human resources,* edited by S. Gleason. East Lansing, Mich.: Michigan State University Press.

Lax, D.A. and J.K. Sebenius. 1986. *The manager as negotiator.* New York: The Free Press.

Miller, J.B. 1976. *Toward a new psychology of women.* Boston: Beacon Press.

Neale, M. and M. Bazerman. 1991. *Cognition and rationality in negotiation.* New York: The Free Press.

Northrup, T. 1991. *Relationality and self-interest: The implications of gender for conflict theory.* Paper presented at the Conference on Gender and Conflict, George Mason University, Fairfax, Va., January 1991.

Pruitt, D. 1981. *Negotiation behavior.* New York: Academic Press.

Pruitt, D.G. and P.J. Carnevale. 1993. *Negotiation in social conflict.* Pacific Grove, Calif.: Brooks/ Cole.

Putnam, L.L. 1994. Challenging the assumptions of traditional approaches to negotiation. *Negotiation Journal* 10(4): 337-346.

———. 1990. Reframing integrative and distributive bargaining: A process perspective. In *Research on negotiation in organizations,* vol. 2, edited by M. Bazerman, R. Lewicki, and B. Sheppard. Greenwich, Conn.: JAI Press.

———. 1985. Bargaining as organization communication. In *Organizational communication: Tradition themes and new directions,* edited by R.D. McPhee and P.K. Tompkins. Beverly Hills, Calif.: Sage

Putnam, L.L., S.R. Wilson and D. Turner. 1990. The evolution of policy arguments in teacher's bargaining. *Argumentation* 4: 129-152.

Putnam, L.L. and M.E. Roloff. 1992. *Communication and negotiation.* Newbury Park, Calif.: Sage.

Raiffa, H. 1982. *The art and science of negotiation.* Cambridge, Mass.: Harvard University Press.

Robinson, R., J. Keltner, L. Ross. In press. Misconstruing the views of the "other side:" Real and perceived differences in three ideological conflicts. *Journal of Personality and Social Psychology.*

Roloff, M.E. and J. M. Jordan. 1992. Achieving negotiation goals: The "fruits and foibles" of planning ahead. In *Communication and negotiation,* edited by L.L. Putnam and M.E. Roloff. Newbury Park, Calif.: Sage.

Ross, L. and C. Stillinger. 1991. Barriers to conflict resolution. *Negotiation Journal* 7(4): 389-405.

Rubin, J.Z. and B.R. Brown. 1975. *The social psychology of bargaining and negotiation.* New York: Academic Press.

Rubin, J.Z. 1991. Some wise and mistaken assumptions about conflict and negotiation. In *Negotiation theory and practice,* edited by J.W. Breslin and J.Z. Rubin. Cambridge, Mass.: PON Books.

Rubin, J.Z., D. Pruitt, and S.H. Kim. 1993. Social conflict. New York: McGraw-Hill.

Schelling, T.C. 1960. *The strategy of conflict.* Cambridge, Mass.: Harvard University Press.

Sebenius, J. K. 1992. Negotiation analysis: A characterization and review. *Management Science* 38(1): 18-39.

Smith, W., J. Pikakis, and J. Miller. 1993. The impact of close relationships on integrative bargaining. Unpublished paper, Vanderbilt University.

Thompson, L 1990. Negotiation behavior and outcomes: Empirical evidence and theoretical issues. *Psychological Bulletin* 108(3): 515-533.

Walton, R. and R. McKersie. 1965. *A behavioral theory of labor negotiations.* New York: McGraw-Hill.

Thinking About Interdisciplinary Inquiry On Culture and Disputing

Neal Milner and Vicki Shook

Neal Milner is a Professor of Political Science and Affiliate and former Director in the Program on Conflict Resolution at the University of Hawaii. He is also a mediator for Hawaii's Center for Alternative Dispute Resolution. He is, with Sally Merry, the co-editor of *The Possibilities of Popular Justice* (1993). His present research is on the regulation of alternative and complementary medicine. He recently published a paper on exorcism on the contemporary Church of England.

Vicki Shook, MA , was formerly the Assistant Director of the University of Hawaii Program on

This article first appeared in *Negotiation Journal*, April 1989: Volume 5, Number 2, pages 133-147.

"How does an interdisciplinary group inquire about disputing?" As we look back at two years of co-leading the Comparative Seminar on Disputing in Asia and the Pacific, the answer is "Not the way we expected!" The experience taught us valuable lessons about interdisciplinary inquiry, comparative analysis, and theory building.

Initially, the seminar was conceived as a project within the newly formed Program on Conflict Resolution (PCR) at the University of Hawaii. The aims of this multidisciplinary program are twofold: to engage in research that furthers an understanding of disputing and dispute settling practices; and to encourage the practice and testing of a variety of dispute resolution procedures.[1] Hawaii is an ideal environment for multicultural studies, so PCR also committed itself to emphasizing the cultural aspects of disputing, particularly in the Pacific and Asia. However, there was one major problem: None of the initial program participants had done work focusing on the confluence of culture and disputing. Some individuals had studied various cultures and others had looked at disputing, but no one had explicitly joined the two. The seminar was conceived to direct some of the research toward the cultural contexts of disputing. Therefore, the seminar's goals for the first year were: (1) to attract Asian and Pacific scholars from the university and community to explicitly examine disputing phenomena; and (2) to develop a cadre of researchers to initiate projects in disputing in Asia and the Pacific. The projects could be individual or collaborative. It was implicitly understood that the seminar's inquiry was to be comparative in nature, although this assumption was later questioned and became a focus of discussion itself.

In this article, we are attempting to reconstruct and understand what happened. How and why did our assumptions change as the seminar progressed? What guided our inquiry? Rather than illustrate specific disputes, we will stress the process of the seminar itself, in an effort to "think about our thinking." Because lenses are instruments used to form images, they are a useful metaphor for the different approaches the group used to gain a culturally grounded understanding of disputing.

91

Conflict Resolution and the co-leader of the Seminar on Disputing in Asia and the Pacific. For the past ten years she has been working with the Hospice Caring Project of Santa Cruz County, most recently as the Coordinator of Training. Her publications in the dispute resolution field related to this article include: *Ho'oponopono: Contemporary uses of a Problem Solving Process* (UH Press, 1985), "Ho'oponopono: Straightening Family Relationships in Hawaii" (with Kwan) in *Conflict Resolution: Cross Cultural Perspectives* (eds. Avruch, Black and Scimecca; Greenwood, 1991) and "What Mediation Training Says—or Doesn't Say— About the Ideology and Culture of North American Community Justice Programs" (with Milner) in *The Possibility of Popular Justice* (eds. Merry and Milner; University of Michigan Press, 1993).

Through the Lenses

In retrospect it appears that there were three phases in the seminar:

Many lenses, many phenomena
(or, "This is my view. What's your view?")
Everyone arrived at the seminar with their own lens, forged from their disciplinary background and particular experience. Each lens was directed toward different phenomena: The Communication-Legal Anthropology lens focused on Fijian society; the Political Science-Law and Society lens focused on the influence of legal institutions on individual rights; the Macro-Sociologist lens examined American mediation; the Mental Health-Communication lens looked at Hawaiian problem solving; and so forth. The emphasis was on presenting and establishing various individual perspectives.

One lens, many phenomena
(or, "Lets try to find a grand scheme.")
In time, the group members struggled to find a common lens through which to view many different disputing phenomena. They tried to find a basis for generalizations and to establish the ideal taxonomy. This grand taxonomy would have categories clear and distinct enough to allow for comparisons across cultures, and be robust enough to permit the richness of cultural distinctiveness to shine through. In effect, we were seeking to create the dispute resolution field's equivalent of the Diagnostic and Statistical Manual (DSMIII) for mental health clinicians. Once the taxonomy was constructed, we expected to be able to plug in American mediation, Hawaiian *ho'oponopono* (a family conflict resolution process), and Thai patterns of community influencing, and see where the similarities and differences lay.

The prism (or, "Let's see if we can keep our preferences and yet link our views together somehow.")
This was a shift toward examining a common case or set of phenomena from different points of view, and then establishing the interrelationships of the views. A prism is a complex set of lenses, both contiguous and reflexive. It can act as a single lens if held steady and unwavering, but if moved even slightly, the shimmering reflections produced by the other facets intrude and reveal

variations in the phenomena's shape and color. The prism as a metaphor here is a reminder that the relativity of the researcher's stance—whether the point of view is narrow or broad—will affect the perception of any phenomena. The slightest shift of the prism reveals a new variation of the image, suggesting the interdependence and complexity inherent in the relationship between viewer and viewed in ways both intriguing and discomforting. Whereas looking at a scene through a single lens affords a clear, seemingly undistorted view, looking through a prism reminds us that such simplistic views are deceiving—that there truly *is* more there than meets the eye. The problem is that, although the view through the prism can be bewitching and delightful, it is difficult to contend with the multiplicity of patterns, shapes, and colors for any length of time. Our eyes and minds aren't used to handling sense data in that fashion. We learned to compromise by holding the prism steady for a time, to give the ease and clarity of a single lens, and then inducing periodic tremors, to remind us of the other facets, or points of view, that make up a whole.

How would these phases translate into interdisciplinary inquiry? In returning to our objective of doing comparative work on disputing, one could examine a Chinese mediation from multiple perspectives—one that emphasized the communication interactions between the mediator and the parties, another that looked at the relationship of government policy and legal structure on village mediation committees, and yet another that looked at how the dispute emerged and developed over time. Then the different views could be placed in a larger context in order to examine the relationships between them. Then a picture could emerge that would be more than any of the singular perspectives would have allowed. As with the prism, the perspectives would be contiguous and affect one another. As one's view shifted with the turning of the crystal, new images would be revealed and a more complete spectrum of understandings would coalesce. The stability of any view would be tenuous, unlikely, and not necessarily desirable.

Before we explore these metaphors and attendant phases in more detail—particularly the tensions that seemed to propel us from one to the other—we will give a brief overview of the composition of the seminar membership and our topical orientation.

Reflections

Our comments are based on our experiences since the seminar ended.

If we were to organize such a seminar again, we would be much more explicit about the complexity of the "prismatic" approach to inquiry and about the problems inherent in examining the concept of culture. The disparity between practitioners' ideas of culture and the concepts that have evolved out of the social science and historical research are still profound. While the nonpractitioner literature stresses the nonreification of culture and the porous nature of boundaries among groups, the practitioners continue to talk of culture as if it is a bounded, static, easily identifiable thing, as in "African American culture" or "Japanese culture." Practitioners convert an analytical device into a hardened reality, while the more academic literature pays little attention to the transfer of cultural practices, like alternative dispute resolution, from industrialized countries to other places.

We are not arguing that this movement is necessarily harmful, rather that its impact is insufficiently considered. There is not enough understanding of how new ideas and processes are adapted, accommodated, or resisted, whether these are rock music, global capitalism, human rights, or alternative dispute resolution. There remains insufficient appreciation of how the global and the local interact in the process of dispute resolution. The interaction between local settings and attempts to globalize human rights is a promising analogy to alternative dispute resolution

Today's cross-cultural seminar would look more closely at the

The Seminar: Who We Were and What We Did

Although the group changed a little over the two-year period, about 15 individuals attended on a fairly regular basis, and a few others would drop in for a session or two. Most individuals were invited to attend because of their interest in exploring the intersection of culture and disputing. Most had lived in Pacific or Asian countries outside of Hawaii, and many had done some field work or other research in the region. The majority had a social science background; a few individuals came from the field of law.[2] Most were regular faculty members; a few were lecturers or PCR staff; some were employed in the community but had regular ties to the university; and four were graduate students.[3]

A number of members shared an interest in the practice of mediation and 11 had training and experience as mediators for nonprofit agencies. Their experience ranged from public disputes to interpersonal, family disputes. The practitioners had a solid interest in the theoretical aspects of disputing as well, so it is perhaps too simplistic to suggest that the practitioners' views diverged widely from the others. The distinction between practitioners and theorists did emerge from time to time, but not consistently.

Given the broad nature of the seminar purpose and our lack of expertise in the specific subject matter, the task of designing an approach to the seminar was problematic. Prior to the first meeting, members were informally polled for ideas about structuring the sessions and for suggestions about reading material. We then adopted a general direction that might be called "planned ad hoc". Before each meeting, we distributed a memorandum describing the topic to be addressed and a general strategy for the discussion. At the end of each session, the co-leaders summarized where the group seemed to be heading and asked for suggestions about the next meeting. In between sessions, the agenda was confirmed and communicated to the participants. However, we did not establish a long-range conceptual or strategic outline for the sessions. Although this produced some discomfort as we searched for some guiding concept or theme, the process actually worked out to the satisfaction of most participants.

During the first year, the discussions were generated by readings, films and videotapes, and presentations by members or invited guests on a wide variety of dispute-related subjects. The second year began with an attempt to categorize many of the recurring questions into three areas: (1) an analysis of mediation; (2) the natural history of disputes; and (3) the relationship between formal and informal approaches to dispute resolution. These themes indicated that pervasive orientations had begun to emerge. We had begun to emphasize disputing as part of a longer narrative. In our view, the nature or dynamics of the disputing process could not be understood outside the context of this narrative, or "story," as it was commonly called in the seminar. This focus on context both reflected and reinforced a deepening sense that any generalizations about culture and disputing needed to be qualified and must take individual circumstances into account.

Although the choice of themes was based on a careful analysis of the previous year's work, the division of the material was less helpful than we anticipated. We soon discovered that these were not actually discrete categories; instead each overlapped with the others. However, the categorization became a useful way to distinguish a preferred emphasis of inquiry. As we proceeded we felt hampered by the lack of a solid core of literature on culture and disputing and, although the group continued to use readings, there was more emphasis on short, one-page reaction papers prepared by the participants to sharpen the discussions.

Half-way through the year, the group decided to focus on a single case, a suggestion that had been made a few times before. There was not a consensus to engage in actual research on the case, but the group did spend a few months exploring what a group research agenda might look like. The seminar concluded with the task of designing a comparative disputing interview approach to be used at a PCR workshop on Disputing in Asia and the Pacific.[4]

The Phases: A Closer Look
Many Lenses, Many Phenomena: Strutting Our Stuff
The seminar began with the notion that our goal was to develop a single frame of reference, and then put specific Pacific and Asian examples of disputing into the taxonomy. In other words, the plan was to reach what we have called "Phase Two," the common

burgeoning global/local literature and consider how it applies to questions like the following:

What does "Hawaiïan culture" mean in a context of multiple influences, porous boundaries, between "Hawaiïian" and "Non-Hawai'ian" norms and values? (Substitute any culture you want here.)

In everyday life, how do people develop, borrow, and change ideas about conflict, disputing, rights, and justice?

The other issue that is based on our experiences since the seminar is about work routines and agendas. It is one thing to raise consciousness and interest in a seminar. It is quite another to change people's research, teaching, and practice priorities. The Program on Conflict Resolution has been less influenced by the seminar than we had wished. This has nothing to do with lack of productivity. Quite the contrary. Well before the seminar began, even though it began early in PCR's history, PCR people already had busy, full agendas. Only a few people then and now look at culture in any explicit way.

What is interesting and a bit ironic about this is that all of the PCR people as well as the practitioners in Hawai'i "do culture" all the time, as does everyone else working in this field anywhere. Everyday in myriad and often subtle ways, we negotiate our realties so that in small but crucial ways it affects the meaning and disposition of culture.

The moral of all of this may very well be that having multidisciplinary discussions about culture is relatively easy. Even getting people to concede that other viewpoints enhance their understanding and research is likely. But creating a context and working

lens, and stay there. In our early meetings, we attempted to discover what our individual concerns were and what kinds of common questions and issues we might raise to transcend our particular perspectives. This was the orientation period.

The following list of issues emerged very early and dominated the seminar's agenda for most of the two years. Although these questions were not discussed explicitly each week they provided a foundation, an undercurrent of both insight and frustration that came up repeatedly.

•How do we broaden our knowledge about alternative dispute resolution (ADR) and understand our own cultural assumptions, as a necessary prelude to studying disputing cross culturally?
•What are the implicit or explicit values in the ADR movement? How is ADR used as an agent of socialization? What is really meant by "neutrality" is the U.S.?
•How valid are the claims of ADR?
•Is the basic vocabulary of ADR—for example terms such as mediator, conflict, dispute—culture-bound?
•What is the influence of U.S. ADR on other countries? Does the popularization of U. S. mediation threaten the existence of indigenous forms of dispute resolution around the world (through its naiveté about the use of other processes, as well as a lack of awareness of the cultural boundedness of its own produces)?
•What should the process and outcome of the seminar be?
•How do we reconcile the tensions between inquiry that tries to make generalizations and inquiry that is more specific and more concerned with cultural context?
•How can we overcome the problems of the lack of information in the existing ethnographic and ADR literature to help us address our concerns and assess our skepticism?

The questions raised are a mix of issues, and these issues were seldom separated cleanly in the discussions. In fact, the constant reemergence of these concerns in different configurations at once strengthened our conviction that we were onto something, and indicated that the problems they suggested were not ones that we were going to be able to resolve in the course of the seminar.

At this stage, it is more important to understand the process of our struggle to answer these questions than it is to consider the answers themselves. Looking at how and why the questions emerged helps us to understand how this interdisciplinary seminar concerned with comparative analysis came to see itself and to function.

Initially, the search for common issues was seen as a way of overcoming the idiosyncrasies of the individual disciplines represented in the seminar. Since many in the group were not familiar with the pertinent literature, we began by identifying works that might bring us to some common understanding and bridge gaps in our knowledge. We soon discovered that there was very little culture and disputing literature, and that the body of work on disputing in Asia and the Pacific was particularly scanty. Some members of the group had worked in various locales in which we were interested, and they concurred that few area ethnographies singled out disputing as a particular social activity. Many of the existing studies did have examples of disputes or dispute resolution processes in them, but they were not categorized or labeled primarily as disputes. Instead, the examples were used to illustrate a variety of societal features like political organization, kinship patterns, and religious beliefs.

The discussions that grew out of the readings, films, and videotapes were an attempt to find a common language in which to talk about the issues. All definitions and terms were up for grabs as members questioned one another about the meaning and implications of concepts. We were operating under the assumption that we were moving toward finding a common framework, an "etic" viewpoint.[5] Once we found the common language, a framework upon which we could generalize, we believed we would be able to use the ethnographic works and our own knowledge of various cultures to fill in the culturally specific features. However, the discourse of comparison that dominated did not lend itself to the development of generalizations. Although we were all interested in unfamiliar cultures, and even in trying to make some generalizations, each of us was anchored in our own specific intellectual experiences, and we talked in terms of our own rather limited roots.

environment for talk that generates a real shift in thinking, research, and practice is tough. If we were to try it again, the cross-cultural seminar would have to be built on a more up-front agenda of systematic reflection and experience of self and work. Building on our previous experiences, this agenda would have a better chance of really penetrating the assumptive veils.

Here are two examples of typical discussion during the first semester. The first exchange was part of a discussion of reactions to a videotape of *ho'oponopono,* a family conflict resolution process.

A. "This is definitely a social work model. Look at the amount of directiveness used."
B. "The Solomon Islands paper mentions the same pattern of directiveness in a cultural context that is not affected by social work."
C. "*Ho'oponopono* reminds me of a '60s encounter group."
D. "Or family therapy."
B. "Like confession in the Catholic Church."

The next example comes from a session on coercion and social control. At this point in the discussion, the group was trying to figure out how to proceed.

A "It would be interesting to look at the difference between mediation in the U.S. and China."
B. "That's what bothers me—how different are they?"
C. "I remember an article about a rape in a Chinese factory where the mediator was the work foreman and the solution was for the girl to marry her attacker... changing your perspective to eliminate the problem of rape."
D. "It's interesting to look at Japan, where the Asian background has merged with a modern, western, business context. Instead of arbitration, as in America, they have 'conciliation.' In Japan it's acceptable for the mediator to use all his moral suasion to force an agreement to comply with social values. In America it's not acceptable. We don't like to admit bias."
A "Maybe it's just a matter of style or degree. It's not okay to state it openly, but the same values and concerns are brought into mediation here through the questions; the outcomes may be the same."
B. "You could investigate by looking at cases at the justice center compared with the Japanese."

This conversation continued to sashay around the globe, touching on the Catholic Church, Hawaiian adoption, Samoa, New Zealand, the Solomons, British judges, U.S. case law, the Philippines, Rajaneesh, Al Capone, the Tikopia and the Yanomamo—all within approximately 15 minutes. Although it may seem amusing when lined up in this fashion, the dialogue is illustrative of how far we were willing to range to locate a connecting thread and find a common place to stand. No one in the seminar identified him or herself as a country specialist. Each of us felt that our own particular disciplines transcended single countries. Yet, as the examples show, individual countries and contexts dominated our professional lives and furnished us with the bulk of vignettes, examples, and analogies that we brought to the discussion. These sets of experience reinforced our growing skepticism toward generalization. Even when we were willing to take leaps, we often did not have the language.

One Lens, Many Phenomena: The Rise and Fall of the Common Lens
The best way to understand the dynamics of this stage of the seminar is to return to our own original conception of it. At the outset, we thought of the common lens as the goal. We would measure our success by the extent to which we developed a shared set of generalizations that could be applied to our own specific interests. These generalizations would be accompanied by a shared language—a common intellectual currency we could all exchange.

What happened instead in this crucial stage was something quite different. Almost immediately, it became apparent that many of the seminar participants had doubts about the approach. The doubts developed into a full-blown critique of the notion of a comparative "common lens."

Many of the seminar's key and overriding issues were raised in our concern with comparative analysis. As the title of the seminar indicated, one of its purposes was to find ways to talk comparatively about disputing and conflict. From the outset, however, comparative analysis was seen as problematical, full of pitfalls and culture-bound traps. No one denied that looking across cultures was a good idea, but when we did so, or when we studied the comparative disputing literature, we had serious misgivings about the outcome of the attempts.

To understand what this trouble was about, it is necessary to consider ways comparative analysis might work and how it tended to work in the seminar. Comparative analysis can be seen as a search for universals and generalizations, an attempt to develop general categories and general statements or positions. What holds across cultures? On the basis of 20 cultures' experience with disputing, what general statements can we make? This "etic" emphasis is the sort of comparative analysis we initially thought would be our focus. There is, however, another side to comparative analysis. Comparisons can reveal differences rather than similarities. Such analysis stresses finding exceptions or showing the importance of particulars, like a specific culture or a set of historical circumstances peculiar to a place.

The two approaches to comparative analysis are not mutually exclusive. Indeed all of us agreed that both were essential—part of the same inquiry. The trouble was that such a claim to nonexclusivity is easier made than carried out. Seminar members differed over the importance of culture or history. To some, culture was a variable that could be rather easily incorporated along with other variables in developing a taxonomy. As one member put it, "Let's develop some taxonomies and see how 20 or 30 cultures can be located according to these." That never happened. Most other participants did not rule out the development of such categories but, when push came to shove, many did not feel comfortable with any categories they saw, nor were we able to develop our own. We were also unable to build generalizations on the basis of our knowledge about specific cultures.

Comparative analysis, in the etic sense, became not simply a difficult chore but one that gave rise to much misgiving. The most obvious reason for this was the lack of good literature. The group remained unconvinced that existing attempts to generalize on the basis of exhaustive review of disputing behavior across cultures were very useful. Its reaction to the Abel (1974) piece is a good example. The seminar participants were awed by Abel's attempt but found many exceptions to his generalizations, questioned his terms and, most of all, were skeptical about the usefulness of his taxonomies. "The categories do not work" was one objection. As one person skeptically put it, "Has anybody used his approach?"

The ethnographies on Asian and Pacific cultures were of limited use in developing taxonomies and generalizations because most of them did not focus on conflict as a conceptual category. There were conflicts in many of these works, but the stories are embedded in analysis of the rest of the culture. We frequently found ourselves debating the value of separating out conflicts or disputes as an analytical device, for many of us felt that the merging of categories and events is precisely the orientation needed to study disputing—if, in fact, one can single out disputing at all as a focus of inquiry We came to see this lack of focus on disputing as a lesson rather than a problem—yet another example of the importance of understanding a dispute as a situation with roots in other social processes, as opposed to something to be examined alone. Members of the seminar would often talk of the need to study the "natural history" of a dispute. At other times, the influence of the ethnographic literature would lead many of us toward the view that, rather than "imposing" criteria for deciding whether something is a dispute, we should focus on how the participants define things. Do they perceive a conflict? What does it mean to them?

The orientation or limits of the literature itself was only part of the reason that seminar members had so much trouble with work that tried to build generalizations. Although anthropologists were a minority in the group, they were disinclined to risk generalization and emphasized the need to understand a phenomenon as part of its own specific cultural context. The seminar's earliest look at exercises in cross cultural generalizations (a report on psychotherapy across cultures) was greeted with some skepticism. Indeed, the person who gave the report and who was engaged in such research was the only one of the regular faculty participants who dropped out of the seminar at the end of its first year.

But the concern was not the anthropologists' alone, nor did it reflect a professional provincialism. This skepticism, increasingly shared by others in the group, was a manifestation of a fundamental epistemological issue that began to pervade the seminar early on and became crucial during our second semester. We became increasingly concerned with the degree of attention that any inquiry should pay to culturally and individually constituted definitions of reality, and the degree to which analytical categories should be developed outside of the actors' and culture's own frame of reference. It is an accurate enough shorthand to call the view that emphasizes the importance of culturally and individually constituted meanings an "interpretative" or "naturalistic" approach. While the seminar did not devote a specific session to interpretative social science, this approach was often discussed in terms of the difficulties of looking across cultures.

Interpretative approaches were also important in our discussions about just what it was we were trying to study. Some members were not very interested in the social and political process by which something emerges as a conflict, while others felt that this process was the key—or at least that dispute resolution could be understood only as part of a long narrative, a "natural history."

Some of the most interesting and fruitful attempts comparison were efforts to accommodate these two approaches. There was indeed a great deal of accommodation and shared learning and a consensus that the approaches are not mutually exclusive. The works of Felstiner, Abel, and Sarat (1980/81) and Mather and Yngvesson (1980/81) were quite influential because they addressed themselves to the concerns of these two approaches, suggesting general categories and exploring the process by which a situation becomes a dispute. However, in the opinion of those primarily interested in disputing as a culturally anchored narrative, neither of these works gave enough insight into the process of dispute transformation. Still, the seminar found the work of these authors to have the greatest potential for cross cultural comparison.

As the discussion of the interpretative approach indicated, this failure to develop a discourse of comparison arose very much from the epistemology that began to dominate the seminar. All of us were constantly comparing our knowledge and experiences with others, but the emerging emphasis on the importance of a specific cultural context and on long narratives typically led us to see broad comparisons as facile rather than useful.

Something else reinforced this concern with the specifics and depth of culture, even among those who were relatively optimistic about developing generalizations. All of us— those who were trained mediators and those who were not—were skeptical of the claims made by advocates of ADR, particularly in the United States. The doubt centered on the contentions that ADR is neutral and that there would be a great demand for the process if people only knew of the opportunities ADR offered them. Cross-cultural literature and films of dispute processes in other countries allowed us to see that values are a very explicit part of the process, both in the U. S. and elsewhere.

A discussion of the Public Broadcasting Service film on China from the *Heart of the Dragon* series examined the degree of influence state policies had on the mediation of a couple's marital dispute. China has an official policy encouraging the "one-child" family. Since the couple in the film already had one child, a divorce and possible remarriages that could lead to more children would violate the policy. The outcome of the mediation was "successful"—the couple reconciled, and the one-child policy was upheld. This led to a discussion of the values that are a part of family mediation in the United States.

Cross cultural studies (Merry 1982) indicate that the distance from the parties that U. S. mediators seem to seek is quite atypical. The group became convinced that this particular value, along with others, had to be "unpacked"—that is, the assumptions ought to be made explicit. Mediation should not be seen as an activity carried out by value-laden parties and a neutral mediator; instead, it should be conceptualized as an interaction among value-laden participants. The mediator's values may or may not have explicit ties to the values of the state, but the link is worth investigating.

Our dissatisfaction with the typical discussion of ADR in the United States was thus related to our feeling that the study of mediation must be broadened to include the values of both the mediator and the state. We tried to unpack the values that appear to be a part of ADR in the United States, and in the process we examined the work of the critics of "delegalization" (Abel 1980). Although we found that work outdated and insufficiently grounded in empirical data, its claims I were no less based on solid evidence than are the contentions of those advocating ADR. The seminar members were also disappointed in a critique by Delgado et al. (1985).

Some of our doubts about ADR were related to its advocates' stances regarding culture and interpretation. Some were rooted in Neo-Marxian notions of the role of formal and informal processes in a capitalist society. But what united us all in our skepticism was the lack of studies that could assess the claims of both the critics and the proponents.

The Prism: Forming New and Fragile Alliances
This phase emerged with the decision to use a single case as the subject of inquiry. By this point, the co-leaders had for the most part given up on the original aims of the seminar; that is, to do comparative work in the way the first two phases suggested. Although we were not certain what exactly would replace these more "objective" aims and outcomes, we did sense that things were rolling and that we should continue with the evolving, organic way the group was heading.

The dispute we settled on had occurred a few years before and involved the multiple uses of land adjacent to a cemetery in a neighboring community.[6] It was brought before the group by two seminar members who had been directly involved as meeting facilitators and mediators. The case seemed amenable to our purposes because the research site was close to campus, which meant that many seminar members were familiar with the community; the dispute was complex and interesting from a multicultural point of view; and the original mediators were able to reconstruct some of the process of the dispute, thus giving us an actual case history to examine. The disputants included representatives from a Chinese civic organization that owned the land and the cemetery, staff from a private preschool that leased a building on the cemetery land, government agency officials, a city council member, and neighbors of various ethnicities and socioeconomic levels. We later became aware of inherent drawbacks to this case, primarily a lack of data, including transcripts of the meetings. And, because the seminar members were not willing to do the field work and interviews that would be necessary to conduct an actual study, what emerged instead was an exercise in constructing possible approaches to interdisciplinary research on this case. All of the activities were prefaced by qualifications like, "If we were to actually do research, and some resources and time were available, what would you do?"

What follows below is an outline of our sessions on the Chinese Cemetery Case. Once again, there was no prior grand scheme about how the inquiry would unfold. The themes developed as we went along, based on reflections at the close of each session about what the next step should be.

Session One. Presentation of case summary. Participants were asked to prepare a paper on "What else do you want to know about the case?"

Session Two. Discussion of papers. Emphasis was on the rationales for the research, as well as on the questions themselves.

Session Three. Presentation of brief research proposals. Individuals presented two-page proposals that included their central research questions, the rationale for their selected focus, and their proposed methodological approach. (Time and financial limitations had been specified for all proposals to make them more practical and roughly comparable in scope.)

Session Four. Reactions to proposals. Questions asked were: "What were the similarities and differences among the proposals?" "Have any of them influenced the way you would now do your research?" "Do you see any feasibility of designing a group research project?"

Session Five. Discussion of the feasibility of a group project. "How might the group arrive at a single research statement and what might it look like?"

Session Six. Presentation of individually prepared group proposals. Each person presented his or her ideas about what a group project might look like. There were some similarities among the proposals, but no consensus about focus, rationale or methodology.

Session Seven. Formation of research subgroups. Individuals grouped themselves into one of three subgroups to focus on (1) conflict resolution practices (the mediation process in the case); (2) the dispute's "natural history," meaning the community interaction before, during, and after the dispute; or (3) the relationship of the dispute to the social, political, and cultural context of the community. Each group was instructed to outline its own research project, and to think about how the other groups' research would benefit, amplify, or extend its own researches and outcomes.

It was the experience of this final session that led the co-leaders to see interdisciplinary research as a prism-like phenomenon. Over the course of the case study sessions, there was a subtle shift in how we thought about research. We recognized that each person had begun with a predilection toward certain kinds of questions and methodologies. Although these predilections held fairly constant throughout the sessions, members did seem to shift their orientations in ways that made the relationships between different research approaches more explicit. For example, a person who relished doing in-depth interviews destined to reveal nuances of meaning in disputing speech was unlikely to give that up in favor of conducting large-scale survey research designed to examine the relationships of variables like ethnicity or educational attainment to the likelihood of using mediation services. However, we did discover, particularly in the last session, that a person might begin to see how others' research could amplify or otherwise enhance the conclusions that he or she might draw about a dispute context or event. This reflected for us a new kind of group effort. individuals were seriously committed to talking to one another regularly about their work. But rather than aspiring to group research with a common focus, we determined that the final decision on how another's information was to be used (or not used) rested with the individual. The seminar provided both the structure and continuity necessary for this collaboration to occur. To return to the prism analogy, each person had his or her own lens, which revealed a particular facet of the phenomenon. Isolated, it remained fragmentary, just one aspect of a whole. Only when each individual perspective was brought into relation with others did it contribute to the prism, which is capable of producing the full spectrum of light.

A Retrospective View: Shifting Epistemologies
What emerged from the seminar was not a body of comparative analysis that could easily bond a variety of researchers across cultures. In retrospect, that goal appears to have been based on a good deal of naiveté, both about the dynamics of a multidisciplinary seminar and about the epistemological issues that dominated the discussions. Multiple lenses are chaotic, but the single lens of generalization and taxonomy did not develop. This made our "product" more elusive, and it is difficult to describe our accomplishment in a terse statement.

What emerged in the seminar was the dominance of the naturalistic paradigm of inquiry: Thus far in this article we have avoided the use of such terms because the seminar did not start out in such a self-consciously epistemological vein. We do not want to leave the impression that there was a sure and steady movement toward this paradigm, or that we even discussed it in such terms. Nonetheless, it is useful to apply this notion in retrospect because the idea of the naturalistic paradigm "fits" as a description of what took place. The following table by Lincoln and Guba (1985:37) summarizes the axioms of the naturalistic and positivistic paradigms.

Table 1. Contrasting Positivist and Naturalist Axioms

Axioms About	Positivist Paradigm	Naturalist Paradigm
The nature of reality	Reality is single, tangible, and fragmentable.	Realities are multiple, constructed, and holistic.
The relationship of knower the known	Knower and known are independent, a dualism. inseparable.	Knower and known are interactive.
The possiblity of generalization	Time- and context-free generalizations (nomo-thetic statements) are possible.	Only time- and context-bound working hypotheses (ideographic statements are possible).
The possiblity of causal linkages	There are real causes, temporarily precedent to or simultaneous with their effects.	All entities are in a state of mutual simul-taneous shaping, so that it is impossible to distinguish causes from effects.
The role of values	Inquiry is value-free.	Inquiry is value-bound.

Reprinted from Lincoln and Guba (1985)

   The seminar members' objections to taxonomies and generalizations were argued very much along the lines of these naturalistic axioms. Two of the strongest themes in the seminar stressed the need to understand the multiple and shifting realities of those involved in a dispute, and the need to understand a dispute as part of a "longer story" that is anchored in a rich and specific history and culture. Our analysis of disputing typically stressed how insepa-rable the dispute was from other events happening simultaneously (for example, changes in the community, other attempts to the issue, and the nature of the family relationship).
   The value-laden aspect of ADR was also a dominant theme, particularly in our concern about the lack of self-awareness among the advocates of ADR in the U. S. We blanched at the facile use of terms like efficiency and neutrality. We also tried to think about

mediation as an interactive process between mediator and parties, though we were hampered by the lack of literature on this point. Our observation of the Chinese mediation case was a key event because it was such an explicit example of an attempt to bring state policies to bear on a process that purports to be both informal and noncoercive.

In a haphazard but ultimately powerful way, we severely questioned the axioms of positivism, but the break from positivism was certainly not clean, unanimous, or even very well understood. The emphasis on context, specifics, and the inseparability of the knower and the known left us floundering for general guiding principles. Is there a way to have such principles without succumbing to the pitfalls that positivist-oriented taxonomies create?

The "prism" approach, the third stage of the seminar, can be seen as our attempt to find this compromise. In our discussion of the cemetery dispute, individuals tried to link their own interests to those of the rest of the group, yet there were few pretensions that this would build theory or even afford much generalization. Particularly in the latter sessions, we stressed how one context or one set of research proposals implicates others. Implication is a less rigorous standard than those normally used in comparative analysis, which searches for general taxonomies. There was constant movement back and forth from individual orientations toward what was interesting about the cemetery dispute and what others found interesting. Though there were very strong assumptions that each of us would learn from the others, there was, finally, almost no feeling that we would come even close to a common framework.

Conclusion

The members of the seminar were by no means satisfied with this not very definitive result, but our final ambiguity, as well as the interesting intellectual and social process that emerged during the case study, appears to be a logical outgrowth of the seminar's ultimately dominant epistemological stance. If the seminar had been run by an acknowledged expert in the field, the group might have gravitated toward a more common ground. If we had conducted a more comprehensive survey of the literature, perhaps we would have found cross- cultural generalizations about conflict that made us all comfortable. On the other hand, the skepticism that dominated our group reflected some serious and increasingly powerful epistemological views. At the same time, that skepticism bolstered a strong spirit of accommodation toward the work of each group member. Our doubts unified us. Anyone who was deeply attached to a single set of approaches had trouble. Consequently, the spirit of inquiry was very open.[7]

Since the outcome of the seminar was not what we had expected, it is not surprising that its role in the overall scheme of the Program on Conflict Resolution is likewise not what we expected. The seminar has become the informal intellectual core for PCR. That does not mean that it serves as some sort of all-purpose theory-developer or idea-generator. Rather, it has become an important forum in which PCR participants can talk about the broader context of their work. The seminar's structure and membership appear to have a great deal of staying power, and to have a wider impact than we could have imagined.

Our experience may also be of interest to other university dispute resolution theory-building programs. From our discussions with other researchers, we discern that programs are not yet very comfortable with the idea of theory building. This discomfort stems from two major concerns: the relationship between theory and practice, and the pitfalls of moving toward grand theoretical designs.

At a 1987 Hawaii conference of university dispute resolution programs supported by the Hewlett Foundation, it was apparent that many of the participants shared a desire to avoid the exploitative relationships that positivistic social science creates. Yet the participants wanted to do something that is cumulative. They were eager to use the insights of one another's research, whether that inquiry was from their own program or from others. Comments were made about the important relationships between theory and practice, researcher and subject, knower and known.

There was a desire to maintain some fluidity to research boundaries, so that a variety of endeavors could flourish, and yet a discomfort about this persisted. How can a university program integrate a desire for openness to various approaches into a pragmatic, research agenda within an interdisciplinary organizational framework? Comments like the following reflected how many of us were getting caught in the dilemma "Oh, you're interested in social justice issues? Go talk to the Michigan folks." "Culture stuff? The Hawaii group does that." As we learned in our seminar, it is much easier to reject the positivist way of doing theory than it is to develop the organizational and intellectual tools necessary to work in other ways.

What do our seminar experiences have to say about the nature of interdisciplinary inquiry? First, it is better to describe our endeavors as multidisciplinary rather than interdisciplinary. We were a group of individuals with well-developed perspectives. In the seminar we brought these perspectives and ideas to bear on common issues, but, as time went on, we did not come close to adopting a single lens or a single definition of problems. Each of us acted like a federated state. Like federated states, however, we shared a set of common values (an unwritten constitution?) that increasingly bound us. These values induced shared orientations toward comparison and generalization, as well as a consensus that integration of perspectives was far more valuable than the establishment of hard and precise boundaries.

The "prismatic" orientation that emerged protected the autonomy of "federated" individuals by allowing them to gaze with comfort at issues from the perspectives they had developed prior to the seminar. At the same time, the prismatic approach reminded us that each of us wished to be implicated in the values and perspectives of the others, that no one was alone. One is reminded of the way the U. S. Constitution was celebrated during its 200th anniversary—as a document that binds people together yet fosters autonomy.

Multidisciplinary inquiry requires this kind of delicate balancing act. It is very easy to drop the whole idea of such inquiry because people constantly quibble about the way things are going. At the same time, it is easy to impose a false consensus or, in disputing terms, a false peace, by claiming that there is a unified perspective. The somewhat organic develop-ment of our prism metaphor suggests a useful middle ground. When consensus emerges slowly enough, participants have plenty of opportunity to figure out what the shared values are and where opportunities for individual and collaborative interests lie. There is still much to be done on the relationship between culture and disputing. Our seminar experience indicates that the substantive issues regarding the culture-disputing link cannot be separated from a consideration of fundamental epistemological questions.

Acknowledgment

The authors would like to thank Jim Crowfoot, Jack Bilmes, and Karen Watson-Gegeo for helpful and encouraging comments about early drafts.

Notes

1. PCR is funded primarily by a grant from the William and Flora Hewlett Foundation. The foundation has demonstrated substantive commitment to the dispute resolution field by supporting practice, education, and research organizations. The University of Hawaii' s pro-gram is one of a group of Hewlett-funded interdisciplinary university programs. Similar programs are currently located at George Mason University, Harvard University, the Univer-sity of Michigan, the University of Minnesota, Northwestern, Rutgers, Syracuse, and the University of Wisconsin, Madison.

2. The 19 seminar members represented the following disciplines (or combinations of disciplines): Anthropology (4); Psychology (4); Law (2); Political Science (2); Political Science/ Planning (2); Sociology (2); Anthropology/ Law/Communication (1); Communication (1); and Planning (1).

3. Two of the graduate students expressed some anxiety about their role in the group, questioning whether they were sufficiently prepared to engage in the discussion, or wonder-ing if others perceived them as "second class" members. Only one student participated throughout the two years.

4. Due to logistical and interview design problems that emerged during the workshop, the interview was not carried out as planned

5. Etics and emics arc constructs borrowed from linguistics to denote generalizable categories (etics) and cultural-specific expressions and categories (emics). For example, "family system" is an etic construct; 'ohana is the Hawaiian emic construct.

6. Most of the actual case detail is omitted, because, although interesting, it doesn't further the discussion about how our inquiry proceeded.

7. Although the discussions were very open, in terms of intellectual inquiry, there was a lack of self-disclosure about how we personally handled disputes. We can only speculate about the reasons for this. One issue the group also skirted, even though it was bought up several times was gender and disputing. A few of the women noted that the style of discourse in the

seminar tended to seem "male." In fact, whenever a particular type of "put down" bantering occurred some men and women began to laughingly point it out as "M. T.," or "male talk." We believe it would be fruitful to explore this issue in future seminar sessions.

References

Abel, R. 1974. A comparative theory of dispute institutions. *Law and Society Review* 8:250-347.

————. 1980. Delegalization: A critical review of its ideology, manifestations, and social consequences. In *Alternative rechtsformer und alternativen zum recht*, ed. by Erhard Blankenberg, Ekkehard Klausa, and Hubert Rottleuthner. Opladen, F R G.: Weiss Deutscher Verlag.

Delgado, R.,C. Dunn, P. Brown, H. Lee, and D. Hubbert. 1985. Fairness and formality: Minimizing the risk of prejudice in alternative dispute resolution. *Wisconsin Law Review* 1359-1404.

Felstiner, W., R. Abel, and A. Sarat. 1980/81. The emergence and transformation of disputes: Naming, blaming, claiming ... *Law and Society Review* 15: 631-664.

Lincoln, Y. and E. Guba. 1985. *Naturalistic inquiry*. Beverly Hills, CA: Sage.

Mather, L and B. Yngvesson. 1980/81. Language, audience and the transformation of disputes. *Law and Society Review* 15: 775-821.

Merry, S. 1982. The social organization of mediation in nonindustrial societies: Implications for informal community justice in America. In *The politics of informal justice*, vol. 2, ed. R Abel. New York: Academic.

Teaching Negotiation
with a Feminist Perspective

Elaine M. Landry and Anne Donnellon

Elaine M. Landry is Assistant Professor of management at Babson College, Babson Park, Mass. 02457.

Anne Donnellon is Associate Professor of management at Babson College.

Negotiation teachers encourage their students to be inventive, improve agreements, and push outward on the "Pareto frontier." Likewise, teachers can improve their practice by seeking value, sometimes in other disciplines. In general, negotiation is taught through a combination of lectures with simulation exercises and debriefings. Feminist pedagogy enhances this normative model of teaching negotiation. This article links the traditional method of teaching negotiation with four key principles of feminist pedagogy.

Negotiation courses continue to grow in popularity. They are a part of the curriculum of most university professional programs and many undergraduate programs. In addition, negotiation training seems to be the ubiquitous offering in most corporate training institutes. The success of such courses is due, at least in part, to the increased awareness of conflict in the workplace and of the requirements for effective negotiation of these conflicts.

Negotiation training has also become popular due to an emerging consensus about what constitutes the constructive handling of conflict (Kolb and Putnam 1997). This shared understanding has led to a common emphasis on the development of individual skills in negotiation. These skills are typically developed through a normative approach that combines a conceptual framework with extensive experiential learning. Indeed, the expectations of participants are generally met by this paradigm.

However, there is mounting, albeit anecdotal, evidence that the typical paradigm for teaching negotiation can be problematic in several ways. In this article, we shall describe the typical pedagogy and identify several concerns we have with it; then, drawing on a feminist-theoretical framework, we shall present an alternative pedagogical approach.

The Typical Approach

The typical contemporary approach to teaching negotiation, especially within management curricula, has been to present a specific

This article first appeared in Negotiation Journal, January 1999: Volume 15, Number 1, pages 21-29.

111

framework for negotiating effectively and to provide opportunities for students to practice and improve their individual ability to use the prescribed skills in "real-world" situations. Materials are usually selected by the instructor on the basis of their ability to illustrate the prescribed framework. Understanding of the framework is developed and refined through lectures and commentary by the instructor.

Commonly, this approach includes case discussion, lectures and simulation exercises; the outcomes of the latter are scored or otherwise compared across individual participants and-or groups. Key learnings about the framework are reinforced in the debriefing of these exercises by focusing on specific aspects of the interaction.

The conceptual framework that undergirds this normative approach emphasizes the transactional nature of negotiations and provides guidance on maximizing one's own self-interest. This paradigm postulates that to achieve self-interest, one must make an exchange with those with whom one is negotiating. The succinct prescriptions for negotiating in this way account for much of the success of this approach.

The experiential pedagogy characterizing this paradigm fits well with the framework. Simulations have been especially effective in enhancing one's ability to identify self-interest and the underlying interests of others in the effort to calculate good exchanges and deals. Good simulations provide extremely efficient opportunities for practice by creating concrete mutual experiences that stimulate action by participants that reinforces their conceptual learning.

Despite the success of the normative approach to teaching negotiation, it is problematic in several ways. Generally, the instructional scheme that surrounds simulation experiences tends to place a premium on logic and rationality. Problems in negotiation are interpreted as the result of cognitive bias (Bazerman and Neale 1992). Students are, therefore, taught to be aware of their own biases and to take advantage of the biases of other negotiators. Bargainers are assumed to operate invariably out of self-interest, and so learn to assess inputs and outcomes of the parties concerned. The problem is that negotiations outside the classroom are rarely the objective transactions that simulations model. Students prepared well to handle those are often blindsided by the effects of self-image and emotion on the behavior of all concerned.

This transactional focus of the dominant teaching model also ignores other important outcomes of negotiation—specifically, relational outcomes. As researchers who study the social construction and evolution of disputes in organizations point out (see Kolb and Bartunek 1992), a pedagogy that prizes a single perspective and a narrow range of transactional outcomes fails to teach students about the most common form of negotiating, those that occur in the context of relationships. Subtly, the normative approach indicates that relations are the inputs, constraints, or instruments in the negotiation, rather than outcomes to be gained or lost. This implication can affect student perceptions of the importance of any but transactional outcomes.

A related problem occurs as a byproduct of the obvious need for efficiency when using simulations. Because of time constraints, the authors of simulations typically reduce the contextual complexity of most negotiations. The result of this simplification is that novice negotiators are unprepared to consider how organizational politics, status, and emotion may influence their ability to realize desired outcomes. The role assumed by the instructor in the normative approach often reinforces this limitation.

Perhaps because learners place such a premium on improved skill, negotiation instructors often operate from an "expert" model. Knowledge and expertise are disseminated by the instructor, with learners customarily speaking only in response to questions or to seek answers to their own. Most evident in the debriefing of simulations, this approach limits the potential for learners to explore and exchange views fully on how their own emotions or self-perceptions affect the process of their negotiation. Thus, the opportunity to learn from a more robust model of negotiations, one that considers the specifics of the people as well as of the dispute, is missed. The instructor-centered learning experience is also problematic in that it unavoidably reflects the instructor's own cognitive biases and emotional make-up. For students who are markedly different from the instructor (in terms of culture, gender, race, or socioeconomic status, for example), the chances of them being able to develop their own repertoire of negotiation strategies and tactics are narrowed.

The difficulty of adapting generic strategies to one's own personality, status, or social position is typically overlooked by the normative approach. A pedagogy that guides students in the analysis of how contextual and social realities reconfigure the general prescription is admittedly "messier." At a minimum, instructors must be comfortable with ambiguity as to the questions, viewpoints, and outcomes that may be generated. We have found, in fact, that providing opportunities to observe and discuss the effects of these realities in the classroom has great benefits. Other pedagogical approaches might overcome some of the shortcomings of the normative teaching approach we have described. Specifically, we argue one positive alternative is an approach to teaching negotiation that shares common roots with feminist theory.

Feminist Theory

What is feminist theory and how can it inform the teaching of negotiation? Although recent analyses recognize important differences among feminist theories (Gray 1994; Harding 1986; Kolb and Putnam 1995), four core principles can be gleaned from the path-breaking work that has been done in this area.

The first focuses on the critical nature of context to the understanding of social phenomena (see Northrup 1995; Warren and Cheney 1991). The basic argument is that behavior observed and interpreted in isolation will produce very different findings from that which is examined in light of the context in which it occurs, particularly the social context. This principle recognizes the role of relationship and interdependence in shaping both behavior and its interpretation. For instructors, the implication is that explicit attention is given to the context of the classroom itself, looking at the process in addition to the content of the course. This involves careful design of the course, attention to the reaction of individual students, and facilitation of discussion in the class of the group process.

A second pillar of feminist theory is the recognition of multiple realities. This argument asserts that reality is essentially subjective and that one's meanings result from social experience (Mustin and Maracek 1990). Thus "reality" varies according to one's social position. Learning is enhanced by recognition of multiple realities in human experience through a process that combines critical analysis of course materials and a synergistic examination of the multiple perspectives on the material that students, among others, bring to the subject.

Thirdly, feminist theory asserts that the distribution of social power profoundly shapes the evaluation of experience, legitimizing and privileging some, at the expense of others. Power thus reinforces itself by defining not only what constitutes knowledge, but also the rules for producing it, and participation in setting those rules and generating that knowledge (see, for example, Calas and Smircich 1991; Ferguson 1984; Flax 1990; Gray 1994; Harding 1986). Instructors, therefore, must be prepared to redistribute power in the classroom in order to legitimate perspectives on the subject matter that social differences among students may otherwise suppress. Instructors may also need to share their power occasionally to create the capacity and incentive for students to be proactive in shaping a rich, diverse dialogue.

The fourth principle (and the underlying objective of feminist theory) is the goal of redistributing social power and achieving social equity (Calas and Smircich 1991; Gray 1994; Flax 1987). One of the primary pedagogical objectives in the feminist classroom is to create some degree of social change as a result of the course. Therefore, the teaching must create a new understanding of social phenomena, as well as the ability for, and interest in creating change.

These four principles of feminist theory are inconsistent with a pedagogical approach based on the assumption that education is the transmission of canonical knowledge by an expert to a group of novices who are not expected to vary except in their command of the material. On the contrary, feminist theory has very different implications for teaching.

Teaching Negotiation with a Feminist Perspective

How would these pedagogical tenets be manifested in the teaching of negotiation? In our view, student learning can be enriched if course designs specifically address the principles of feminist theory. We shall briefly discuss ideas for applying these tenets in each of the following areas: course materials, the instructional role, improved practice, and the learner experience.

Course materials should encompass a wider range of perspectives with particular attention to exercises and discussions, which take account of relational situations and concerns. Within this category, instructors need to consider a broader mix of classroom events, including more frequent use of student-designed case situations. When students share their own conflicts, it helps to make visible what may remain invisible in exercises that focus primarily on the transactional perspective.

Materials reflecting a wide range of personal and professional situations are increasingly available to instructors and students often resonate to well-chosen examples. Heavy reliance on course material generated outside the students' personal experience, however, forecloses on the possibility for deeper learning that occurs when their own cases are incorporated into the course. In addition, the iterative process of writing, evaluating, and discussing these cases between instructor and learner significantly enhances the potential for personal learning.

The instructional role can shift away from an expert model through the instructor's decision to model inclusiveness. The instructor can work toward this goal in a number of ways, such as: acknowledging that there are many valid interpretations and reactions to class events; a willingness to be vulnerable personally; and providing alternate paths for learner reaction—for example, by offering a mix of assessment and feedback inputs on course activities throughout the course.

Instructors may also limit their individual control over learning outcomes and enhance inclusiveness by encouraging students to serve as consultants and advisers in working on their personal conflicts together. This practice heightens student learning by exposing them to a range of strategic and analytic choices that may not be modeled by the instructor. Further, it provides opportunities for feedback and reflection about the learner's ability to engage in these roles.

As one goal of feminist pedagogy is to produce change, the negotiation instructor should be particularly concerned with assisting learners with experiences that allow them to emerge from the classroom with more confidence and a heightened ability to address social disparities. In addition to choosing a wide spectrum of voices for study and discussion, instructors can also increase the likelihood that they will evoke participation from a myriad of learners' voices. Through assignments and in-class discussion, instructors can provide opportunities for students to reflect on, and gain legitimacy for, their identity and their role.

Since access to these opportunities may not always be replicable in the classroom, the instructor may also encourage students to seek opportunities to practice the manner in which they address real-world challenges to their gender, race, and other identification characteristics. Students might be assigned to community service or other types of internships during the course in order to be able to report on these experiences and both test and debrief their skills in a supportive atmosphere. In the absence of these opportunities, guest speakers, readings and work in other media may be selected to close the gap in experience.

Finally, feminist pedagogy asserts that the classroom reflects process in a very tangible way. In practice, the instructor should work to achieve this goal by: engaging and maintaining a respectful relationship; generating ground rules with the group; and insuring that the process by which the course unfolds is explicit, discussed, and negotiated. Students have a similar responsibility. Often, however, it takes students several sessions to engage in a fully interactive setting. The instructor's orchestration of the early classes where "unfreezing" of existing attitudes and assessment of learner competency takes place is particularly crucial. For example, if an instructor resists the temptation to provide prescriptions (in terms of either process or outcomes) early in the course, learners often become comfortably self-critical. Further, they are more likely to open themselves up to exploring and integrating new ideas. The resulting practice they develop is enriched through periods of self-reflection, appreciation of new ideas, and commitment to continuous learning.

Possibilities and Rewards of Teaching
Negotiation with a Feminist Perspective
As instructors, we often encourage our negotiation students to aim for agreements which reflect a fully realized attempt to maximize joint interests. In so doing, we urge them toward the "Pareto frontier." We counsel our students that these results are only achievable by negotiators who are open in sharing information about themselves and who are tenacious in their efforts to incorporate creatively the concerns of all parties (Lax and Sebenius 1986; Fisher, Ury, and Patton 1991).

Originally adapted from the utility concept in economics (and named after Vilfredo Pareto), many negotiation theorists use the notion of a "Pareto frontier" (Lax and Sebenius 1986; Raiffa 1982; Fisher, Ury and Patton 1991; Rubin, Pruitt, and Kim 1993) to illustrate the degree to which an agreement has maximized possible gains (see Figure One).

Using this concept as an overlay to our discussion is a useful way to illustrate the potential of the ideas we have presented. Figure Two, for example, shows where various outcomes related to instructor-learner interactions lie on the diagonal "Pareto frontier." We use this figure as an adapted version of the "Pareto frontier" graph to illustrate the assumptions described in this brief essay, and, in particular, to illustrate the key features which affect a range of learning outcomes.

Figure 1. Negotiator Outcomes Displayed on an
Adapted Possibilities Frontier
Instead of representing the concerns of two constituencies, we have designed the essential tension to be the value placed on attention to substance versus the value placed on attention to the instructor/learner relationship: Obviously, *Point 0* represents the unfortunate convergence of inattention to either, perhaps caused by instructor incompetence but certainly creating learner escape from the learning context. *Point 1* illustrates that common pedagogical elements (such as an acontextual framework, development of tactical skill, and value-neutral instruction) often achieve minimal learning outcomes.

In this design, the learner is restricted to an experience of assimilation—adoption of the instructor's perspective and style. *Point 2* illustrates a learning environment in which diversity is accepted and where learners can surface their point of view but one in which there are no changes related to the traditional authority structure of teacher and learner. In this

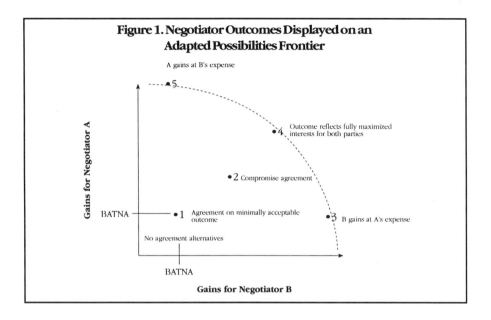

Figure 1. Negotiator Outcomes Displayed on an Adapted Possibilities Frontier

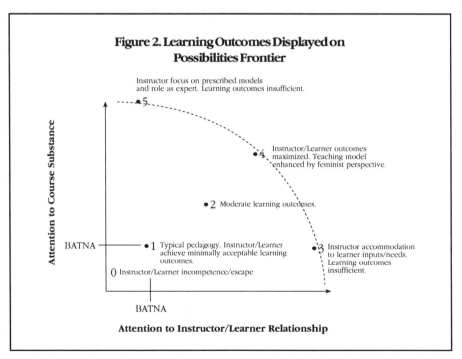

Figure 2. Learning Outcomes Displayed on Possibilities Frontier

occurred if the power dynamics were modified. *Point 3* illustrates that learning goals also remain insufficient when instructors focus too heavily on teaching style and accommodate learning needs to the exclusion of substance. *Point 5* illustrates an environment in which the learning process is blunted by an over-reliance on objective knowledge and the expert model of instruction. Finally, *Point 4* illustrates that learning outcomes are maximized when instructors and learners deliberately seek out and value the range of experiences and perspectives; when they collaborate in their endeavor to create personalized knowledge; when transformational goals are entwined with content; and, when both parties actively seek to learn from— and with—each other.

As described here, the specific actions that theorists identify as effective in moving negotiators toward the frontier mirror the characteristics of negotiation pedagogy as informed and guided by feminist principles. We should add that many of these same principles from feminist pedagogy are also advocated in the negotiation literature as the components that facilitate good agreements. For example, feminist pedagogy suggests that sharing the task of learning about each other's interests and that openness about experiences supports learning. Additionally, feminist pedagogy advocates that techniques such as questioning, listening, testing perceptions, and making room for emotion, can assist instructors in shifting from a sole focus on their own expertise and toward a collaborative and fuller exploration of the substance as well as the student's developmental needs in negotiation skill building.

In conclusion, linking feminist principles with theory that describes creation of value in negotiation illuminates a path interested instructors can take in the effort to become more effective teachers. Moving toward the "possibilities frontier" of learning outcomes is a complex enterprise. Partners in education, just as partners in negotiation, after all, engage in learning without a road map of what opportunities for cooperative action there are to exploit.

There is a complex set of tasks to manage in the early phases of any learning venture. Selecting the most effective learning tools—both content and teaching strategies—is an organic process each time you engage it. Faulty moves in enacting routine instructional jobs (e.g., choosing when to intervene; question selection; or overly constructing situations to yield specific lessons) may foreclose on private value for an individual and/or common value for the group. And, although instructors bear more of the burden for creating a forum that will unmask the learning possibilities, optimal results occur only if there is an exchange of efforts by instructors and learners and only if the learning exchange is congruent with instructional goals.

To summarize, our premise is that, while we are encouraging our students to pursue joint gains in their negotiation experiences, our pedagogy often does not incorporate these principles with similar rigor. As a result, many learning gains are unrealized. By adopting feminist principles as a guideline for our teaching strategies, we are congruent with the negotiation prescriptives we espouse and, more importantly, we begin to explore the frontier of deeper learning we aim to achieve.

References

Bazerman, M. and M. Neale, 1991. *Negotiating rationally.* New York: The Free Press.

Calas, M. B. and L. Smircich, L., 1990. Rewriting gender into organizational theorizing: Directions from feminist perspectives. In *New directions in organizational research and analysis,* edited by M. I. Reed and M.D. Hughes. London: Sage.

Ferguson. K.E., 1984. *The feminist case against bureaucracy.* Philadelphia: Temple University Press.

Fisher, R., W. Ury, and B. Patton, 1991. *Getting to YES: Negotiating agreement without giving in.* 2d ed. New York: Penguin.

Flax, J. 1987. Postmodernism and gender relations in feminist theory. *Signs* 12(4):621-643.

———. 1990. *Thinking fragments: Psychoanalysis, feminism, and postmodernism in the contemporary West.* Berkeley: University of California Press.

Gray, B., 1994. The gender-based foundations of negotiations theory. In *Research on negotiation in organizations,* vol. 4, edited by R. Bies, R. Lewicki, and B. Sheppard. Greenwich, CT: JAI Press.

Harding S., 1986. *The science question in feminism.* Ithaca: Cornell University Press.

Hare-Mustin, R.T. and J. Maracek, eds., 1990. *Making a difference: Psychology and the construction of gender.* New Haven: Yale University Press.

Kolb , D. M. and J. Bartunek, J., eds., 1992. *Hidden conflict in organizations: Uncovering behind-the-scenes disputes.* Newbury Park, Calif.: Sage.

Kolb, D.M. and L.L. Putnam, 1997. Through the looking glass: Negotiation theory refracted through the lens of gender. In *Workplace dispute resolution,* edited by S. Gleason. East Lansing: Michigan State University Press.

Lax, D. A. and J.K. Sebenius, 1986. *The manager as negotiator.* New York: The Free Press.

Northrup, T., 1994. *The uneasy partnership between conflict theory and feminist theory.* Syracuse University.

Raiffa, H. 1982. *The art and science of negotiation.* Cambridge, Mass.: Harvard University Press.

Rubin, J.Z., D. Pruitt, and S.H. Kim, 1993. *Social conflict.* 2nd ed. New York: McGraw-Hill.

Warren, K.J. and L. Cheney, L., 1991. Ecological feminism and ecosystem ecology. *Hypatia* 6: 179-197.

From Theory to Practice: Critical Choices for "Mutual Gains" Training

Raymond A. Friedman

Raymond A. Friedman is
Assistant Professor of
Business Administration
at the Harvard Business
School, Soldiers Field.
Boston, Mass. 09163.
He is currently finishing
a book on the rituals of
labor negotiations and
efforts to change those
rituals, including
training in mutual gains
bargaining.

"Mutual Gains Bargaining" (MGB)[1] has captured the imagination of many prominent negotiators, consultants, and scholars around the country. The MGB process appears to offer a sensible, productive, and rational way of negotiating that can be used in contexts ranging from purchasing used cars to locating a waste disposal site to determining child custody after a divorce.

Mutual gains bargaining also offers an alternative to traditional labor negotiations. The traditional approach, which includes elaborate rituals of conflict (Friedman 1989) and only very private and subtle forms of cooperation (Friedman 1992), does not fit comfortably with the emerging consensus that labor relations must be more cooperative if unions (and the industries they dominate) are to survive (Heckscher 1988). A better way of bargaining is an essential ingredient in any effort to change the basic structure of labor relations.

In spite of this general interest in MGB and its place in our hopes for a new future in labor relations, the process is proving rather difficult to disseminate to labor negotiators in an effective way. One constraint has been the ideas themselves: While they are powerful ideas that can easily capture the imagination, how they are to be applied in practice may be more difficult for negotiators to understand. Another problem is cost: Training may be more expensive than many bargaining units can afford. A third constraint is the structure of labor negotiations, in particular: Constituents are often highly mobilized, leaders are usually "professionals" who are expert in their established way of negotiating (Kolb 1984), and labor laws place requirements on bargainers to act in certain ways.

These constraints raise several questions. How do we bring MGB ideas successfully into the labor relations context? What are the choices available to interventionists, and what are the implications of those choices? And, what are some of the patterns that have worked and in what contexts have they worked?

This article first
appeared in
Negotiation Journal,
April 1992:
Volume 8, Number 2,
pages 91-98.

121

My answers to these questions are based on data from several sources: observations of three test cases of joint labor-management training sponsored by the Department of Labor (DOL); discussions among MGB trainers and researchers at a December, 1990 meeting sponsored by the Harmon program at Harvard's Kennedy School of Government; a survey of those seminar participants (conducted by Charles Heckscher); and, more recently, telephone interviews with these and other trainers.

Lessons from Three Test Cases

In 1988, the Program on Negotiation at Harvard Law School received a grant from the U.S. Department of Labor to bring MGB training to three contract negotiations. The hope, as expressed in the original proposal, was to "develop an approach to negotiation and training which can foster the needed movement from adversarial to cooperative labor relations." At the time, the Department of Labor had developed a broad portfolio of between-contract services to help companies and unions in their effort to be more cooperative. What the agency was missing was a program that addressed the negotiation process itself.

Faculty of the Program on Negotiation had developed an expertise in MGB training (covering many areas of dispute resolution) and a set of teaching techniques (primarily negotiation games and role playing) designed to let students practice MGB in a relatively safe atmosphere. For the Department of Labor project, these techniques would be applied to the training of labor and management negotiators just prior to their actual negotiations.

In general, three stages were intended for each training program. First, both parties would be interviewed and a customized bargaining game would be written that would provide a realistic simulation of their bargaining problems. Both parties would then attend a two-day negotiation workshop that included lectures, several bargaining simulations, and debriefings of those simulations. During the simulation, negotiators would reverse roles—they would be asked to take the perspective of their opponents, arguing their views, and seeing their own views from the opponents' perspective. After the simulations, trainers would debrief the exercises and help negotiators develop their own set of rules for their upcoming negotiations—based on both the core MGB ideas and their experiences during the simulations.

If these training sessions worked, it would show that a few powerful ideas could be conveyed in a short period of time and have an impact on actual negotiations. I call this approach to training a "minimalist" model.

In practice, this short-term, high-impact model did not actually happen. On the front end, entry into the three cases was far more complex than expected. In one case, for example, the union would commit to the training only after a day of open debate among constituents and with the Program on Negotiation trainer. In another case, the trainers had to get involved in extensive on-again, off-again negotiations with the company and union before they would agree to try using MGB, and they had to add, as part of those negotiations, a day of "pretraining" training. And, in the third case, additional days of training needed to be scheduled given the large number of constituents whom the parties felt had to be involved. Even if the "training" might take only several days, the prework required to set up those several days was extensive.

I should point out that, as difficult as the entry process was in these cases, we can expect it to be even more difficult in other cases. This project had the advantage of full funding by a third party (the Department of Labor) before initial contacts were even made. The value of MGB is likely to be challenged even more aggressively when thousands of dollars in training costs are part of the equation; labor and management debates over who should pay the bulk of those costs have not been uncommon in such cases. And if, as is likely, management ends up paying more than the union, the neutrality of the trainers can be called into question.

During training, the trainers faced several different problems. The simulations generally went well, but in one case it became complicated by some relatively minor, but gnawing complaints: at times the customized case was deemed too unlike their real situation, but at other times too close to the real situation. And, when it came time to do the simulation, this group refused to reverse roles. The details of the simulation became a forum for playing out conflicts and anxieties that generally made negotiations difficult for this group. These dynamics led to a second problem: while the events were designed to deal primarily with negotiations, much of the discussion inevitably drifted toward the state of the relationship and what did or did not happen "last time."

These discussions proved fruitful—they were essential in order to clear away the emotional underbrush for MGB—but they were not always part of the training plan; they dealt with issues beyond negotiations per se (requiring different kinds of training skills); and they occurred in spite of explicit attempts, in some cases by lead negotiators, to avoid touchy issues from the past.

After training, it was hoped that the ideas and lessons from the training session would in themselves change the negotiations process, but this was more the exception than the rule. In most cases, negotiators needed additional ongoing support, either to clarify how the ideas were to be implemented in practice or to help them work through difficult moments when they felt stuck in spite of trying very hard to do MGB. The transition from simulations to real negotiations is very difficult and is inevitably fraught with unforeseen ambiguities and complexities. Even negotiators who get past the difficult starting phase can be caught off guard by constituent pressures or by an overwhelming sense of lack of time. (See Ancona, Friedman, and Kolb (1991) for an analysis of the effects of constituent and time pressures on MGB negotiations.) In these instances, they called for extra help from the trainers, who were able to provide assistance, either by phone or in person.

As the trainers moved through this series of test cases, they found themselves being involved more extensively than initially anticipated—before, during, and after the training. Negotiators' actions and concerns drove trainers away from the minimalist model. These developments point to several alternative approaches to MGB training—alternatives that are currently emerging in practice.

Alternative 1: Expand Involvement

The Program on Negotiation's experience points out that trainers cannot enter a situation, spend a few days, leave, and, thereby, change the way labor and management negotiate. They are part of a larger system of relations. This means that trainers must become involved with more people and over longer periods of time (i.e., throughout the course of negotiations). Before negotiations, trainers must be more proactive and interact with a broader range of constituents. During negotiations, they will have to be involved in ongoing, real-time training, possibly serving as quasi-process mediators. And, after negotiations, trainers should continue the relationship, helping the parties implement changes—both in content and process—that were agreed upon or proposed. (See Susskind and Landry 1991.)

This is indeed an optimal model for MGB training, but there are several drawbacks. The model requires significant financial resources to cover the fees for such extensive consulting, and if labor and management have a hard time agreeing on how to manage several days of training, it will be even more difficult for them to agree on a large-scale, all-encompassing consulting project. In many cases, too many barriers to entry may exist for this more inclusive training approach, and entry may be possible only for the most prominent and established trainers in the field.

Alternative 2: Expand Behavioral Clarity

A second alternative is to expand not the extent of trainer involvement, but the specificity of the recommendations that are provided. If it is not possible—because of political, financial, or time constraints—to be involved as extensively as would be ideal, it is important to provide negotiators with a very clear and detailed set of guidelines for conducting negotiations.

While the minimalist approach is to let negotiators develop their own rules of action (so that the rules would be most appropriate to their situation and participants would be committed to those rules), alternative 2 emphasizes the need to provide, a priori, a more complete behavioral road map for conducting negotiations.

Barrett (1991) has developed an MGB training program along these lines. In his program, negotiators are told to carry out specific "steps," and his simulations model those steps very explicitly (negotiators are moved, in a fairly structured way, through stages of generating issues, defining interests, developing options, setting standards to evaluate the options, and arriving at a settlement). The advantages of this approach are that these ideas can be taught relatively quickly and that the training costs are minimal. Also, this approach will be attractive to parties who truly do not want to jointly examine their broader relationship. For these reasons, it is more likely to actually be taught to negotiators. Most important, unlike the minimalist model, negotiators are provided with a detailed action plan that is relatively unambiguous.

The risk of this approach, of course, is that little work is done with constituents or around problems in the relationship that tend to plague efforts to use MGB. This approach may also be too concise—participants may learn behaviors without mastering principles.

Alternative 3: Expand Control

In a few cases, trainers have been able to expand both their involvement and the behavioral clarity of their recommendations; they have stepped in and told negotiators exactly what to do before or during negotiations (including how to relate to constituents) and remained available to negotiators throughout the negotiations, watching and/or directing their activities. What was distinctive in these cases was the high level of control achieved by the MGB trainers.

Two trainers who have approached MGB training in this way are Kathryn Tooredman, of the National College of Education, and Don Power, of the Federal Mediation and Conciliation Service (FMCS). In Tooredman's approach (1990), negotiators are required to go through a series of ten phases, beginning with a meeting between the college president and the faculty (she works only with schools), moving through several weeks of "protocol discussions" and group "retreats," and ending in contract writing and a "victory party."

Her formula is detailed and specific: for certain meetings, the exact number of people who should attend is stated, the activity and product of each meeting or retreat is defined, and the length of time allotted for subcommittee work is specified. Most strikingly, she requires the key management constituency—the school's board of trustees—to be present. Negotiators develop some steps for themselves (they determine the "protocols" to be used), but much is determined by the trainer as a condition for doing the training.

Power (1990) also specifies a series of steps and requirements. Most important, before negotiations, he requires each side to engage in a structured issue identification process (using his forms and a computerized data "assembly" process); an issue classification process; and a data compilation and feedback process. The result is a joint bargaining manual.

During negotiations, each issue is resolved separately (no tradeoffs are allowed), and wages are required to be the first item discussed. During the ratification process, both formal and informal agreements are presented to constituents and, after negotiations, a joint contract follow-up committee is formed. As in Tooredman's model, negotiators choose how they want to negotiate (Power calls it their "consensus guidelines"), but much of the MGB process is very tightly controlled.

In both the Tooredman and Power models, the trainers maintain a high degree of control; they determine much of what happens before, during, and after negotiations and remain involved throughout. This kind of control enables these trainers to drive the process, ensure that MGB gets done, and guarantee that constituent relations are managed. No behavioral ambiguities exist.

Such control depends on some structural conditions that are unique to their situations. Each is a full-time staff member of an organization that provides these training services to organizations that want them. Participants do not have to pay the trainers, so they are less likely to want (or need) to limit the time that trainers spend helping them, and they do not have to negotiate over who pays the costs. From the trainers' perspective, their income does not depend on generating clients, so they can more easily demand that subjects follow prescribed steps and reject cases where participants refuse to follow those ground rules.

Finally, both Tooredman and Power have worked primarily with relatively small units, where they are likely to have more leverage than would be the case with larger clients. These structural conditions may not exist in many cases or for many trainers.

Table 1 provides an outline of the differences among these three approaches, including their areas of emphasis, costs, the likelihood of being initiated and implemented, and the kinds of skills or background needed by the trainer. Note that this formulation does not represent all of the subtleties of each approach or all of the ways that each might be enacted, but rather represents basic differences among the approaches as they have been enacted so far. Also, no attempt is made to evaluate which has done "better" in practice; as is implied by the table, the answer to that question would depend on whether "better" means more likely to be used, more readily available to a broad range of bargaining units, more likely to have a lasting impact, or some other criterion.

Views of Trainers

Are there any aspects of MGB training about which trainers agree? Based on a survey of more than a dozen trainers who attended the Harmon seminar on MGB, trainers in general agree that: (1) simulations are a necessary ingredient to training; (2) role reversals during the simulations are useful; and (3) at least some outside facilitation is needed after training.

Trainers who came from a labor relations background expressed different views on two points; they, more than others, felt that training had to include constituents (not just the negotiators) and that the simulations should reflect the parties' real issues (rather than being safe, issue-neutral exercises). And trainers who had been doing short, intensive training programs believed that a few days of training could be effective (while others thought more time was necessary).

Trainers' views were even more varied regarding conditions that made MGB successful. Some thought that the probability of success was increased if the bargaining unit was white collar, if participants were more highly educated, or if bargainers did not have too much experience with old bargaining traditions; others disagreed. Some thought it could be useful to train one side (if that was all that was possible); others disagreed. And, on a hopeful note, while most trainers thought that MGB could not be implemented if relations between the parties were really hostile, the few trainees in the survey stood out in their clear disagreement with that assessment.

Observations

The distinction between "interests" and "positions" is a powerful idea and the core element of an MGB alternative to traditional labor negotiations. In spite of the simplicity of the idea, however, getting people to understand and use it can be daunting in its complexity. The

Table 1. Intervention Strategies

	High involvement	High clarity	High control
Helps with constitutent problems	yes	no	yes
Addresses relationship?	yes	no	maybe
Provides a priori behavioral clarity?	Recommendations evolve	yes	yes
Provides guidance during negotiations?	yes	no	yes
Provides support after negotiations?	yes	no	maybe
Costs of process	high	low	low for clients medium for sponsor
Likelihood of beginning training	low	high	medium
Likelihood of implementing MGB after training	medium	medium	high
Likelihood of long-term impact	high	low	medium
Trainer skills needed	•training •process management •reputation	•training	•training •process management •power and independence

initial minimalist model of training was based on the hope that the idea, in itself, could change the negotiation process. We know now that that is not enough. Negotiators need additional support, either in terms of more broad involvement by trainers or more clearly specified and concrete behavioral recommendations by them. Current modifications of MGB training differ in the degree to which they emphasize these forms of support.

Each approach has advantages and disadvantages. Greater involvement in constituent relations and the actual negotiation process can be highly effective but poses great risks to the parties and represents large costs, so that only large bargaining units, willing to face great changes, will sign up for this training. Training that focuses on providing, up front, a few concrete steps for taking action is not as likely to have as broad and sustained an impact on the parties but is cheap enough and simple enough that many bargaining units may actually try it. Each approach may be appropriate, depending on the size and wealth of the bargaining unit, the degree of risk that is viable, and the availability of trainers with the appropriate skills and level of credibility.

It is possible to provide both greater clarity and greater involvement, but that is rather atypical; to do so the trainer must have a great deal of control over the negotiators and a high degree of availability, which seemed to occur only when the trainers were full-time staff supplied by a parent agency rather than independent consultants. This suggests that more should be done by policy makers, the Federal Mediation and Conciliation Service, and other servicing organizations to develop a staff of full-time MGB trainers. In the meantime, however, most trainers are outside consultants, and as such, they have to find ways to be effective within the cost, time, and political constraints they face.

Clearly, the data is not all in yet; each attempt to bring MOB into labor negotiations offers new ideas, new insights, and new opportunities for improving labor relations.

Note

1. "Mutual Gains Bargaining" is one of a number of terms (others include "principled negotiation," "interest-based bargaining," "all-gain," or "win-win" negotiation, and "integrative bargaining") used to describe an approach to the negotiation process developed and popularized by Fisher and Ury (1981), Susskind and Cruikshank (1987), and numerous others in recent years.

Key elements of this approach to negotiation include a focus on interests, not positions; separating the person from the problem; working collaboratively to create options that satisfy mutual interests; and insisting on objective criteria.

References

Ancona, D. G., R. A. Friedman, and D. M. Kolb 1991. The group and what happens on the way to "Yes". *Negotiation Journal* 7:155-173.

Barrett, J. Y. 1991. *Past is future: A model for interest-based collective bargaining that works!* Falls Church, VA.: J.Y. Barrett

Fisher, R. and W. L. Ury 1981. *Getting to YES: Negotiating agreement without giving in.* Boston: Houghton Mifflin.

Friedman, R. A. 1989. Interaction norms as barriers of organizational culture: A study of labor negotiations at International Harvester. *Journal of Contemporary Ethnography* 18 (1): 3-29.

———. 1992. The culture of mediation: Private understanding in the context of public conflict. In *Hidden conflict: Uncovering behind-the-scenes disputes*, edited by D. Kolb and J. Bartunek. Newbury Park, Calif.: Sage.

Heckscher, C. 1989. *The new unionism.* New York: Basic Books.

Power, D. 1990. Target-specific bargaining process. Paper presented at Mutual-Gains Bargaining Seminar, Harvard Kennedy School of Government, 14 December.

Kolb, D. 1984. *The mediators.* Cambridge, Mass.: MIT Press.

Susskind, L., and J. Cruikshank 1987. *Breaking the impasse.* New York: Basic Books.

Susskind, L., and E. M. Landry 1991. Implementing a mutual gains approach to collective bargaining. *Negotiation Journal* 7: 5-10.

Tooredman, K. J. (1990). Win-win bargaining: Techniques and impact. Paper presented to the Gateway Chapter of the Industrial Relations Research Association, St. Louis, 22 February.

Can "Mutual Gains" Training
Change Labor-Management Relationships?

Larry W. Hunter and Robert B. McKersie

Larry W. Hunter is
Joseph Wharton
Lecturer in Manage-
ment at the Wharton
School of the University
of Pennsylvania,
Philadelphia, Pa.,
19104.

Robert B. McKersie is
Professor Emeritus at
the Sloan School of
Management, Massa-
chusetts Institute of
Technology, Cambridge,
Mass. 02139.

Over the past decade, "mutual gains bargaining" (MGB) has
attracted growing interest from practitioners and students of
negotiation, including those interested in collective bargaining
and labor relations. Briefly, MGB encourages parties in a negotiation to focus on interests rather than positions; agree on
objective criteria for evaluation of settlements; separate problems from the people involved; and explore solutions without
early commitment (Fisher and Ury 1981; Susskind and
Cruikshank 1987). It has been suggested that joint labor-management training in MGB techniques can improve collective
bargaining relationships and outcomes (Susskind and Landry
1991; Friedman 1992).

Historically, calls for reexamining the process of labor
negotiations occur when the country has experienced an up-
surge in strike activity or when negotiated settlements appear to
be out of line with a nation's macroeconomic objectives. In the
United States today, the symptoms of difficulty in collective
bargaining are different but the problems are no less acute.
Consider, for instance, the following:

(1) Skyrocketing health care costs continue to be a problem that
labor and management have not addressed adequately. Leading
industrial relations professionals have nearly given up on the issue,
advocating throwing the problem into the lap of government.

(2) Several decades of evidence indicate that new work systems
and more flexible arrangements for the deployment of labor
provide performance advantages. Still, despite severe competitive pressures and threats to long-run employment security in
many industries, the transformation process continues to move
slowly.

(3) Evidence also suggests that unless unions are able to engage in strategic decisions that are traditionally the province of
management, they will be increasingly unable to represent their
members' concerns effectively. Yet unions have made few successful steps in this area, using the collective bargaining process
to engage such issues only rarely.

This article first
appeared in
Negotiation Journal,
October 1992:
Volume 8, Number 4,
pages 319-330.

131

Adversarial styles of collective bargaining are widely considered to be impediments to the parties in meeting their interests in areas like those just mentioned (Kochan, Katz and McKersie 1986; Heckscher 1988). Thus it seems reasonable that changes in the process of labor negotiations—away from distributive bargaining tactics, toward processes incorporating aspects of mutual gains bargaining—may begin to address these concerns.

"Pivotal events," which cause parties to rethink their relationship with one another, may initiate the process of a transformation toward more cooperative labor-management relations (Cutcher-Gershenfeld 1988). Or parties may express strong interests in changing the ways they negotiate—perhaps where one or both sides recognize that their emphasis on distributive bargaining prevents a more cooperative approach in other aspects of labor-management relations. Where such momentum for change exists, MGB training may be particularly effective and may also serve as a complement to deeper industrial relations transformation. Cases where the parties are actively interested in change, however, represent only a subset of the collective bargaining arena. MGB training, as a "new game in town," may also attract the interest of experienced industrial relations practitioners secure in more traditional labor-management relationships.

In this brief article, we describe a training intervention in which neither party expressed an interest in altering their adversarial style of industrial relations. The experience has implications both for trainers interested in disseminating MGB techniques and for those interested in broader changes in labor-management relationships. The case supports an argument made by Heckscher and Hall (1992): Changes in the process of negotiation (what Heckscher and Hall refer to as "Level 1") are unlikely to endure without changes in the practice of industrial relations ("Level 2").

Where industrial relations are conducted in a traditional fashion, MGB processes are difficult to introduce or to sustain, and MGB training alone is unlikely to be successful in addressing transformation in underlying industrial relations practices. Though the training may begin a process of change, the difficulties associated with achieving such change and in implementing MGB techniques should be acknowledged. There remains more to learn about the general effectiveness of MGB training, and challenges remain for trainers in conceptualizing, communicating, and finding paths to achieve deeper structural changes.

The Site

In 1988, the U.S. Department of Labor sponsored joint labor-management MGB training in three sites to serve as test cases for the introduction of MGB techniques into labor relations. One of the three sites was the Northrop Precision Products Division in Norwood, Massachusetts. The Northrop site differed in one important respect from the other two. At the other two sites, the parties had already sought outside help in improving their relationship, and the Department of Labor training was proposed in response to the request. At Northrop, the trainers offered the joint program, unsolicited, to the management of the division and to the bargaining committee of United Auto Workers (UAW) Local #1596, which represents over 700 hourly workers at the division.[1]

Northrop industrial relations managers expressed considerable interest in the training. The division's main customer, the U.S. Department of Defense, had moved from encouraging the adoption of total quality management (TQM) in its suppliers to the verge of mandating such programs. The industrial relations staff was under considerable pressure from top management to secure union cooperation in TQM. The union had withdrawn from an earlier program, and industrial relations managers envisioned the training as a way to reintroduce the issue to the union. Northrop managers also hoped that the training would encourage local union leaders to be more assertive, both in sorting out valid grievances within their own membership and in exercising independence from the outside UAW representatives upon which the committee relied heavily. Management partially funded the training sessions, and the vice president for industrial relations emphasized that the customized simulation should explicitly address the issue of quality.

The union was less enthusiastic. Committee members claimed that in the previous contract negotiation, the company had induced them to accept a lump-sum bonus ("service premium") rather than a percentage raise, with the assurance that managers would also receive the premium rather than a raise. A few months after the contract was ratified, salaried workers received percentage raises, and union trust in management plunged. At the time the trainers approached the union, any program which gained the interest of management was likely to be received skeptically. MGB training was no exception, but the union committee eventually decided they had nothing to lose and agreed to participate. Curiosity about the training, particularly the simulation, provided the incentive, though the union never contributed toward the cost of the training, and several of the committee members made it clear that the customized simulation should not approach their own real concerns too closely.

Neither side expressed much interest in changing the labor-management relationship more generally. Rank-and-file workers placed little pressure on their leaders to move toward more cooperative arrangements; rather, the members encouraged the union leaders to reverse the results of the previous negotiation. Union leaders felt they had been burned over the service premium, and the committee was preparing to mobilize worker indignation over the issue and to use this resentment as a source of distributive bargaining power.

On the other side of the table, line managers preferred to leave dealing with the union to the industrial relations professionals. While agreeable to suggestions that they pursue MGB training, the line managers had little interest in broader changes. The industrial relations managers, in turn, were satisfied that their traditional, distributive approach to issues was effective. Although interested in bringing the union in on a TQM program, the industrial relations staff was not convinced of the need for broad changes in their relationship with the union. Both sides explicitly branded the training as an exercise; with contract negotiation still more than six months away, the parties agreed jointly not to use the training to raise contract issues early.

MGB Training

The First Session

In the first meeting, which lasted one day, the trainers introduced MGB principles to 15 union and 15 management participants through lecture, discussion, and two role-playing exercises.[2] Training in the techniques produced a variety of reactions ranging from interest to deep skepticism. Late in the day the trainers encouraged the parties to explore ways in which their relationship either impeded or fostered adoption of the techniques they had just learned. A lengthy discussion of tactics used in the previous negotiation followed and began to center on the issue of the service premium in the prior contract.

Discussion of the service premium effectively violated the agreement that the training not be used for real-life issues or prenegotiation. Some union leaders later expressed concern over the airing of the issue, fearing it may have compromised their ability to use indignation over the premium as a source of leverage in the upcoming negotiation. Though a number of union leaders participated in the discussion, the union committee alternate who was most active in raising the issue and in exploring reasons for the conflicting accounts of the previous negotiation was not invited by union leaders to attend the second training session.

While management may have benefited tactically from this premature discussion, the issue also surfaced splits among the managers. The production group raised questions about the handling of the last negotiation by the industrial relations staff, asking whether this had made it more difficult to secure the cooperation of the union in TQM. At the end of the meeting, management stated its interest in continuing the training, while the union committee was unwilling to commit to a second session.

After the session, the industrial relations managers resisted the trainers' private suggestion that they make a low-cost change in the calculation of the service premium paid to retiring workers. Although it was clear that the union would have taken such a change as a key indicator of good faith, management preferred to hold any such concessions for the actual contract negotiation.

The Second Session

Both sides acknowledged that the first session had some positive effects. Upon reflection, both union and management were intrigued by MGB techniques, and both sides believed that the training had done some good by getting the two groups together in a new forum, off site, where they could get to know one another better. Management expressed interest in continuing the training, again requesting that the customized simulation address quality.

The union committee, following a lengthy discussion with MGB trainers, and nearly a month of deliberation, agreed to further training. However, the union representatives rejected proposals for a simulation featuring role reversal or designed for teams with mixed union-management membership, perhaps because they were suspicious that they were being asked to gain sympathy for a management perspective. Both parties agreed with the trainers' suggestion that the case be realistic enough that they could experiment with

MGB skills in a plausible setting, but the parties continued to stress that the case should not address issues that were likely to surface during the next negotiation.

Following interviews with representatives of both groups, the trainers developed the case of "The Stimson Company," and sent background materials to the parties two weeks before the second session. "Stimson" had a few similarities with the Northrop situation: it was a New England manufacturing company, and the case focused on three issues. By mutual agreement of the parties, one of the issues in the case was the introduction of a total quality program. Despite the apparent connection to the Northrop situation, the union committee readily agreed to the inclusion of this issue. It had no intention of negotiating over a quality program in its upcoming contract, indicating the extent to which the labor-management relationship was bound by tradition.

The other central issues in the Stimson simulation—a two-tier wage system, and employment security provisions—had been identified as extremely unlikely to emerge in the actual negotiation. Real-life issues that the parties had warned would be contentious, such as the health plan, work rules, and the service premium, were not described in the case.

Nevertheless, upon receipt of the materials, the union committee claimed that "Stimson" was too close to the real situation at Northrop and threatened to withdraw from the training. Through further discussion, the trainers persuaded the union representatives that any case would have certain similarities to their own situation, and the committee agreed to continue.

The second session began with more presentations and another exercise designed to reinforce MGB techniques and principles.[3] It also included a presentation on union involvement in TQM by a highly respected former national leader of the United Auto Workers. Union representatives viewed this talk as a sign that the trainers were considering union as well as management interests; managers were interested to hear the official describe a role for the union that few of them had envisioned. Following the presentations and drill, three labor-management groups bargained the Stimson case.

The three groups had varied success with MGB. In one, a particularly vocal union committeeman with whom most managers had difficulty working had been openly skeptical of the training program. He had been quiet during most of the first session, but in this second session he emerged as the leading spokesman for his group and tried out many of the MGB concepts in bargaining the simulation. The management group also began to work with the concepts fairly successfully.

In the other two groups, many of the participants hesitated to adopt the roles the case called for. Their experiences with collective bargaining at Northrop tended to overwhelm both the more abstract MGB concepts and the details of the Stimson case. One group had considerable difficulty experimenting with the ideas and adopting the conditions in the simulation. The participants spent much of the simulation haggling over minor details in the Stimson contract, complete with technicalities around scheduling and bidding rights that were not even mentioned in the case. They confronted the issues in the case only briefly.

The third group had mixed success with the techniques. The managers in this group were especially quick to adopt the language and jargon of MGB, though such techniques as exploring interests and exchanging ideas without commitment remained difficult for them to employ.

The training concluded with union and management participants discussing, first separately, and then jointly, elements that could facilitate further adoption of MGB principles that they believed might be useful in achieving their interests in the upcoming negotiation. In their separate meetings, each party agreed that some of the MGB techniques could prove useful in achieving their interests and indicated that they would pursue these techniques in the upcoming negotiation. In the joint session, the trainers attempted to direct the parties toward a more cooperative relationship by suggesting they agree to a set of principles, showing them a protocol that had been agreed to by union and management in another training site. Neither side, however, was willing to commit to the use of MGB techniques in the upcoming negotiation.

The Actual Negotiations
A few months after the training, the new contract was settled. Agreement was reached early and with little brinkmanship. Both sides professed to be pleased with the outcome. The parties claimed that the negotiations were more professional than ever; the process featured fewer emotional outbursts, less acrimony, and more sensible discussion. The MGB training had "cleared the air," they said, and the joint meetings had alerted each group to the seriousness of the breakdown in trust following the previous negotiation.

Substantively, however, the bargaining was conducted traditionally; it was positional and distributive. Researchers who observed the negotiation agreed that MGB techniques were adopted much less at Northrop than at the other two Department of Labor training sites.

One critical problem was that some key negotiators had not been involved fully in MGB training. Two of the seven union committeemen did not attend the training, while just before bargaining began, the UAW assigned a new servicing representative to the Northrop site. The new representative expressed scant interest in mutual gains techniques, saying that he "didn't have time to try this stuff," and the local committee did not press him to learn more about the MGB approach.

On the other side, the industrial relations vice president continued to lead the management team although he had been more an observer than a participant in the training process. As in the past, he emphasized the presentation of a large body of management-compiled data on wage comparability. Rather than addressing his arguments to the interests expressed by the union, or searching for joint agreement upon standards, he repeatedly stressed the rationality of his own position, just as in previous negotiations.

Even where the parties took tentative steps toward the adoption of MGB, the experimentation caused some difficulty. For example, some of the negotiators began to explore possible joint gains using a process they called "supposals," or proposing suggestions without commitment. After a few steps in this area, however, the new servicing representative attempted to hold management to one of its more experimental suggestions. This traditional, distributive tactic ended the "supposal" process and undermined management interest in MGB for the duration of the negotiation.

Some substantive changes in the labor-management relationship followed the contract settlement. Management secured the cooperation of the union in pursuing the total quality program. Union committee members noted that MGB training, including the presentation by the UAW official, had encouraged them to think of ways they could use a quality program to achieve their own goals. At about the same time, the union committee chair stepped down, and the membership elected the committee representative who had taken to the MGB approach during the second training session. Management had earlier feared this change in leadership, being extremely doubtful that it would be able to work constructively with the new chair. However, the interest of the new chair in the MGB techniques as tools to achieve his own goals softened management doubts. The relationship got off to a better start than either side had predicted.

Conclusions

Heckscher and Hall (1992) point out that "Level 1" changes in the negotiation process are unlikely to be durable unless they are supported by changes in "Level 2"—the underlying structure of collective bargaining and labor relations. At the Northrop site in Massachusetts, the MGB training program addressed negotiating technique but not this deeper structure; indeed, the parties had declared substantive issues "off limits" for the trainers. No constituency for change in the bargaining process was created, and pressures for traditional distributive bargaining prevailed even though many of the trainees had, by the end of the training, been convinced that (at least in principle) there was some merit in the MGB approach.

Table 1 illustrates some of the tension between the two approaches at each of the two levels. In traditional labor negotiations, the parties focus on issues narrowly. They generally limit discussions to the set of issues that are mandatory subjects for bargaining. MGB requires that all items of interest be on the table. This, in turn, requires new ways of thinking about such issues as production quality and job security. At Northrop, even in the experimental training exercise, the parties found it difficult to confront these issues; they were constrained by their traditional tools for framing collective bargaining problems, bound by what they believed should belong in a labor contract and what should not.

Engaging the parties in broader and potentially complicated issues takes substantial time. Indeed, it has been argued that in order to transform industrial relations in this way, negotiations must move from "episodic showdowns" held every two or three years to continuing exercises in conflict resolution (Walton, Cutcher-Gershenfeld, and McKersie, forthcoming). Yet it may be difficult to move the parties away from the showdown model. At Northrop, for example, both union and management declined opportunities to turn the training program into an effort that would include prenegotiation problem solving.

Production managers at the Northrop site have moved neither toward more extensive participation in negotiations nor continuous problem solving with union representatives. In fact, labor-management issues continue to be addressed separately from production problems. For example, while the industrial relations function was instrumental in securing union cooperation for the new quality program, the industrial relations staff is not integrated into TQM, and the new initiative has few mechanisms for the accommodation of union concerns. Adhering to their traditional system, production managers continue to assert control over job rules, transfers, and bidding rights. The union responds in kind by demanding elaborate protection through contractual language.

This traditional behavior leads to an "obey-and-grieve" mentality rather than to mutual problem solving; and, since the parties cannot solve thorny work rule problems jointly, issues accumulate. Problems continue to end up in third-party arbitration, which the parties still approach in a distributive, adversarial fashion.

The inability of the old system to accommodate continuous negotiation over production issues and work rules illustrates another general problem. Traditional collective bargaining is conducted by agents for the interested parties. MGB principles suggest that all interested parties participate in negotiation, but it is difficult—if not impossible—to bring all who are interested to the actual negotiations (or even to the training). For example, Northrop's rank-and-file workers, who knew little about the training program, brought their usual "laundry list" of demands to the union committee prior to the first actual negotiating session. The committee, in its traditional role as representative, dutifully presented this elaborate set of demands to management at the opening of bargaining, and this aspect of traditional negotiations did not help the parties focus on their most important interests.

Committee members said later that the MGB training encouraged them to move away from this list of demands to focus on their most important interests more quickly than in the past. However, the norms of the traditional relationship and the expectations of the rank-and-file did not change enough to permit the committee to sort out its interests in advance. More generally, union leadership has been slow to take responsibility for sorting out grievances and priorities internally, and the membership continues to press the committee with detailed demands for action on particular issues. The committee thus finds it difficult to focus on interests rather than positions. Management, in turn, has difficulty ascertaining the union's most important interests and in achieving joint gains by developing packages that would meet those interests.

A small but potentially important further problem lies in keeping MGB negotiations on track. Although it is helpful, perhaps necessary, for the parties to have MGB process consultants available during actual negotiations (Susskind and Landry 1991), labor and management negotiators who have not sought help initially—particularly experienced agents— are unlikely to enlist such consultation.

In the Northrop case, neither the researchers (some of whom had been MGB trainers, and who had access to nearly the entire negotiation) nor the federal mediator (who

Table 1. Two Approaches to Labor-Management Negotiations
(suggested by Heckscher and Hall, 1992)

	Subject Area	Traditional Collective Bargaining System	Mutual Gains Bargaining/ Transformed
Level 1: **Negotiation** **Process**	Agenda	Narrow, "mandatory" subjects	Broad range of topics
	Bargaining Characteristics	Short, intense, positional	Long process, exploratory, interest-based
	Parties to the Negotiation	Small number at at the table	Anyone with with an interest
Level 2: **Collective** **Bargaining** **Structure**	Contract Language	Focused on details; specific language important	Focused on principles; "living document"
	Locus of Dispute Resolution negotiation	Grievances and episodic, formal problem solving	Continuous and informal joint
	Representatives	Professional negotiators, national repsconcerns	Locally chosen; sensitive to local

attended the training and expressed considerable interest in MGB concepts) were able to assist the parties in proceeding with MGB during the actual negotiations. The parties had made no mutual commitment to use the techniques. Thus, though the mediator had expressed interest in pursuing MGB further, he did not feel he had approval from the two sides to push them toward new approaches. He maintained a more traditional mediator's role, and made only tentative suggestions toward the use of MGB.

MGB training programs may be effective in persuading individuals of the value of new concepts. But generally, where parties have not sought an intervention, forces for continuing to exhibit traditional behaviors can be expected to inhibit innovation in negotiation processes. Even in such traditional relationships, however, mutual gains bargaining is a powerful educational tool.

As a new and fashionable approach, MGB intrigues both labor and management representatives sufficiently that experienced negotiators can be convinced to devote substantial time to training in the concepts. MGB techniques provide trainers with a unique point of entry into a relationship. The offers of expert training in MGB principles and of the development of a customized simulation piqued the parties' interests even in a relationship as tradition-bound as the one at Northrop.

Training may produce some positive effects, even where there is little explicit implementation of MGB. Both sides at Northrop credited the techniques with helping them to listen better and to avoid unproductive cycles of argumentation that characterized previous rounds of bargaining. Settling well within the deadline, in an amicable and business-like fashion, is now associated with the MGB approach in the minds of the key Northrop negotiators. The approach may thus be utilized more fully in future negotiations.

Byproducts of intervention may also be serendipitous. It would have been difficult to predict the election of the new union chair at Northrop, for example, or the extent to which the training eased managers' reservations about working with him.

Though MGB training focuses on specific skills, even a "boiler-plate" program raises choices for trainers, particularly around the extent to which they attempt to engage deeper changes in the relationship. To take one such choice point, a simulation designed to serve as the centerpiece of a training session may vary in its proximity to the parties' own experience. At Northrop, the realism of the simulation nearly derailed the second training exercise before it began. And, even though union agreement to participate was eventually secured, some of the break-out learning groups were not successful in experimenting with the concepts because the players drew too closely upon their own experience. Still, this simulation had value as a realistic analog to the parties' situation: It engaged participants more fully than a less specifically tailored exercise might have and was particularly effective in the subgroup which included the labor leader who eventually chaired the union negotiating committee.

As an intervention which brings the parties together for a considerable length of time, in a social as well as a group learning environment, MGB training can strengthen trust by enabling each party to gain perspectives on the other's interests and positions. Although the union at Northrop was adamant in its opposition to using the sessions for any "real time" negotiations, the training nevertheless became an arena in which the parties to begin to shape their relationship for the onset of formal bargaining.

However, in situations where management and union leaders agree, as in this case, that the training will not be used for real-time bargaining, opportunities for improving the relationship within the context of training (for example, the suggestion that the Northrop managers modify the service premium) may not be fully exploited. Indeed, the emergence of such opportunities may push the parties back into traditional behaviors during training itself. Only where the parties have agreed that the training should address not only negotiating skills but the broader relationship will its potential as an intervention be fully realized.

At Northrop, and at other potential sites, the implementation of MGB depends ultimately on the success in realizing broader changes in "Level 2" in industrial relations. Yet, convincing parties to make such changes may be considerably more difficult than convincing them of the effectiveness of MGB techniques, especially where no traumatic events or pressing concerns provide the "unfreezing" impetus that is a necessary condition for change (Schein 1987).

A specific, isolated focus on the bargaining process can be viewed as an entry point to begin the transformation of a complex industrial relations system. However, without other system changes, it will be difficult to institutionalize the MGB techniques themselves—even where they will produce gains for both sides. Based on our experience at Northrop, we conclude by offering these four caveats to MGB trainers in the labor relations arena:[4]

•For significant and lasting changes in labor negotiations to occur, there must be fundamental changes in other—Level 2—aspects of labor-management relations.

•It is feasible to use the inherent appeal of MGB to labor and management practitioners in order to gain entry into a relationship, and, from here, to begin to discuss more general issues of transformation. However, further pressure, perhaps even some degree of crisis, is necessary to motivate the parties to apply the new concepts and to foster other supporting changes.

•Where possible, trainers should encourage the parties to think about and discuss how changes in their traditional practices might support negotiation techniques that would produce joint gains. Conversely, the parties and trainers must surface impediments to change during the training program. While such practices may be controversial, they are also necessary.

•MGB represents a new tool in the portfolio of intervention strategies aimed at creating more constructive labor-management relations. Clearly, much more experimentation is in order to better understand how MGB training can be combined successfully with other approaches to transformation.

Notes

1. Trainers came from the faculty of the Program of Negotiation at Harvard Law School and had considerable experience in the teaching of mutual gains bargaining. At each site, the training involved two or three days of training and included the creation of a role-playing bargaining exercise designed expressly for the two parties. For more details on the Department of Labor project, see Susskind and Landry (1991) and Friedman (1992).

2. The exercises were standard role-playing games distributed by the Clearinghouse of the Program on Negotiation. The "Pepulator" bargaining game, a simple, individually scored exercise designed to illustrate the advantages of developing trust and bargaining for mutual gains, was used for the first exercise. The second exercise, called the "AMPO" negotiation,

was a more complex team exercise featuring multiple issues in a collective bargaining setting.

3. This exercise, called "Eazy's Garage," was another simple, individual game designed to reinforce the principles of MGB: focusing on interests rather than positions, agreeing on objective criteria, and exploring solutions without early commitment.

4. These caveats are particularly applicable to trainers who are not able to realize the "high control" strategy for intervention described by Friedman (1992). Where mediators, trainers, or consultants are able to exert considerable control over the negotiation process, the results may be considerably different from those described here. But, as Friedman observes, the structural conditions that facilitate high control intervention by a third party are uncommon.

References

Cutcher-Gershenfeld, J. 1988. *Tracing a transformation in industrial relations.* Washington: U.S. Department of Labor.

Fisher, R. and W. L. Ury. 1981. *Getting to YES: Negotiating agreement without giving in.* Boston: Houghton-Mifflin.

Friedman, R. A.1992. From theory to practice: Critical choices for 'mutual gains' training. *Negotiation Journal* 8: 91-98.

Heckscher, C. C. 1988. *The new unionism: Employee involvement in the changing corporation.* New York: Basic Books.

Heckscher, C. C. and L. Hall. 1992. Paper presented at the 44th Annual Meeting of the Industrial Relations Research Association, New Orleans, 4 January.

Kochan, T. A., H. Katz. and R. B. McKersie. 1986. *The transformation of American industrial relations.* New York Basic Books.

Schein, E. H. 1987. *Process consultation (vol. 11): Lessons for managers and consultants.* Reading, Mass.: Addison-Wesley.

Susskind, L. and J. Cruikshank. 1987. *Breaking the impasse: Consensual approaches to resolving public disputes.* New York: Basic Books.

Susskind, L. and E. Landry. 1991. Implementing a mutual gains approach to collective bargaining. *Negotiation Journal* 7: 5-10.

Walton, R. J. Cutcher-Gershenfeld and R. B. McKersie (forthcoming). Negotiating the social contract: A theory of change in labor-management relations. Draft manuscript.

Teaching Strategy
in Negotiation

Allan E. Goodman

Allan E. Goodman is the President and Chief Executive Officer of the Institute of International Education (IIE), the nation's largest educational and cultural exchange agency with an annual budget of over $100 million and 400 employees. The Institute designs and implements fellowship, training, and technical assistance programs for sponsors that include government agencies, corporations, foundations, universities, and international organizations.

This article first appeared in *Negotiation Journal*, April 1990: Volume 6, Number 2, pages 185-188.

Any attempt at negotiation requires decisions about what is to be sought, how best to achieve objectives while minimizing costs and risks, and the approach that should guide the effort. In other words, negotiating requires an overall plan of action or strategy. Ideally, the strategy should be conceived well in advance of sitting down at a bargaining table and should focus on the "big picture": It should relate all elements of the situation to what the negotiator wants or is instructed to get, and how this can best be achieved.

Most negotiators, however, have little time for strategy. Conducting a negotiation, whether in the public or private realm, involves so many practical considerations that practitioners today have a tendency to think in tactical rather than strategic terms (see, e.g., Habeeb 1988; Raiffa 1982 and 1984; and Zartman 1984). Negotiation training courses also emphasize that in most cases "it is often hard to tell whether a particular move is a bit of strategy or a tactic," (Nierenberg 1973:147; see also Fisher and Ury 1981, and Karass 1970).

For ten years I have taught a course on the "Theory and Practice of International Negotiation" to seniors and graduate students at Georgetown University's School of Foreign Service and lectured on this topic at the Foreign Service Institute and the National War College. Teaching strategic thinking has consistently proved to be the most difficult part of my job. In my opinion, no text handles the subject well for the student of international affairs (see, e.g., Ikle 1964 and Lall 1966). The literature in the fields of business, decision science, law, and labor relations also tends to give short shrift to the analysis of how to formulate strategy or teach about it in the classroom (Edwards and White 1977 and Zartman 1976).

So I think there would be a clear benefit if teachers of courses on negotiation developed a literature on strategic analysis and exchanged views on how best to convey its importance to different professional audiences. In the hope that others who

Reflections

In the year after this article appeared, I received about a dozen letters. Half of the correspondents wrote in sympathy, saying that they, too, encountered problems with teaching strategy and had shied away from it. The rest said that they suspected that teaching by the case method was a good way to get students thinking about the big picture. And this was the approach to which I gravitated, too.

What I got, however, was only better tactical thinking. And because many of my cases were drawn from negotiations where students could learn of the actual outcome, there was an even greater reluctance to second guess strategy.

The way I eventually got around this was to ask students at the outset—and before they were fully aware

readers of this journal, I offer my own approach. It involves asking students to discern the strategies that might be applied in specific situations that diplomats frequently encounter.

I ask my Georgetown class to consider the following example:

> Two countries of unequal size and resources are about to enter a negotiation over the terms on which an agreement covering a military base to which the more powerful country currently has access can be extended. The smaller country wants to receive a substantial increase in the rent paid for this base and to demonstrate clearly that, while permitting the larger country the access it requires, it has not surrendered sovereignty. It is essential to be clear about this because the leadership of the smaller country does not want to be vulnerable to charges by opposition groups that it is being manipulated by external pressure. The larger country does not think of itself as paying rent at all, since the base contributes to the security of the smaller country and generates considerable employment. And while it is willing to increase military and economic assistance programs in the country, the larger country's parliament will not permit increases in the amounts likely to be demanded. Each country wants to reach an agreement.

Policy Planning

Strategy can be detected by asking why certain goals are being sought. But as is the case in the example I use—as in many instances involving international negotiation—numerous and even conflicting goals are being pursued simultaneously. One way to reconcile and accommodate such differences and priorities is to engage in a "policy planning" session.

I ask my class to imagine that they are behind the closed doors of a meeting for those planning to conduct the negotiations for each government. At such a meeting there would undoubtedly be a discussion of what policy—i.e., strategy—to follow. I ask the students to consider this question: If you were involved in such policy planning, what strategy would you recommend?

Later in the term, we return to this same question when the class participates in a three-week simulated military base negotiation. The simulation is organized by my colleague, Ambassador Andrew Steigman, and based on material developed by Paul M. Kattenberg, another former State Department official, for the International Studies Association (Kattenberg 1975). Of course, any hypothetical example could be used, but I think it important to select one that will apply to a number of cases and examples discussed throughout the course. This avoids giving the student the impression that the need for strategic thinking is rare or requires superhuman intellect.

The initial discussion in the class is about everything but strategy. Many students begin by saying what it is they want to get in the negotiations and how they would use this or that element of pressure to achieve their objective. In other words, they—like most of us—tend to think about goals and tactics. They want to get right to the heart and heat of the bargaining and think it essential to do so, especially when they are put on the spot and asked for a practical recommendation.

of the outcome—to do a short memo predicting the outcome of the negotiation. I asked each to make a forecast of how things would turn out, and then used it to discuss why they thought that was going to be the case. With some, I urged them to build, in fact, a scenario that got them from the present to the forecast outcome. As they did this, strategy emerged.

Keep Focus on Strategy

The teacher's role at this point is to insist that the class focus on strategy first. When the shortcomings of the initial responses to the question are pointed out, many students are literally at a loss for words that might be used to describe a strategy for dealing with the situation posed above. It is important here to be patient, and to give students a few minutes for reflection before resuming class discussion. If taking a class break is appropriate, ask students to use it to discuss in smaller groups the meaning of strategy, and how one could be developed for this particular situation.

Eventually, most students come to the point of recognizing the need for a guiding principle to organize the negotiator's proposed actions in a way that relates what they want to achieve with the resources they have to apply toward those objectives. And it is from a discussion of what these principles ought to be that a strategy emerges for each side in the negotiation.

In the particular case I use, class discussion usually results in three alternative strategic approaches:

- *accommodation*—reaching agreement by recognizing the legitimacy of the other side's position and objectives, then creatively trying to find ways that they can be satisfied;
- *pressure*—working to get the best deal possible for one side, but getting a deal no matter what; and
- *standing firm*—using whatever means necessary to get an agreement, but also being prepared to walk away if the other side cannot be persuaded to accept the proposed terms.

Initially, most students do not opt for a strategy of accommodation. But neither do they tend to think that standing firm is inherently appropriate or likely to assure success. The evident preference for a strategy of pressure tends to grow out of the mock policy-planning session mentioned above. For it is in the process of examining goals and debating how they can most effectively be achieved that the students come to realize the sources of leverage they may have over the situation posed, as well as the limits to which they can go in trying to impose their will.

When we return to the problem later in the course via a three-week simulated military base negotiation, the learning process resumes. Delegates on both sides tend to enter the negotiation with a strategy of pressure. Usually the first meetings go quite poorly as a result. Tensions run high, cross-cultural differences are accentuated, and virtually no progress is made toward preliminary agreement.

As the individual delegations take stock of what their strategy produced in the first round, however, they also tend to re-evaluate policy. Despite numerous intradelegation pressures to get the best deal for the special interests each person is assigned to represent, the negotiators also recognize that they have a mandate to reach an agreement. While tough bargaining continues, the strategy followed in weeks two and three of the negotiation tends toward accommodation.[1]

How Do Others Teach Strategy?

I would like to learn about other approaches to teaching strategy. What interactive approaches are currently in use? Are these approaches fundamentally different if the context of the negotiation is domestic rather than international, or if the issues are of an economic and commercial nature rather than political or military in character? And does thinking strategically really enhance the prospect for successful negotiating outcomes? Are there instances/situations where such thinking is, in fact, counterproductive? And do others note a trend toward accommodation as the predominant style of negotiators today?

Note

1. Elsewhere, Ambassador David Newsom and I have suggested that there is a growing tendency toward accommodation and conflict resolution in world politics generally, and that this is a reflection of systemic changes in international affairs. See our article, "Why Diplomacy Works" in *The Diplomatic Record*, edited by David Newsom. (Boulder, CO: Westview Press, forthcoming).

References

Edwards, H. T. and J. J. White. 1977. *The lawyer as a negotiator.* St. Paul, Minn.: West Publishing Co.

Fisher, R. and W. L. Ury. 1981. *Getting to YES: Negotiating agreement without giving in.* Boston: Houghton Mifflin.

Habeeb, W. M. 1988. *Power and tactics in international negotiation: How weak nations bargain with strong nations.* Baltimore: The Johns Hopkins University Press.

Iklé, E. C. 1964. *How nations negotiate.* New York: Praeger.

Karass, C. 1970. *The negotiating game.* New York: Thomas Y. Crowell Publishers.

Kattenberg, P. M. 1975. *Diplomatic practices.* New York: Consortium for International Studies Education of the International Studies Association.

Lall, A. 1966. *Modern international negotiation: Principles and practice.* New York: Columbia University Press.

Nierenberg, G. I. 1973. *Fundamentals of negotiating.* New York: Hawthorne Books.

Raiffa, H. 1982. *The art and science of negotiation.* Cambridge, MA: Harvard University Press.

———. 1984. Teaching the art and science of negotiation. *In International negotiation: Art and science,* ed. by John W. McDonald, Jr. Washington: Foreign Service Institute, U.S. Department of State.

Zartman, I. W. (ed.) 1976. *The 50% solution: How to bargain successfully with hijackers, strikers, bosses, oil magnates, Arabs, Russians, and other worthy opponents in this modern world.* Garden City, N. J.: Anchor Press.

———. 1984. Negotiation: Theory and reality. In *International negotiation: Art and science,* ed. by John W. McDonald, Jr. Washington: Foreign Service Institute, U.S. Department of State.

Interpersonal Expectancies, Nonverbal Communication, and Research on Negotiation

Robert Rosenthal

Robert Rosenthal is Distinguished Professor, University of California, Riverside, and Edgar Pierce Professor of Psychology, Emeritus, Harvard University. His research and scholarly interests are in the substantive areas of interpersonal expectancy effects and nonverbal communication and in the methodological areas of the use of statistical procedures in the social sciences and especially in contrast analysis and in meta-analysis.

This article first appeared in Negotiation Journal, July, 1988: Volume 4, Number 3, pages 267-279.

Only with the greatest diffidence can a research psychologist with no experience in research on negotiation accept an invitation to contribute to a symposium of experts in the field. My only hope is that some of the concepts and some of the methods I have been employing in my own research may prove to be useful in research on some processes and some outcomes of negotiation.

For the past 30 years, my collaborators and I have been studying some processes of social influence that are primarily unintended, subtle, covert, and, to a great extent, nonverbal. Most of the research we have conducted has been on dyadic, or two-party, interactions, such as those between psychological researchers and their research subjects, teachers and their students, physicians and their patients, psychotherapists and their clients, managers and their subordinates, and judges and their juries. A power imbalance existed in all these dyadic interactions in that one participant controlled the outcomes to a greater extent than did the other. In more recent years, we have also studied more power-balanced dyads of same-sex and opposite-sex peers who have known each other for varying periods of time.

One of the major concepts we have been investigating over the years has been the concept of interpersonal expectations: the idea that one person's expectations for the behavior of another can come to serve as a self-fulfilling prophecy. For example, when experimenters conducting behavioral research are led to expect certain responses from their research subjects, they are more likely to obtain those responses from their research subjects. Likewise, when teachers are led to expect certain levels of intellectual achievement from their students, they are more likely to obtain those levels of achievement from their students.

Interpersonal Expectancy Effects

Long before there were experimental studies of this phenomenon, various theorists suggested its operation. The great

Reflections

What's New?

A lot can happen in a dozen years of empirical research and scholarship in the social and behavioral sciences. The purpose of this commentary is to draw attention to recent developments that have strong implications for research on the processes and products of negotiation. These developments are broadly of two types: substantive and methodological.

Substantive Developments, Individual Studies

There are dozens of specific studies of nonverbal communication and interpersonal expectations that have great potential relevance to a better understanding of negotiation. Here there is space only to be illustrative, choosing our examples from classrooms, courtrooms, and consulting rooms.

In classrooms, Ambady and Rosenthal (1993) found that the observa-

contemporary sociologist Robert Merton (1948), for example, introduced to the social sciences the concept of "the self-fulfilling prophecy." A person prophesies an event and the expectation of the event then changes the behavior of the prophet in such a way as to make the prophesied event more likely. The late Gordon Allport (1950), a founder of contemporary social and personality psychology, applied the concept of interpersonal expectancies to an analysis of the causes of war. Nations expecting to go to war affect the behavior of their opponents-to-be by the behavior which reflects their expectations of armed conflict. Nations that expect to remain out of wars, at least sometimes, manage to avoid entering into them.

Drawn from the general literature, and the literatures of the healing professions, survey research, educational research, organizational research, and laboratory psychology, there is considerable evidence for the operation of interpersonal self-fulfilling prophecies. This evidence, while ranging from the anecdotal to the experimental, has been reviewed elsewhere (Rosenthal 1966; 1985a). The basic paradigm of the experiments designed to investigate interpersonal expectancy effects has included the experimental induction of special expectations—in the minds of, for example, psychological experimenters or teachers in classrooms—so that we might learn the effects of those induced expectations on the performance of those for whom the expectations were held (Rosenthal and Rubin 1978). For instance, in one type of study teachers were led to expect unusually good intellectual performance from students who had been arbitrarily represented to their teachers as having "special potential for intellectual growth." At the end of the school year of the experiment, these "special" children had, in fact, gained more IQ points than had the children of the control group (Rosenthal and Jacobson 1968).

Implications for Research on Negotiation

Methodological implications

Among the implications for research on negotiation are some quite general implications for research methods in the social sciences (Rosenthal and Rosnow 1984). These have to do with the threats to the validity of our research by the expectations of the investigator. If the investigator holding such expectations is in direct contact with the research subject for whom the expectations are held, the investigator may unwittingly treat the subject in such a way as to bring about a self-fulfilling prophecy. Details of this source of threat to research validity have been presented elsewhere, along with procedures to minimize the threat (Rosenthal 1966).

Substantive implications

It seems reasonable to suspect that participants in the negotiation process may influence one another in quite unintended ways as well as in the quite obvious ways in which they intend to influence each other. One source of these unintended influence processes might well be the expectations the negotiators hold for each negotiator's behavior. It might be valuable to conduct both experimental and observational studies in which the independent variables are the expectations held for one another's behavior. Experimental studies have the advantage that they permit clear causal inference to a far greater degree than do the nonexperimental observational studies (Cochran 1983). However, unless a field experiment is possible, experimental studies have the disadvantage that they often lack the natural quality or ecological validity of the nonexperimental observational study.

Design implications

Research on the effect of interpersonal expectations on the outcomes of processes of negotiation can be classified along two independent dimensions: (a) the *naturalness of the setting* in which the research is conducted; and (b) the degree of *clarity of causal inference* that can be drawn from the research.

Naturalness of setting could vary continuously from a laboratory analogue in which students pretend to be negotiators all the way to actual high-level negotiations. The disadvantage of the laboratory analogue approach in general is that it may be a poor model for the real thing. The advantage is that features of the context can be controlled in such a way that random error or "noise" in the system can be reduced. The disadvantage of the "real thing" negotiation is that features of the context cannot be controlled; thus, the noise level of the research is likely to be greater. The advantage is that we are at

tion of *30 seconds* of silent videos (or of tone of voice alone) of college teachers teaching their classes allowed highly accurate predictions of how those teachers would be rated by their entire class at the end of the semester.

In courtrooms, building on the brilliant work of Peter Blanck, Alan Hart and Andrea Halverson showed that the expectation or belief of a judge in the guilt of a defendant could function to increase dramatically the conviction rate by jurors exposed to the nonverbal behavior of the judge delivering instructions to jurors. Techniques were also developed to reduce the biasing expectations of the judges (Halverson, Hallahan, Hart, & Rosenthal 1997).

In the consulting rooms of surgeons and primary care physicians, it was possible to tell from the doctors'

151

tone of voice alone which ones were more likely to have been sued two or more times (Ambady, LaPlante, Nguyen, Chaumeton, Rosenthal, & Levinson 1999).

Meta-Analytic Findings More than is possible for any individual study, meta-analyses are able to provide far more definitive conclusions about what is shown in the empirical literature (Rosenthal 1991; 1994; Rosenthal & Jacobson 1992). Three such meta-analyses serve as illustrations of results relevant to a better understanding of negotiation processes and products.

Ambady and Rosenthal (1992) found that in several dozen studies very "thin slices" of nonverbal behavior could serve accurately to predict subsequent behavior of interpersonal consequence.

Harris and Rosenthal (1985) in their 31 meta-analyses, found

least studying the topic we really want to know about—the actual negotiation. Note that nothing about the naturalness of setting necessarily has any implications for the clarity of causal inference that can be drawn. Variation in that clarity depends specifically not on the setting but on the research paradigm.

Variation in the research paradigm ranges from randomized experiments to observational studies. Randomized experiments provide the greatest leverage for drawing strong causal inference. That is their great advantage. Their disadvantage is that randomized experiments are not always feasible, especially in real-life settings of classrooms, clinics, offices, factories, or negotiation tables. Observational studies offer the advantage that they are usually easier to implement and especially so in real-life settings. They suffer from the disadvantage, however, that they provide weaker leverage on drawing causal inference. Just as there are actually many possible degrees of naturalness of setting, there are many possible degrees of clarity of causal inference that may be drawn from various research paradigms. For example, some observational studies provide only synchronic or cross-sectional or "one-shot" observations of variables which are then examined for their relationships. A stronger basis for causal inference emerges from diachronic or longitudinal, or "follow-up" type research (Rosenthal and Rosnow 1984).

Four Types of Research
The combination of the two dimensions of naturalness of setting and the research paradigm yields four types of research labeled A, B. C, and D. In this section, I shall examine examples of each type of research that could be conducted on negotiation processes and outcomes.

Type A
In research on teacher expectation effects, Type A designs have often involved real teachers interacting with students in a laboratory situation. For half the students, teachers are led to expect especially good intellectual performance; for the remaining students, teachers are given no particular expectations at all. In research on negotiation processes and outcomes, real negotiators could be brought together to negotiate agreements. For half

the negotiations, negotiators are led to expect favorable agreements; for the remaining negotiations, negotiators could be given either no particular expectations or actively negative expectations. (In research with children, negative expectations are ordinarily avoided for ethical reasons.)

Type B

Type B designs have often involved real teachers interacting with their own students in an actual classroom situation. For half the students, teachers are led to expect especially good intellectual performance; for the remaining students, teachers are given no particular expectations at all. In research on negotiation processes and outcomes, randomized experiments are possible only in those situations where multiple negotiations can be meaningfully employed as in student-faculty negotiations at different schools or labor-management negotiations at different work sites. In these studies, half the negotiations are entered into by negotiators for whom positive expectations for achieving favorable agreements have been created; the remaining negotiations are entered into by negotiators for whom no special expectations have been created. (In these real-life negotiation situations, the creation of negative expectations for outcomes appears to be ethically indefensible.)

In both Type A and Type B research, then, the independent variable is the experimentally created and randomly assigned level of interpersonal expectation (e.g., very favorable vs. control). The dependent variables include—but are not limited to—favorableness of negotiation outcome, negotiators' ratings of one another and of the probability that they could achieve favorable outcomes in future negotiations. Nearer-term dependent variables include the verbal and nonverbal behavior of the negotiators during the process of negotiation. Detailed methods useful in the study of such behaviors are available elsewhere (Rosenthal, 1987).

Type C

Type C designs are nonexperimental studies conducted in laboratories. The limitations on drawing strong causal inference of observational studies coupled with the loss of ecological validity in employing laboratory settings make the Type C design scientifically unattractive under most circumstances. Type C stud-

specific behaviors to serve as likely mediators of interpersonal expectancy effects.

Kramer and Rosenthal (1999) found that while it was indeed true that group problem solving was, on average, superior to individual problem solving, about 80% of the advantage of the group had nothing to do with the group's interaction per se, but was due to the simple averaging of individuals' problem solutions.

Methodological Developments
The methodological developments since our earlier report are such as to reinforce our earlier caution that in the field of negotiation research, causal inferences are hard to come by. The methodological developments requiring special caution have fostered the erroneous belief

that quick-fix, high tech statistical procedures are now available that allow us to draw causal inference without the hard work of random assignment or other procedures that are quasi-experimental (but not too quasi.)

These high tech seductive procedures, (e.g., structural equation modeling) can't really do the job, but they are fancy enough, and sophisticated-appearing enough, that many social scientists (but very few top flight statisticians) have been led astray by them. As the Task Force on Statistical Inference of the American Psychological Association has reported, fancy data analytic procedures, when clearer, simpler, more focused procedures are available, are neither good science nor good statistics (Wilkinson, et.al. 1999; see also Rosenthal, Rosnow, & Rubin 2000). It should

ies, however, may be useful as a source of new hypotheses, a proving ground for new procedures or measures, and as a source of preliminary data relevant to the planning of future studies— e.g., information on basic noise levels to aid in power calculations, etc. (Rosenthal and Rosnow 1984).

Type D

Type D designs are nonexperimental studies conducted in nonartificial settings. Despite the limitations on drawing strong causal inference, Type D designs at least offer the advantage of involving real-life settings. Among the best of the Type D studies of teacher expectancy effects are those in which teachers' reports of their expectations for pupils' intellectual performance are correlated with pupils' subsequent intellectual performance after adjusting for pupils' prior intellectual performance (e.g., Crano and Mellon 1978). By the use of such stronger methods for causal inference we can make the best of the situation where randomized experiments may not be possible. Such stronger Type D studies are possible in research on negotiation process and outcome where multiple negotiations can be meaningfully employed. In these studies, negotiators' expectations are not induced experimentally but are assessed before the negotiations begin. These prior expectations are then correlated with negotiation outcomes and other dependent variables but with statistical adjustment for the prior probability of a favorable outcome.

Combination of Types

Sometimes combinations of types are particularly effective. For example, pairing a Type A with a Type D design yields particularly strong scientific benefits. When the results point in the same direction we have achieved the combined benefits of strong causal inference and minimization of noise (i.e., experimental precision) from the Type A study and of ecological or real life validity from the Type D study.

The Role of Nonverbal Cues

Channels of Influence

Many of the experiments on the operation of experimenter expectancy effects employed a standard photo rating task in which subjects were asked by their experimenter to rate the degree of success or failure that appeared to be reflected in the ten or more photographs of faces shown to the subject by the experimenter. One of the earliest and strongest hints that nonverbal cues were probably involved in the mediation of these expectancy effects came from the fact that all experimenters read the same standard instructions to their subjects; despite this precise standardization of the *verbal* content of experimenters' communications, subjects responded in accordance with the expectations we had experimentally induced in the minds of the experimenters. If the words did not differ as a function of experimenters' expectations, then the *nonverbal* cues must be critical, we felt (Rosenthal 1966).

A good many subsequent experiments were designed specifically to show which channels of communication or influence were likely to be involved in the transmission of the expectation held by the "expecter" to the "expected." These studies provided strong evidence that nonverbal cues such as facial expressions, body movements, and tone of voice were all likely to be involved (Rosenthal 1985b).

Implications for Research on Negotiation
Expectancy mediation. To the extent that negotiators' expectations may have direct effects on the processes and outcomes of negotiations, it appears likely that the mediation of their expectancy effects will depend at least in part on their nonverbal behavior toward the other negotiators with whom they are in interaction. A fuller understanding, then, of both the processes and outcomes of negotiation may well depend on a fuller understanding of processes of nonverbal communication.

Other outcomes. There are, of course, many other negotiator variables that may have unintended effects on the processes and outcomes of negotiation. Among such variables are the sex, race, ethnicity, experience, ability, personality traits, and states of the negotiators, all of which may affect the processes and outcomes of negotiations. The evidence is very suggestive that, in a variety of real-life contexts, such attributes of the interactants may well be associated with different patterns of nonverbal behavior which, in turn, may well be associated with different outcomes (Blanck, Buck, and Rosenthal 1986).

be noted that the caution about causal modeling procedures are not critical of the mathematics employed, but rather of their use to draw causal inference. More useful procedures to draw causal inference when randomization is impossible (e.g., for ethical reasons) have been described by Holland (1986), and by Rubin (1990a, 1990b). These procedures, while no substitute for randomization, at least provide some valuable leverage on drawing causal inference, a fundamental goal of negotiation science.

References
Ambady, N., & Rosenthal, R. 1992. Thin slices of expressive behavior as predictors of interpersonal consequences: A meta-analysis. *Psychological Bulletin,* 111: 256-274.

Ambady, N. and Rosenthal, R. 1993.

Half a minute: Predicting teacher evaluations from thin slices of nonverbal behavior and physical attractiveness. *Journal of Personality and Social Psychology,* 64:431-441.

Ambady, N., LaPlante, D., Nguyen, T., Chaumeton, N., Rosenthal, R., and Levinson, W. 1999. Physicians' affect and malpractice claims in primary care and surgery. (Unpublished manuscript).

Harris, M. J., and Rosenthal, R. 1985. The mediation of interpersonal expectancy effects: 31 meta-analyses. *Psychological Bulletin,* 97:363-386.

Halverson, A. M., Hallahan, M., Hart, A. J., and Rosenthal, R. 1997. Reducing the biasing effects of judges' nonverbal behavior with simplified jury instruction. *Journal of Applied*

Design implications. The systematic study of the role of nonverbal cues in the processes and outcomes of negotiations requires that the nonverbal behavior of the participants be at least observed and, ideally, recorded via videotape for careful subsequent study. Details on the use of such observations are described in the following section of this article and, in more detail, elsewhere (Rosenthal 1987).

The 10 Arrow Model and the Study of Negotiator Expectancy Effects

Based on the extensive research on the variables underlying the operation of interpersonal expectancy effects, a preliminary model was constructed that has proven useful in pointing out questions most in need of attention before we can understand better: (a) the variables serving to moderate or alter the magnitude of interpersonal expectancy effects, and (b) the variables serving to mediate or transmit the operation of interpersonal expectancy effects (Rosenthal 1981).

The model is described here as applied to research on negotiator effects in general and negotiator expectancy effects in particular. The hope is that it may serve as a useful way of thinking about different types of needed research in the domain of negotiation where the focus is on the personal and interpersonal behavior of the negotiators.

This system, called the "10 Arrow Model," utilizes an underlying dimension of time for the study of negotiator expectancy effects. This factor may give the impression that the model depends on a particular data analytic procedure (e.g., path analysis), but that is not the case. The model does not imply any particular data analytic method. One purpose of the model is to make explicit the classes of variables that must be examined in relation to one another before we can achieve any systematic understanding of the social psychology of negotiator expectation effects. The basic elements of the model include: (A) background and (B) foreground independent (or predictor) variables; (C) mediating (or transmitting) variables; and (D) short-term and (E) long-term dependent (or outcome) variables.

Classes of Variables

Background independent variables refer to such more stable attributes of the expecter (e.g., negotiator, teacher) or expectee (e.g., fellow negotiator, student) as sex, status, race, ethnicity, ability, and personality. It should be emphasized that background independent variables refer to stable attributes of the expectee as well as of the expecter. That increases the power of the model by allowing us to make use of expectee attributes as moderating or altering variables.

The foreground independent variable in this model generally refers to the variable of interpersonal expectation—especially expectations that have been varied experimentally rather than those that have been allowed to vary naturally When expectations are simply measured rather than varied experimentally, a correlation between background and foreground variables is introduced (e.g., negotiators usually expect superior outcomes where initial positions are close to begin with, and teachers usually expect superior performance from brighter students). This correlation makes it virtually impossible to disentangle the effects of interpersonal expectations from the effects of attributes of the expectee or of the difficulty of the task; thus, the effects of interpersonal expectations *per se* become unassessable without the aid of elaborate data analyses (e.g., adjusting for covariates).

Mediating variables refer to the processes by which the expectation of the expecter is communicated to the expectee. These, then, are like the process variables of the psychotherapy research literature or the teaching behavior research literature and our focus is on the behavior of the expecter during interaction with the expectee. By constraining the nature of the verbal communication permitted between expecter and expectee, many studies have shown that these mediating variables must, to a great extent, be nonverbal in nature.

Short-term dependent variables refer to the behavior of the expectee shortly after interaction with the expecter has occurred. A significant relationship between these variables and the experimentally varied foreground independent variables is what we mean by an interpersonal expectancy effect. We should note that the behavior of the expectee (D), including the nonverbal behavior, may have important feedback effects on the behavior of the expecter (C) and the expectation of the expecter (B).

Psychology, 82:590-598.

Holland, P. W. 1986. Statistics and causal inference. Journal of the American Statistical Association, 81, 945-960.

Kramer, S. and Rosenthal, R. (1999). Why are two heads better than one? A meta-analytic comparison of individual, statistical group, and interacting group problem solving. (Unpublished manuscript).

Rosenthal, R. 1991. Meta-analytic procedures for social research. Newbury Park, CA: Sage.

Rosenthal, R. 1994. Interpersonal expectancy effects: A 30-year perspective. Current Directions in Psychological Science, 3:176-179.

Rosenthal, R. and Jacobson, L. 1992. Pygmalion in the

classroom. Expanded edition. NY: Irvington.

Rosenthal, R., Rosnow, R. L., and Rubin, D. B. 2000. Contrasts and effect sizes in behavioral research: A correlational approach. New York: Cambridge University Press.

Rubin, D. B. 1990a. Formal modes of statistical inference for causal effects. Journal of Statistical Planning and Inference, 25: 279-292.

Rubin, D. B. 1990b. Neyman (1923) and causal inference in experiments and observational studies. Statistical Science, 5: 472-480.

Wilkinson, L., and the Task Force on Statistical Inference, APA Board of Scientific Affairs. 1999. Statistical methods in psychology journals. American Psychologist, 54:594-604.

Long-term dependent variables refer to outcome variables obtained in follow-up studies (e.g., the one-year follow-up testing in the Pygmalion research by Rosenthal and Jacobson 1968). We can present the model diagrammatically as in Figure 1.

The 10 Arrows

The 10 arrows of the model summarize some of the types of relationships that are to be examined before any claim to a thorough understanding of interpersonal expectancy effects in the negotiation context can reasonably be made. As will be shown, each of the arrows is usually of social psychological significance, with the exception of arrow AB which is often of only methodological significance. An overview of the meaning of the 10 arrows follows.

AB. These relationships are often large in studies not manipulating interpersonal expectations. Thus, in studies in which teachers are asked to state their expectancies for pupils' intellectual performance, high correlations between teacher expectations (B) and pupil IQ (A) are inevitable. These high correlations make it difficult to conclude that it is the teacher's expectancy rather than the pupil's IQ that is "responsible" for subsequent pupil performance. Covariance analysis, cross-lagged panel analyses, and related procedures can be useful here, however, and have been creatively employed (e.g., Crano and Mellon 1978). When expectancies are varied experimentally, the expected value of the AB correlations is zero since neither the attributes of the expecter nor of the expectee should be correlated with the randomly assigned experimental conditions. A non-zero correlation under these circumstances serves as a methodological warning of a "failure" of the randomization procedure.

AC. These relationships describe the "effects" on the expecter's interactional behavior of various characteristics of the expecter, the expectee, or both. The joint "effects" of teacher susceptibility to biasing information and pupil ability on the teacher's subsequent behavior toward the pupil serve as illustration.

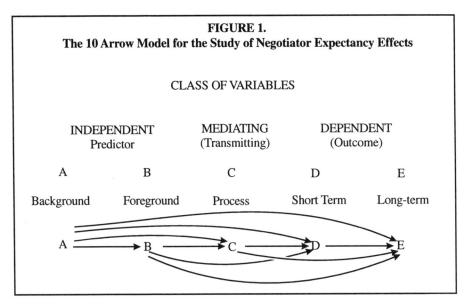

FIGURE 1.
The 10 Arrow Model for the Study of Negotiator Expectancy Effects

AD. These relationships describe the effects of (usually) the expecter's characteristics on the subsequent behavior of the expectee. A relationship between teacher attitude and/or ability and pupil learning would be an illustration.

AE. These relationships are like those of AD except that behavior E occurs at some time in the future relative to D.

BC. These relationships describe the effects on the expecter's behavior toward the expectee of the expectation that has (often) been induced experimentally in the expecter.

BD. These relationships define the phenomenon of interpersonal expectancy effects when the expectancy has been experimentally manipulated. These relationships may be self-moderating over time as when expectee behavior (D) affects the subsequent expectation of the expecter (B).

BE. These relationships define the longer term effects of interpersonal expectations. There are very few studies of this type available.

CD. These relationships provide suggestive clues as to the type of expecter behavior that may have effects on expectee behavior. It is often assumed that CD relationships tell us how teachers, for example, should behave in order to have certain desirable effects on pupil behavior. Except in those very rare cases where mediating variables are manipulated experimentally, such assumptions

159

are unwarranted. Finding certain teacher behaviors to correlate with certain types of pupil performance does not mean that teachers changing their behavior to emulate the behavior of the more successful teachers would show the same success with their pupils. These relationships may also be self-moderating over time as when expectee behavior (D) affects the subsequent behavior of the expecter (C).

CE. These relationships are like the CD relationships except that the outcome variables are of the follow-up variety.

DE. These relationships may merely assess the stability of the behavior of the expectee, as when the measures employed for D and E are identical. When these measures are not very similar, the DE relationship may yield an index of predictive validity that is of substantive interest.

Of the 10 arrows of the model, three are clearly most important and should ideally be included in most studies of negotiator expectancy effects: BC, BD, and CD.

The BD relationship tells us the degree to which interpersonal expectancy effects occurred. The BC relationship tells us the degree to which the (preferably experimental induction of) expectancy was a determinant of a particular type of behavior of the expecter toward the expectee. The CD relationship tells us the degree to which certain behaviors of the expecter are associated with changes in the behavior of the expectee. If the BC results show an increase in behavior X due to the induced expectations, and the CD results show that increases in behavior X by the expecter are associated with changes in the performance of the expectee, behavior X becomes implicated as a candidate for status as a mediating variable.

It should be emphasized that the 10 Arrow Model is designed to help think about the type of research we might want to conduct. It tells little about the specification of variables (except for the variable of expectancy, and even that can be specified in a wide variety of ways). Variables to be employed in a given study can vary tremendously on such dimensions as time duration and molarity, for example. Thus, for time duration, studies may range from employing ten-second clips of a videotape of a psychotherapy session as the source of verbal or nonverbal mediating behavior all the way to employing hundreds of hours of observation of a continuing negotiation process. For levels of molarity, studies may range from employing the heart rate of a participant to employing the outcome of an international summit negotiation.

Measuring Sensitivity to Nonverbal Cues
Individual Differences
As discussed earlier, much of the research on interpersonal expectancies has suggested that mediation of these expectancies depends to some important degree on various processes of nonverbal communication. Moreover, there appear to be important differences among experimenters, teachers, and people generally in the clarity of their communication through

different channels of nonverbal communication. In addition, there appear to be important differences among research subjects, pupils, and people generally in their sensitivity to nonverbal communications transmitted through different nonverbal channels.

If we knew a great deal more about differential sending and receiving abilities, we might be in a much better position to address the general question of what kind of person (in terms of sending abilities) can most effectively influence covertly what kind of other person (in terms of receiving abilities). Thus, for example, if those teachers who best communicate their expectations for children's intellectual performance in the auditory channel were assigned children whose best channels of reception were also auditory, we would predict greater effects of teacher expectation than we would if those same teachers were assigned children less sensitive to auditory nonverbal communications.

Ultimately, then, what we would want would be a series of accurate measurements for each person describing his or her relative ability to send and to receive in each of a variety of channels of nonverbal communication. It seems reasonable to suppose that, if we had this information for two or more people, we would be better able to predict the outcome of their interaction regardless of whether the focuses of the analysis were on the mediation of interpersonal expectations or on some other interpersonal process.

Our model envisages people moving through their "social spaces" carrying two vectors or profiles of scores. One of these vectors describes the person's differential clarity in sending messages over various channels of nonverbal communication. The other vector describes the person's differential sensitivity in receiving messages in various channels of nonverbal communication.

In general, the better persons A and B are as senders and as receivers, the more effective will be the communication between persons A and B. However, two dyads may have identical overall levels of skill in sending and receiving and yet may differ in the effectiveness of their nonverbal communication because the sender's skill in one dyad "fits" the receiver's skill better than is the case in the other dyad. One way to assess the "fit" of skills in dyad members is to correlate the sending skills of A with the receiving skills of B, and to correlate the sending skills of B with the receiving skills of A. Higher correlations reflect a greater potential for more accurate communication between the dyad members since the receiver is then better at receiving the channels which are the more accurately encoded channels of the sender.

The mean (arithmetic, geometric, or harmonic) of the two correlations (of A's sending with B's receiving and of B's sending with A's receiving) reflects how well the dyad members "understand" each other's communications. That mean correlation need not reflect how well the dyad members like each other, but rather only that A and B should more quickly understand each other's intended and unintended messages, including how they feel about one another.

As a start toward the goal of more completely specifying accuracy of sending and receiving nonverbal cues in dyadic interaction, an instrument was developed that was designed to measure sensitivity to various channels of nonverbal communication: The Profile of Nonverbal Sensitivity, or PONS. The details of this test, its development, and the results of the extensive research that has been conducted employing the PONS are given elsewhere (Rosenthal 1979; Rosenthal, Hall, DiMatteo, Rogers, and Archer 1979). Here we can give only a brief overview.

The Profile of Nonverbal Sensitivity

The PONS is a 45-minute, 16 millimeter sound film (or videotape) comprised of 220 two-second auditory and/or visual segments. The printed answer sheet employed by the viewer has 220 pairs of descriptions of real-life situations. From each pair of descriptions, the viewer circles the description that best fits the segment that has just been seen and/or heard. Twenty scenarios are each represented in the 11 nonverbal "channels" that include face alone, body alone, face plus body, tone of voice, and various combinations of face, body, and tone of voice.

The 20 scenarios were selected such that half were judged to communicate positive affects and half were judged to communicate negative affects. Orthogonally to this dimension, half the scenarios were judged to reflect a dominant interpersonal orientation and half were judged to communicate a submissive interpersonal orientation. Thus, there are five scenarios in each of the following four quadrants: Positive-Dominant, Positive-Submissive, Negative-Dominant, and Negative-Submissive.

An Overview of Some Results

For 133 samples comprised of 2,615 subjects, sex differences favored females very consistently. Females were especially superior to males at judging cues of negative affect. In general, younger children were less accurate than older children and young adults at decoding nonverbal cues. However, younger samples showed a relative advantage at judging audio as opposed to video cues, a result suggesting that the ability to read vocal nonverbal cues may be developmentally prior to the ability to read visual nonverbal cues.

PONS performance was not highly correlated with intellectual ability, though it did tend to be correlated with cognitive complexity. Further, people scoring high on the PONS tended to be better adjusted, more interpersonally democratic and encouraging, less dogmatic, more extroverted, more likely to volunteer for behavioral research, more popular, and more interpersonally sensitive as judged by acquaintances, clients, spouses, or supervisors. These results, based on dozens of studies, contribute strongly to the construct validity of the PONS.

Implications for Research on Negotiation

It would be interesting to learn whether the outcomes of negotiation might be predictable, at least to some degree, from a knowledge of the patterns of negotiators' sensitivity to nonverbal cues. Should that prove to be the case, instruments are now available to help in the selection for and training in negotiators' sensitivity to a variety of channels of nonverbal communication (Rosenthal 1979).

Research on the effects of negotiators' sensitivity to nonverbal communication could be easily carried out in conjunction with any of the four types of research described earlier. It would only require that, in laboratory or actual settings, negotiators take the PONS test prior to the negotiation. The processes and outcomes of the negotiations could then simply be correlated with negotiators' scores on the POINTS.

Other Topics with Implications for Research on Negotiation
There are, of course, many topics in the domain of nonverbal communication that may prove relevant to a fuller understanding of the processes and outcomes of negotiation. Here I shall touch on only a few, selected for their having well-developed research literatures of their own, though not necessarily with direct reference as yet to negotiation research.

Deception
Negotiators must be acutely aware of the possibility of deception—their own and that of others. The evidence is compelling that deceptions can be detected by both verbal and nonverbal behavioral cues given off by the deceiver (DePaulo, Zuckerman, and Rosenthal 1980; Zuckerman, DePaulo, and Rosenthal 1986). From this evidence we learn that speech cues (verbal and nonverbal) are the best source of cues to catch lies, that body cues are also valuable cues to deception, but that facial cues may be more an aid to deceiving than to detecting deception.

Rapport
Although investigated more often in a context of clinical interaction than in the context of negotiation, the construct of rapport and related constructs such as empathy also show a rich tradition of research and theory (Tickle Degnen and Rosenthal 1987). While many of the findings of this literature are well-known and intuited by most, some are little known and more subtle. Examples of the former include findings such as: greater rapport is positively correlated with participants' leaning toward each other, smiling, and having eye contact. Examples of the latter include such findings as: greater rapport is positively correlated with participants' appearing to move their bodies "in time" to one another, creating an impression of a kind of "interactional dance" (Bernieri, Reznick, and Rosenthal 1988).

Sex Differences
There is a growing literature on the important differences between the nonverbal sensitivity and the nonverbal behavior of females and males (Hall 1984). Differences in the ways in which male and female managers' tone of voice changes in their speaking to bosses, peers, and subordinates may have direct implications for the process and outcome of mixed sex negotiations (Steckler and Rosenthal 1985). Even the tone of voice in which people speak about nonpresent others appears to be determined by the sex of the person spoken about (Goldberg, Gorgoglione, Isen, and Rosenthal 1987).

Design Implications
All three of these topics—deception, rapport, and sex differences in negotiation—could be investigated in settings varying in degree of naturalness and in research paradigms varying in degree of clarity of causal inference. Thus, for example, in laboratory or more natural settings, the sex composition of the negotiation teams can be varied experimentally or simply assessed and recorded as it occurs naturally. Sex composition of the negotiation teams then serves as the independent variable and various processes of verbal and nonverbal communication can serve as mediating variables. Serving as dependent variables would be favorableness of agreements reached or probabilities of future negotiation outcomes. The 10 Arrow Model offers a guide for further details on such a design.

Conclusion
Research on interpersonal expectancy effects and on the processes of nonverbal communication that often play a role in the mediation of these expectancy effects may prove relevant to a better understanding of the processes and outcomes of negotiation. Psychological researchers who investigate these topics have much to learn about social interaction from social scientists who study negotiation. In return, these psychological researchers can bring some interesting bodies of literature and some interesting research methods to bear on the problems of negotiation research. Productive collaboration seems to be a natural and happy consequence.

Acknowledgment
Preparation of this article and much of the research described has been supported in part by the National Science Foundation.

References
Allport, G. W. 1950. The role of expectancy. In *Tensions that cause wars*, ed. H. Cantril. Urbana, IL: University of Illinois Press.

Bernieri, F. J., J. Reznick, and R. Rosenthal. 1988. Synchrony pseudosynchrony, and dissynchrony: Measuring the entrainment process in mother-infant interactions. *Journal of Personality and Social Psychology* 54:243-253.

Blanck, P. D., R. Buck, and R. Rosenthal, eds. 1986. *Nonverbal communication in the clinical context*. University Park, Penn State Press.

Cochran, W. G. 1983. *Planning and analysis of observational studies*. New York: Wiley.

Crano, W. D. and P. M. Mellon. 1978. Causal influence of teachers' expectations on children's academic performance: A cross-lagged panel analysis. *Journal of Educational Psychology* 70: 39-49.

DePaulo, B. M., M. Zuckerman, and R. Rosenthal. 1980. Detecting deception: Modality effects. In *Review of personality and social psychology* vol. 1. ed. L. Wheeler. Beverly Hills, CA: Sage.

Goldberg, S., J. M. Gorgoglione, A. M. and R. Rosenthal. 1987. *Speaking of women.* manuscript submitted for publication.

Hall, J. A. 1984. *Nonverbal sex differences.* Baltimore, Md.: The Johns Hopkins University Press.

Merton, R. K. 1948. The self-fulfilling prophecy. *Antioch Review* 8: 193-210.

Rosenthal, R. 1966. *Experimenter effects in behavioral research.* New York: Appleton-Century-Crofts.

————, ed. 1979. *Skill in nonverbal communication.* Cambridge, MA: Oelgeschlager Gunn & Hain.

————. 1981. Pavlov's mice, Pfungst's horse, and Pygmalion's PONS: Some models for the study of interpersonal expectancy effects. In *The Clever Hans phenomenon.* ed. T. A Sebeok and R. Rosenthal. New York: Annals of the New York Academy of Sciences, no. 364.

————. 1985a. From unconscious experimenter bias to teacher expectancy effects. In *Teacher expectancies.* ed. J. B. Dusek. Hillsdale, NJ.: Lawrence Erlbaum Associates.

————. 1985b. Nonverbal cues in the mediation of interpersonal expectancy effects. In *Multichannel integrations of nonverbal behavior.* ed. A. W. Siegman and S. Feldstein. Hillsdale, NJ.: Lawrence Erlbaum Associates.

————. 1987. *Judgment studies design, analysis, and meta-analysis.* New York: Cambridge University Press.

Rosenthal, R., J. A. Hall, M. R. DiMatteo, P. L. Rogers, and D. Archer. 1979. *Sensitivity to nonverbal communication: The PONS test.* Baltimore, Md.: The Johns Hopkins University Press.

Rosenthal, R., L. and L. Jacobson. 1968. *Pygmalion in the classroom.* New York: Holt, Rinehart and Winston.

Rosenthal, R. and R. L. Rosnow. 1984. *Essentials of behavioral research.* New York: McGraw-Hill.

Rosenthal, R. and D. B. Rubin. 1978. Interpersonal expectancy effects: The first 345 studies. *The Behavioral and Brain Sciences* 3:377-386.

Steckler, N. A. R. and R. Rosenthal. 1985. Sex differences in nonverbal and verbal communication with bosses, peers, and subordinates. *Journal of Applied Psychology* 70:157-163.

Tickle Degnen, L. and R. Rosenthal. 1987. Group rapport and nonverbal behavior. In *Group processes and intergroup relations.* Vol 9: *Review of personality and social psychology.* ed. C. Hendrick. Beverly Hills, CA: Sage.

Zuckerman, M., B. M. DePaulo, and R. Rosenthal. 1986. Humans as deceivers and lie detectors. In *Nonverbal communication in the clinical context.* ed. P. D. Blanck, R. Buck and R. Rosenthal. University Park, PA.: Penn State Press.

II. Curriculum Design

Teaching Negotiation and Dispute Resolution in Colleges of Business: The State of the Practice and Challenges for the Future

Roy J. Lewicki

Roy J. Lewicki is the Lorraine Tyson Mitchell Professor in Leadership and Communication and former Dean at Max M. Fisher College of Business at Ohio State University. His research interests include business ethics, leadership, dispute resolution and negotiation, and managing change.

In this paper, I will review the pedagogical development of teaching negotiation in schools of business. Since I initiated one of the first applied negotiation courses in an American business school and have been teaching it consecutively for over 20 years, I will trace the evolution of both content and methods from a personal perspective. I will identify three phases in the growth and development of this field: the first decade (1975-85), in which the field developed; the second decade (1986-1995), in which the field matured; and the emergence of the third decade (1996 and beyond), for which I identify some key challenges and opportunities for the field.

The Formative Decade (1975-1985)

I taught my first negotiation course, "Dynamics of Bargaining," in 1973 at the Amos Tuck School of Business at Dartmouth College. I had joined the Amos Tuck School faculty a year earlier and learned early that teaching MBAs bore absolutely no resemblance to facilitating discussion in a research-oriented doctoral seminar. Theory *had* to be supplemented with some kind of case or experience to hold student attention and facilitate the application of principles. No discipline of "managerial negotiation" or even "applied negotiation" existed at the time. The field of social psychology had enjoyed a boom in experimental studies of bargaining and conflict behavior in the late 1960s; however, a minimal literature was available to practitioners, and there were almost no training vehicles in the field. The classroom materials were primitive simulations adapted from social psychological research paradigms and matrix games, such as Prisoners' Dilemma, the Acme Bolt trucking game, simple coalition bargaining games, and case studies on labor relations, real estate, and industrial marketing. (See Lewicki 1975.)

This chapter first appeared in Deborah Kolb, editor, *Negotiation Eclectics: Essays in Memory of Jeffrey Z. Rubin*, PON Books, 1999.

169

Core theory was drawn from the fields of labor relations (Walton and McKersie 1965; Douglas 1962), early game theory (Luce and Raiffa 1957; Rapaport 1960; Seigel and Fouraker 1960); social psychological research on conflict and its resolution (Deutsch 1973; Rubin and Brown 1975), international relations (Schelling 1960; Fisher 1969); community affairs (Alinsky 1971) and materials on community organizing, real estate, purchasing, and related disciplines. A few of the early practitioner books on negotiation (Nierenberg 1973; Karrass 1974) seemed almost completely removed from anything written in the academic literature.

In the early 1980s, courses in negotiation were beginning to emerge at other major business schools[1]. A clear momentum of interest had begun; books, professional organizations, and funding for research began to emerge. Books such as Raiffa (1982) and Fisher and Ury (1981) gained considerable visibility and continue to be core resources in negotiation courses. A small group of scholars, lead by Max Bazerman, began presenting papers at professional meetings and decided to organize their own research conference in order to bring negotiation and conflict management topics into the mainstream of behavioral science research in business schools. Jeff Rubin was among the invited speakers to the first conference, which produced the first volume of edited research papers (Bazerman and Lewicki 1983). A biannual conference and research volume have followed, encouraging both a strong research tradition and a strong conceptual base for pedagogy.

The success of the research conferences encouraged several academics to call for the organization of a Power, Negotiation and Conflict Management Interest Group within the Academy of Management. Over 500 Academy members responded with interest (Edelman 1989). The group was recognized in 1988, creating a forum for teachers and scholars to organize regular paper sessions, symposia, and workshops on negotiation research and pedagogy.

In the period 1983-1986, the National Institute for Dispute Resolution (NIDR) initiated its grants program. Its expressed purpose was to stimulate creation and dissemination of pedagogical materials in dispute resolution that could be used in core behavioral science courses in business, law, and public policy schools. Faculty from several disciplines (management, applied economics and planning, and law) created role play scenarios and accompanying instructional notes, and then conducted workshops at major professional meetings (cf. Brett, Greenhalgh, Kolb, Lewicki, and Sheppard 1985). Over 600 copies of the business volume were disseminated. NIDR's effort in support of the development of teaching materials was timely and instrumental in bringing high quality pedagogy to many behavioral science courses.

In 1984, a second major funding agency, the Hewlett Foundation, began its program of financially underwriting interdisciplinary dispute resolution centers. Several of these centers—particularly at Northwestern and Harvard—have made major contributions to pedagogy. In addition, the Ph.D. programs from many Hewlett-funded centers have produced a stream of new scholars with advanced expertise in teaching negotiation who have contributed to the enrichment and expansion of the field.

By the mid-1980s, the number of negotiation and dispute resolution courses had grown from a handful to approximately 100, and by the end of the decade, to 200. An increasingly rich pool of resource materials had been developed and marketed, trade books had proliferated, doctoral programs had produced new streams of negotiation research and new faculty to meet the increasing course demand. The professional field of dispute resolution grew significantly beyond the labor relations sector and practitioner training in law schools (Edelman 1989).

The Dominant Pedagogy in the Field
Most instructors in the management field take an eclectic approach to pedagogy. They use a combination of lecture and discussion, role play, and case presentation. Most courses, in one way or another, employ the classic "experiential learning" methodology (Kolb 1974). This incorporates four types of activity: concrete experience, reflection on this experience, derivation of concepts and theoretical principles, and planning for active experimentation and application of these principles to new settings. Many negotiation and conflict courses implicitly (or explicitly) follow this model by intertwining presentations of theory and research with simulated practice (Lewicki 1986).

Many instructors are quite explicit about including the components of the model in designing their course outline, although they may be less explicit about how these activities "flow" through the different stages. Course designs create learning cycles that include a dose of theory, a role play or simulation that highlights the key issues and dynamics of that theory, a "reflection paper" or journal entry of some form to help the student tie theory and experience together, and a mandate for personal goal setting which is designed to improve their future negotiating behavior. This format has become the dominant model for teaching negotiation. However, as noted below, questions still linger about its impact and effectiveness.

Thematic Orientation and Course Content
At the risk of oversimplifying what has become a very diverse and eclectic panoply of approaches, it is possible to identify two dominant orientations for negotiation courses within the business school environment today. The first treats negotiation as a decision-making process; emphasizes the more cognitive and rational dimensions of decision making, and predominantly employs an economics/game theory paradigm (employing resources such as Bazerman and Neale 1992; Murnighan 1991; Raiffa 1982). The second has a more social psychological thrust and emphasizes the interpersonal dynamics between negotiators and the contextual factors that shape these interactions (employing resources such as Lewicki *et al.* 1993, 1994; Rubin, Pruitt, and Kim 1994).

Both groups often supplement the academic materials with one or more practitioner-oriented books (e.g., Fisher, Ury, and Patton 1991). Themes in these courses are likely to include:

• an introduction to conflict theory, including the basic dynamics of interpersonal and intergroup conflict;
• an introduction to game theory, noting the behavioral and decision-making dynamics in simple matrix games;
• an overview of the strategy and tactics of competitive, distributive negotiation;
• an overview of the strategy and tactics of cooperative, integrative, principled negotiation;
• time-series or "stage" models of the negotiation processes, addressing the critical elements that need to occur at each stage;
• an assessment of the individual differences (cognitive processes, communication and persuasion processes, and differences in negotiator personality and gender) and contextual factors (power differences, national culture differences, and structural considerations) that tend to enrich and complicate negotiations beyond these basic approaches;
• negotiation within and between groups and organizations; and
• an overview of the procedures for moving deadlocked negotiations from impasse toward resolution, including procedures the parties can use themselves, and the key roles played by third parties.[2,3]

Trends in the Second Decade (1985-1995):
The Development of the Field
Negotiation courses have enjoyed success in business schools for several reasons. First, students become heavily involved in the role plays and simulations. Competitive dynamics are engaged, and the focus of attention moves from the "abstract" (as in discussing theory, or reading a case) to the "real" (as in actual exchanges with each other, and living with the consequences of those exchanges). Students remember these experiences long after the course is over, and they create a strong reputation for the course. Second, the courses meet the need for students to learn both skills and theory. As a result, negotiation courses are often embraced by business school deans as models in the curriculum for the effective teaching of theory and practice (Porter and McKibbin 1988). Finally, students often see the negotiation course as being directly helpful and relevant to their career aspirations in a variety of professional disciplines.

In the second decade, content and pedagogy remained relatively stable. Textbooks, cases, and role plays proliferated. The organization and presentation of material was improved, providing better guidance to instructors on how to use and adapt the materials. Applications have been developed in almost every area where negotiation and conflict management skills are practiced.

During this period, major innovations in the use of instructional technology (videotape, computers, and integrations between the two) were applied to negotiation.

Videotape

Many instructors use videotape to record student negotiations and provide opportunities for either classroom viewing or private review. Orchestrating this taping process is often time-consuming, labor intensive, and difficult to accomplish because of large class size or inadequate facilities. Providing direct feedback to individual students is even more difficult given these conditions. While the opportunity to see and review one's own negotiating activity is critical to skill development, the labor-intensive nature of this process limits its applications.

    Another way to use videotape is to utilize commercially available productions which show unfolding negotiations in different sectors and contexts. Using tape in this manner permits the teaching of negotiation as a dynamic process. The presentation can be stopped at any point to discuss appropriate responses, strategic choice points, or tactical alternatives. Unfortunately, many of the videotapes developed in this decade are very simplistic and talk at the learner rather than providing real or simulated role models in realistic, complex negotiation sequences. A strong and viable market remains for producers and publishing houses to create effective materials in this area.

Computers

Computers can be used in two major ways to facilitate teaching: unilateral and bilateral applications. Unilateral applications pace negotiators through a sequenced strategic planning process that helps negotiators prepare for an upcoming deliberation (e.g. *Negotiator Pro* 1993). These applications present a series of screens that require participants to define the issues, develop priorities among them, set targets and resistance points, identify interests, invent options, profile opponents, and anticipate their positions and interests.

    A computer may also be used bilaterally for scenarios in which both sides use it as a simulation tool and as a data base. Work in both of these areas is in its infancy, and applications to teaching need to be expanded. (See Shell 1995 and Wheeler 1995 for recent reviews of the state of the field.)

Integrating Computer and Video Media

An example of work integrating the two media is the McGill Negotiation Simulator (Saunders and Roston 1993). This ambitious computer-based simulation provides a major interactive negotiation training device. Using computer and laser-disk technology, the simulator creates a realistic opponent whose complex, preprogrammed responses effectively duplicate the behavior of a real opponent in a multi-issue negotiation, played out on a large video monitor. Since the student's choice of alternatives is recorded as she works her way through the simulator, the tool not only teaches strategic interaction, but also can measure what skills were acquired and developed through the simulator, and how durable and generally applicable those skills are.

In addition, the simulator offers an important opportunity for educators to debate what patterns of responses *should* be programmed into the simulator to make it as effective as possible. The simulator may be used to sharpen the pedagogical focus on effective and ineffective strategic response alternatives. Saunders and Lewicki (1995) review the issues and problems in teaching from this medium.

An Interdisciplinary Focus
During this period, business schools and disputing courses were becoming increasingly interdisciplinary. However, because negotiation and dispute resolution are processes in search of contexts, considerably more work was necessary to apply the processes to practice areas such as public policy and legislation, regulation, environmental management, and other areas of social concern. This integration was difficult to acheive, particularly in traditional universities, given shrinking resource bases and the absence of incentives for faculty members to work across disciplinary lines. For example, at Ohio State University we have designed a successful, high-enrollment interdisciplinary course on social conflict taught by faculty from City and Regional Planning, International Affairs, Natural Resources, and Business. Yet only two of the four faculty members can get any formal credit for teaching that course from their own academic units, because the course is interdisciplinary and not mandated by the primary academic units.

The Seven Challenges for the
Third Decade (1996 and Beyond)
The next decade holds a number of challenges. The first four of these are substantive, tied to critical shifts in emerging theory and research; three are procedural.

1. More emphasis will be placed on negotiation within relationships, rather than transactional negotiations.
In the business disciplines, there seems to be a significant shift away from market transactions between individuals and organizations, and toward the establishment and maintenance of long-term relationships between individuals within and across organizational boundaries. This shift in emphasis strongly parallels the emergence of new organizational forms in the marketplace. These forms stress collaboration within teams and across business units, an increased focus on customers, and the development of strategic alliances and joint ventures. These transitions have mandated an examination of the "transactional" negotiation models, for example, of distributive and integrative negotiation (Walton and McKersie 1965; Lewicki et al. 1994); of claiming and creating value (Lax and Sebenius 1986); and of similar approaches (e.g. Fisher, Ury, and Patton 1991). Investigators have questioned the adequacy of these approaches for explaining the challenges of managing disputes in the context of long-term relationships.

It is common wisdom that practicing the strategy and tactics of traditional distributive negotiation in the context of a long-term relationship is likely to kill it. The context demands more interest-based approaches, but even in this setting, the negotiation approach may need to be dramatically reframed. For example, Sheppard and Tuchinsky (1995) note a number of deficiencies in the current "transactional" theories when we apply them to negotiations in a relational context:

First, current research has focused on single-issue distributive negotiations, regarding them as cool, economic, rational calculations. However, within relationships, single-issue discussions can be very "hot"; how they are settled in a relationship can have dramatic implications for the future.

Second, single-issue distributive negotiations can be transformed by trade offs over time. Parties consistently trade off against the past or trade off for the future in dealing with tough, nondivisible problems. Time—past and future—becomes a much more critical factor in understanding how parties manage relational conflicts.

Third, negotiations within relationships may never end. Some deals are never "done"; they are reopened, rediscussed, replanned, as external factors shift the parties' preferences and priorities over time.

Fourth, separating the person from the problem (Fisher, Ury, and Patton 1991) may be not only undesirable but also impossible. Each side needs to learn as much about the other person as possible, learn how to increase their value to the other, and develop plans that incorporate the interests of both sides.

Fifth, in many relationships, the person is the problem. Time and attention must be devoted not just to negotiating a solution to the problem but on changing the behavior of the key person to minimize future problems.

Sixth, relationship development leads to multiple interdependencies, enabling each party to exercise different kinds of power over the other (cf. Zartman 1997). Because of these multiple interdependencies and linkages, "surfacing interests and inventing options" may be far more difficult to do than it has been presented.

The instructional challenge is not only to decide whether our theory is adequate for representing the dynamics but also to find ways to use traditional simulation methodology to "insert" students into long-term, relationship-based role plays and help them grasp the history, parameters, and key dynamics of that relationship. This may be a problem that is better suited to "scripted" negotiations on videotape or CD ROM, in which the context and relationship is extensively elaborated before the specific negotiation challenge is specified.

2. Selected aspects of interpersonal relations that have been neglected in research to date, but which are critical to negotiation within these contexts, will be targeted.
Many aspects of interpersonal relationships are relevant to negotiation; two important examples, discussed below, are the role of emotionality and the development of trust.

First, the field of negotiation has been dominated by approaching it as the science of decision making. This approach has emphasized the nature of cognitive dynamics, assumptions of rationality, and decision biases which occur because negotiators are not as rational as they should be (cf. Raiffa 1982; Bazerman and Neale 1992). Yet real negotiation is often more than the rational exchange of information and decisions based on that information. It may involve feelings and emotional attachments which strongly affect a negotiator's preferences and which can be used tactically.

Researchers have tended to treat emotion as a negative or extraneous factor in research on negotiation They have treated it as the producer of random variance, or as a "nonrational" component which confounds the predictions made by the economic/cognitive models. However, a recent book by Goleman (1995) has made the concept of "emotional intelligence" accessible and demonstrated how qualities of self awareness, control of emotions, persistence, enthusiasm, and empathy actively contribute to a high "E.Q." and to personal and professional success.

Trade books on negotiation and conflict have not ignored the role of emotion. Jeff and Carol Rubin's book on family disputation (1989) directly dealt with the critical role of emotion and prescribed strategies to manage emotionality. In summary, not only do we need to significantly incorporate emotional dynamics into our theories, but also we need to spend more time focusing on how emotions, in addition to cognitive preference functions, shape negotiator decision making.

Second, whether we are talking about achieving successful principled negotiation in a transaction or building and strengthening a long-term relationship, trust is the glue that binds the processes together. While there is growing research interest in trust and its importance to relationship development and maintenance, for example in the compilation of Kramer and Tyler (1996), we know remarkably little about how to build trust, what not to do if you want to sustain trust, or how to repair broken trust.

Our own work on trust (Lewicki and Bunker 1995, 1996; Lewicki, Bunker, and Stevenson 1997; Lewicki and Stevenson 1997; Lewicki, McAllister, and Bies 1997) has proposed that trust is a multidimensional concept, that we can understand its developmental dynamics, that trust and distrust are different phenomena, that there are clear steps to building trust in negotiations, and that trust can be repaired under the right circumstances. We believe this work is fundamental to helping parties in relationships understand exactly what they need to do to build trust, maintain trust, or repair trust which has been damaged.

3. Our models of negotiation are dominantly Western and dominantly male. We have made some modest inroads into gender differences and cultural differences, but we tend to treat these as "variations" on the western male motif.

The past decade has seen some significant shift in research attention toward understanding international differences in approaches to negotiation approach strategy (e.g. Hofstede 1991; Foster 1992; Janosik 1987; Weiss and Stripp 1985; Weiss 1993, 1997). This work has created a language that allows us to compare cultural differences in negotiation style and approach and to understand how to interpret the impact of culture on negotiation process and outcomes. Almost all negotiation courses now address international differences in some manner and an increasing number focus exclusively on multinational negotiations.

It is not yet clear whether the dominant tenets of our Western theory apply to all cultures, or whether that theory should be reconstructed for different international contexts. The shift from a transactional to a relational view of negotiations, noted above, can in part be attributed to a better understanding of how Asian negotiators have utilized the advantages of that approach. We may see similar shifts in the future.

Efforts to understand gender differences have progressed at a slower pace. Early research on gender differences has been highly equivocal, but ambiguous findings could be attributed to research paradigms that obscured or minimized gender differences. Theory work, on the other hand, has clearly argued for gender differences (Kolb and Coolidge 1991). Investigators have suggested that women a) have a more relational view of negotiation, b) tend to see negotiations as more embedded in relationships, c) use power in a way that is more empowering than controlling of the other, and d) pursue negotiation dialogue in a manner that is more like problem solving than like confrontation. Again, similar to our discussion of international differences, it is not clear whether we need to significantly reconstruct the core principles of negotiation in pedagogy, but the debate has been engaged.

4. Raising issues of ethics and values in our teaching of negotiation is an essential instructional challenge.
The content and methods of negotiation courses in business schools are clearly consistent with utilitarian and capitalistic values. Many negotiation courses are really courses in "applied social influence", in which we are teaching students how to "design and execute a strategy to get what they want." The very fact that we bill our courses as such, and gain large MBA enrollments, argues for the general success of our mission.

Much of the success of negotiation in the second decade has been the result of a clash of cultures in the classroom. The humanistic, power-equalizing, conflict resolution-oriented values of most of the faculty were at odds with the pragmatic, economic, and often power-seeking values of the students. Many of the faculty who began teaching negotiation courses in the 1980s received their education in the 1960s, mostly in applied social science disciplines; most of them bring a very strong humanistic, cooperative orientation to their subject. For years, this humanistic frame ran headlong into the more conservative and pragmatic value system of a younger generation of MBAs.

In the short term, the results were disastrous; in the 1970s and early 1980s, many organizational behavior courses were the worst-rated courses in the curriculum and were roundly criticized for being "soft" on management issues of conflict, power, and assertive leadership. Many of the faculty members began to teach negotiation, hoping that this course would support a strongly normative, pro-cooperation perspective. But the conflict continued, particularly in the pro-business environment of the late 1980s and early 1990s.

I would argue that this clash was often responsible for much of the classroom excitement. Students entered the course believing that they needed negotiation skills for career success, to help them "win"—i.e., be more successful competitors, both for their employers and themselves. Faculty members designed their courses to convert students, subtly or not-

177

so-subtly, from a competitive to a more cooperative world view.

This is often accomplished through role play and simulations in which students experience the long-term consequences of short-term distributive behavior. Students learn how to be competitive *and* collaborative, strategic and tactical, and to understand the virtues (and limitations) of both the distributive and integrative approaches to conflicts and their resolution. These dialogues have been transformative for both the students and faculty involved.

In the consumption-oriented 1980s, many MBAs began to argue that we were doing them a disservice by overstressing cooperation and integrative negotiation in a world that rewarded them for getting everything they could, and by any means. In retrospect, I am glad we did not accede to their demands. It is clear that collaborative and integrative skills are the ones required to build and manage teams, strategic alliances, joint ventures, and other cooperative business relationships which have become the hallmarks of successful management in the late 1990s.

Still, few professors are really comfortable addressing the ethical and value issues that arise as students pursue aggressively competitive strategies with each other. Several years ago, at a professional meeting, we conducted a workshop on how negotiator ethics should be taught in our courses. To engage the audience on an early Sunday morning, we staged the discussion as a debate and forced the audience to take a position on whether faculty should "preach" what is ethically right in negotiation or be ethically neutral and encourage students to do "whatever works." Audience passions rose rapidly; half of the 80 academics in the room willingly committed themselves to one side or the other. Clearly this issue requires further exploration, first among the professorate, then in the classroom.

5. We need to dissect "negotiating skill" into specific skill sets which we can measure, drill, and then reassemble into strong overall negotiator behavior.
Remarkably, we have almost no "best practices" study when it comes to teaching negotiation. There is a lot of normative theory but not much direct empirical testing of the theory. Part of the problem may be that negotiation is not one single skill. Effective negotiation is a complex collection of skill elements that entail aspects of planning, strategizing, advocacy, communication, persuasion, and cognitive packaging and repackaging of information. The skills required to be an effective negotiator include the ability to:

• understand the issue under dispute;
• determine one's own interests, values and preferences related to the issue;
• define or frame the issue in an appropriate manner;
• define/reframe the issue if such a redefinition might lead to a better outcome (for one or both sides);
• determine the relational context in which the negotiation is embedded, including who the other is, the level of trust in the relationship, what role the past and future relationship

plays, and the key aspects of the organizational and cultural context;
• construct a line of argument to support one's preferred outcome;
• organize and persuasively present this line of argument;
• listen effectively to the other side;
• ask questions to gain information from the other side and probe for their interests and preferences;
• analyze the total pool of shared information so as to understand points of agreement and disagreement;
• package and trade off issues and concessions;
• creatively brainstorm and invent options to bridge these areas of disagreement; and
• articulate and record a final agreement.

Numerous other skills are called into play to keep negotiations from growing out of control, to deal with opponents who are "difficult," to effectively handle multiparty disputes, and so on.

We seldom pay attention to helping students diagnose, develop, or refine critical skill subsets. Significant progress in improving skill definition and acquisition, and measurement of progress will require several key steps.

We need to isolate the key skill components of effective negotiating. (We see some efforts to begin to do this in the Saunders and Roston simulation.) Few articles in either research or pedagogy have focused on "what successful negotiators do," (e.g., Rackham 1980), and these works have not reported very convincing data.

Then, we must create training that specifically addresses the underlying skill clusters. For example, if there was widespread acceptance of a skill list such as that proposed above we could specifically provide competency-based training in listening, asking questions, cognitive repackaging and creative thinking, building trust, engaging in advocacy and debate, and persuasive communication. I believe our colleagues in the law school have made more progress in this domain than we have.

Third, we must improve our ability to measure skill acquisition. Few, if any, negotiation education programs provide actual measures of improvement on the key skill clusters they purport to teach. Rather than measure student learning by traditional exams and papers, we should enact a negotiation in-basket exercise, videotape the results, and evaluate skills in handling those problems.

Finally, skill training is time and resource intensive. We need to design technology that will enhance the instructor's ability to demonstrate, train, and drill students on the key skill activities without incurring expensive instructor time. This is an area in which videotape and other computer/simulation technology can make a huge contribution, in creating significant behavior models of best skill practices, exhibiting the key behaviors that negotiators should exhibit, and providing students with personalized feedback against these standards of performance.

I understand that negotiation is ultimately complex, far more than the sum of its parts. I am suggesting that we may not do justice to the education process by trying to teach that complexity all at once (through large-scale and complex simulation dynamics). The novice negotiator may be better served if instruction began with simple component skill development.

6. We must revive and sustain an ongoing dialogue about teaching in the profession.

Unfortunately, unlike in the legal field (as noted by Williams and Geis, in this volume), there has been little, if any, systematic polling and tracking of what is taught, how it is taught, or discussion of what should be taught in a negotiations course or seminar within the management discipline. There are probably several reasons for this failure to structure a dialogue.

First, the field has been highly successful. Instructors teaching this subject at major business schools are saturated with student demand and are able to meet the demand with the existing course models.

Second, the field has been truly profitable for many of us. Not only are we able to teach an elective course which significantly overlaps our research interests, but we can often marry the two by collecting data in the classroom for research publications. Moreover, with a little spit and polish, the approach translates easily into executive education modules and customized in-house corporate training programs. We are certainly not about to behead the golden goose while it is still laying eggs!

Third, there is no organized group of professional practice, as there is in law, which is evaluating, critiquing, or accrediting relative to what the profession requires of graduates. While there has been some pressure to adapt the discipline to the changing nature of the organizations noted above, there are no minimum standards of any kind to which we are accountable. The market success of the product is the only ongoing standard of accountability we have.

Fourth, though negotiation is an applied professional discipline, the predominance of research values in academic institutions has constrained inquiry on pedagogy. We have simply not encouraged faculty in our own original disciplines to evaluate the adequacy of our pedagogy. The field would be considerably healthier if both master researchers and master teachers came together to discuss what and how we are teaching in negotiation and sought to move beyond the simple amalgamation of approaches and techniques to some clearly distinct strategies whose effectiveness can be measured and tested.

7. We should try to determine whether the current "eclectic model" of teaching negotiation—theory, role playing and practice, and back-home applications—actually produces changed cognitions and changed behavior.
Coincident with a major dialogue on pedagogy is an effort to undertake the "dismal" science of evaluation research. While this field has relied very heavily on the experiential learning methodology featuring role play and simulation, we have no idea whether the learning derived from these courses and seminars really "takes." Can those who go through this

180

training translate their new-found skills into more effective real-world negotiation? This is a major issue for both the training of students and managers.

Few of us have ever seriously followed up with students or executives to determine whether they were more capable of effectively negotiating as a result of the training. My experience with one consulting client sheds some light on this problem. After training approximately 40 sales managers in several multiple-day seminars, management and I monitored their negotiations on the job. Most *thought* they had developed a moderately sophisticated understanding of how to convert their sales negotiations from transactional events into customer-focused dialogues which actively pursued needs and interests, yet managed to hold the line on the price of the product.

However, in both simulated and real sales calls, most could not successfully achieve this outcome when dealing with a simulated customer, let alone a real one! Working with the client's sales training staff, my colleagues and I needed six months of ongoing effort to train and develop these skills in a small "high potential" group of sales people. We extensively employed one-on-one clinical observation and coaching, videotape analysis, and apprenticeship with senior sales managers before they were clearly ready to effectively address a variety of complex customer deals.

In short, my own experience indicates that much negotiation training is involving and fun, but at the same time largely cosmetic and superficial, particularly if we really hope to develop the acquisition of strong skills that can be transferred to new problems.[4] It is remarkable, I think, that neither our corporate clients nor our students have demanded greater accountability, given the total dollars invested in this industry. And if this is the problem that exists among those of us who are university-based, imagine what may (or may not) result from those whose only exposure to negotiation training is through "how to do it" books, one-day seminars, or audio tapes! We deserve to ask these questions of our own profession, and we deserve to examine the answers with an open mind. We may find that we are having far more impact than we think—but we also may find the opposite.

Summary

This chapter has outlined the development of pedagogy in negotiation, particularly in the management and business disciplines. The past two decades have witnessed a boom economy in this field, characterized by a rapidly growing research base to support the pedagogy, a surge in demand for courses and seminars, and a rich collection of texts, role plays, and cases. After two decades of success, we are seeing a research shift toward understanding negotiation less as a transactional process, and more as a process embedded within long-term business or personal relationships, and within specific relational contexts. As theory and pedagogy attempt to embrace the additional (but important) complexity introduced by the relational context, (e.g. gender and nationality of the negotiators, long-term objectives of the relationship, etc.), we will see a shift not only in how we create meaningful negotiation training, but also in what we consider to be most relevant.

181

This theoretical shift also requires us to focus more strongly on training methods and training effectiveness and to test the appropriateness of the theory, the amalgamation of methodologies, and our overall effectiveness in training people to be more effective negotiators.

Acknowledgment

Selected parts of this paper were previously presented at a tribute conference to Robert Coulson upon his retirement from the American Arbitration Association, March 1994.

Notes

1. For a review of the approaches to teaching negotiation in the early 1980s, including key themes, contributing disciplines, and available resource materials, see Lewicki (1981).
2. Elsewhere, I argue that these are also the dominant research themes for the past three decades (Lewicki, Weiss, and Lewin 1992).
3. Dispute resolution courses in business schools are dominantly courses in negotiation. Third party roles are often addressed within this context, but usually not extensively. With the exception of specific courses in dispute settlement taught in labor relations programs, few if any courses in third-party behavior exist in business schools.
4. The problem is not unique to negotiation training; the broad field of executive education has periodically come under similar criticism (cf. Fuchsberg, *Wall Street Journal,* September 10, 1993).

References

Alinsky, S. 1971. *Rules for radicals.* New York: Random House.
Bazerman, M. and R. J. Lewicki. 1983. *Negotiating in organizations.* Beverly Hills, CA: Sage Publications.
Bazerman, M. and M. Neale. 1992. *Negotiating rationally.* New York: Free Press.
Brett, J., L. Greenhalgh, D. Kolb, R. J. Lewicki, and B. Sheppard. 1985. *The manager as negotiator and dispute resolver.* Washington, DC: National Institute for Dispute Resolution.
Deutsch, M. 1973. *The resolution of conflict.* New Haven, CT: Yale University Press.
Douglas, A. 1962. *Industrial peacemaking.* New York: Columbia University Press.
Edelman, P. B. 1989. *Evaluation of the program in higher education of the National Institute for Dispute Resolution.* Washington, DC: National Institute for Dispute Resolution.
Fisher, R. 1969. *International conflict for beginners.* New York: Harper & Row.
Fisher, R. and W. Ury W. 1981. *Getting to YES.* Boston, MA: Houghton Mifflin.
Fisher, R., W. Ury, and B. Patton. 1991. *Getting to YES.* 2nd edition. Boston, MA: Houghton Mifflin.
Foster, D. A. 1992. *Bargaining across borders: How to negotiate successfully anywhere in the world.* New York, NY: McGraw Hill.

Fuchsberg, G. 1993. Taking control. *Wall Street Journal Special Reports,* September 10.

Goleman, D. 1995. *Emotional intelligence.* New York: Bantam Books.

Hofstede, G. 1991. *Culture and organizations: Software of the mind.* London, UK: McGraw Hill.

Janosik, R. J. 1987. Rethinking the culture-negotiation link. *Negotiation Journal* 3: 385-395.

Karrass, C. 1974. *Give and take.* New York: Thomas Y. Crowell.

Kolb, D. A. 1974. Management and the learning process. In Kolb, D. A., J. Z. Rubin, and J. McIntyre (eds.) *Organizational psychology: A book of readings.* Englewood Cliffs, NJ: Prentice Hall.

Kolb, D. and G. G. Coolidge. 1991. Her place at the table: A consideration of gender issues in negotiation. In J. Z. Rubin and J. W. Breslin (eds.) *Negotiation theory and practice.* Cambridge, MA: Program on Negotiation at Harvard Law School.

Kramer, R. and T. Tyler. 1996. *Trust in organizations.* Thousand Oaks, CA: Sage.

Lax, D. and J. Sebenius. 1986. *The manager as negotiator.* New York: Free Press.

Lewicki, R. J. 1975. A course in bargaining and negotiation. *The Teaching of Organizational Behavior* 1(1):35-40.

Lewicki, R. J. 1981. Bargaining and negotiation: A review of the literature. *Exchange: The Organizational Behavior Teaching Journal* 6(3): 33-42.

Lewicki, R. J. 1986. Challenges of teaching negotiation. *Negotiation Journal* 2(1):15-27.

Lewicki, R. J. and B. B. Bunker. 1995. Trust in relationships: A model of trust development and decline. In Bunker, B. B. and J. Z. Rubin (eds.) *Conflict, cooperation and justice: A tribute volume to Morton Deutsch.* San Francisco: Jossey Bass.

Lewicki, R. J. and B. B. Bunker. 1996. Developing, maintaining and repairing trust in work relationships. In Kramer, R. and T. Tyler. *Trust in organizations.* Thousand Oaks, CA: Sage.

Lewicki, R. H., B. B. Bunker, and M. H. Stevenson. 1997. *The three components of interpersonal trust: Instrument development and differences across relationships.* Working Paper Series, The Ohio State University.

Lewicki, R. J., J. Litterer, J. Minton, and D. Saunders. 1994. *Negotiation.* 2nd edition. Burr Ridge, IL: Richard D. Irwin.

Lewicki, R. J., D. Litterer, D. Saunders and J. Minton. 1993. *Negotiation: Readings, exercises and cases.* Second Edition. Burr Ridge, IL: Richard D. Irwin.

Lewicki, R. J., D. McAllister, and R. Bies. 1997. *Trust and distrust: New relationships and realities.* Working Paper Series, The Ohio State University.

Lewicki, R. J. and M. H. Stevenson. 1997. Trust development in negotiation: Proposed actions and a research agenda. Paper presented to a conference, "Trust in business: Barriers and Bridges." Loyola University, February.

Lewicki, R. J., S. Weiss, and D. Lewin. 1992. Models of conflict, negotiation and third party intervention: A review and synthesis. *Journal of Organizational Behavior* 13(3): 209-254.

Luce, R. D. and H. Raiffa. 1957. *Games and decisions: Introduction and critical survey.* New York: John Wiley.

Murnighan, K. 1991. *Dynamics of bargaining games.* Englewood Cliffs, N.J.: Prentice Hall.

Negotiator Pro. 1993. Brookline, MA: Beacon Expert Systems.

Nierenberg, G. 1973. *Fundamentals of negotiating.* New York: Hawthorn.

Porter, L. and L. McKibbin. 1988. *Management education: Drift or thrust into the 21st Century?* New York: McGraw Hill.

Rackham, N. 1980. The behavior of successful negotiators. In Lewicki, R., J. Litterer, D. Saunder, and J. Minton. *Negotiation: Readings, exercises and cases.* Burr Ridge, IL: Richard D. Irwin.

Raiffa, H. 1982. *The art and science of negotiation.* Cambridge, MA: Harvard University Press.

Rapaport, A. 1960. *Fights, games and debates.* Ann Arbor, MI: University of Michigan Press.

Rubin, J. Z. and B. E. Brown. 1975. *The social psychology of bargaining and negotiation.* New York: Academic Press.

Rubin, J. Z. and C. Rubin. 1989. *When families fight.* New York: Morrow.

Rubin, J., D. Pruitt, and S. Kim, 1994. *Social conflict: Escalation, stalemate and settlement.* New York: McGraw Hill.

Saunders, D. and R. J. Lewicki. 1995. Teaching negotiation with computer simulations: Pedagogical and practical considerations. *Negotiation Journal* 11(2)159-167.

Saunders, D. and J. Roston. 1993. *The McGill Negotiation Simulator.* Montreal, Qu: McGill University.

Schelling, T. 1960. *The strategy of conflict.* Cambridge, MA: Harvard University Press.

Seigel, S. and L. E. Fouraker. 1960. *Bargaining and group decision making: Experiments in bilateral monopoly.* New York: McGraw Hill.

Shell, R. G. 1995. Computer-assisted negotiation and mediation: Where are we and where are we going? *Negotiation Journal* 11(2): 117-121.

Sheppard, B. H. and M. Tuchinsky. 1995. Micro-OB and the network organization. In Kramer, R. and T. Tyler. *Trust in organizations.* Thousand Oaks, CA: Sage.

Walton, R. E. and R. B. McKersie, 1965. *A behavioral theory of labor negotiation.* New York: McGraw Hill.

Weiss, S. E. 1993. Analysis of complex negotiations in international business: The RBC perspective. *Organizational Science* 4: 269-300.

Weiss, S. E. 1997. One impasse, one agreement: Explaining the outcomes of two international joint venture negotiations. In Lewicki, R. J., R. Bies and B. H. Sheppard. *Research on negotiaiton in organizations,* Vol 6. Greenwich, CT: JAI.

Weiss, S. and W. Stripp. 1985. *Negotiating with foreign businesspersons: An introduction for Americans with propositions for six cultures.* New York, New York University Graduate School of Business Administration, Working paper #85-6.

Wheeler, M. 1995. Computers and negotiation: Backing into the future. *Negotiation Journal* 11(2):169-176.

Zartman, I. W. 1997. The structuralist dilemma in negotiation. In Lewicki, R. J., R. Bies, and B. H. Sheppard. *Research on negotiaiton in organizations,* Vol 6. Greenwich, CT: JAI.

A Conflict Management Curriculum
In Business and Public Administration

C. Gregory Buntz and Donald L. Carper

C. Gregory Buntz is
Professor of Public
Management in the
School of Business and
Public Administration at
the University of the
Pacific, Stockton,
California 95211.

Donald L. Carper is
an Associate Professor
of Business Law in the
Department of Organi-
zational Behavior and
Environment at Califor-
nia State University,
Sacramento, Californira
95819.

New methods of dispute resolution are being developed and applied to an ever-widening array of problems, from family to commercial disputes and a growing number of public interest disputes. In addition to these new methods and applications, managers in growing numbers are recognizing that conflict is not pathological, that it need not be avoided, and that it can be managed toward productive ends.

In many ways, it seems that practice is leading theory in this field—or is, at least, leading teaching and research in management schools. Consequently there is a need to synthe-size theory and experience and to think systematically about education, training, research, and service in conflict management and dispute resolution. In this article, our goal is to explain why managers need to be competent in conflict management and dispute resolution, the particular competencies they need, and approaches to teaching those competencies. Though our focus here is on the teaching of conflict management and dispute resolution skills in business and public management educa-tion, we believe many of these ideas will be of interest to edu-cators from other disciplines.

The Need in Management Education

Conflict is an inevitable part of organizational life; indeed, one could argue that conflict is necessary to sustain dynamic and viable organizations. As such, managers in both the public and private sectors are regularly faced with intra- and interorganizational conflict situations that must be managed in order for their organizations to achieve missions and goals effectively.

There is a need for generalist managers who can think broadly about conflict (i.e.. about both its productive and its de-structive consequences) and who can apply conflict management skills to direct organizational conflict to productive ends. There is also a need for persons who possess specific dispute resolution

This article first
appeared in
Negotiation Journal, April
1987: Volume 3,
Number 2, pages
191-204.

skills—negotiation and mediation skills for example—to apply those skills as neutrals in disputes (for example, mediators, arbitrators, ombudspersons, or administrators of dispute resolution organizations). Each of these two types of managers will now be addressed in turn.

The Generalist Manager

All managers are, to some extent, conflict managers and dispute resolvers. "General managers," for instance, might have to deal with a dispute between a design engineer and a production supervisor over the introduction of a design innovation. Or, consider supervisors of social workers who have to manage the conflict associated with the introduction of a new evaluation system for case workers.

Effective managers in either the private or public sectors must have a broad view of the world which allows them to think comprehensively and strategically about conflict and conflict management as opposed to narrowly and bureaucratically (Green 1984). As an example, consider the popular television show "Hill Street Blues." Captain Furillo, the general manager of Hill Street Precinct, is a public manager who is called on daily to mediate in a swirl of conflicting interests. He must deal with:

•an egomaniac chief of police who regularly places his personal interests above those of the department and public he is supposed to serve;
•some of his own detectives who skate an ethical fine line in the pursuit of the law enforcement mission (Lt. Buntz, for example);
•a psychopathic, and at times pathetically hawkish Lt. Hunter, and a sympathetic, and at times self-righteous Lt. Goldblume;
•a variety of personalities and personal problems among his uniformed officers;
•an overburdened court system that many of his officers see as unduly restrictive;
•a public defender (who happens also to be his wife) whose duties often place her in conflict with Furillo and his officers;
•an unappreciative and suspicious public;
•youth gangs and other law breakers;
•social agencies, the missions of which are frequently in conflict with law enforcement; and
•overhead agencies within the police department (accounting, budgeting, personnel) which often restrict his free-flowing and nonbureaucratic style.

Like many generalist public managers, Furillo, to be effective in terms of his organization's mission, must, at various times, be a facilitator, a problem solver, a decision maker, a collaborator, a negotiator, a confessor, a counselor, a stimulator of change, and an administrator who can maintain order in a highly chaotic situation. In short, Furillo must be a conflict manager. This means he must value conflict for its productive possibilities and be wary of its destructive potential. He must understand how his approach to conflict management will affect his relationship with those with whom he must work (and live), and how it will affect the relationships among the others "on the Hill."

Frank Furillo is a character from fiction, but his character seems to be a fairly good reflection of the reality of life for many public managers. City managers, for example, must mediate the conflicting interests of their staff members, their elected bosses, the constituents of various city departments, "good government" and other interest groups, personnel and budget agencies, other communities, and various intergovernmental actors (for instance, state and federal officials who often mandate organizational mission without providing budget support). In order to work effectively with all of these groups, and to keep the diverse units of local government operating effectively and efficiently, city managers must be conflict managers with vision.

Private managers may not be required to reconcile competing interests in quite as public a way as public servants, but the complexity of interests to be considered is similar. Both the interorganizational and extra-organizational environments are spawning grounds for conflict as the result of the many diverse interests that exist and frequently compete there. Private managers often must reconcile short-term with long-term goals. They must deal with the competing demands of majority and minority shareholders, directors, employees, consumers, government, competitors, and the general public. The need for private organizations to have management generalists who can reconcile social interests may be critical to organizational prosperity. As just one example, consider the current social concern about divestiture of U.S. business interests in South Africa. Additionally, other organizations are being required to deal with product-tampering problems which potentially could devastate the market for those products. The skills and abilities required to deal with such problems should be part of the educational preparation of generalist business managers.

Historically, there seems to have been little interest in teaching conflict management skills to managers and evaluating managers on the basis of those skills. Generations have studied and discussed leadership, communications, and interpersonal skills in depth without recognizing that, until recently, these add up to an ability to find "win-win" solutions to organizational problems. It now appears that conflict management may be one of the most important things managers do, and their success at it may be a major reason for their ability to ascend and stay atop the organizational hierarchy.

The Specialist Dispute Resolver
Besides generalist managers who have well-developed conflict management skills, there is a corresponding need for specialists who can serve as administrators of dispute resolution processes or as third party dispute resolvers. All such conflict managers should be able to function in both public and private sector disputes.

Specialist dispute resolvers are gradually becoming common in the United States. Though one might not expect this service area to experience the same phenomenal growth that occurred in a related field—the consulting firm—one can't ignore the fledgling private and public entities that are arising specifically to assist others in resolving their problems. These new organizations may or may not become strong and permanent enterprises; eventually, however, we suspect that such organizations will be available on a routine basis for ad hoc extrajudicial assistance. In addition, permanent staff interveners are increasingly being suggested as part of a management team.

Most major disputes requiring third party intervention cross public and private lines. For example, ADR has been used to help settle community, criminal and civil disputes, divorce and child custody problems, adoptions, personal injury cases involving both private and governmental entities, and environmental and siting disputes. It's also been used as a tool in social service agency administrative hearings and in negotiated rule making by governmental regulatory agencies. Persons skilled in negotiation, mediation, facilitation, or collaborative problem solving could serve as neutrals to assist the parties in resolving disputes in any of these areas. Graduates of programs who undertake an emphasis in conflict management and dispute resolution could also be effective managers of public or private dispute resolution organizations in all three sectors (public, private, and private not-for-profit).

Managers skilled in conflict management and dispute resolution could also be called on to intervene in commercial conflicts, such as those over the terms of construction contracts; in interorganizational disputes, such as those between a parent company and a subsidiary; and in the negotiation of business deals in any number of settings, including those in the international arena. Some of these may lie clearly in the private sector, but many will spill over into the public.

Given the fledgling status of ad hoc dispute resolution, the background and skills of persons offering themselves as conflict intervenors can perhaps best be described as varied. However, a significant number of individuals providing their services as specialists in dispute resolution have backgrounds in law or labor relations. Lawyers familiar with the formal dispute resolution processes of the courts provide a ready resource of professionals with an inclination toward problem processing, if not resolution. Lawyers will also often carry the biases and inclinations of the formal system with which they are most familiar. Conflict resolvers who have emerged from a labor/management background likewise have a familarity with a particular type of conflict. With that background they also potentially carry biases about how best to resolve conflict. Specialist training in conflict management in the universities should provide managers with skills to act as dispute resolvers with knowledge of a variety of processes and without vested interests in any one type of forum.

What Do Managers Need to Learn?

While there might be some debate over the specific skills and knowledge needed by conflict managers, there is widespread agreement that they need a combination of theoretical knowledge and practical skills gained through study in the classroom and application in the field. This is true both for specialists and generalists. There is clearly also agreement on the fact that the knowledge base for managers of conflict is multidisciplinary. Forming much of this knowledge base are such areas of study as decision theory, logic, interpersonal and organizational behavior, game theory, communications, and legal reasoning and processes, among others. On the practical side, managers of conflict also need skills from a multidisciplinary list. Topics on such a list would include negotiation, strategy formulation, facilitation, argumentation, persuasion, fact finding, systems analysis, and the ability to take risks and creatively put together integrative agreements.

As an aid to thinking systematically about the range of knowledge, skills, values, and behaviors needed by conflict managers consider the outline shown in Figure 1. This list was modeled on a matrix developed in 1974 by the National Association of Schools of Public Affairs and Administration (NASPAA 1974) as an indicator of competencies needed by graduates of master's degree programs in public administration.

The outline lists competencies in six major subject matter areas. They are:

(1) the disputing context (the broad environment within which the dispute takes place);

(2) analytical tools (such as decision analysis and game theory which are useful for understanding disputes and selecting interventions);

(3) individual, group, and organizational dynamics (behavioral areas useful for understanding such elements of conflict management as the dynamics of conflict escalation and third party intervention);

(4) intervention tools (techniques, strategies, and tactics useful for managing and resolving conflicts);

(5) communications (includes the study of methods of information transmission and behaviors designed to facilitate problem solving); and

(6) management processes (the use of concepts such as planning and organizational development in conflict and conflict management).

Within each of these areas are listed divisions of knowledge (awareness and understanding); skills (conceptual, analytical, and interpersonal abilities); conflict management values to which conflict managers and dispute resolvers should be committed; and behaviors (personal attitudes and actions of the manager) which should be evidenced by managers committed to conflict management.

Figure 1 reflects our synthesis of current thinking on the competencies needed by both generalist and specialist conflict managers. Both the subject matter headings and the specific elements in this outline represent an amalgam of the work of many different authors. In addition, Figure 1 represents the results of a search of recent literature on teaching in this area and to a lesser extent some of the ideas contained in the original NASPAA matrix. This outline is not intended to represent a complete degree program, nor even a specialty within a degree program. Also, it is doubtlessly neither complete nor perfect. However, we believe it does represent a good start at identifying the knowledge, skills, values, and behaviors which professionally competent conflict managers should possess. Clearly, some will need to be more skilled than others in various elements of the subject matter. Just how much, and where to place the emphasis, depends upon whether one is intending to specialize in dispute resolution or be a generalist manager. The emphasis will also depend, to some degree, on whether the eventual goal is work in the public or private sector.

Figure 1. Professional Competencies Needed by Conflict Managers

Disputing Context
1. Knowledge of:
    a. Conflict sources, dynamics, productive and destructive consequences
    b. Cultural and social mores and norms including law
    c. Political and social values and processes
    e. Economic systems, incentives, and controls
    f. Governmental institutions, powers procedures, and relationships
    g. The impact of environmental factors on the process of conflict
2. Skills in:
    a. Analysis and interpretation of environmental forces and trends
    b. Application of knowledge about the context to conflicts and disputes
    c. Conflict analysis—party, problem, and interest identification
3. Conflict management values represented by knowledge of and commitment to:
    a. Fairness/justice/equity
    b. Peaceful resolution of disputes
    c. Alternatives to litigation as a means of dispute resolution
    d. Equal access to dispute resolution processes
    e. Ownership of the dispute by the parties
    f. Standards of professional conduct and ethics
4. Behavior represented by:
    a. Tolerance of diverse views of other persons and groups
    b. Tolerance of ambiguity and complexity
    c. Capacity to be flexible and to adjust to changing needs and demands
    d. Ability to function as a facilitator of change

Analytical Tools
1. Knowledge of
    a. Game theory, decision theory, logic, modeling
    b. Social exchange theory
    c. Economic analysis, tradeoff analysis, benefit/cost analysis
    d. Systems analysis, organizational and interorganizational analysis
    e. Fact finding and legal research
2 Skills in:
    a. Conflict analysis and diagnosis
    b. Problem identification
    c. Application of conceptual analytical knowledge
    d. Design of problem-solving systems

e. Recognizing integrative possibilities in distributive situations
3. Conflict management values represented by knowledge of and commitment to:
   a. Objectivity and rationality
   b. Impartial inquiry and investigation
   c. Working to keep problems solved
   d. Principled bargaining
4. Behavior represented by:
   a. Personal involvement in data collection and analysis
   b. Familarity with a variety of research methods
   c. Use of the results of analysis to forge agreements
   d. Use of the art and science of creative problem solving

Individual/Group/Organizational Dynamics
1. Knowledge of:
   a. Individual and group behavior; e.g., individual motivation, dynamics of groups, leadership, power and influence
   b. Organizational structure, processes and dynamics
   c. Communications theory and processes
   d. Interorganizational theory and behavior
   e. The phenomenon of psychological entrapment and methods of avoiding it
   f. Systems thinking
2. Skills in:
   a. Motivation and leadership
   b. Interpersonal and group relationships
   c. Identification of sources of organizational and personal power and influence
   d. Organizational design
   e. Application of appropriate models of leadership, decision making and change
   f. Organizational systems analysis
3. Conflict management values represented by:
   a. Protection of individual rights
   b. Fostering of individual welfare
   c. Promotion of efficiency, effectiveness, and equity
   d. Reconciliation of individual interests and needs with group and organizational interests and needs
   e. Recognizing that organizational conflict is neither good nor bad per se

4. Behavior represented by:
    a. Genuineness and integrity in personal and organizational
       relationships
    b. Action designed to preserve and enhance relationships
    c. Positive attitudes concerning the contribution conflict can
       make to personal and organizational growth
    d. An unwillingness to let conflict deteriorate into personal
       attacks and psychological or physical injury
    e. Recognition and understanding of the fact that there is no
       "one best way" to manage organizational conflict

Intervention Tools
1. Knowledge of:
    a. The problem-solving process
    b. Traditional forms of dispute resolution, e.g., litigation
    c. Alternative conflict handling modes, e.g., competition, compromise,
       accommodation, avoidance, and collaboration
    d. The negotiation process and the principal forms of
       bargaining—distributive and integrative
    e. Bargaining strategy and tactics
    f. Mediation, facilitation, arbitration, and other forms of alternative
       dispute resolution
2. Skills in:
    a. Fact-finding
    b. Facilitating group decision making
    c. Communication—oral and written
    d. Interpreting needs and interests
    e. Advocacy
    f. Negotiation, mediation, arbitration and collaborative problem
       solving
3. Conflict management values represented by:
    a. Adherence to standards of justice and fairness
    b. Belief in principled bargaining
    c. Adherence to high ethical standards whether participating as a
       neutral or an advocate
    d. A willingness to search long and hard for alternative solutions
       to problems
    e. Respect for the legitimacy of opponent's interests

4. Behavior represented by:

a Openness and risk taking in problem-solving situations

b. A principled approach to bargaining wherein attempts are made to create rather than claim value

c. The creation of trusting and supportive environments for problem solving

d. Engaging in alternative thinking—"brainstorming" alternative solutions and consequences

e. Action taken to expand problems so as to bring uncontrolled variables under control

Communications

1. Knowledge of:

a. The communications process

b. Barriers to effective communication and methods to overcome them

c. The role of perceptions in communication

d. The role of questioning in negotiation

e. The importance of information exchange and the impact of location and setting on problem-solving behavior

2. Skills in:

a Oral and written communications, persuasion, and argumentation

b. Dealing with barriers to effective communication

c. Active listening

d. Interpretation of body language

e. Formulation of effective questions and answers

3. Conflict management values represented by:

a. A commitment to openness and honesty

b. Measures to increase the level and quality of participation in meetings

c. Concern for the level of accuracy in communications

d. Procedures for disclosure of an appropriate level of information

4. Behavior represented by:

a. An ability to synthesize and integrate information toward common objectives

b. Active participation in problem-solving meetings

c. Engaging in active listening

d. Rewarding risk taking and the honest sharing of feelings

e. Being trusting and supportive as opposed to defensive and negative

Management Processes
1. Knowledge of:
   a. Methods of planning and implementation
   b. Management systems and processes including leadership, decision making, and organizational development and change
   c. Monitoring and evaluation (in order to "keep problems solved")
2. Skills in:
   a. Conceptualizing, goal setting, program development and entrepreneurship
   b. Program/problem assessment and review
   c. Making decisions and managing change
3. Conflict management values represented by knowledge of and commitment to:
   a. The role and use of organizations and management processes to resolve disputes
   b. Standards of individual and organizational integrity and performance
   c. A working environment conducive to conceptualizing, planning, and collaboration
4. Behavior represented by:
   a. Openness to new ideas and proposals
   b. Long-term thinking
   c. Planning and preparation prior to entering negotiations
   d. Recognition and consideration of strengths and weaknesses of one's self and others

Teaching Conflict Management and Dispute Resolution in Business and Public Administration Programs

Some conflict management skills and behaviors may be best learned through experience; knowledge of theory, and methods of application, however, are best taught in the classroom. Values are learned in a variety of ways. Those related to professional socialization are perhaps best taught through a combination of experience and classroom exposure. Others are well ingrained long before students arrive at the doors of academe.

This all suggests that an eclectic program that combines theory and practice through lectures and exercises in the classroom with internships, field or clinical work, and student research efforts is the appropriate model in this field. This would seem to be true whatever the disciplinary base of the program. In fact Eric Green (1984, p. 245), in describing his law school seminar on ADR, notes that he focuses on "building a conceptual framework of dispute resolution within which one can understand the essential characteristics and dynamics of the full range of dispute resolution processes in an interdisciplinary course that attempts to unite the conceptual with the practical." A number of authors writing on the teaching of negotiation and related conflict management subjects recommend a similar multidisciplinary/theory-related-to-practice/clinical and classroom approach (Davis and Dugan 1982; Hall 1986; Patton 1985; Raiffa 1985; Riskin 1984; Sander 1984; and Wedge and Sandole 1982).

In this article, our primary focus is on training business and public managers to be conflict managers/dispute resolvers within the context of existing degree programs. We recognize, however, that nondegree-related training can (and indeed should) be provided through seminars, workshops, and certificate programs offered through the auspices of schools of management. The number of such programs currently in existence is testimony to the importance of the subject matter to working business and public managers.

As just two examples, consider the Northwestern University program on managerial negotiations and a recent Santa Clara University Business School program on alternative dispute resolution in business. The Santa Clara program highlighted dispute resolution in the Silicon Valley of California and considered ways for lawyers, businesspersons, and engineers to collaborate in dispute resolution and resolving technology-related disputes. The Kellogg School of Management (Northwestern) program was designed to help managers learn techniques for analyzing and preparing for negotiations, and to enable them to practice mediation and negotiating skills. To be sure, there are others, and there are excellent and long-standing programs offered in other disciplinary settings, but these are examples of what is being done within the context of training in management.

In terms of pedagogy, there is widespread agreement that effective learning in the field of conflict management/dispute resolution depends upon the use of simulations, exercises, and cases that will give participants experience in negotiation, mediation, or whatever particular subject is being taught. Our own experience with the experiential approach bears this out. It is also highly recommended that video technology be used as teaching/learning aids both to show examples of dispute resolution in action (e.g., tapes produced and distributed by the American Arbitration Association), and to tape classroom negotiation sessions for later review and critique. We have found this to be a highly effective way to help students learn and develop conflict management skills and behaviors—it also adds some fun and excitement to the learning.

What is Currently being Done?
Curricula
Within the context of management education, we know of no nonlabor degree programs or concentrations in dispute resolution, though courses in negotiation and bargaining have been in existence in business schools for a long time. Courses in managerial negotiation are a newer phenomena, and do seem to be taking hold. A recently published directory of dispute resolution courses and internships in Northern California (Hastings College of Law 1986) lists some 44 nonlabor courses in conflict resolution and negotiation offered through

a variety of academic departments in some 33 Bay Area universities. The 1986-87 directory of Boston area courses and internships lists approximately the same number (Program on Negotiation at Harvard Law School 1986).

A recently completed survey of over 500 institutions of higher education in the U.S. identified "838 courses taught by 636 instructors in 294 institutions across 43 states" (Wehr 1986). It appears that close to 800 of these are nonlabor courses. The survey, conducted by researchers at the University of Colorado, also reports that approximately 40 percent of the courses are offered in business and public administration-related disciplines. About 35 percent are offered in the fields of law, sociology/anthropology, and communications/speech. The remaining 25 percent are spread among 15 other disciplines.

Figure 2 shows the distribution of courses found by the Colorado research team in business and public administration fields.

Figure 2. Conflict Resolution Courses in Business Degree Programs in the U.S.

Discipline	Courses	Percent
Government/political science	126	15.0
Business/Commerce	94	11.2
Management/Organization	70	8.3
Administration/Planning	35	4.1
Human Resources Management	9	1.0

In addition to courses, law and other nonmanagement schools are offering certificate programs, specializations in conflict and alternative dispute resolution, and in at least one case a master's degree in conflict management. For example, George Mason University offers a Master of Arts in Sociology with a concentration in conflict analysis and conflict management as well as a Master of Science degree in Conflict Management. The University of Colorado offers a concentration in Social Conflict in its graduate and undergraduate programs in sociology. And, at Harvard University and the Massachusetts Institute of Technology, a joint Ph.D. program in dispute resolution is in the very early discussion stages.

Development of Course Materials
In 1985, the National Institute of Dispute Resolution (NIDR) began a modest grant program to support, among other things, the development of course materials on dispute resolution. NIDR has awarded 19 grants to develop teaching materials, five textbook grants, and has commissioned and published two volumes of dispute resolution teaching materials for business schools. Most of these materials would seem to be appropriate for both business and public management schools. Some excellent case materials applicable to both the public and private sectors are also available from the Program on Negotiation at Harvard Law School (1985).

Among the newer texts on the subject of conflict management and dispute resolution, the reader will probably find books by the following authors particularly helpful: Brown (1980); Goldberg, et al. (1986); Juergensmeyer (1984); Moore (1986); Lax and Sebenius (1986); Pruitt and Rubin (1986); and Lewicki and Litterer (1985a and 1985b).

Integration Into a Specific Course
One course that is taken by virtually all business administration and many public administration students is law. Whether the law course is called business law, law for business or legal environment of business, part of the content will include an introduction to legal process, systems and theory.

The modern trend in such courses is to increase foundational material and also introduce both legal reasoning and elementary ethical reasoning. In addition, almost every law course provides some investigation of formal dispute resolution processes. Until recently, such study was done without any consideration of alternative processes. This practice probably continues in most courses where study is focused on the courts as formal institutions and the manner in which the court system is used to process disputes. Many courses also cover the less formal (in most cases) administrative law hearing process.

The integration of material on alternative approaches to formal legal resolution of disputes fits perfectly as part of this introductory law course. There are two ways such integration becomes both logical and important. First, it serves as an early introduction to management of organizational problems. It suggests to students that even legal disputes often lend themselves to direct action by management rather than passive delegation to legal specialists. Second, early introduction of students to ADR (even if done only briefly) should encourage student receptivity to further consideration of such concepts in the remainder of their program of study. At least two recent texts in this area suggest that some authors are aware of the importance of the early introduction of conflict resolution techniques (Fisher and Jennings 1986; and Lieberman and Seidler 1986). This contrasts with most texts which provide usually no more than a paragraph on ADR, with arbitration the only technique covered.

Recommendations
We recognize that there is no one best way to structure and deliver programs for business and public managers in the area of conflict management and dispute resolution. We also recognize, however, that the need is great and we urge faculty and administrators in management schools to consider their options and do something. Programmatically, that "something" could include: (1) a concentration or emphasis area in conflict management and dispute resolution similar in structure to concentrations in functional areas such as personnel or marketing; (2) an integrative approach in which topics from the outline of professional competencies shown in Figure 1 are blended into existing management courses; (3) the creation of a certificate program that would include courses from the school of administration and other schools, and which would enable students to pursue their own degrees as well

as the certificate; (4) the addition of a required course (or an elective if administrative constraints prohibit a new requirement) in conflict management and dispute resolution that would survey the essential topics; or (5) the creation or strengthening of joint degree programs, such as between law and business or law and public administration, which emphasize ADR along with legal training.

Typically; concentrations in business or public management include four courses. A concentration in conflict management/dispute resolution, then, might consist of the following:

Conflict and Conflict Management
A survey of the theoretical literature on conflict emphasizing its productive as well as destructive consequences. A focus on integrative approaches to conflict management which recognizes conflict stimulation and conflict resolution as management techniques.

Alternative Dispute Resolution
In-depth study of modern ADR techniques including negotiation, mediation and arbitration. A focus on applications in a number of areas including environmental, commercial and international disputes.

Managerial Negotiations
An experiential course which focuses on the role of the manager as negotiator. Coverage would include readings and cases and exercises in distributive and integrative bargaining.

Seminar in Conflict Management
A case analysis course which would integrate material from the other three and which could involve students in the resolution (or simulated resolution) of some particular dispute of current interest.

One example of an integrative approach has already been given with the case of business law. There are a number of other courses in the typical business and public management curricula where such integration could take place. Among the most obvious are the organization and management course where knowledge and skills in disputing and the management of conflict could be introduced in the discussion of individual and group dynamics. Personnel courses are also obvious candidates for the introduction of material on interpersonal conflict and its management. The business and society or administrative ethics courses could also benefit from the introduction of conflict theory and alternative approaches to conflict management. The cases which are typically studied in such courses frequently involve public interest disputes and students could benefit from the application of conflict based analytical frameworks with such case studies.

With regard to the certificate idea, the bounds of courses and disciplines represented in such a program are limited only by the imagination and biases of the originators and the administrative and political dragons they must slay to put a program together. In a perfect world, we would design a certificate program to include seven courses. One to three courses would be required, and the remainder would be carefully chosen to reflect the interests of the student and the best available courses on campus or on the campuses of collaborating institutions.

We believe there are three key considerations in the design of certificate programs. First, there must be an introductory course which all students would take and it would be desirable to include a required capstone seminar. Second, one cannot simply throw together courses on the basis of catalog descriptions. The courses must be carefully and logically chosen, and instructors must be aware that their particular courses are being included in the program. Third, the program must truly be multidisciplinary so that students can take advantage of the best available courses from throughout the university.

Courses and/or programs should blend theory and applications through experiential exercises and cases and through internships, field trips and experiences, and the appropriate use of guest lecturers. The American Arbitration Association, and local chapters of the Society of Professionals in Dispute Resolution and similar organizations can be quite helpful in this regard.

Students, whether they are in degree programs or short courses and seminars should have the opportunity to take advantage of available technology such as films and tapes, the videotaping of their own dispute resolution sessions, and computer software which is beginning to emerge. Again, the American Arbitration Association is a good source for films and tapes, and an interesting negotiation planning program for the IBM PC is available from the Negotiation Institute (1985).

Notes

The authors wish to thank University of Pacific students Robert Oakes and Amy McKenzie for the library research and other assistance which they provided.

1. Descriptions of these materials and information on how to obtain them can be found in Dispute Resolution Forum. Washington, D. C.: National Institute for Dispute Resolution, April, 1986, pp. 12-16.

References

Brown, L. D. 1983. *Managing conflict at organizational interfaces*. Reading, Mass.: Addison-Wesley.

Davis, H. E. and M. A. Dugan. 1982. Training the mediator. *Peace and Change* 8:81-90.

Fisher, B. and M. Jennings. 1986. *Law for business*. St. Paul, Minn.: West Publishing Co.

Goldgerg, S. B., E. D. Green and F. E. A. Sander. 1985. *Dispute resolution*. Boston: Little, Brown.

Green, E. D. 1984. A comprehensive approach to the theory and practice of dispute resolution. *Journal of Legal Education* 34: 245-58.

Hall, L. 1986. Preliminary thoughts on graduate programs in dispute resolution. *Negotiation Journal* 2:207-11.

Hastings College of Law. 1986. *Dispute resolution directory: Courses and internships in Northern California.* Berkeley: University of California.

Juergensmeyer, M. 1984. *Fighting with Gandhi.* New York: Harper and Row.

Lax, D. and J. Sebenius. 1986. *The manager as negotiator.* New York: The Free Press.

Lieberman, J. K. and G. Siedel. 1986. *Business law and the legal environment.* New York: Harcourt. Brace, Jovanovich.

Lewicki, R. J. and J. A. Litterer. 1985a. *Negotiation.* Homewood, Ill.: Richard D. Irwin.

————. 1985b. *Negotiation: Readings, exercises, and cases.* Homewood, Ill.: Richard D. Irvin.

Moore, C. W. 1986. *The mediation process.* San Francisco: Jossey Bass.

National Association of Schools of Public Affairs and Administration.1974. *Guidelines and standards for professional masters degree programs in public affairs/public administration.* Washington, D.C.: National Association of Schools of Public Affairs and Administration.

Negotiation Institute. 1984. *The art of negotiating software program.* New York: Negotiation Institute Inc.

Patton, B. 1984. *On teaching negotiation.* Program on Negotiation Working Paper Series 85-6. Cambridge, Mass.: Program on Negotiation at Harvard Law School.

Program on Negotiation at Harvard Law School. 1985. *Case clearinghouse catalog.* Cambridge. Mass.: Harvard College.

Program on Negotiation at Harvard Law School. 1986. *Dispute resolution directory: Boston area courses and internships.* Cambridge, Mass.: Program on Negotiation at Harvard Law School.

Pruitt, D. G. and J. Z. Rubin. 1986. *Social conflict: Escalation, stalemate, and settlement.* New York: Random House.

Raiffa, H. 1984. *A hypothetical speech to a hypothetical audience about a very real problem.* Program on Negotiation Working Paper Series 85-1. Cambridge, Mass.: Program on Negotiation at Harvard Law School.

Riskin, L. L. 1984. Mediation in the law schools. *Journal of Legal Education* 34:229 36.

Sander, F. E. A. 1984. Alternative dispute resolution in the law school curriculum: Opportunities and obstacles. *Journal of Legal Education* 34:259-67.

Wedge, B. and xJ. D. Rubin. 1982. Conflict management: A new venture into professionalization. *Peace and Change* 8: 129-38.

Wehr, P. 1986. Conflict resolution studies: What do we know? Dispute Resolution Forum. Washington D.C.: National Institute for Dispute Resolution.

Negotiation Skills Training in the Law School Curriculum

Gerald R. Williams and Joseph M. Geis

Gerald R. Williams is professor of law at the J. Reuben Clark Law School, Brigham Young University.

Joseph M. Geis is a graduate of the Clark Law School.

It is difficult to imagine what would be more useful to negotiation teachers than to see at first hand how their colleagues at other institutions are teaching. The next best thing would be for teachers to get together for a few days to share experiences, an event we hope to see in the future. Until then, the best alternative is to see what various teachers have written about how they teach their courses. The purpose of this chapter is to report on these writings as they pertain to teaching negotiation in law schools. We have drawn primarily upon two sources of information: articles by law professors on how they teach negotiation and syllabi that various teachers were willing to share with us.

The information from these sources is so fertile that it is difficult to communicate adequately. No single description can capture the richness of what individual teachers are doing in the negotiation classroom. To make this information as accessible to the reader as possible, we have summarized our gleanings in a detailed chart appended to this chapter. The chart compares key aspects of the courses taught by 20 law teachers. Comparisons include type of course, place in curriculum, class size, course objectives, teaching methods, grading criteria, use of outcome information, aids to self-understanding, assigned readings, and use of journals or other writings for reflective learning.

Entries in the chart also include page number citations to the published materials for the benefit of readers who would like more detail about any given practice. In this paper, we highlight some of the information included in the chart. However, for a more complete comparison, please refer to the appendix. Please be aware that negotiation teachers are continually learning from their experience and revising their courses as they go. For this reason, even the more recent published accounts may fail to reflect the current practices of their authors. In this chapter, an assertion that a negotiation teacher practices in a certain way really means that he or she reported that practice in a written source.

This chapter first appeared in Deborah Kolb, editor, *Negotiation Eclectics: Essays in Memory of Jeffrey Z. Rubin,* PON Books, 1999.

The Beginnings of Negotiation Instruction in Law Schools

It has now been 50 years since negotiating skills were introduced into legal education. According to published sources, the first teachers were Professors Mueller and James at Yale Law School, who taught negotiation as part of a case presentation seminar, and Professor Robert Mathews at Ohio State University, who taught the first course dedicated exclusively to legal negotiation (Mueller and James 1948; Mathews 1953). These forward-looking educators were considerably ahead of their time. There is a lapse of 20 years before we find the next published descriptions of negotiation courses, one of them taught by Professors James J. White and Carl P. Malmquist at the University of Michigan (White 1967) and the other by Professors Cornelius J. Peck and Robert I. Fletcher at the University of Washington (Peck 1972).

At this point, negotiation began to enter the mainstream. Reports of negotiation courses appeared at an increasing rate and published teaching materials proliferated. Today, teachers can choose from nearly a dozen textbooks on legal negotiation; from several books on lawyering skills and alternative dispute resolution that include useful chapters on negotiation; and from a number of excellent books written for broader audiences. Many of these resources are discussed later in this chapter and are also listed in the references.

In the days before negotiation was offered as a subject in law school, it was expected that young lawyers would learn such skills on the job after graduation. It was assumed that these skills could only be learned by experience, ideally under the tutelage of more experienced lawyers. It should come as no surprise, then, that the objective of early teachers was to improve upon raw experience and to devise teaching methods that would enhance student learning of negotiation skills. They were treading new ground. One early teacher described the situation in these words:

> There is no literature, no teaching material, little faculty
> experience or skill. Whatever solution there is would seem
> to lie in active student participation under conditions so well
> simulated as to convey a sense of actuality, of real loss or
> gain, of stakes seriously at issue (Mathews 1953:99).

Developing a Body of Negotiation Theory and Practice

From the perspective of today, we might wonder why these early teachers didn't draw from the bodies of theoretical and experimental work on negotiation we are familiar with today and which was summarized many years ago in such works as Walton and McKersie (1965), Rubin and Brown (1975), Young (1975), and Zartman (1976). The answer, of course, is that negotiation was an equally new topic in other disciplines as well.

The discovery of negotiation as a discrete object of study in these disciplines actually occurred during these same years, the late 1940s and early 1950s. The early teachers of legal negotiation faced the daunting task of developing a substantive basis for the study of negotiation as they went along. In his pioneering article, "Negotiation: A Pedagogical Challenge," Mathews (1953) sets the stage for these developments. The broad scope of his interest in negotiation was confirmed in his working definition of the topic:

> Negotiation may be tentatively described...as a process
> of adjustment of existing differences, with a view to the
> establishment of a mutually more desirable legal relation
> by means of barter and compromise of legal rights and
> duties and of *economic, psychological, social and other interests*
> (Mathews 1953: 94) [italics added].

With this definition, Mathews seemed to anticipate developments in negotiation theory that were shortly to come from many disciplines. He also reminds us that law teachers will need to be attentive to these developments as they unfold in their respective disciplines. Mathews offered an initial description of the negotiation process, enumerated some basic negotiating skills, identified personal qualities negotiators should seek to develop, and raised ethical issues he felt to be inherent in legal negotiation.

It isn't possible, in this short chapter, to trace the unfolding of the substantial legal literature on negotiation itself, much less the extensive literature in such fields as economics, business, communications, the behavioral sciences, and other disciplines. It is possible, however, to offer a few generalizations about the content of negotiation courses for law students.

Law professors have produced about a dozen books tailored exclusively for courses in legal negotiation or for other courses that include a segment on negotiation. Taken as a whole, they have much in common with one another, but some distinguishing themes do occur. For example, Edwards and White (1977) were the first to deal systematically with issues of culture, race, and gender in legal negotiation. In his book, Williams (1983) reports extensive empirical research about the negotiating patterns of lawyers. Bastress and Harbaugh (1990) go the furthest to integrate negotiation with client interviewing and counseling.

No list of teaching materials would be complete without including several additional works generally written by scholars outside the legal profession for use in a variety of educational and business settings and which are frequently adopted or recommended in courses on legal negotiation. Among these are several classics, including Fisher, Ury, and Patton, *Getting to YES* (1991), Raiffa, *The Art and Science of Negotiation* (1982) and Lax and Sebenius, *The Manager as Negotiator* (1986). Among their many contributions to the field, participants in Harvard's Program on Negotiation have developed many excellent teaching materials for general educational use, most notably Landry, Kolb, and Rubin (1991) and Hall (1993).

Of all these works, *Getting to YES* is undoubtedly the book most widely used in law school negotiation courses. There is an apparent split between negotiation teachers who see *Getting to YES* as the only acceptable approach and those who see it as just half of the picture, with the other half being occupied by the more competitive or manipulative model described

205

by White (1967) and documented empirically by Williams (1983). With respect to this split, Jeffrey Z. Rubin (1994) suggested that while these two approaches have widely different, and even conflicting, orientations, each model is appropriate under different circumstances. In his view, "[n]ot only is it unnecessary to *choose* between the two, it is foolish to do so." As reflected in the appendix, most negotiation teachers agree with Rubin and teach both approaches.

It is clear that no single book is comprehensive enough to satisfy the teachers of stand-alone negotiation courses. As detailed in the bottom row of the chart in the appendix, most teachers require a rich selection of readings from a wide variety of sources. One of the most eclectic is Galanter (1984), who, in addition to the usual kinds of readings, also assigns materials on real-life negotiations, such as Stern's *The Buffalo Creek Disaster* (1997), telling the story of the preparation and settlement of a complicated tort case on behalf of 600 flood victims, and a "generous" dose of newspaper clippings.

When and in What Context Should Negotiation Skills Be Taught?

There is a healthy variety in the ways negotiation is taught in law schools. One of the basic choices is whether to teach negotiation as a stand-alone course or to include it in the context of a larger substantive or skills-oriented offering. For example, at the University of Missouri-Columbia School of Law, negotiation is included as part of a program that integrates alternative dispute resolution across the entire first-year curriculum (Riskin and Westbrook 1989). Even in the absence of a comprehensive program such as Missouri's, individual teachers have taken the initiative of incorporating negotiation skills into their courses, both in the first year (Little 1981; Barken 1990) and in upper-division classes (Moore and Tomlinson 1969).

Aside from substantive courses, negotiation skills are typically included as part of lawyering skills courses, where they are taught in the context of a wider range of skills, including interviewing and counseling, pretrial practice, trial advocacy, and others (Bellow and Moulton 1978; Mauet 1995; Haydock et al. 1996). In a similar vein, negotiation is included in courses and seminars on alternative dispute resolution. Negotiation skills are also included in clinical law courses in which students handle actual cases under the watchful eyes of supervising attorneys. Clinical students have two enormous advantages over all other students of negotiation. First, they have the experience of representing an actual client; second, they often have the opportunity to engage in real-life negotiations with counsel on the opposite sides of their cases.

The most sustained and intense exposure to negotiation comes in courses devoted exclusively to the topic. Some readers may worry that there is not enough content or substance to sustain, say, a two-credit course in negotiation. Experience is to the contrary. Those who teach such a course admit that the work amounts to more than is normally required for two credits (Craver 1993). Some law professors who began teaching negotiation as a two-credit course have now moved it to three (Ortwein 1981), and negotiation is currently taught as a three-credit class in several law schools.

Based on the literature, it appears that all of the stand-alone courses on negotiation are offered as upper-division elective courses. Some teachers have restricted enrollment to third-year students on the theory that third-year students are closer to graduation and are beginning to feel a keener interest in preparing for the practice of law (Williams 1983; Sabin 1987). Otherwise, there appear to be no prerequisites for taking the course, although it has been suggested by at least one teacher that a prerequisite course in professional responsibility should be required of students taking the negotiation course (Ortwein 1981).

Obviously, it would be wrong to suppose that negotiation should only be taught as part of other courses or that it should only be taught as a course in its own right. It is clear that students who are first exposed to negotiation, say, as a small unit in a first-year contracts course would benefit from later taking a course devoted exclusively to negotiation. It is also apparent that students who have had a free-standing negotiation course would also gain from revisiting negotiation in the context of some other course in the curriculum. As a basic rule, we could say that some exposure is better than none, and the more the better.

Use of Simulations

Mathews (1953) gave the first description of a course devoted exclusively to legal negotiation. In a class of 12, students are assigned in groups of two and are further assigned to take the role either of lawyers or of clients. After extensive preparations, two teams attempt to reach a negotiated solution while the instructor and the rest of the class observe. The class period that follows is dedicated to critiquing the two negotiators' performances, sharing lessons learned from the exercise, and discussing ways to improve (Mathew 1953:93-101). Elements of this approach are still used, in whole or in part, in most negotiation courses today.

The next advance in simulation methodology in law schools was to apply the concept of a duplicate tournament to negotiations. In this model, rather than have some students negotiate while others observe, all students in the class are assigned to negotiate the same problem simultaneously (White 1967). A ranking of results is generally distributed to students afterwards so they can compare their outcome to those of other students in the class. Professor White takes the concept to its logical extreme and uses monetary outcomes of each negotiation as the sole basis for each student's grade in the course.

Peck and Fletcher (1968) also use the duplicate tournament method, but rather than give students all of the facts of the case up front, they add realism to the preparation phase of the process by handing out only the information attorneys would normally obtain in an initial discussion with the client. From this point it is up to each student to discover the remaining facts by asking specific questions. The professors play the roles of all parties and witnesses, providing written responses to students' written inquiries about the facts of the case. The professors are as consistent as possible in their responses so that different students posing the same questions get the same answers. The first time through, this process is very time-intensive for the professors. In subsequent years a teaching assistant or secretary is able to field most of the questions by referring to "data banks" containing a list of all the questions asked in previous years and giving out the corresponding answers. The instructors are available to respond to novel inquiries.

In his two-credit course, Professor Ortwein (1981) has students negotiate four simulations derived from the closed-case files of local attorneys. As is the case in most negotiation courses, the problems are negotiated during class time. Ortwein allocates three two-hour class sessions to each problem. In the first session, the students negotiate the problem; in the second, the attorney who handled the actual case shares with the students interesting facets of the case; and in the third session, students view a videotape of one team's negotiation and discuss their own experience in negotiating the problem.

Many negotiation teachers use videotape to enhance instructor feedback. Moberly (1984) notes that while many teachers use videotaping, very few contemplate actually observing or critiquing *all* student performances in a systematic way. He believes students learn the most from professorial and peer feedback on their negotiation and feels that it is a waste of resources "to ask students to negotiate a problem and then fail to provide feedback from the professor and the other participants." (Moberly 1984:320). He claims his method is not overly burdensome or time-consuming. With a class of 24 students, his method enables him to critique 15 to 30 minutes of videotape of every negotiation for all of his students within the amount of time normally allotted to teaching a law school course. He does not require written reports or examinations on the reading materials; he has found that emphasizing negotiation and professorial critique is more valuable.

Sabin (1987) uses an interesting combination of student observation and simultaneous negotiation. For each negotiation exercise, he assigns all teams except one to negotiate the problem outside of class. When they have finished, the remaining pair negotiates the same problem in front of the class. Afterwards, class members critique the performance. Once or twice during the semester, rather than having class members negotiate in front of the class, Sabin brings in practicing attorneys to negotiate the same problem that was just negotiated by the all of the students. Sabin assigns eight problems during the semester and prefers exercises based on actual cases so the "real" outcomes can be shared.

Craver (1986) uses the duplicate tournament structure but lets students first gain negotiation experience by completing three or four nongraded simulations. He includes both zero-sum and non-zero-sum problems to assure students gain experience with a sufficiently wide range of bargaining situations.

In evaluating the use of the duplicate tournament method, Galanter (1984) believes it gives students a unique opportunity to see the effect of interactions between negotiators who have different goals, expectations, and styles. This conveys the variability of the process and the power of various contingencies to shape the results. On the other hand, Galanter also sees limitations in the use of simulation games, such as the lack of ongoing relationships between the negotiators, inadequate time for things to develop, artificial deadlines which prevent using time as a sanction or reward, and the inability to use normal lawyering moves such as filing of actions, discovery, and so on (Galanter 1984).

Negotiation teachers cannot avoid wondering what impact their course is having on students. Craver (1986) did a statistical study of legal negotiation training and future negotiation success. Using data from two years, the study tested the correlation between students' prior legal negotiation skills training and results in a subsequent negotiation exercise in a different class. The results showed that students who had previously taken the negotiation skills course achieved more favorable results on a later negotiation exercise than the other class members. Craver concludes that basic lawyering skills can be effectively taught in an academic setting.

How Many Students Should be Permitted in the Class

In the first years of teaching negotiation in law schools, classes were limited to 10 or 12 students. This can be attributed to the experimental nature of such courses and the fact that they relied so heavily on providing realistic experience as contrasted to more formal training in negotiation theory and practice. The literature shows that most teachers today feel comfortable with somewhat larger classes, typically in the neighborhood of 24 students. However, as the interest in negotiation has grown, many teachers have sought ways to open the course to larger numbers of students.

At Harvard, the solution has been to enroll students in groups of 24 but to offer as many as a half-dozen sections, each of them headed by a well-trained teaching assistant under the instructor's close supervision (Mnookin syllabus 1996). Craver (1986) has taught as many as 60 students in a class, but he prefers to keep class size down to a more manageable 20 to 40 students. Williams (1983b) has designed his course to accommodate larger class sizes and comfortably teaches classes with as many as 85 students.

Two determining factors regarding class size are instructor supervision and simultaneity of negotiations. For example, if the instructor is determined to have all class members negotiate at the same time and within an area small enough for the instructor to look in on the negotiations, then class enrollment is limited by the number of small rooms available at any one time in the day. However, if the teacher gives class members a number of days to complete the exercise, there is no need to provide rooms for the negotiators, much less contiguous rooms, and larger class sizes can easily be accommodated. Some trade offs are possible. Providing open times for larger class sizes sacrifices the benefit of debriefing the case immediately upon its completion, the ability of the instructor to view the negotiations, and the confidentiality of the negotiation process. When class members are permitted to spread the negotiation, on their own, over a period of several days, there is a danger that settlement offers and outcomes from early negotiators will leak out, greatly diminishing the value of the exercise for the remaining students. Instructors who run simulations in this way have developed rules for reducing the incidence of such problems. (See Williams syllabus 1996.) The great advantage is that by offering the course every semester with essentially unlimited enrollment, Williams is able to make negotiation training available to virtually every interested student.

What to Grade in Negotiation Courses

One of the areas of greatest variation among negotiation teachers is how they assign grades in their courses. It is also one of the most important. Grading policies strongly influence what students learn from the class (Williams 1984). There is a continuing tension around using outcomes as a basis for part or all of the grade. At one end of the spectrum are teachers who base most of the grade on their observations of their students' performances in negotiation. For example, Mathews (1953) evaluated negotiation performance using subjective criteria such as command of the facts, perception of limits on bargaining position, manner, poise, organization, and order of presentation. His assessment of the student's negotiation performance counted for 46 percent of the grade, written critiques of other students' in-class performances made up 36 percent, and a self-critique made up the remaining 18 percent. Moberly (1984) is the most vigorous advocate of professorial review. Nevertheless, in his course, student performance counts less than 35 percent of the grade, and outcomes count 65 percent. It is interesting that despite the emphasis Moberly puts on the professorial review of the student's performance, he assigns much greater weight to outcomes than performance in the grading process.

One concern raised by rating student performances is the subjectivity of a teacher's evaluation. To address this problem, Fisher and Siegel (1987) have developed a "process grading scale" with explicitly delineated criteria by which they rate students while viewing videotapes of student performance. Their method probably results in the most consistent instructor feedback. Full details of the system are included in their 1987 article.

At the other end are teachers who use outcomes as the determinant of most or all of the grade. Professor White (1967) uses the outcome as the primary determinant of the student's entire course grade. White's method focuses on creating an objective standard for grading student performance. Consistent with this goal, students are compared only with students negotiating the same side of the problem. Craver (1986) also uses duplicate tournament method and compares students only with other students negotiating the same side of the problem. Students are ranked and assigned points after each negotiation problem. For example, if 15 students negotiated the same side of the problem, the one with the highest score receives 15 points, the one with the second highest score receives 14 points, etc. The scores are tallied at the end of the semester and ranked. Two thirds of the grade is determined by ranking the outcomes of the negotiation exercises, while the remaining one third comes from a 12- to 15-page term paper describing the impact of theoretical factors on the student's negotiating experience.

Williams (1983b) also gives weight to outcomes but assigns them only a trivial role, 10 percent of the final grade. He finds this token amount is sufficient to bring out the competitiveness in students who are so inclined, but not so much as to outweigh all other considerations.

Of the 19 courses described in the appendix, less than half calculate outcomes as part of the final grade. Teachers using this method acknowledge the degree of competitiveness it encourages in students may become excessive, but they feel this simulates the pressures and incentives lawyers will face in the real world. They want their students to begin making conscious choices about it now, before they are representing actual clients. Professor Ortwein (1981) uses problems with defined point structures, and uses outcomes of these exercises as the main factor in grading. He raises the concern that when students negotiate for their grades, the result is hostility. He asks if there isn't a better way of grading. In his article, he contemplates experimenting with a pass/fail grading system, which he believes would de-emphasize grades enough to alleviate some of the competitiveness and allow students to view the process more objectively and realistically. Sabin (1987) has class members participate in the grading process by evaluating themselves and also those with whom they have negotiated. Students submit written reports responding to specific questions about their negotiation experiences.

Summary

In reviewing 50 years of negotiation skills training in law schools, we can see that the general approach has proven relatively stable. From the beginning, teachers have focused on two main objectives. The first is learning by doing. Students are assigned to negotiate problems similar to those they will encounter in law practice; they receive feedback about their performance and outcomes from the instructor and from other class members; and they participate in debriefing sessions to discuss their experiences. The second main objective is to expose students to the best available substantive knowledge about negotiation.

Fifty years ago, when negotiation was just being recognized as a potential field of knowledge in law and in other disciplines, there was very little information to draw upon. Today there is an abundance. Beginning with Mathews (1953), most law teachers have recognized the interdisciplinary nature of this topic and, since White (1967), have drawn significant portions of their course content from the behavioral sciences. They have sometimes team-taught with psychiatrists or psychologists.

In a similar vein, many teachers have recognized that negotiation is more than just a set of skills and a body of substantive knowledge. It is also a basic form of human interaction that offers an opportunity for students and teachers to gain greater self-understanding as well as a greater appreciation for others. This has led many teachers to emphasize the use of written journals for reflective learning. A few teachers use psychological tools such as the Myers-Briggs Type Indicator and the Thomas Kilman Conflict Mode Instrument.

The most glaring weakness in negotiation training today is the continuing absence of the client in all settings except clinical classes. A few teachers address this problem by playing the role of client, by assigning class members to take turns as clients, or by hiring drama students to play the role of clients, but this area calls for further attention.

References

Auerbach, J. S. 1983. *Justice without law?* New York: Oxford University Press.

Barken, M. E. 1990. Integrating contract and property fundamentals with negotiation skills: A teaching methodology. *Journal of Legal Studies Education.*

Bastress, R.M. and J. D. Harbaugh. 1990. *Interviewing, counseling, and negotiating skills for effective representation.* Boston: Little, Brown & Co.

Bellow, G. and B. Moulton. 1981. *The lawyering process: Negotiation.* Mineola, NY: Foundation Press.

Binder, D. A., P. Bergman, and S. C. Price. 1991. *Lawyers as counselors: A client-centered approach.* St. Paul, MN: West Publishing Co.

Breslin, J. W. and J. Z. Rubin, eds. 1991. *Negotiation theory and practice.* Cambridge , MA: Program on Negotiation Books.

Casse, P. 1980. *Training for the cross-cultural mind.* Washington, DC: The Society for Intercultural Education, Training and Research (SIETAR).

Cohen, H. 1980. *You can negotiate anything.* New York: Bantam Books.

Coleman, N. A. 1980. Teaching the theory and practice of bargaining to lawyers and students. *Journal of Legal Education* 30:470-491.

Craver, C. B. 1986. Clinical negotiating achievement as a function of traditional law school success and as a predictor of future negotiating performance. *Journal of Dispute Resolution* 1986: 63-71.

———. 1993. *Effective legal negotiation and settlement.* 2nd ed. Charlottesville, VA: The Michie Company.

———. 1993b. *Effective legal negotiation and settlement: Teachers manual.* 2nd ed. Charlottesville, VA: The Michie Co.

Edwards, H. T. and J. J. White. 1977. *The lawyer as a negotiator: Problems, readings and materials.* St. Paul, MN: West Publishing Co.

Fisher, M. and A. I. Siegel. 1987. Evaluating negotiation behavior and results: Can we identify what we say we know? *Catholic University Law Review* 36: 395-453.

Fisher, R., W. Ury, and B. Patton. 1991. *Getting to YES.* 2nd ed. New York: Penguin Books.

Follett, M. P. 1942. *Dynamic administration: The collected papers of Mary Parker Follett.* H. C. Metcalf and L. Urwick (eds.). New York: Harper & Row.

Freeman, H. A. 1964. *Legal interviewing and counseling.* St. Paul, MN: West Publishing Co.

Freund, J. 1992. *Smart negotiating: How to make good deals in the real world.* New York: Simon and Schuster.

Galanter, M. 1984. Worlds of deals: using negotiation to teach about legal process. *Journal of Legal Education* 34:268-276.

Gifford, D. G. 1989. *Legal negotiations: Theory and applications.* St. Paul, MN: West Publishing Co.

Goldberg, S. B., F. E. A. Sander, and N. H. Rogers. 1992. *Dispute resolution: Negotiation, mediation, and other processes.* 2nd ed. Boston: Little, Brown and Co.

Goldman, A. 1972. *Processes for conflict resolution: Self-help, voting, negotiation, arbitration, labor relations and social problems.* Washington, DC: Bureau of National Affairs.

Guernsey, T. F. 1996. *A practical guide to negotiation.* National Institute for Trial Advocacy.

Hall, C. S. and V. J. Nordby. 1973. *A primer of Jungian psychology.* New York: Mentor.

Hall, L., (ed.) 1993. *Negotiation: Strategies for mutual gain.* Newbury Park, Calif.: Sage Publications.

Harbaugh, J. D. 1990. *Interviewing, counseling, and negotiating skills for effective representation.* Boston: Little, Brown & Co.

Harbaugh, J. D. and B. Britzke. 1984. *Primer on negotiation: A video handbook.* New York: Practising Law Institute.

Haydock, R. S. 1984. *Negotiation practice.* New York: Wiley Law Publications.

———, P. B. Knapp, A. Juergens, D. Herr, and J. Stempel. 1996. *Lawyering: Practice and planning.* St. Paul, MN: West Publishing Co.

Hermann, P. J. 1965. *Better settlements through leverage.* Rochester: Aqueduct Books.

Kanowitz, L. 1986. *Cases and materials on alternative dispute resolution.* American Casebook Series. St. Paul, MN: West Publishing Co.

Landry, E. M., D. M. Kolb, and J. Z. Rubin. 1991. *Curriculum for negotiation and conflict management—instructor's manual.* Cambridge, MA: The Program on Negotiation at Harvard Law School.

Lax, D. A. and J. K. Sebenius. 1986. *The manager as negotiator: Bargaining for cooperative and competitive gain.* New York: The Free Press.

Lewicki, R. J. and J. A. Litterer. 1985. *Negotiation.* Homewood, IL: Richard D. Irwin.

Little, J. W. 1981. Skills training in the torts course. *Journal of Legal Education* 31:614-45.

Mastenbroek, W. F. G. 1991. Development of negotiating skills. In *International negotiation: analysis, approaches, issues.* Victor A. Kremenyuk (ed.) San Francisco: Jossey-Bass Publishers.

Mathews, R. E. 1953-54. Negotiation: a pedagogical challenge. *Journal of Legal Education* 6:93-101.

Mauet, T. A. 1995. *Pretrial.* 3rd ed. Boston: Little, Brown & Co.

Meltsner, M. and P. G. Schrag. 1973. Negotiating tactics for legal services lawyers. *Clearinghouse Review* 7:59-63.

Moberly, R. B. 1984. A pedagogy for negotiation. *Journal of Legal Education* 34:314-325.

Moore, D. R. and J. Tomlinson. 1969. The use of simulated negotiation to teach substantive law. *Journal of Legal Education* 21:579-86.

Mueller, A. and F. James, Jr. 1948. Case presentation. *Journal of Legal Education* 1:129-135.

Murray, J. S., A. S. Rau, and E. F. Sherman. 1996a. *Processes of dispute resolution: the role of lawyers.* 2nd ed. Westbury, NY: The Foundation Press, Inc.

———, A. S. Rau, and E. F. Sherman. 1996b. *Negotiation.* (reprinted in part from *Processes of dispute resolution: The role of lawyers.* 2nd ed. Westbury, NY: The Foundation Press,

Inc.

Ortwein, B. M. 1981. Teaching negotiation: A valuable experience. *Journal of Legal Education* 31: 108-127.

Peck, C. J. 1972. *Cases and materials on negotiation, labor relations and social problems.* Washington, DC: Bureau of National Affairs.

———, and R. L. Fletcher. 1968. A course on the subject of negotiation. *Journal of Legal Education* 21: 196-206.

Peters, E. 1955. *Strategy and tactics in labor negotiations.* New London, CT: National Foreman's Institute.

Raiffa, H. 1982. *The art and science of negotiation.* Cambridge, MA: Harvard University Press.

Riskin L. L. and J. E. Westbrook. 1987. *Dispute resolution and lawyers.* American Casebook Series. St. Paul, MN: West Publishing Co.

———, and Westbrook, J. E. 1989. Integrating dispute resolution into standard first-year courses: The Missouri Plan. *Journal of Legal Education* 39:509-521.

Ross, H. L. 1980. *Settled out of court: The social process of insurance claims adjustment.* New York: Aldine Publishing Co.

Rubin, J. Z. 1994. Models of Conflict Management. *Journal of Social Issues* 50:33-45.

———, and B. R. Brown. 1975. *The social psychology of bargaining and negotiation.* New York: Academic Press.

———, D. G. Pruitt, and S. H. Kim. 1994. *Social conflict: Escalation, stalemate and settlement.* 2nd ed. New York: McGraw-Hill.

Sabin, A. 1987. Pragmatic aspects in the teaching of negotiations. *Legal Studies Forum* 11:337-346.

Stevens, C. M. 1963. *Strategy and collective bargaining negotiation.* Westport, CT: Greenwood Press.

Stern, G. M. 1977. *The Buffalo Creek disaster.* New York: Vintage Books.

Susskind, L. and J. Cruikshank. 1987. *Breaking the impasse: Consensual approaches to resolving public disputes.* New York: Basic Books.

Tamsitt, G. 1987. Interviewing and negotiation revisited. *Journal of Professional Legal Education* 5: 177-185.

Teply, L. 1992. *Legal negotiation in a nutshell.* St. Paul, MN: West Publishing Co.

Ury, W. I. 1991. *Getting past no: Negotiating with difficult people.* New York: Bantam Books.

Walton, R.E. and R. B. McKersie. 1965. *A behavioral theory of labor negotiations.* New York: McGraw-Hill.

White, J. J. 1967. The lawyer as a negotiator: An adventure in understanding and teaching the art of negotiation. *Journal of Legal Education* 19:337-53.

Williams, G. R. 1983. *Legal negotiation and settlement.* St. Paul, MN: West Publishing Co.

———. 1983b. *Legal negotiation and settlement—teacher's manual.* St. Paul, MN: West Publishing Co.

———. 1984. Using simulation exercises for negotiation and other dispute resolution courses. *Journal of Legal Education* 34: 307-314.

——. 1992. *A lawyer's handbook for effective negotiation and settlement.* 4th ed. (privately published).

——. 1996. Negotiation as a healing process. *Journal of Dispute Resolution* 1996: 1-66.

Young, O. R. 1975. *Bargaining: Formal theories of negotiation.* Chicago: University of Illinois Press.

Zartman, I. W. 1976. *The 50% solution.* Garden City, NY: Anchor Press.

	Mathews	White	Peck & Fletcher	Ortwein
	(1953)	(1967)	(1968)	(1981)
Type of Course	Negotiation "Practice Course"	Negotiation Skills Course	Negotiation Skills Course	Negotiation Skills Course
When	2L/3L	2L/3L (prefers 3L)	2L/3L	3Ls who have taken professional responsibility
Teaching Methods	Class observes one pair of students negotiate each of 5 or 6 problems	Negotiation problems structured as duplicate tournament; attorney-client negotiation exercise (p.342); taped negotiation sessions	Study of case histories (p.197, 201-04); simulations (duplic. tournament) w/ open data banks providing fact gathering and client interviewing experience (p.198); taped negotiation sessions	Simulations (duplic. tournament); each problem uses (3) 2-hr classes (p.119); more focus on skills -- best developed through actual performance -- and less on theory (p.116); guest lectures from practitioners (p.119)
Class size (no. of students)	10-12	24 (2 groups of 12 each -- 6 two-person teams) (p.338)	unlimited	26 max.
Course Objectives, Goals, and Elements	Active student participation in conditions that simulate actual practice (p.99)	Develop student's ability to manipulate others (p.348); simulate the real thing as much as possible & add teaching supplement to help students learn from experience (p.337)	Discuss a variety of methods through case histories (p.201-04); effective negotiation entails discovering other party's settling limits while creating uncertainty about one's own (p.203)	Awareness of various negotiation techniques, interpersonal relationships, and ethical dilemmas; self-awareness; disagrees with White's view that negotiation is manipulation; course focus is to expose students to negotiation process (p.127)
Grading Criteria	Subjective performance 46%, critiques 36%, self-critique 18% (p.100)	Students negotiated with one another for their grades (p.338 & 341)	Grades depend to large extent on outcomes of simulations (p.199)	Outcome based grading caused excessive competitiveness will try pass/fail (p.122)
Use of Outcomes		Compared against students negotiating same side only; table of results distributed after each negotiation (p.341)	Negotiation results announced after each exercise (p.205)	Unsettled cases decided by instructor/judge -- monetary outcomes of such cases reduced by litigation fees (p.123)
Aids to Self-Understanding		Co-taught with a psychiatrist (p.338 n.3 & p.345)	Enlisted the help of psychiatrists -- experienced difficulties, but of great importance (p.198 & 204)	Some psychiatrist or psychologist involvement is essential for explaining certain concepts (p.125)
Course Reading Materials		Hermann (1965); Peters (1955); Stevens (1963); other selections from psychology, social psychology, and psychiatry (p.338 & 347)	Case histories of negotiated settlements (10); selections from Freeman (1964); Hermann (1965); articles on psychology, collective bargaining, and evaluating personal injury and automobile accident claims (p.198)	Selections on strategies & techniques, psycho-dynamics of negotiation, nonverbal communication from Edwards & White (1977); other readings: problem specific information, ethical aspects (p.115)
Written Reflection	Class members submit 2-6 page critiques for each negotiation observed (p.100); negotiators do a self-criticism (p.100)			

Page numbers in parentheses refer to the professor's published article

	Little	Galanter	Moberly	Craver
	(1981)	(1984)	(1984)	(1986)
Type of Course	Torts		Negotiation Skills Course	Negotiation Skills Course
When	1L		2L/3L	2L/3L (usually 3L)
Teaching Methods	Single simulation problem done in pairs	Consciously eclectic: negotiation simulations of disputes, films and videotapes, reports of researchers, accounts by visitors, analysis of readings (theory, "how to" accounts, newspaper clippings) (p.270)	Systematic videotaping, faculty observation and detailed critique of every student negotiation simulation (duplic. tournament); student self-critique (p.316)	Simulations (duplic. tournament); two-person teams to simulate attorney-client interaction (p.65)
Class size (no. of students)	unlimited		24 (2 groups of 12 each -- 6 two-person teams) (p.318)	60 (prefers 40)
Course Objectives, Goals, and Elements	Students received "Negotiating Tactics for Legal Services Lawyers" which extolled such tactics as: make your first demand very high, appear irrational where it seems helpful, raise some of your demands as the negotiations progress, etc. (p. 615, 636-38)	Distributional and integrative. Negotiation is a family of processes and not a single set of skills. Make students reflect on their negotiating; give them markers, mnemonics and analytical tools to apply to a variety of bargaining arenas (p.272)	Develop student's capacity to move between cooperative and competitive behavior and to determine when each is appropriate (p.323); "principled" negotiation (p.322); develop capacity to evaluate and learn from their own behavior (p.319)	Distributional and integrative; gender issues
Grading Criteria	Simulation was unsupervised and not evaluated (p.614-15)		Simulations outcomes 65-75%, Improvement, participation, professor evaluation 25-35% (p. 324-25)	Simulation outcomes 67%, Term paper 33% Can opt for P/F, but cannot divulge to other students (p.65)
Use of Outcomes	Outcomes not ranked		Each team is ranked against other teams in group (p.318)	Example: class of 15 students: 15 pts for 1st place, 14 pts. for 2nd place, etc.
Aids to Self-Understanding			Psychologist discusses selected topics; has team-taught course with psychologist -- useful, but not essential (p.322, n.26)	Impact of psychological factors upon the negotiation process discussed (p.64)
Course Reading Materials	Only negotiation readings excerpted from Meltsner and Schrag (1973) (p.615 & 636-38)	Ross (1970); Stern (1977); Bellow & Moulton (1981); Williams (1983); and numerous newspaper clippings (p.270)	Selections dealing with communication, psychology, ethical issues: Raiffa (1982); Edwards & White (1977); Fisher, Ury & Patton (1991); Williams (1983) (p.322)	Edwards and White (1977); Craver, Fundamentals of Effective Legal Negotiating
Written Reflection	Students submit report on negotiation experience	Record estimates, goals, and strategies before each simulation	Students write critiques of own and others' performance after each negotiation (p.320)	Students prepare 12-15 page term paper on the impact of theoretical factors upon their negotiation experiences (p.65)

Page numbers in parentheses refer to the professor's published article

	Sabin	Fisher & Siegel	Riskin & Westbrook "Missouri Plan"	Hall
	(1987)	(1987)	(1989)	(1993)
Type of Course	Negotiation Skills Course	Negotiation Skills Course	1L Substantive	Negotiation & Dispute Resolution Course
When	3L -- maturity & closeness to practice (p.338)	appears 2L/3L	ADR topics in all 1L courses	2L/3L and nonlaw students
Teaching Methods	In-class & out-of-class simulations, practitioners negotiate simulation exercises in front of class (p.341)	Simulations video taped	Part of a comprehensive program to teach basic dispute resolution knowledge and skills in all first year courses. Negotiation simulations used in Torts, Contracts, and Criminal Law courses (p.512-14)	Lecture & discussion (1/3), guest lecturers (1/3), exercises and simulations (1/3)
Class size (no. of students)	20 max. (prefers 12 or 16; multiples of four) (p.338)		unlimited	
Course Objectives, Goals, and Elements	Distributional and integrative		Overall program goals: to acquaint students with alternatives to traditional litigation and emphasize lawyer's role as a problem solver (p.510)	Teach students a range of effective negotiation practices; distributional and integrative; participants become aware of own and others' behaviors; effective communication (p.177)
Grading Criteria	Students are asked to grade selves (overall grading criteria not discussed)	"Process Grading": professor rates student performance using "Process Grading Scale" while viewing video (see article)	Each professor decides own grading criteria: graded, nongraded, posting of negotiation results, final exam question (515-16)	
Use of Outcomes		"Process Grading" as described above	Some professors ranked outcomes	
Aids to Self-Understanding				
Course Reading Materials	Eclectic assortment of practical selections: Cohen (1980); Auerbach (1983); Bellow & Moulton (1981); Book of Genesis, Gandhi's autobiography, etc. Limited material on statistical analysis and theory (p.339)			Fisher, Ury & Patton (1991); Raiffa (1982); Rubin & Pruitt (1994); Susskind & Cruikshank (1987); Casse (1980) and numerous articles (p.177-84)
Written Reflection	Students fill out "Negotiation Report" and "Response Questionnaires" for each simulation (p.340-43)			Journal (p.178)

Page numbers in parentheses refer to the professor's published article

	Barkai	Cagle	Hoffman	Liebman
	(syllabus, 1996)	(syllabus, 1996)	(syllabus, 1996)	(syllabus, 1996)
Type of Course	Negotiation, Mediation, Arbitration & Meeting Facilitation	Negotiation/ Mediation Skills Course	Negotiation Skills Course	Simulation/Workshop
When	2L/3L	2L/3L	2L/3L	2L/3L
Teaching Methods	In-class and out-of-class simulations, videos, guest speakers	Simulations, videos, guest speakers	Simulations, videos, guest speakers (judge, negotiator, mediator), fishbowl negotiations, interviews	Simulations, videotape demonstration, exercises, review of videotapes of student negotiations
Class size (no. of students)	unlimited (40-60)	26 max. (prefers 24) (25-30% nonlaw students)	24 (approx.)	20 per section, 4 sections (three taught by adjuncts)
Course Objectives, Goals, and Elements	Distributional and integrative	Distributional, integrative, problem solving and "hybrid" approaches; students learn who they are, how to understand others, how to develop a workable plan for each negotiation; discuss ethical issues	Prepare students to handle a variety of bargaining situations: distributional, integrative, and problem solving; gender, cultural/ international, multi-lateral	Exposure to a variety of models; emphasis on Lax & Sebenius' tension between value creating and value claiming; self-critique of own negotiating experience; effects of one's background on negotiations; ethics, culture and gender
Grading Criteria	Final exam 65% "Create-a-Simulation" in which students write and analyze a conflict situation, class participation, journals 35%	Midterm exam, final exam, video, sketchbook (journal), class participation, small percentage on simulation outcomes	Class participation, writing assignments 30% Journal or paper 30% Out-of-class outcome-based simulations 30% Attendance 10%	Class participation & role plays 25-30%; Journal 20-25%; Final project (paper, creation of role play, or exam) 45-55%
Use of Outcomes	Outcomes not ranked	Outcomes not ranked		Outcomes not ranked
Aids to Self-Understanding	Myers-Briggs Type Indicator	Myers-Briggs Type Indicator	Thomas Kilman Conflict Mode Survey	
Course Reading Materials	Fisher, Ury & Patton (1991) and photocopied material including cross-cultural selections	Fisher, Ury & Patton (1991); Cohen (1980); Freund (1992) and supplemental materials by Cagle and others	Fisher, Ury & Patton (1991); Lewicki & Litterer (1985); Williams (1983)	Lax & Sebenius (1986); Fisher, Ury & Patton (1991); Murray, Rau & Sherman (1996b); Meltsner & Schrag (1973) and extensive photocopied material including material on cognitive psychology (barriers to agreement, etc.)
Written Reflection	2-3 writing submissions over the semester	"Sketchbook" (journal); analyze negotiations from own environment and news events	Journal or 15 page paper	Journal

Page numbers in parentheses refer to the professor's published article

	Mnookin	Riskin	Stuckey	Williams
	(syllabus, 1996)	(syllabus, 1996)	(syllabus, 1996)	(syllabus, 1996)
Type of Course	Negotiation Workshop	Negotiation Theory & Skills Course	Negotiation Skills Course	Negotiation Skills Course
When	Law and other graduate students	2L/3L	2L/3L	2L/3L
Teaching Methods	Simulations, demonstrations, communication exercises, videos	Demonstrations, simulations, videotape students, guest lecturers	Out-of-class simulations, portion of students videotaped, watch videos of actual lawyers	Lectures, demonstrations, videos, fishbowl & out-of-class simulations (duplic. tournament), group debriefings of simulations
Class size (no. of students)	144 students taught in groups of 24	20 (approx.)	24-36 (multiples of 4)	unlimited (60+)
Course Objectives, Goals, and Elements	By combining theory and practice, help students improve understanding of negotiation and effectiveness as negotiators	Adversarial & problem-solving (identifying interests) negotiation with overriding emphasis on Lax & Sebenius' tension between value creating and value claiming	Distributional, integrative and problem solving	Empirical data on cooperative and aggressive patterns; distributional and integrative; students encouraged to be proficient in and know how to deal with both negotiation styles; objectives range from settlement to healing from effects of conflict
Grading Criteria	Pass/fail or letter grade based 2/3 on class participation and one-third on final paper	Journal 35% Negotiation case study or paper 65%	Final exam (written question, video/transcript critique) -- simulations not graded because unsupervised & students' first attempt	Journal 45% Simulation results 10% Midterm 25% Final 20%
Use of Outcomes	Outcomes not ranked	Ranking of adversarial simulations only	Outcomes not ranked	Based on deviation from mean settlement amount, students scored for each problem
Aids to Self-Understanding	Interpersonal Skills exercise with psychological consultants; Thomas Kilman conflict mode survey; videotaped sessions	Lecturer discusses stress management; psychologist discusses Neuro-Linguistic Programming (NLP)		Emphasis on Jungian psychology; psychologist explains results of Myers-Briggs Type Indicator
Course Reading Materials	Mnookin, Peppet & Tulumello (unpublished); Fisher, Ury and Patton (1991) and other workshop readings	Fisher, Ury & Patton (1991); Ury (1991); Riskin & Westbrook (1987); and other photocopied material. Optional: Freund (1992)	Harbaugh & Britzke (1984); Gifford (1989).	Binder, Bergman & Price (1991); Hall & Nordby (1973); Fisher, Ury & Patton (1991); Lax & Sebenius (1986); Williams (1983); Williams (1992); Williams (1996)
Written Reflection	daily journal and final 7-10 page paper	"Working File" (journal) -- submitted during semester, bound & resubmitted at end of semester		Journal on readings and simulations; submitted during semester & bound for final grade

Page numbers in parentheses refer to the professor's published article

The Course on Negotiation at the Faculty of Law, University of Limburg, Maastricht, The Netherlands

Huub Spoormans, Job Cohen, and Jos Moust

Huub Spoormans is Dean of the Faculty of Law of the Netherlands Open University.

Job Cohen is Junior Minister of Justice in the Dutch central government.

Jos Moust is educationalist at the Faculty of Health Sciences of Maastricht University

A course on negotiation is uncommon in Dutch law faculties; currently, the Faculty of Law in Maastricht is the only Dutch law faculty teaching negotiation as a part of the regular curriculum, albeit as an optional course. In general our faculty pays more attention to skills training than other law faculties do. (For information about the skills program of our faculty, see Cohen et al. 1987.) In professional practice, settling disputes through negotiation instead of through litigation is becoming more commonplace. Increasingly, lawyers strive for negotiated settlements. Consequently, four years ago the faculty decided to start offering a course on negotiation.

Originally, the course could be taken during the third year of the four-year curriculum. The students could choose between this course and one on drafting contracts. In recent years, our students may take the negotiation course as a part of the moot court course. The negotiation portion contributes about a quarter of the credits earned in the moot court course.[1] Presently, the course on negotiation is quite popular: about three-quarters of the students at Limburg's Faculty of Law take it. In part, the popularity of the course is probably due to the fun of the experience. We should add that the other part of its popularity is probably due to the fact that students consider it an easy way to meet part of their obligations.

Goals

The major goal of the negotiation course is to give our students a general idea about the impact of negotiating in society, and especially of the role lawyers play in avoiding and settling disputes through negotiations. Recognizing the huge impact of negotiating in society is rather new for law students, who during their training are encouraged to look at society through exclusively legal glasses. Every dispute and every question is taken

This article first appeared in *Negotiation Journal*, July 1991: Volume 7, Number 3, pages 331-337.

Reflections

The Rijksuniversiteit Limburg no longer exists. That is to say, after the Treaty on the European Union of 1992 the university changed its name to Universiteit Maastricht. The course on negotiation of its Faculty of Law as described in this 1991 article hardly changed, though. Uncoupled from the moot court program, the negotiation course is standing on its own nowadays as a part of the third- and fourth-year curriculum. Some 100 students participate in the course each year. Revisions have been made only on some minor points. The main change consists of the introduction of Alternative Dispute Resolution in one of the cases, as it becomes more and more important in the professional practice of Dutch lawyers. Therefore, the negotiation exercise

as a legal dispute, to be solved by legal means. This (mis)representation of reality is the predictable result of the emphasis given in the curriculum to the law.

Therefore, the course on negotiating primarily is meant to give our students a new, nonlegal perspective: it is worthwhile to examine whether disputes, although abundant with undoubtedly legal elements, can be solved through nonlegal means. Most students are not aware of the psychological, economic, and social elements that play an important role in the settlement of, for instance, injury damages, divorce cases, or applications for a license. Getting the gist of those psychological, social, and economic elements and becoming more sensitive to the constraints, problems, and possibilities of negotiating are the primary goals of our course.

Another major course goal is to give students insight into the process, tactics, and phases of negotiating. Students must acquire knowledge about the theoretical aspects as well as develop some competence and effectiveness in basic negotiating skills. In particular, they must become more sensitive to and aware of their own personal style of communicating with clients and other parties to the negotiating process.

In gaining this insight, other subgoals are met: the students acquire knowledge of the theoretical aspects of the art of negotiating and develop personal negotiating skills, or at least get experience-based knowledge about the kinds of skills that may suit each person. At the end of this article, we offer an evaluation of our success in reaching these goals.

Design

The original design of the course emphasized the acquisition of skills. We gave no lectures and assigned only a small amount of reading; by far, most of the class time was dedicated to negotiating exercises. Every week, the class met for three hours. Half or more of that time was originally dedicated to exercises; the rest of the time we discussed the actual negotiations. Presently, we take more time for theoretical viewpoints, which means that the time for negotiating exercises has decreased.

During the early years, almost all of the course consisted of a series of simulated negotiation assignments, in which students were the negotiators. The design of those assignments has not been changed: starting off with very small and rather simple disputes (in the beginning hardly with a legal context), the exercises become more and more complex, and the students increasingly need to use their legal knowledge and legal skills to handle them. We move from such subjects as a case of traffic damages,[2] to divorce, a dispute on positive discrimination, and finally even to unfriendly takeovers of companies by stockholders and to negotiations about the reform of a parliamentary bill.

Contrary to the university system in the commonwealth countries,[3] law faculties in continental Europe have relatively large numbers of students. This means that the classes on negotiation also have to be relatively large. Nevertheless, we decided to have no more that 32 students in each class, each of which is taught by two teachers. This still is, of course, a large number in relation to the design and the goals of the course. However, we cannot afford smaller classes.

But thinking about this number of students on the one hand, and the goals of the course on the other, we came up with the idea of dividing each class into two halves by composing teams of two students each. In each exercise, every two-person team plays the role of one party. This does not mean that every team plays as if it were composed of only one person; only one person plays while the other observes and gives feedback to the other team member. Before playing, the two are allowed—and even encouraged—to outline their strategy together, which may stimulate them to think better and more explicitly about the goals they want to reach and the means they want to use. We offer literature about observing and giving and receiving feedback. We offer observation pads and handouts to make it easier to observe and to give feedback. Although, as we discuss later, the results of the observation and feedback were less than we would have wished, we nevertheless think that the idea of dividing the class by forming teams was good. With only 16 players, the class is easier to handle; at the same time, students like to work together

Student preparation for the negotiations in our course does not differ from other negotiation courses we know of. In advance, each team receives a written instruction containing a general description of the case and an agenda for specific items

concerning divorce with opposing lawyers, has been changed to an exercise in which one lawyer has to settle arrangements with both parties.

How to explain this lack of change in a course that is almost ten years old? There is a benevolent and a critical answer to this question. The former refers to the program evaluation outcomes showing that students are quite satisfied with the content as well as the process of the course. Students notice that the negotiation course was an eye-opener, giving them an opportunity to become more aware about the way people behave in situations of opposing interests and interdependent relationships. Students also say that the course was a powerful stimulus to reflect on their own behavior in professional circumstances. When asked what should be changed in the course, students showed a preference for small-scale negotiation exercises. However, the teaching staff, consisting of five to six faculty members (lawyers and social scientists), decided to maintain the structure of the course, as described above. One might say that this resistance to change is inspired by the claim "Never change a winning course."

Here, the critical answer to our question comes in. The lack of change might also be explained by the fact that in Maastricht there is no single staff member having negotiation as a primary task in his or her teaching and/or research duties. The design of the course is agreed upon by the consensus of the teaching staff, who all have other important obligations. Changes in the format or content still have to be made by compromise in a world preferring non-intervention rules.

for negotiation. In addition, each team receives confidential materials not disclosed to the other party. Within each team, the students read the (legal) materials pertinent to the subject matter of the case and prepare the negotiations by setting goals to be reached and outlining a strategy. They also decide which member of the team will be the negotiator and which the observer. Afterward, they evaluate their performance, first within their own team and next with the members of the adversary team. In this evaluation, the feedback about the players' negotiating style from the observers of course plays an important role. This is followed by a general discussion with all the participants in the course and the teachers about the results obtained and the process followed.

All teams simultaneously negotiate the same problem in different parts of the room. During each exercise, one group is videotaped. Significant parts of this tape are shown to and discussed with all the participants during the next meeting.

During the originally six-week, now eight-week course, the exercises become more and more complex and difficult. First, the number of parties involved in the negotiation process increases. The course starts with two-party exercises and ends with a five-hour simulation game in which twelve parties are involved. Second, the legal subject matter involved becomes more complicated with each session. Starting with quite simple exercises not requiring specialized legal knowledge, the course ends with a rather complicated case concerning the introduction of a reform bill. For this, the students have to study statute and case law in order to handle the content adequately.

Finally, with each session, more and different aspects of the negotiation process are discussed and taught. Students are forced to feel the atmosphere, to gauge the balance of power between the parties, and to apply the empirical rules and procedures pertinent to each negotiation. During one of the exercises, for example, students experience the real difficulties of the role of the advocate, positioned between his client on the one hand and legal constraints on the other. During another session, the students in some of their roles experience the lack of power, while in others they feel the balance, the possibilities, and the constraints of the "do ut des" position. Sometimes they get a sense of the importance of atmosphere and feel the shadow of the future. The exercises are designed to emphasize these various aspects, which we discuss following the exercises. At times, however, we have to admit that we find it difficult to link the theoretical points with the performances of the students.

Would some form of specialization among the staff make a difference? The answer to this question is not up to the authors, because they are no longer with the Faculty of Law.

Changes

Although the goals and the overall design of the course have remained unchanged, we introduced a number of changes based on our first experiences. The main changes were revisions of some role-plays; more explicit discussion of negotiation theory; more background literature pertinent to the case involved; and introduction of "warming-up" lectures.

Revisions in Role-Play Exercises
Some role-plays were revised, or even replaced with others, because on reflection they did not fit our learning objectives very well. A role-play is designed to direct the students' attention to specific problems. In some cases, however, students did not do what we expected them to do. A labor-contract case, for example, proved to induce students to dwell on technical details. Their energy became absorbed by the quest for technical solutions instead of focusing on negotiating. We learned that a role-play should not be too complicated, for otherwise it may distract the student's attention from the process of negotiating.

On the other hand, a role-play should not be too simple, either: For a while, we experimented with cases developed by students. This, however, did not work out very well because the cases proposed were generally too simple and, consequently, not challenging enough. A simple case does not stimulate students to invest energy in finding a "solution." Therefore, a certain degree of complexity exists; the appropriate complexity depends on the learning objectives and the position of the case in the course as a whole. Besides, it is difficult to predict whether a role-play will function as intended. We are learning through trial and error.

Emphasis on Negotiation Theory
At first we did not pay very much attention to negotiation theory. As the course was part of the skills training program of

the faculty, theoretical knowledge was de-emphasized in favor of learning-by-doing. We still hold that practical exercise is, and should be, the kernel of our course.

However, in order to heighten the value of the experience of the students during the role-play, and to evaluate the role-play in a more systematic manner afterward, it seemed helpful to rely on some elementary concepts of negotiation theory. In addition to a videotape (concerning empirical rules of negotiations) to be presented during the second meeting, in evaluating the role-plays we began to emphasize conceptual matters more. Like the video-tape, the texts on negotiations do not present grand theory but offer instead practical guide-lines and suggestions on how to negotiate more effectively.

We intended to present the students with some insights and clues that would help them understand their own (successful or unsuccessful) actions. We hoped that students would use these insights spontaneously while evaluating their own behavior. Whether we succeeded in the first we do not know for lack of test results. In reaching the second objective, we definitely failed. Once again, we think that the introduction of some basic theoretical concepts is required in order to make practical experiences during the role-plays more valu-able. We will return to this problem in the last section of this article.

Additional Background Literature

In addition to a more explicit discussion of negotiation theory, we began to add more literature on the legal substance of the cases involved. We paid attention to three specific aspects, in particular.

First, students should be knowledgeable about the relevant legal provisions of a case. The reason for this is twofold: On the one hand, students must take into account relevant legal provisions when negotiating; on the other hand, they must discover that legal provisions often leave room for different solutions, which means that the result depends more on the negotiator's skills than on the law involved. Secondly, we supplied the students with information on how similar cases are handled and resolved in the real world. What kind of practical, nonlegal rules do people follow, for example, in adjusting traffic damages? We want the roles being played to be as "real" as possible, and thus, we supply students with rules of conduct as they are used in the real world.

Finally, our students have to deal with relevant psychological, social, and other aspects that may influence the negotiation process. Psychological stress, for example, is a factor in our divorce case, which involves strained relations that might result in escalating claims. The shadow of the future lies upon the industrial dispute with inevitable questions of power and prestige, which must be dealt with somehow in order not to thwart future negotiations. Lobbying, tactical maneuvering, and compromising turn out to be important elements in the introduction of a reform bill.

"Warm-Up" Lectures

Contrary to our initial intention, we ultimately introduced concise lectures at the beginning of each meeting. We did this not because we decided to abandon the learning-by-doing principle, but rather in order to deepen the learning process. These lectures enable us to accomplish three interrelated goals: to give additional information on the cases involved, to summarize and discuss the main points of the literature read by the students, and above all, to motivate the students. The lectures serve the "warming-up" function. They are given by a staff member acquainted with the problems of the case under consideration. Thus, the lecturer gives "inside information" and elaborates on the latest developments. The case of company raiding, for instance, is introduced by a specialist in company law, and the case of positive discrimination is introduced by a staff member involved in the project on women and law. In comparison with written materials, an (enthusiastic!) oral introduction seems to better stimulate students.[4]

Evaluation
We see two weak points in our course. First, we do not succeed well in relating the theoretical aspects of the process of negotiating to the practice of it. Although we inserted more and more theory into the course, it remains a problem to show the students how these theoretical aspects are reflected in the exercises they perform themselves. We think this is due partly to the large number of students we have to work with. As a result, the teachers do not have enough time or opportunity to monitor in great detail all the exercises of all students. Consequently, feedback they can give often lacks detail.

Although one of the reasons to form teams was the idea of giving feedback to one another, this often does not work well either. Here, we touch on the second weak point of the course: we feel that students do not succeed in giving feedback among themselves on the level we had hoped. Moreover, our students do not have enough experience to relate negotiation theory to the practice themselves. All this means is that the course is too large on the one hand (with respect to student numbers) and too short on the other hand (lasting only three hours per week during eight weeks plus a few hours for preparation) to really influence the negotiation skills of the students.

However, our goals are far more modest than preparing skilled negotiators. We want only for our students to get some idea of and feeling for the process of negotiation. In this respect, our learning-by-doing approach is successful: the skills approach is useful in introducing to our students the sensitivities involved in negotiation processes.

Secondly, the course succeeds in offering our students the opportunity to see other than legal aspects relevant in dispute settling. We are convinced that this is important: we offer law students, with their primarily legal perspective, another pair of glasses through which they can observe the world. With these they become better prepared to tackle disputes. Once again, we stress that our course offers only a starting point for obtaining the experiences necessary to becoming really skillful at negotiating. But it offers more than only the beginning of experience: it also offers some tools (and their theoretical background) to work with.

In the third place, the course offers the students an opportunity to relate the world of law to the world of negotiating. They learn to see that solving disputes can be influenced by using nonlegal skills, although the law usually plays an important role in the background of the kind of disputes that lawyers are expected to help solve. Also in this respect, we think that the perspectives the students hold on the law change during the course.

In the fourth place, most students like to be videotaped and to watch themselves working. For quite a lot of them, it is the first time they can watch and hear themselves. Although this is often a sort of shock therapy, they seem to find it useful. Again, we must add that the time devoted to playing of tapes is short, and that the groups of students are so large that they can watch themselves only once or twice during the course, which means that videotaping does not serve the purpose of improving performances through repeated training.

Finally, the course is both fun and directly related to issues that are important to our students. The last role-play, for example, focuses on the question whether a new Civil Code should be introduced or not, which has been quite an issue in The Netherlands for the past decade. All the students are involved in playing one of 12 different roles, ranging from the ministers of Justice and Finance, civil servants, and members of Parliament, to different lobbyists and members of the press. The role play requires considerable knowledge of the subject matter, calls upon all kinds of negotiation skills, and demonstrates the influence or lack of it of the different players. Each time this role-play, which lasts an entire day, is performed, the participants are exhausted at the end. But they also feel good about their participation and the fun of playing: it is an experience that few forget easily. In many respects, that is the best that can happen in education.

Notes
An earlier version of this article was presented at the December, 1989 Nottingham (England) Conference as "The Effective Negotiator: Theory, Research and Practice."

1. The moot court course is a new element in the curriculum: while students play the roles of the advocates and the public prosecutor, and members of the teaching staff take the roles of clients and judges, the cases develop in much the same way that real cases do. In moot court cases, everything is allowed, within the constraints of Dutch law.
2. We use a dispute between a university and a car driver: the car driver severely damaged his tires when he drove his car on the property of the state university over a set of spikes, intended to prevent him and others from parking in front of the main building of the university (photographs included).
3. For example, the law faculty of Limburg University has an influx of 400 students a year, the faculty being one of the smaller ones in the country. The largest is the Leyden faculty, with an influx of more than 1000 students a year.
4. Readers interested in a week-by-week outline of the course may obtain a copy by writing to Huub Spoormans, Faculty of Law, Limburg University. P.O. 616, 6200 MD Maastricht, The Netherlands.

Reference

Cohen, M. J., et al. 1987. Skills training at the Limburg University Faculty of Law. *Journal of Professional Legal Education* 5(2):135-150.

Bridging the Gap Between Negotiating Experience and Analysis

Daniel Druckman

Daniel Druckman is Professor of conflict resolution and coordinator of the doctoral program at George Mason's Institute for Conflict Analysis and Resolution. He has published widely on such topics as international negotiation and ancient diplomacy, nationalism and group processes, nonverbal communication, political stability, peacekeeping, and modeling methodologies including simulation. He is the editor (and an author) of the August 2000 issue of

This article first appeared in *Negotiation Journal*, October 1996: Volume 12, Number 4, pages 371-383.

A perennial challenge for teachers of negotiation courses is to relate the analysis of negotiation to the experiences of their students. Students often come to a class on negotiation with some personal experience or information about particular negotiations and nostrums from "how-to" books. Few students, however, come to class with analytical skills or knowledge about research on the topic.

The central theme of my graduate course on negotiation processes, taught at George Mason University's Institute for Conflict Analysis and Resolution (ICAR), is to demonstrate how analysis complements experience and contributes in important ways to an understanding of negotiation. The purpose of the course is to develop analytical skills that will increase students' understanding of the research and theoretical literature as well as to make them more sensitive observers of negotiation. The course is not intended specifically to make students more effective negotiators, although any contributions made to sharpening these skills would be welcome.

The students and I work to achieve our goals by moving in sequence from the specific to the general, and then back to the specific. In other words, starting with the students' experiences, we construct a framework that is then used to analyze a number of cases, and conclude with judgments about the extent to which the framework and analysis have contributed to an understanding of their experiences or of particular cases. This approach is an alternative to using experiential games or role-play exercises to accomplish similar goals. My choice of this approach was influenced by the results of studies showing small long-term learning outcomes from participating in interactive games or simulations. (See Druckman 1995 for a recent review of evaluation studies.) This article describes how the approach is implemented in a semester-length graduate course.

the *American Behavioral Scientist* on "Public and Private Cooperation in the Beltway." He may be contacted at the Institute for Conflict Analysis and Resolution, George Mason University, Fairfax, VA 22030-4444. Phone: 703-993-3655; Fax: 703-993-1302; e-mail: ddruckma@gmu.edu

Reflections

The teaching approach described in this article still guides the course. More recently, however, I have encouraged students to spend more time on group research projects. Among the projects completed in my Spring 2000 class were a comparative case study of post-settlement processes, evaluating a framework for the analysis of turning points in international and domestic cases, developing a typology of impasses and the way they are resolved in a variety of types of negotiation, and the

Negotiating Experience

On the first day of class, students are asked to describe a negotiating experience that involved them or that they observed closely. Among the wide-ranging examples that this request stimulates are: negotiating over the price of a bicycle or a computer; resolving disputes among family members over shares in a family-owned business; negotiations between students and faculty in a department over travel funds to be allocated to students; budget disputes among federal agencies; territorial disputes between factions in a boy's camp; environmental negotiations among national representatives over issues with global consequences; issues concerning the role of local citizens in school decisions; negotiating changed relationships with parents; and vying to negotiate a lease for a highly-prized apartment. Many of these examples deal with tangible resource-allocation issues or purchases; a few concern relationship issues or describe complex negotiations within organizations or institutions.

Students are asked a number of questions about these experiences: What were the issues? What was the outcome? What happened during the process of negotiating? Was there bargaining and, if so, how did it occur? How did the parties prepare to negotiate? What were some factors in the situation that may have influenced the negotiation process or its outcome? Has the agreement (if attained) lasted? And, did the negotiation affect the parties' relationship and, if so, how? The answers to these questions identify factors common to many of the students' experiences as well as some that were unique to particular experiences.

Most of the students focused on the issues, processes, situation, and outcomes. In discussing the issues, they dealt primarily with such content-specific topics as "differences over price," "the role of school employees," or "space and territory." In characterizing the process, they used such terms as "discussion," "formal or informal," "note-passing or face-to-face," or "a series of meetings with alternating personnel." The situations were described often in terms of the parties, such as "six sellers and one buyer," "multiple groups with consultants," "team stability or change," or "the influence of NGOs." With regard to the outcomes, they referred to the "agreed price," "the proposal on the table" (if no resolution occurred) or "the creation of a program."

Many of these descriptions are nonanalytical. They depict aspects of the specific negotiating examples rather than more generic categories such as large or small issues, concession exchange or problem-solving processes, time pressures, or whether the agreements were comprehensive (all issues resolved) or partial. Many factors about which research has been done were not mentioned and few students seemed to have a conception of relationships between processes or situations and outcomes. Based on these descriptions, I recognized the need for a broad analytical framework in which relationships among parts of the negotiating environment and processes are depicted.

respective influences of national and professional cultures on negotiating behavior.

Building on these descriptions, the students and I develop a vocabulary that consists of a listing of factors in the situation, process, issues, and external events operating in any negotiation. In a second round of responding to the questions noted earlier, the students are encouraged to group aspects of their negotiation into the categories of issues (e.g., large or small); process (e.g., bargaining, debate); outcomes (e.g., proportionate division, impasse); situation (e.g., time pressures, team stability); and implementation (e.g., provisions for protecting the agreement). These questions are also asked by researchers. But, in addition, the researchers add questions about relationships between the process and its outcome or between factors in the situation and the process or outcome. The exercise introduces students to the idea of relationships among various parts of a negotiation, emphasizing that these connections are discovered through empirical research done on a large number of cases, not on the basis of a single negotiating experience.

Developing a Framework

Negotiation is depicted in most of the literature as a complex process which, when thought about analytically, consists of many related parts. The parts and their relationships can be depicted by a framework that connects factors that, in general, occur at three different time periods:

- antecedent (preparation, issues, background factors);
- concurrent (processes such as bargaining, conditions such as time pressures or external events); and
- consequent (including the outcomes and implementation provisions).

The framework shown in Figure 1 (based originally on the format developed by Sawyer and Guetkow [1965]) provides a structure for the course by organizing research on the topic and providing a tool for comparing diverse cases.

This approach is more eclectic than specialized in terms of one or another disciplinary orientation. However, while synthesizing several research traditions, the framework emphasizes social psychological factors. The Sawyer-Guetzkow (1965) framework serves these purposes well. But we also review other candidate frameworks, including those by Randolph (1966), Walton and McKersie (1965), Iklé (1964) and various modified versions of the Sawyer and Guetkow framework, such as the ones developed by Druckman (1977, 1993), Ramberg (1978), and Bonham (1971).

Figure 1. Influences and Processes of Negotiation: A Framework

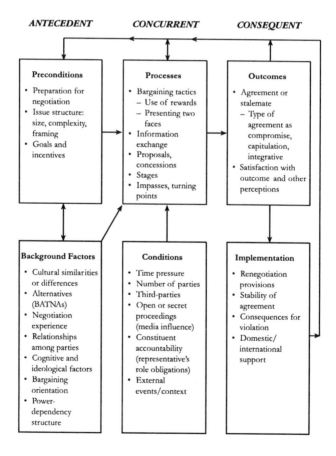

ANTECEDENT   CONCURRENT   CONSEQUENT

Preconditions
- Preparation for negotiation
- Issue structure: size, complexity, framing
- Goals and incentives

Processes
- Bargaining tactics
  - Use of rewards
  - Presenting two faces
- Information exchange
- Proposals, concessions
- Stages
- Impasses, turning points

Outcomes
- Agreement or stalemate
  - Type of agreement as compromise, capitulation, integrative
- Satisfaction with outcome and other perceptions

Background Factors
- Cultural similarities or differences
- Alternatives (BATNAs)
- Negotiation experience
- Relationships among parties
- Cognitive and ideological factors
- Bargaining orientation
- Power-dependency structure

Conditions
- Time pressure
- Number of parties
- Third-parties
- Open or secret proceedings (media influence)
- Constituent accountability (representative's role obligations)
- External events/context

Implementation
- Renegotiation provisions
- Stability of agreement
- Consequences for violation
- Domestic/international support

I note that the frameworks contain many of the factors identified by the students in their own experiences plus other factors identified by the research but not thought to be present in their examples. I then revisit the students' examples by asking class members to describe their negotiation experiences again, this time in terms of the frameworks: What were some preconditions? Background factors? Aspects of the process? Conditions? Types of outcomes? I also ask the students to develop hypotheses about how these factors might be related in the context of their examples.

The same students who described the content of the issues at stake in their examples now distinguished (in the case of multiple-issue negotiation) between the large and small issues as well as between complex and simpler issues. Instead of referring to the process as a "discussion" or "formal," they conceptualized it in terms of concession exchanges, the frequency of threats used or accommodations made, and as phases going from developing agendas to an endgame.

Features of the situation or conditions now included whether the talks were public or private, divisions within teams (for bilateral examples) or coalitions (for multilateral examples), and stresses on the negotiators. Outcomes were now discussed in terms of the number of issues resolved, whether resolutions were compromises, asymmetrical distributions, or integrative agreements, and whether packages (for complex examples) were balanced or imbalanced. The students also noted the extent to which parties were satisfied with the outcome.

Going beyond reconceptualization, we then explore the idea of relationships among these factors. For example, a relationship between issues, process, and outcome may take the following form: bargaining is more likely to occur over tangible (material as opposed to ideological) issues leading to either compromises or outcomes that favor one or another of the parties. These are the sorts of relationships investigated by researchers, and we turn next to a review of the studies.

Reviewing the Research Literature

Examples of published research studies designed to investigate relationships among most of these factors and outcomes are reviewed in conjunction with the framework — and as a prelude to discussions of the research literature listed in the syllabus. Topics discussed include the experimental studies on constituent accountability (e.g., Ben-Yoav and Pruitt 1984); the experiments done on the effects of time pressure (e.g., Carnevale and Lawler 1986); work on the way negotiating teams perform tactical moves (e.g., Hilty and Carnevale 1993); case study analyses of the influence of external (compared to internal) events (e.g., Hopmann and Smith 1978); the way that alternatives to negotiated agreements are developed and used (e.g., Pinkley et al. 1994); and the role of experience in previous negotiations as analyzed by Thompson (1993).

These examples of research studies begin an excursion into the literature which is organized into several parts. Readings from the Kremenyuk (1991) volume are supplemented with journal articles including reports of experimental studies in the Journal of Conflict Resolution and the case studies presented in *Negotiation Journal*. The first part of the course, thinking about negotiation, consists of an introduction to four research traditions: game and decision theory, bargaining games, organizational bargaining, and systems approaches. (See Druckman and Hopmann [1989] for an overview of these traditions.)

In discussing these approaches, students are encouraged to use their examples and to seek parallel illustrations from other domains. Regarding game theory in terms of puzzles to be solved, I ask the students to think of their examples as choice dilemmas for both (or all) the "players." The choice may be similar to that confronting United States and Soviet Union negotiators during the Cuban missile crisis—to concede or to hold firm (Snyder and Diesing 1977). Or, it may be between choosing to negotiate or to obstruct negotiations as illustrated by the Iran hostage crisis game (Brams 1993). Many of the students' examples involved a bargaining process in which concessions were exchanged until an agreement was reached. In negotiating over the price of a computer or over claims for space, bargainers respond to each other's moves in a manner similar to the way arms control negotiators exchange proposals from one round to another (Jensen 1988).

The students' examples of conflicts within universities or federal bureaucracies illuminate bargaining within organizations. In these examples, negotiators are representatives who must attempt to resolve the competing demands of one's own and others' constituencies. This boundary-role dilemma is common in labor-management negotiations (Walton and McKersie 1965) but is also illustrated by the two-level game in international politics (Putnam 1988).

When describing global environmental negotiations or deliberations involving the International Red Cross, the students show how negotiations can be used to manage international relations or to bridge cultures. They are made aware of systems approaches by reading other cases where context and process are merged in attempts to negotiate regimes (Jervis 1983) or to redesign international structures (Strauss 1977).

The next part of class discussion and readings—rhythms and patterns of negotiation—exposes students to experimental and case studies on role constraints, preparation, framing, concession-making, tactics, and phases and turning points. The discussion of tactics raises questions of ethics in negotiation. Many tactics used in distributive and intraorganizational bargaining (including some from the students' examples) involve manipulation, deception, and coercion. Competitive bargainers often convey misleading impressions, withhold information, fabricate commitment, exaggerate achievements, and interpose obstacles to communication with opponents and constituents. The ethical dilemmas posed by these tactics have led many authors to reject distributive bargaining in favor of a process of open communication leading to integrative agreements (Kressel et al. 1994; Hopmann 1995).

Students are challenged to develop strategies that encourage sharing of information without risking being exploited. They are helped by reading Walton and McKersie's (1965: 358) discussion of trust, which is a key element in both distributive and integrative bargaining: "The fact is that trust appears to be an unmixed asset in negotiations. There is little to commend a policy of fostering distrust, from either the perspective of attitudinal structuring or from that of the other processes." These issues are considered also in relation to flexibility in negotiation, a topic addressed in some detail in a recent special issue of the Annals of the American Academy of Political and Social Science (Druckman and Mitchell 1995).

Next, the analysis of complex cases is treated in conjunction with the class project outlined in the following section. A part on applications (training, decision support, and how-to-negotiate books) precedes a summary discussion on retrospect—what we know to date—and prospect—uncharted topics and areas.

Analyzing and Comparing Cases

When I introduce the subject of complex cases, I return to the framework, built from both experience and research findings, which I now use as an analytical tool for comparing diverse cases. Referred to as a "new research frontier," the students are taken on an intellectual journey in which they go beyond the single case study in order to develop theories that apply broadly across cases. The comparative approach addresses such questions as: What are the features (issue area, number of parties, conference structure) that distinguish the cases in terms of similarities and dissimilarities? What are the processes (stages, concession exchanges, procedures) and situations (media coverage, time pressures, stakes) that distinguish the cases in terms of the outcomes produced? What are the key drivers of the negotiation process, for example, external or internal factors? Do the findings obtained with one set of cases apply also to another set not yet analyzed?

The idea of comparing cases is introduced in terms of the students' experiences. They are asked to think about the similarities and differences between, for example, negotiations over departmental budget allocations and competing with other buyers in negotiations with an agent for an apartment. The interplay between framework and empirical research, illustrated by this project, is similar in many ways to the well-known CASCON project designed by Bloomfield and Beattie (1971) to help analysts deal with local conflicts.

The cases used in classes taught to date were compiled from such sources as the Johns Hopkins Foreign Policy Institute monograph series and the declassified negotiation transcripts now contained in the Library of Congress archives under U.S. Foreign Policy, as well as at a number of university libraries. Other sources for case material used by the students are the case chronologies and events described by negotiators in the Foreign Service Institute's "lessons learned" projects (Bendahmane and McDonald 1986; McDonald and Bendahmane 1990); articles in the case studies section of this journal; book-length accounts of arms control (e.g., Talbott 1984) or environmental negotiations (e.g., Benedick 1990); the several edited collections of case analyses sponsored by the Processes of International Negotiation (PIN) project at the International Institute of Applied Systems Analysis (e.g., Faure and Rubin 1993; Sjöstedt 1992; Zartman 1994); and the Pew Foundation-sponsored series of cases in international diplomacy.[1]

237

It is important to distinguish between the interpretive analyses presented in most published sources and the original documentation found in archives, retrospective reporting by the negotiators, or in government or international organization files. When available, original documents, transcripts, memoranda, or direct observation are preferred sources of data for the kinds of comparative analyses done in this class project. These materials provide a window into what actually took place. The published case studies are often filtered through the lens of an analyst's conceptual approach.

Framework categories are translated into coded variables and applied to the description of the processes and events surrounding the cases. We ask about the structure of the negotiation (e.g., number of delegations), the issues (e.g., number and size), the situation (e.g., existence of deadlines, media attention), role of external events (e.g., linkages to other talks), the process (e.g., bargaining or problem solving, use of hard or soft tactics), and outcomes (e.g., agreement or stalemate, binding or nonbinding agreements, partial or comprehensive agreements).

Each student reads, summarizes, and codes three cases, enabling us to accumulate a sufficient number for statistical analysis. They also write descriptive summaries of the cases which are presented orally to other students in the class. This insures that everyone benefits from learning about all the cases used in the project.

Class members perform two kinds of analyses. One consists of charting trends in moves or rhetoric for identifying negotiation stages. The second involves discovering general dimensions or clusters from correlations computed among the cases (across the coding categories) and among the coding categories (across the cases).[2] Each is discussed in turn.

Stages
A more detailed analysis is performed on the aspect in the framework's process box referred to as "stages of negotiation" (see Figure 1). For each case where actual conversations are available, students place the negotiators' statements into the coding categories of the bargaining process analysis system developed by Walcott and Hopmann (1978). These categories distinguish between, on the one hand, the "hard" bargaining tactics of commitments, threats, and demands and, on the other, the "softer" problem-solving categories of perspective-taking, brainstorming, and reframing. By dividing the cases into time periods or phases, it is possible to discern patterns in the incidence of bargaining or problem-solving behaviors used by the different negotiating parties.

For example, in the World War II-era negotiation among the United States, Great Britain, and Switzerland over a blockade of Nazi Germany, we found that, over the course of six meetings, the British negotiators were consistent hard bargainers; the U.S. negotiators were consistent problem solvers; and the Swiss were mixed, bargaining in the early meetings and problem solving in a "mediator" role during the later meetings. In a post-World War II negotiation over establishing basic laws for Germany, different patterns were found for each of three stages: going from establishing each party's limits to brainstorming in attempts to establish common ground to reframing and commitments in a final stage. Such cases as the Austrian State Treaty talks from 1952-1955 showed more complex patterns of party behavior through various time periods. Other cases showed the well-known "phase movement pattern" found to characterize small problem-solving groups, identified initially in early research conducted by Bales and Strodtbeck. That pattern consists of certain acts or behaviors which occur most frequently during particular stages of negotiation. (See Enders 1988 for a review and application.)

These analyses made students aware of rhythms and patterns that characterize the negotiation process. Using their own examples, the students are asked to think about the relative incidence of different kinds of acts at different times in the negotiation. The phase-movement hypothesis is used for comparison. For example, the extent to which giving and asking for information (referred to as orientation acts) occurred most often during the early phase, whether opinions were given (evaluation statements) most frequently during the middle phase, and if decisions were made (control actions) primarily during the final phase.

As suggested also by the phase-movement hypothesis, positive and negative expressions of emotion were seen to increase from the early to the later phases in many of the examples. By applying various stage conceptions to actual negotiations in this way, the exercise also brings to life the theoretical debates in the literature about the number and types of negotiation stages.

Dimensions
Students also code the cases in terms of such characteristics as power differences among the parties, issue area, number of issues, deadline pressures, and outcomes. In this exercise, we demonstrate how statistical analysis can be used to organize a set of cases in terms of key dimensions. With the help of a statistical software package, students compute correlations and participate in a multidimensional scaling analysis.

In one class project, using 15 cases from the Foreign Policy Institute monograph series, we discovered that the cases were organized in terms of two issue dimensions: the number of issues in contention and the complexity of the issues. Examples of cases with many complex issues are SALT I and the Mutual and Balanced Force Reduction talks; those with many, not complex issues are the 1977 Panama Canal negotiations and the 1972 Simla talks between India and Pakistan. Cases with a few complex issues include the 1975-76 base rights talks between Spain and the United States; and, those with a few, not complex issues are Sinai II and the 1983 agreement over Lebanon.

In another class exercise, using the 12 cases from the U.S. Foreign Policy archival collection, we discovered that the cases were organized in terms of whether the focus was on long or short-term issues (e.g., economic aid vs. establishing governing structures) and whether the outcome was a general framework agreement (e.g., some repatriation and trade agreements) or was technical, concrete, and specific (e.g., base-rights agreements).[3]

The negotiation codings are also used to diagnose negotiating flexibility and estimate possible negotiation outcomes for each case. (See Druckman 1993a, for details on how this is done.) These analyses introduce students to some ways in which computers can be used as aids for comparing and dealing with the complexity of a variety of types of negotiation cases. With regard to their own experiences, the students appreciated the value of computers as devices for keeping track of moves over time (particularly in complex talks), for content-analyzing verbal statements to gauge commitment and flexibility, and for calculating reservation prices.

Lessons Learned

I proceed then from the general to the specific by returning to the earlier descriptions of students' experiences. The students are asked to ascertain the extent to which the general results—across the set of cases—apply to those particular experiences as well as to particular cases in the set analyzed. They attempt to reconceptualize their own experiences, described earlier, in terms of the analytical categories used in the project.

One example is an understanding of the decision dilemma of balancing alternatives to negotiated outcomes against time pressures when bargaining over, for example, the price of a computer. More attractive alternatives in the face of time pressure may enhance bargaining power which can, in turn, lead to a better outcome for the more powerful bargainer. Another example is the way that cooperative or competitive communications during the bargaining process affects future negotiations among family members. More cooperative processes improve relationships even when negotiated outcomes are nonoptimal. A third example deals with the facilitating effects of mediating roles played by moderates on both sides of a departmental budget dispute. Collaborating moderates can reduce the polarization between parties, making negotiated agreements possible. A fourth example concerns the effects of audiences on the flexibility displayed by representatives of disputing community groups. Students were able to attribute the apparent lack of compromising in this example to the presence of audiences during the talks.

Other examples included the role of cognitive differences in international environmental negotiations and the role played by preparation for negotiating complex issues. Students learned that cognitive differences are particularly difficult to bridge through compromise. They also became aware of how unilateral strategy development prior to negotiation can reduce understanding of the others' positions and, thus, reduce the chances of obtaining an integrative agreement. Each of these examples is also supported by the research studies reviewed earlier in class.

While emphasizing these particular processes in the context of their examples, the students also learn to eschew single-factor explanations for negotiating behavior. They develop an appreciation for the way that several factors in the situation and process interact to influence both short and long-term outcomes. This is illustrated by the framework in Figure

1 as well as by simulation exercises designed to explore the impacts of multiple interacting factors on negotiation decisions (e.g., Druckman 1993).

A "lessons learned" session, moving between the particular or experiential and the general or analytical bases for understanding negotiation, concludes the class. During this discussion, students are encouraged to consider both similarities and differences between their "everyday" negotiating experiences and the more complex cases used in the comparative analyses. One difference is between conflicts in which bargaining is the primary process (as in many of the students' examples) and conflicts where bargaining takes place only at a later stage in a process that consists also of conceptualizing the problem and constructing alternative packages (as in many of the international cases).

In their course evaluations, students have indicated the usefulness of the project for learning to do analytical work, for achieving a deeper understanding of complex cases, and for supplementing the perspectives gained from the readings. One student commented that "the course outline—personal cases, then general theories, then more specific aspects—was a good approach to the subject." Another remarked that "the class project served as an excellent way of learning a subject that often can be difficult to comprehend." A third student noted that it was "done especially well, giving us a very comprehensive picture of negotiations—and ample sources were available." Although these comments are typical of those made by other participants, they do not substitute for the systematic evaluations that remain to be done.

The results of these analyses also contribute to the research literature on comparative case studies (see Druckman forthcoming). Some students were eager to continue work on the project. In the months following the 1996 class, they coded an expanded set of 30 Pew Foundation-supported cases on 16 dimensions represented in the framework. Preliminary results of the scaling analysis show that the cases are distinguished in terms of Iklé's (1964) taxonomy of types of international negotiation objectives. For future projects, I would like to expand the domain of case materials, focusing in particular on domestic negotiations.

In conclusion, the approach described here is one way to bridge the gap between negotiating experience and analysis. I would like to learn about other teaching approaches to the merging of experience and analysis. Among the questions other teachers of negotiation might consider are: How are the students' experiences used in analyzing negotiations? Are role-play exercises used? If cases are used, what are these cases and how well are they documented? Are statistical techniques used in the analysis? How do students react to or evaluate the exercise? And, are there indications that your students incorporate the analytical approach in their negotiating experiences? If interested colleagues contact me, I would be pleased to communicate what I learn in a future issue of this journal.

Notes

1. Interested readers can obtain the Johns Hopkins Foreign Policy Institute cases by writing to: FPI Publications Program, School of Advanced International Studies, The Johns Hopkins University, 1619 Massachusetts Avenue N.W., Washington, D.C. 20036-2297. Inquiries about publications produced by the PIN Project should be sent to the International Institute of Applied Systems Analysis, A-2361, Laxenburg, Austria. The Pew Foundation-sponsored case studies can be obtained from the Institute for the Study of Diplomacy, Edmund A. Walsh School of Foreign Service, Georgetown University, Washington, D.C. 20057-1052.

2. For a complete listing of the cases analyzed to date, as well as the coding categories and scaling results, contact the author at the Institute for Conflict Analysis and Resolution, George Mason University, Fairfax, Virginia 22030-4444.

3. One student in the class has used this exercise as the basis of a dissertation project being completed at The Johns Hopkins University School for Advanced International Studies (SAIS) in Washington. She is analyzing relationships among processes and outcomes in twelve historical cases from the U.S. Foreign Policy documentation. Interested readers may contact Lynn Wagner at 2922 2nd Street, Apt. D, Santa Monica, Calif. for further information about this project.

References

Bendahmane, D. B. and J. W. McDonald, editors. 1986. *Perspectives on negotiation: Four case studies and interpretations.* Washington: Foreign Service Institute, Department of State.

Benedick, R.E. 1990. *Ozone diplomacy.* Cambridge, Mass: Harvard University Press.

Ben-Yoav, O. and D.G. Pruitt. 1984. Accountability to constituents: A two-edged sword. *Organizational Behavior and Human Performance* 34: 283-295.

Bloomfield, L.P. and R. Beattie. 1971. Computers and policy-making: The CASCON experiment. *Journal of Conflict Resolution* 15: 33-46.

Bonham, G.M. 1971. Simulating international disarmament negotiations. *Journal of Conflict Resolution* 15: 299-315.

Brams, S.J. 1993. Theory of moves. *American Scientist* 81: 562-570.

Carnevale, P. J. and E. J. Lawler. 1986. Time pressure and the development of integrative agreements in bilateral negotiation. *Journal of Conflict Resolution* 30: 636-659.

Druckman, D. Forthcoming. Dimensions of international negotiation: Structures, processes, and outcomes. *Group Decision and Negotiation.*

____. 1995. The educational effectiveness of interactive games. In *Simulation and gaming across disciplines and cultures,* edited by D. Crookall and K. Arai. Thousand Oaks, Calif.: Sage.

____. . 1993. The situational levers of negotiating flexibility. *Journal of Conflict Resolution* 37: 236-276.

____. 1993a. Statistical analysis for negotiation support. *Theory and Decision* 34: 215-233.

Druckman, D. (editor). 1977. *Negotiations: Social-psychological perspectives.* Beverly Hills: Sage.

Druckman, D. and P. T. Hopmann. 1989. Behavioral aspects of negotiations on mutual security. In *Behavior, society, and nuclear war,* edited by P. E. Tetlock et al. New York: Oxford University Press.

Druckman, D. and C. Mitchell, editors. 1995. Flexibility in international negotiation and mediation. Special issue of *The Annals of the American Academy of Political and Social Science.* 542, November.

Enders, J. K. J. 1988. Clarifying the limits of the phase hypothesis: The presence of phase movement in established groups. Unpublished master's degree thesis, Department of Behavioral Sciences, University of Chicago.

Faure, G. O. and J.Z. Rubin, (eds) 1993. *Culture and negotiation.* Newbury Park, Calif.: Sage.

Hilty, J. A. and P. J. Carnevale. 1993. Black-hat/white-hat strategy in bilateral bargaining. *Organizational Behavior and Human Decision Processes* 55: 444-469.

Hopmann, P. T. 1995. Two paradigms of negotiation: Bargaining and problem solving. *The Annals of the American Academy of Political and Social Science* 542: 24-47.

Hopmann, P. T. and T. C. Smith. 1978. An application of a Richardson process model: Soviet-American relations in the test ban treaty, 1962-63. In *The negotiation process,* edited by I. W. Zartman. Beverly Hills: Sage.

Iklé, F. C. 1964. *How nations negotiate.* New York: Harper & Row.

Jensen, L. 1988. *Bargaining for national security: The postwar disarmament negotiations.* Columbia, S.C.: University of South Carolina Press.

Jervis, R. 1983. Security regimes. In *International regimes,* edited by S. Krasner. Ithaca, N.Y.: Cornell University Press.

Kremenyuk, V.A., (ed). 1991. *International negotiation: Analysis, approaches, issues.* San Francisco: Jossey-Bass.

Kressel, K. et al. 1994. The settlement-orientation vs. the problem-solving style in custody mediation. *Journal of Social Issues* 50: 67-84.

McDonald, J. W. and D. B. Bendahmane, (eds) 1990. *U.S. bases overseas: Negotiations with Spain, Greece, and the Philippines.* Boulder, Colo.: Westview.

Pinkley, R. L., M. A. Neale, and R. J. Bennett. 1994. The impact of alternatives to settlement in dyadic negotiation. *Organizational Behavior and Human Decision Processes* 57: 97-116.

Putnam, R. 1988. Diplomacy and domestic politics: The logic of two-level games. *International Organization* 42: 427-460.

Ramberg, B. 1978. *The Seabed Arms Control Negotiation: A study of multilateral arms control conference diplomacy.* Monograph Series in World Affairs, Graduate School of International Studies, University of Denver.

Randolph, L. 1966. A suggested model of international negotiation. *Journal of Conflict Resolution* 10: 344-353.

Sawyer, J. and H. Guetzkow. 1965. Bargaining and negotiation in international relations. In *International behavior: A social-psychological analysis,* edited by H. C. Kelman. New York: Holt.

Sjöstedt, G., (ed) 1992. *International environmental negotiations.* Newbury Park, Calif.: Sage.

Snyder, G. H. and P. Diesing. 1977. *Conflict among nations: Bargaining, decision-making, and system structure in international crisis.* Princeton: Princeton University Press.

Strauss, A. 1978. *Negotiations: Varieties, contexts, processes, and social order.* San Francisco: Jossey-Bass.

Talbott, S. 1984. *Deadly gambits: The Reagan administration and the stalemate in nuclear arms control.* New York: Knopf.

Thompson, L. 1993. The influence of experience on negotiation performance. *Journal of Experimental Social Psychology* 29: 304-325.

Walcott, C. and P. T. Hopmann. 1978. Interaction analysis and bargaining behavior. In *The small group in political science: The last two decades of development,* edited by R. T. Golembiewski. Athens, Ga.: University of Georgia Press.

Walton, R. E. and R. B. McKersie. 1965. *A behavioral theory of labor negotiations: An analysis of a social interaction system.* New York: McGraw-Hill.

Zartman, I. W., editor 1994. *International multilateral negotiation.* San Francisco: Jossey-Bass.

Integrating the Undergraduate Experience: A Course on Environmental Dispute Resolution

Abram W. Kaplan

Abram W. Kaplan is the Anne Powell Riley Director and associate professor in the Environmental Studies Program at Denison University, Granville, OH 43023.

In addition to the environmental dispute resolution course (the subject of this article), he teaches courses on environmental policy and problem solving, geographic information systems, planning and design, and others.

His research interests include the

This article first appeared in *Negotiation Journal,* October 1998: Volume 14, Number 4, pages 369-379.

This paper describes a rigorous undergraduate course on environmental dispute resolution. Students get hands-on experience in negotiation cases, developing skills and building theoretical understanding through a series of exercises. With this foundation, the students advance to an extended role-playing case study on oil exploration in the Ecuadorian rain forest. The course provides an integrative function not only in terms of understanding environmental issues, but also in modeling reality, encouraging action, and building process tools that are essential in addressing environmental and social challenges facing the planet.

Not long ago, one of my students applied for graduate school, looking at the best programs where she might find further training in environmental mediation. After being accepted to the top three schools in the country, she went to visit and talk with relevant faculty members.

At one of these premier universities, she met with a well-known scholar in the field, and told him of her undergraduate training. His reply, she related to me later, was one of disbelief. "There are no such courses in undergraduate institutions," he told her flatly, "and you could have received no such training." She was unable to convince him that she had indeed completed a course on environmental dispute resolution, or that she had already worked her way through a number of the classic negotiation exercises. She quickly chose to attend a different institution, where her skills were accepted without suspicion, and where she could progress in her training instead of starting over.

This article describes that course, "Environmental Dispute Resolution," which is taught as part of the undergraduate environmental studies program at Denison University, a liberal arts college located in Granville, Ohio. This course is distinct not only because of its undergraduate context but

245

role of GIS in environmental dispute resolution, ADR as a facet of leadership, and the persuasive power of familiarity and experience in electric utility adoption of solar energy. His e-mail address is kaplan@denison.edu.

Reflections
This course continues to be successful in integrating issues in an undergraduate setting, yet has evolved because its reputation gained the attention of local government officials. When I recently taught the course, the manager and planner of our community (population, 4,000) asked if my students would help with a local development issue. Midstream, I asked my students to choose between a complex international dispute over oil exploration or a relatively contained local conflict ostensibly over road widening. The

also because of its design. It offers opportunities for students to integrate their understanding of negotiation in a far more interdisciplinary context than is typically available in courses touching on the resolution of conflict. Indeed, courses like this may provide a means to integration that may be useful in a broader educational context as well.

The "Bones" of an ADR Course
Environmental Dispute Resolution is one of a number of mid-level elective courses available to students interested in environmental studies at Denison University. It complements offerings on environmental education, geographic information systems, environmental policy, ecosystem management, and a host of disciplinary courses that deal with relevant issues. The syllabus describes the course goals as follows:

This course examines different means of resolving and managing conflict over environmental issues, drawing primarily on the rubric of alternative dispute resolution (ADR) as an improvement over the conventional judicial system. This course serves as both an intellectual introduction to ADR in the environmental arena, and as an opportunity to gain hands-on experience with the theory and practice of environmental negotiation. For those who wonder if solutions to environmental problems are unattainable, this class provides a hallmark of new directions for the field. It offers an unusual opportunity for undergraduates to gain both a liberal arts, interdisciplinary perspective and a set of marketable skills in the realm of environmental problem solving.

The course relies heavily on current readings from relevant journals (both in negotiation and in the environmental field) plus two commonly used books: Fisher, Ury, and Patton's *Getting to YES* (1991) and Susskind and Cruikshank's *Breaking the Impasse* (1987). Additional reading on a specific negotiation case is required as well, and that case material is described later in this article.

The first ten weeks of the course are devoted to a progressive development of dispute resolution theory and practice (see Table One). Students are introduced to such concepts as: principled negotiation; conflict styles; stakeholder analysis; the Pareto-efficient frontier (Raiffa 1982); deadlock strategies;

assisted negotiation; and culture and gender issues that influence negotiation processes and outcomes.

As each topic is discussed, students undertake increasingly complex, hands-on exercises, drawn largely from the teaching and training materials developed and marketed by two organizations—the National Institute of Dispute Resolution (NIDR) and the Program on Negotiation at Harvard Law School. Only when this sequence is completed are the students given the opportunity (or perhaps the "license") to test the real world of environmental conflicts. The following section describes this evolution, leading to the discussion of the hands-on case the students use to culminate their ADR education.

Sequence of Learning

In the first week of the class, students bring to the discussion their own perceptions of conflict. They are asked to write a summary of conflicts they have experienced, and to identify themes that make conflicts similar or different from one another. Some students, for instance, differentiate between calm and feisty disagreements, while others look at the context of "fights," distinguishing relationship spats from car purchases. In rare instances, they recognize the importance of complexity, or the involvement of third parties as potentially useful elements in the process of dispute resolution. The students also read essays by environmentalists, developers, loggers, and others engaged in particular environmental conflicts, to assess how these writers perceive conflict. This provides an excellent starting point for semester-long discussions regarding conflict typologies and opportunities for resolution.

The next week, these students experience their first hands-on negotiation exercise, a classic known as *Win as Much as You Can*, written by Professor Michael Wheeler of the Harvard Business School. This clever exercise can encourage competition at different levels, and helps students redefine the notion of "winning" from a strictly selfish model to one that fosters cooperation. The exercise is particularly interesting in its ability to expose base personalities among the students: the amoral economist, the pleaser, the "scaredy-cat," the righteous advocate, etc. I am continually struck at the memory students have of each other from this first, simple exercise. Occasionally, they later will avoid a peer

decision process was a fascinating learning opportunity, and the group agreed to work in our backyard.

Our experience in the local project provided a very similar context for addressing ADR issues up close and personal—obviously more so than the Ecuador case simply due to the presence and accessibility of the stakeholders. The students decided on appropriate roles, established role-playing groups, and undertook serious hands-on research to build strategies and analyses in anticipation of the final negotiation session. They interviewed the real players in the case, and typically found that the parties were fascinated with the role-playing process, providing far more details of their interests than

Table 1: Outline of Environmental Dispute Resolution Course

Week	General Topic	Lecture/Discussion Issues	Exercise/Task
1	Perspectives on Conflict	Introduction; Perceptions of Conflict	What Makes it a Conflict? (exercise)
2	The Status Quo	Modes of Conflict; Foundations of Law	Exercise #1: Win as Much as You Can
3	Negotiated Alternatives	Limits of the Litigatory Process	Exercise #2: Development on Bay Island
4	What is ADR? Negotiation	Basics of ADR; Principled process	Debriefing/evaluation
5	Style and Action	Conflict Styles; Stakeholder Analysis	Thomas—Kilmann Test
6	Would You Care to Dance?	Negotiation Dances; Efficient Frontier	Exercise #3: Farmland Conversion
7	Environmetal Applications	ADR—EDR	Exercise #4 Riverside Lumber/DEC
8	Barriers to Agreement;	Obstacles and Deadlocks	Exercise #5: Radwaste
9	Assisted Negotiation	Facilitation & Mediation	Facilitation Building (prep for Ex. #6)
10	Putting It All Together	Negotiation Design Issues	Exercise #6: Dirty/Stuff II
11	Norms of ADR	Culture and Conflict	Exercise #7: Manehune Bay Development
12	Ecuador Oil Exploration	Ecuador Oil Case Startup	Stakeholder analysis/ preliminary hearing
13	Reality Checks	Role of Experts	Ecuador expert input
14	So What? Policy For What?	Opportunities	Ecuador position paper; final prep
15	Final Examination	Culmination of EDR Education	Ecuador Final Negotiated Hearing

might have occurred in a traditional research exercise.

When the final negotiation session took place, every party was represented in the whom they perceived as deceitful in this game, even if the same student's behavior has improved.

Win as Much as You Can is helpful in beginning conversations about different methods of conflict resolution and the conventional means used to resolve differences in our society. We talk about the American legal system, the basis of law, the role of precedent, the limits of the litigatory process, and the evolution of courts to accept, and incorporate, mediated settlements. With only this basic comprehension of the status quo, the students then role play an exercise like *Development on Bay Island*, which is a two-party negotiation with largely distributive issues.

With this exercise, the students gain a first examination of conflict intensity, and they take "baby steps" in the process of formally evaluating and debriefing negotiation exercises. After every exercise, each student prepares a three-to-five page memorandum discussing stakeholder interests, individual strategies, outcome assessments, and reflections on basic negotiation principles. As the exercises get more complex during the semester, the evaluations gain in sophistication as well. Students often refer back to earlier evaluations to gain perspective on the concepts they have learned through the semester.

The group spends considerable time discussing each case in the class session following each negotiation exercise as well. With classes large enough to engage in multiple simultaneous exercises (e.g., five separate four-person participants in a 20-student class), the opportunities to compare among experiences is greatly enhanced. Students often discover that their perceptions of the exercise do not match those of their classmates, or that they misinterpreted the strategy of a counterpart. Often seemingly small idiosyncrasies end up having critical significance in the outcome of an exercise, and students become increasingly perceptive as the exercises unfold. The students learn a tremendous amount from these comparative discussions.

In the ensuing weeks, the class develops better footing in the terrain of dispute resolution, starting from rudimentary principled negotiation (Fisher, Ury, and Patton 1991) and the basics of stakeholder analysis to deadlock handling and the Pareto-efficient frontier (Raiffa 1982). As the concepts get more complex, the exercises follow suit. A case like *Farmland Conversion* introduces additional parties; *Riverside Lumber vs. DEC* makes a conversion from distributive to integrative contexts; and *Radwaste* greatly increases the number of parties (to seven) while continuing to accelerate the complexity of the substance under negotiation.

The last section of the formative training involves third-party intervention through facilitation and mediation. The students learn about the value of assisted negotiation, discuss a variety of cases where it might have helped or hindered effec-

audience and on the evaluative panel: the real participants in the conflict all showed up to watch themselves being role-played by the students. The discussion was a two-hour affair, with a fairly formal structure preset by the students. After the first hour, it was obvious that the students felt they had accomplished little, and that they had misallocated their time. They spent the fifteen-minute break frantically caucusing with the real representatives of their interests, getting pointers and considering alternative strategies. It had a surreal quality about it: previously entrenched stakeholders advising student surrogates about ways to extend their principled approach to a negotiation that had taken on a complete (artificial) life of its own.

At the end of the two-hour session, the

students had not reached a final, mutually satisfying conclusion to the problems at hand, and they felt poorly. Yet the real stakeholders continued to show their fascination with the process, and were seen leaving the classroom talking with each other about the very issues which had divided them for months.

Using a local case was a mixed experience. The students left the class with a sense of inadequacy which could have been overcome with a lengthier case study or a set of follow-up classes to discuss how valuable the final session truly was. The students were so focused on their final exams that they failed to recall the continuing nature of real conflicts: never would a situation like this be finalized with a single meeting! The community found the exercise extremely

tive solutions, and distinguish among types of assistance to understand the idiosyncrasies and boundaries of each approach. With this crash course in assisted negotiation, the students work through two exercises requiring a neutral party, *DirtyStuff II* and *Menehune Bay Development*. In one case, I select the top students in the class to serve as facilitators, sometimes giving two students co-facilitation roles to ease the burden of this responsibility. (Interestingly, the class sometimes objects to the co-facilitator roles, finding that it is far easier to progress in the negotiation when there is a single outsider. In one group, the nervous facilitators became good-cop/bad-cop partners, causing considerable confusion about their roles by all involved.) In the other case, I allow the students to select their facilitators, and I often find that their criteria are inadequate or biased: the most popular male or the most attractive female may win votes, but is not guaranteed to be the most effective—or impartial—facilitator. These exercises do not permit all students to play the neutral party, but the simple act of watching and critiquing their peers provides a reasonable basis for future exposure to this element of negotiation.

Real-World Trials

At the end of this relatively formal and intensive introduction to environmental dispute resolution, the class takes a short breather. I suggest that they now have a solid foundation in the basic theory and practice of negotiation, and perhaps it is time to put their new skills to use. How about if we take on the toughest environmental conflict we can find, and see if principled negotiation can be applied?

The class stops to consider some criteria for a "tough" case: it should be multiparty and multi-issue; it should be international to make for cultural difficulties; it should involve numerous obstacles, even intra-stakeholder conflicts; and so on. We also stipulate that the case should be a current one, so that we might imagine ourselves influencing it in real life, and not just rehashing old business to show our ability to do better than an existing settlement. Thus, fascinating cases like *Exxon Valdez*, Lake Mead, Bhopal, and many others are eliminated from contention. (I involve the class in identifying criteria, but for reasons of preparation and start-up, I choose the case study.)

Instead, the class takes on an incredible case, oil exploration in Ecuador. An OPEC member until recently, Ecuador has considerable oil reserves beneath its lush tropical forests, and numerous international oil companies have explored there, some setting up extensive drilling sites with authorization from the Ecuadorian government. The conflict has come from two sources: environmentalists appalled at the ensuing environmental damage, and native peoples unnerved by the sudden intrusion of machinery, pollution, and foreigners on their sacred lands.

As the native peoples have no formal rights with the government, they lack standing to make a legal complaint. Because the environmental community in Ecuador has strong ties to the United States, American environmental groups primarily have created a stir over the case. In fact, in 1993, the Natural Resources Defense Council (NRDC) filed a $1 billion class action suit in U.S. federal court, claiming that Texaco was contaminating the Ecuadorian rain forest. The lawsuit was filed on behalf of Ecuadorian Indians who could not sue in their native land. The lawsuit was thrown out of court in 1996, but legal wranglings persist to this day, and the Ecuadorian government recently approved oil exploration in Yasuni National Park, opening yet another round of conflicts over rights and environmental protection (Brunschwig 1998).

The case involves extremely challenging issues, ranging from road siting and waste pit specifications to human rights and ecosystem preservation. The stakeholders are far-ranging too: multiple governments (e.g., the United States, Ecuador, Peru); numerous environmental groups (Fundacion Natura and Tierra Viva in Ecuador, and the NRDC, Rainforest Action Network, and Sierra Club in the U.S.); many local Indian groups (Achuar, Cofan, Huaorani, Quichua, and others); international agencies (USAID, World Bank, OPEC); perhaps a dozen multinational oil companies (e.g., Conoco, Texaco, British Petroleum, Maxxus); Ecuador's own government-run petroleum operation (PetroEcuador); pharmaceutical companies and others who have nonpetroleum interests in the rain forests, etc.

A number of fascinating books have been written about this case, including Judith Kimerling's insightful *Amazon Crude* (1991) and Joe Kane's popular *Savages* (1995), which provide somewhat different perspectives on the situation, though both books are sympathetic to the native and environ-

positive. I would readily take on a local case like this again, but would be cautious about the ambitions of the class in resolving a case, for that is neither realistic nor helpful in the pedagogy of interest-based alternative dispute resolution.

251

mental protests. My students read both of these works, and undertake a stakeholder analysis to identify the primary parties, as well as their interests, strategies, and sources of power. The students then narrow the field to a manageable number of parties (depending on class size, so that teams of students can work together in stakeholder groups) and begin their research on the case from the perspective they have chosen. In one recent version of this case study, the class divided itself into six parties: Ecuadorian government; Conoco Oil; Fundacion Natura (Ecuadorian environmental group); NRDC; World Bank (involved in attempting to settle the conflict); and the Huaorani Indians (the native peoples most affected by the oil exploration).

Each team produces its own confidential stakeholder analysis, does in-depth research on the particular needs and interests of its party, and resolves internal conflicts according to the principles learned throughout the term. A preliminary hearing is used to establish the base-line interests among the parties, and allows each group to ask pointed questions of the other stakeholders, in order to develop better strategies toward a mutual gains, or "principled negotiation" solution.

The students then work in their roles to gather all the information they can. I find the participants to be very resourceful: one group telephoned the Ecuadorian Embassy in Washington, and suddenly found themselves speaking directly with the ambassador. He was thrilled to know that students were learning about the case in the context of negotiation, and even released information to the students which was not yet public. Other students endeavored to obtain relevant information from the oil companies (with limited success), and one group broadcast an electronic mail plea for assistance, which netted them a slew of information from largely unknown sources that they then had to review and corroborate.

After the groups have worked on the case for a couple of weeks, I bring to campus an established expert in the case (e.g., Judith Kimerling, who spent three days with us one year) to serve as a consultant to each party, providing reality checks and in-depth advice about strategy, pitfalls, and other facets of the situation. Since it is not feasible to take the students to Ecuador (and even if we had the wherewithal to travel there, it would not be obvious what to study upon our arrival), bringing in someone who has experienced the situation first-hand makes a significant difference. The students work diligently in preparation for the visitor, and are highly motivated to make the best use of the expert's time as they possibly can. I suggest to them that such an expert could easily charge thousands of dollars for a brief consultation and that a great deal can be accomplished in a small amount of time. I have rarely seen students so excited about a visiting speaker as are the Ecuador stakeholders when the expert visits campus.

At the end of the sequence, the students submit a position paper representing the full strategy and orientation of each stakeholder, complete with anticipated negotiation efforts by the other parties in the case. The papers are written by the members of the groups, and are required to follow readings and discussion topics from the formative stages of the semester to show comprehension of the fundamental dispute resolution concepts. Each stakeholder party writes as a team (typically two students), so that they read in a coherent manner, not as a collection of individual reports fastened together. The students learn (in this class, as in others) that solid writing and lucid presentation are fundamental in making a strong case.

The final examination for the class is somewhat unusual: a negotiated hearing of the Ecuador stakeholders before a panel of judges who evaluate the arguments, assess the preparedness of the participants, and recommend ratings for all involved. The judges are typically administrators, local planners, businesspeople, and others who have experience in various types of negotiation, and who can provide perspective on process, if not on the substance of the particular case.

The students go to considerable lengths to prepare for the final hearing, often expanding the purpose of the session so that they can obtain additional feedback on their work. They also typically establish their own groundrules through a participatory process, and, often without recognizing the pattern, use ADR tools to sort out meta-conflicts concerning the structure of the meeting, the arrangement of tables, the dress code, catering, and other logistics of the event.

The event itself lasts three hours, and the students generally leave feeling mentally spent yet invigorated by the proceedings. The session often moves slowly for the first hour, as the parties try to delineate coalitions and common interests. They spend the second hour honing an agreement that appears to satisfy all but one or two parties. The third hour is almost always one of sheer panic, as the agreement breaks down or a party decides to lob a figurative grenade into the discussion. The students find that their emotional involvement in the role-playing magnifies in intensity during this last hour as they struggle to find joint gains that might repair the fissures of recently exploded settlements. Invariably, they long for an additional hour, feeling so close to an ideal outcome, and yet so far from completion. I try to remind them that this is a case that has failed to find even a remotely satisfactory outcome after nearly a decade of attempts, but they are hardly satisfied by such reality checks.

Integration

The Environmental Dispute Resolution course serves an integrating role at our institution on a number of levels. In terms of environmental studies, it is a natural focal point for addressing many issues. It also encourages students to meet three particular goals which I consider rudimentary to the dispute resolution field: learning how to model reality, encourage action, and build process tools (Kaplan 1999).

Dispute resolution is an ideal course in which to model reality. By working through the series of invented exercises in the sheltered classroom, students can build their confidence as they build their skills. But the key is not to stop there, as often happens in courses on this subject. Rather, the students must be challenged to apply their new expertise in a real, unsolved environmental conflict, to test their wits and their understanding of the formative lessons. Certainly, a simpler case than the Ecuador conflict might produce greater self-assurance, but one of this complexity provides other sorts of reality checks. Here students experience a situation where they may not understand the values and norms of stakeholders, and where their ability to digest, decipher, and translate other peoples' experiences may be pivotal in their professional success. I believe this scenario also encourages creativity they might not discover in a case that is comfortable and close to home.

The second theme is encouraging action. This course integrates a solid education with active learning, making sure the students have a hands-on means to experience their texts, not merely a passive relationship with the relevant material. By role-playing the stakeholder parties in the Ecuador case, the students get out of their seats and into an active research mode. With the prospect of a known expert coming to work with them, they accelerate their efforts and act more like an institute preparing for a site visit than a group of students endeavoring for a grade. They know, however, that it is safe for them to experiment with strategy, substantive joint gains, and back-room dealing, and are willing to try out inventive ideas to encourage a mutually satisfactory resolution of the case. The safety net does not inspire wanton or irresponsible actions, for they recognize the social costs of outrageous behavior. Indeed, this is a form of integration that can be translated to many topics in any institution.

Finally, our program values process tools. We strive to integrate these tools in many of our mid- and upper-level courses, so as to help our students assemble a toolbox of options they might select for any given challenge. Dispute resolution, geographic information systems, statistical analysis, interview and survey design, problem definition, bullet writing, and effective communication are all valuable tools, and the more often they appear in different forms, the better able our students are to discern appropriate ones and use them productively. Since a variety of other tools are germane to ADR, students are naturally exposed to more than negotiation in the Environmental Dispute Resolution course—e.g., they must express themselves effectively both orally and in writing, they must perform complex analyses, and they must define elements of a conflict in a holistic way. Conversely, ADR concepts integrate well with other courses to refine the toolkit and educate the whole person for a successful life.

Courses like this offer integration on a higher level as well. In the liberal arts, and in other collegiate settings, there is increasing interest in linking disciplines, bridging perspectives, and encouraging broader critical thinking among students. A course on the facets of negotiation naturally establishes that effect. Students learn about ethics in strategy, about economics of information dispersal, about politics of decision making, about psychology of individual styles, about sociology of interactions, about anthropology of cultural clashes, and many other disciplines along the way.

A course like this is in no way meant to substitute for proper disciplinary training, nor does it provide a complete picture in any specific field of study. Rather, it offers perspective and context, the jargon and currency of many areas. This has the wonderful effect of heightening awareness about new approaches and inspiring students' interest in fields they may have ignored or previously assumed to be uninteresting. Integration can transpire in many ways, fortuitous and by design.

Concluding Thoughts

Dispute resolution is a topic that clearly offers many benefits to students at all levels. While I teach about environmental issues, I cannot avoid the fact that the negotiation skills we discuss are relevant to many other facets of life. I even find my students applying their new-found skills in personal relationships, and discovering whole new ways of communicating that never before occurred to them. There are days in class when I admonish the class for seeming to forget the environmental context: "You guys have gotten so caught up in the idea of principled negotiation that you've forgotten what our focus is. If I hear one more story about how ADR saved your love life, I'm just gonna jump out the window!" But that natural penchant for connecting their studies to other realms of life is precisely the value of teaching it.

ADR can serve the needs of many undergraduate curricula. Students yearn for courses which make sense and which give them something they can use right away. This is a subject area that can be taught from accessible texts, that can be fit to nearly any location or subject area, and that can be brought to life through active learning and real-world application. It has the properties of an ideal teaching topic. I suspect that a distinguished professor at a top university may soon interview more applicants with considerable ADR background, and he might just need to reexamine his dismissal of their qualifications. For, in the spirit of *Field of Dreams*, we have built it, and they are coming!

Note

1. Teaching simulations mentioned in this essay, their authors, and distributors are all listed in a separate section following the references.

References

Brunschwig, F. 1998. Ecuador grants protected land for oil exploration. *Cultural Survival* 22:6.

Fisher, R, W. Ury, and B. Patton. 1991. *Getting to YES: Negotiating agreement without giving in.* 2d ed. New York: Penguin Books.

Kane, J. 1995. *Savages.* New York: Knopf.

Kaplan, A.W., 1999. Teaching environmental problem solving: Perspective, tools, and action. *Environmental Practice.*

Kimerling, J. 1991. *Amazon crude.* New York: Natural Resources Defense Council.

Raiffa, H. 1982. *The art and science of negotiation.* Cambridge, Mass: Harvard University Press.

Susskind, L. and J. Cruikshank. 1987. *Breaking the impasse: Consensual approaches to resolving public disputes.* New York: Basic Books.

Negotiation Exercises Cited

Win as Much as You Can. Michael Wheeler. Cambridge, Mass: The Clearinghouse of the Program on Negotiation at Harvard Law School.

Development on Bay Island. 1989. Rafael Montalvo and Bruce Stiftel. Cambridge, Mass: The Clearinghouse of the Program on Negotiation at Harvard Law School.

Farmland Conversion. 1989. A. Bruce Dotson, David Godschalk, and Jerome Kaufman. Washington: National Institute of Dispute Resolution.

DEC vs. Riverside. 1985. David Lax, James Sebenius, Lawrence Susskind, and Thomas Weeks. Cambridge, Mass: The Clearinghouse of the Program on Negotiation at Harvard Law School.

Radwaste Siting Game I. 1984. Lawrence Susskind, Denise Madigan, Wendy Rundle, Douglas Rae, and Tod Loofburrow. Cambridge, Mass: The Clearinghouse of the Program on Negotiation at Harvard Law School.

Dirty Stuff II. 1993. Jeffrey R. Litwak and Lawrence Susskind. Cambridge, Mass: The Clearinghouse of the Program on Negotiation at Harvard Law School.

Development Dispute at Menehune Bay. 1986. Lawrence Susskind, Tom Dinell, and Vicki Shook. Cambridge, Mass: The Clearinghouse of the Program on Negotiation at Harvard Law School.

Conflict Resolution Training Programs: Implications for Theory and Research

Beatrice Schultz

Beatrice Schultz is Professor *Emerita* in the Department of Communication Studies at the University of Rhode Island. Her research interests focus on group decision-making performance, with a special interest in facilitating group problem solving and decision making and understanding the role of informal groups in promoting creativity and learning.

Interest in methods of conflict resolution has grown significantly in the last decade (Pruitt and Kressel 1985). Some of the more prominent developments include the emergence of public sector labor mediation, family and divorce mediation, and judicial and public resource mediation. This interest is also reflected in the number of courses included in the curricula of schools of law and business, graduate programs in sociology and social psychology, and in interdisciplinary programs focusing on conflict resolution. Additionally, many professionals and lay people in a variety of occupations indicate a strong desire to acquire skills in conflict resolution (Sandole and Sandole-Staroste 1987). To meet these needs, researchers, theorists, teachers, and practitioners in academic and nonacademic settings are holding conferences, conducting research, producing papers, and offering many types of short courses and training programs with such titles as "The Craft of Negotiation," "Mediation of Family and Divorce Conflict," and "Methods of Alternative Dispute Resolution."

In this article, I shall examine four conflict resolution training programs in an attempt to determine to what extent the assumptions, approaches, principles and theories underpinning these programs could form the basis of an economical model that could effectively train a variety of people and groups.

Is there a set of necessary principles for teaching people how to be conflict resolvers? Are there methods of training that encourage the skill development of potential conflict resolvers? How should training programs be evaluated? Are criteria being developed for appraising the effectiveness of training?

The training programs discussed here—each selected because of its distinctive purpose—were offered by expert practitioners for experienced as well as would-be negotiators and mediators. My analysis of the training programs is based on observations of and consultations with trainers and participants, and on my own direct participation in the trainings.

This article first appeared in *Negotiation Jounal*, July 1989: Volume 5, Number 3, 301-311.

Reflections

Since this article was published I have taught conflict resolution in undergraduate classes and honors seminars at the University of Rhode Island. The teaching was more formal in that, in addition to practical advice about the skills and processes of mediation, conceptions about conflict and its resolution through negotiation and mediation were based more on theoretical and experimental studies than on shared learnings.

The training programs examined in the article were largely nonempirical. The diverse actions that mediators undertook were demonstrated clearly in each of the four programs analyzed. The trainees were taught to establish a working alliance with participants and to improve the climate between them. They were shown that a problem-solving

The programs, evaluated during a six-month period from 1986 to 1987 were as follows:

1. The Ethical Society of St. Louis, Missouri.

The participants in this program were mostly lay people interested in learning the skills of conflict resolution for use in their personal lives. One trainer, Professor Neil Katz, associate director of the Program in Nonviolent Conflict and Change at Syracuse University, and a small staff provided an intensive two-and-one-half-day course in interpersonal conflict resolution.

2. The George Meany Center, Washington, D.C.

The participants—union leaders who were serving, or who expected to serve as bargainers for their respective union— were enrolled in a week-long course taught by Thomas Colosi, a vice president of the American Arbitration Association, and several invited guest instructors. The course emphasized learning the skills of negotiation as a way of enhancing the more traditional bargaining styles of union representatives.

3. Educational Relations Commission, Toronto, Ontario.

The Province of Ontario mandates mediation for all teacher-school board disputes. To meet this requirement, the Education Relations Commission carries out ongoing training programs for potential mediators, as well as follow-up sessions for experienced mediators. In the program I observed, a group of beginning and experienced mediators participated in a two-day workshop emphasizing the skills of mediation. In addition to a panel conducted by experienced mediators who shared their perspectives on successful mediation, participants were given instruction in the principles of conflict management and in skills practice by Dr. Christopher Moore of the Center for Dispute Resolution, Denver, Colorado.

4. Chicago Neighborhood Justice Center, Chicago, Illinois.

This not-for-profit organization, one of more than 180 such centers developed over the last decade in the United States, accepts referrals from the courts and community agencies for suits amenable to mediation. Chicago Neighborhood Justice depends on a volunteer group of mediators and, to add to its cadre of mediators, the program offers occasional 48-hour courses conducted over two weekends. The trainings, primarily open to professionals interested in becoming mediators, are taught by experienced mediators previously trained by the center's personnel.

In the following analysis, I shall explore the common and unique features of these training programs, the extent to which the programs are theory-driven, the extent to which they are evaluated for effectiveness, and the implications for theory and research.

Common Features

Defining Conflict

In the opening sessions of each program, attitudes toward conflict and the components of conflict resolution were explored. A recurring theme was the meaning of the term conflict. In general, the material presented by trainers—definitions of conflict, the myths and realities of conflict, and illustrations to differentiate between functional and dysfunctional conflict—correspond with what is found in most introductory chapters of books emphasizing the skills of conflict resolution (Forger and Poole 1984; Hocker and Wilmot 1985).

Conflict Styles

The concept of style, and its implications for resolving conflict, was first suggested by Blake and Mouton (1964) and Hall (1969), and further developed by Kilmann and Thomas (1977). Each trainer discussed the styles identified by researchers—avoidance, compromise, accommodation, competition, and collaboration—albeit with some modification of terminology. Whether stylistic choices were supported with examples, or whether participants completed a self-test, such as the Thomas-Kilmann questionnaire (1974), the purpose appeared to be: (1) to lead participants to examine their own characteristic style of approaching a conflict situation; and (2) to recognize that while each style can be appropriate for some circumstances, it may not be for others. The Washington

approach would assist in addressing the issues, and that the function of negotiation and mediation was to find a way to reach a settlement and to bring pressures to bear toward reaching such a settlement.

Reflecting on how much has been learned by researchers and practitioners in the interim, I believe there would be value in offering more theoretical underpinnings as to what works and does not work in conflict resolution and mediation. The research question is: How does a third party produce a cooperative problem-solving process? For example, using game theory to demonstrate that parties in conflict have interdependent interests and how the course of a conflict will be determined by the mixture of cooperative and competitive processes would provide a substantive understanding of the mediation process. Other learnings from experimental and field studies would also augment the intuitive knowlege that practitioners utilize.

While the skills of mediation were taught in these instances through practice and tutoring, very little of the research data has been incorporated in teaching trainees in a workshop format. My own view is that demonstrating the value of empirical studies offers a rationale for what action is being proposed and would greatly assist a mediator's substantive knowledge and associated skills. Morton Deutch's work on destructive and constructive processes, for example, provides insight as to why a tough approach throughout a negotiation session can lead to a detrimental outcome versus the apparent effectiveness

program, in particular, stressed the implications of competitive and cooperative styles of negotiation.

Communication and Interpersonal Skills

Three of the programs strongly emphasized the impact of communication skills on negotiated agreements, although the content and explication of these skills varied. For example, the St. Louis program stressed listening skills. Participants explored how to improve their listening by practicing paraphrasing and other forms of active and reflective listening. The information they received focused on the need for rapport, empathy, and flexibility in their turn-taking and responses.

The Toronto program, on the other hand, suggested that mediators could enhance their listening skills by learning to summarize, and that by listening well, they could both elicit issues and place them in some type of order. Active listening was depicted as a way to comprehend both the issues and the personalities involved in a dispute.

The Chicago training program informed trainees about the need to develop good communication skills, and especially to establish trust in the initial phases of a mediation session. Opening statements about the function of a mediator, the confidentiality of the proceedings, and the offer of third-party help were presented as essential communicative functions for promoting an interpersonal climate of trust. Also stressed was the need for such skills as brainstorming, summarizing, weighting and categorizing issues, and knowing how to formulate questions that would aid the parties in reaching a settlement. While not explicitly emphasizing interpersonal skills, the Washington program asked participants to recognize the strengths and pitfalls of hard and soft bargaining in the context of whether they were involved in short-term or continuing relationships with their opposite number.

Conflict Resolution as Process

All programs identified the process nature of conflict resolution, but Chicago and Toronto devoted a significant period of time explicating the several phases of negotiation and mediation. Although the St. Louis program outlined the problem-solving process, and indicated that communication and interpersonal skills were necessary to move the parties to a problem-solving process, it did not elaborate on the structure and phases. The Washington program reviewed the process nature of negotiation but concentrated more on various analytic processes that negotiators would find essential for planning negotiation sessions.

The Chicago program, on the other hand, explicitly emphasized the sequential nature of mediation. It identified three phases: a first phase, for establishing the tone and climate of the mediation session; a problem-solving phase for developing issues and suggesting proposals; and a third phase, for securing an agreed-upon settlement, typically in the form of a written and signed document.

Much of the practice of the first phase involved simulations of mediation sessions. In particular, trainees learned how to seat the parties, how to describe the functions of the mediator, and how to determine when a caucus (a meeting with individual parties during the mediation session) would be used. The objective of the first phase was to let the parties know that, although the mediator controls the session, he or she has no power to make decisions or judgments for the parties. Trainees were expected to acquire more knowledge about the other phases from directed practice sessions and from continuing experience as mediators.

The Toronto program stressed that the task of a mediator is always to analyze a situation as it unfolds. Early in a mediation (the first phase), attention is to be given to statements that determine a climate for diagnosis. The second phase focuses on problem solving, especially the unfolding of issues. This is when mediators are expected to devise strategies to elicit issues. The process can be aided by either expanding or dividing issues into smaller units. By helping parties recognize that some progress toward resolution is being made on some issues, a mediator lays the groundwork for further agreement. The third phase represents the conclusion of the mediation, occurring when parties accept procedures for an agreed-upon settlement.

Unique Features

Since each training program was directed at a specific group of participants, I correctly assumed that each would have some specialized feature.

of using a tough approach only at the beginning of a session. Recognizing that threats hinder positive outcomes but that the use of proportionality greatly assists in finding positive outcomes would help explain why a competitive approach seldom accomplishes one's goals. From such empirical studies, participants can realize that many common sense beliefs about conflict and mediation are much too simplistic.

Most training programs are aware that a constructive process of negotiation or mediation is based on cooperative problem-solving processes and bring to their participants the attitudes, knowledge, and skills that promote the resolution of conflict. There is still a need to engage in a more systematic evaluation of the effectiveness of training methods, both the effectiveness of their training programs

and the conse-
quences of such
training as well as its
durability.

The St. Louis Program

The distinctive feature of this program was an examination of, and practice in, communication skills, especially the role of listening in reducing the impact of conflict struggles. Although a standard treatment of paraphrasing and reflective listening was included, the unique offering was a "three-part assertion" model (Watson and Remer 1984). This model, composed of a sequence of statements, stresses the value of description and offers participants a structure for confronting a conflict:

> "When you..." (describe behavior of other person concretely)
> "I feel..." (describe the effect on you specifically)
> "Because..." (provide rationale or indicate consequences of behavior)

The St. Louis program also pointed out that one has choices in behavior. If you are infringed upon, you can seek to modify the environment or your own behavior, you can be aggressive or withdraw, or you can seek the help of a third party. A *leitmotif* of the training was the need to learn to be assertive with skill. The advice given trainees was this: Acquire the communication skills that allow you to be assertive when you are having a conflict and to listen when the other party is describing a conflict. Assertiveness and good listening were presented as essential skills for persuading parties to move to a problem-solving approach.

Washington Program

The salient feature of this program was its emphasis on teaching participants to examine the different realities of parties in conflict. To increase their understanding of how perspectives may differ, trainees completed a questionnaire that categorized their "thinking styles" (Harrison and Bramson 1980). The questionnaire prompted them to recognize that negotiation is dependent on one's understanding that people vary in their preferred modes of thinking—there are realists and idealists; some people are pragmatists; others are analyzers or synthesizers.

Trainees were also presented with a "core model" for probing their own and the other team's likely behavior (Colosi

1983). The model explicates the roles that members of a negotiating team may take on, such as: "stabilizers," individuals who compromise easily to get resolution; "nonstabilizers," those who upset moves toward accommodation; and "quasimediators," individuals with sufficient flexibility in their responses to know when to accommodate, when to demand, and when to use tradeoffs. Another variable of the "core model" explains three types of bargaining demands embedded in the negotiation process: horizontal, or bargaining across the table; vertical, or bargaining with the various hierarchical levels of an organization; and internal, or learning to bargain with one's own negotiating team.

The Toronto Program
Critical points in mediation, particularly the use of probes to break an impasse were emphasized in Toronto. Participants were encouraged to do a "reality" test with such questions as: "What (in your view) would be a reasonable settlement?" "Are there any conditions that would hamper a settlement?" "Is that all there really is in the pot?" "Is that your entire proposal?"

Participants also learned how to reframe issues to alter a stymied mediation session. The rationale behind reframing is that by saying something in a different way—either by changing the syntax or wording of the message, putting issues in a logical sequence, or grouping them according to some common principle—one can lead conflicting parties to re-examine their conflict. The concept of "fractionating," (Simon 1976) a focusing on subsets of problems, was also presented as an important mechanism for moving the parties toward a settlement. Trainees were asked to examine the "size" of a problem. How many issues should be considered? How can a mediator put boundaries on the number of issues? In addition, trainees were reminded that analysis is an ongoing process, and that as mediators, they would continually have to analyze the underlying interests of the parties. The message was that good negotiators are always thinking about potential substantive outcomes.

Chicago Program
This program was organized around role-plays drawn from actual cases. The cases, ranging from tenant-landlord issues and neigbor-neighbor disagreements to problems of custody and visitation rights, were presented in an economical format that encouraged maximum practice for all participants. Each trainee received a handout briefly describing a conflict situation from the perspective of either an "initiator" (plaintiff), "respondent" (defendant), or "mediator."

The unique aspect of this approach was the use of dozens of very brief situations for practicing the role of mediator. The only information provided to the "mediator" were the initial positions of each of the parties to the conflict and some few clues likely to have been revealed in caucus (although such information would not have been available in typical Chicago Justice Center mediation sessions). In this way, trainees learned how to probe for issues in contention, to discover potential remedies, and to work for reasonable settlements. Each simulation was observed by an experienced mediator, who provided an immediate evaluation of the trainee's enactment of the mediator role. Also, after each simultaneous simulation, all participants gathered in a large group session to discuss the types of settlements the different role players had reached and the reasons for the different outcomes.

Theoretical Foundations

The two most important theories influencing these training programs were the treatment of conflict resolution as a problem-solving process and the identification of the communication and interpersonal skills that influence conflict resolution. However, neither explicit theoretical explanations nor discussions of contributions of theorists were included as a formal part of the instruction, although participants did receive handouts containing prescriptive material based on theories and bibliographic sources for further edification.

The focus in all respects was on the practical and the didactic, with a significant emphasis on "how to." Even when participants were given questionnaires directly based on the theories of researchers, neither descriptions of historical and current research findings, nor their strengths and weaknesses, were included in any of the training programs. For example, participants examined models of problem-solving approaches and models for diagnosing conflict situations that borrowed from the works of Dewey (1910), Coser (1956), Maier (1963), Deutch (1973), Filley (1975), Rubin and Brown (1975), and Fisher and Ury (1981), but only Fisher and Ury were identified as the source of their model.

The St. Louis program illustrated a seven-step problem-solving approach with role-play simulations, but did not discuss whether and how such prescriptive models would be useful (Fisher 1980; Poole 1981). The need to use such processes as brainstorming to elicit issues was an essential part of the simulated mediations of the Chicago training program, but neither descriptions nor analysis of the procedure, nor specific practice in brainstorming, were offered. Nor did the training indicate why and how brainstorming would function in mediation and negotiation. Neither the justification of a problem-solving approach nor its evolution and application in analyzing conflict situations informed any of the training programs.

Role-taking and an assessment of role performance was an important focus of the Washington program, but theories of role analysis and role conflict were not discussed. Explanations for why people would assume roles that would result in win-lose solutions were not provided, nor was attention given to such issues as the universal needs of people, which ultimately affect a problem-solving framework (Burton 1986).

Learning to raise questions that would help define issues was an essential ingredient of the Toronto program. However, the complexities of interaction patterns, problems of perception and interpretation, and theories of language usage, both verbal and nonverbal, were not provided. Also absent from consideration were the implications of decision-making patterns, especially strategies that can help the parties assess risks and values. Although trainers would summarize in their brief lectures some of the data extracted from the literature, explicit discussions of conflict theory, decision theory, and communication theory—theories that underpin conflict resolution—were not critical to the training programs.

Evaluation

Just as discussion of theory did not play a significant role in these trainings, neither did evaluative measures for assessing the impact of the trainings. No program incorporated procedures for monitoring whether their methods produced effective conflict resolvers. The evaluations that were undertaken took the form of feedback to participants, typically immediately after a role simulation. Trainees received verbal feedback from observers of their practice sessions, as in the Chicago program, or from each other, as in the St. Louis program. Sometimes, evaluations came from a general analysis of the resolution of a case. The Washington program relied on a two-day simulation of a union-management dispute, which was then analyzed in terms of the different settlements the various role-players worked out. Although simulations were employed in the Toronto program, trainees did not receive individual comments about their performance. What evaluation did take place occurred in a group discussion of how cases could be analyzed and possible remedies proposed.

All programs sought feedback from participants, however. Verbal and written evaluations were collected during the final sessions, but it was unclear how these data would be used. Although trainees informed trainers about how satisfied they were with the programs, the instructors did not assess whether the training increased the participants' knowledge or improved their skills. Some of this information will doubtless be sought for the longer term in the Chicago and Toronto programs since their trainees practice "under fire" when they perform actual mediation assignments. But more evaluation will probably come from word of mouth. Mediators acquire reputations for how well they handle disputes, and generally their accomplishments become the "war" stories of future training sessions.

Implications for Theory and Research

It is clear that these four training programs are based on a number of common elements, while each also stresses a particular element of conflict resolution. What is less evident is the rationale for the choices made. For example, the St. Louis format sought to empower individuals by emphasizing communication and interpersonal skills. It provided important models for learning to listen and to be assertive. The unstated assumption was that the acquisition of these skills would make one a more effective conflict resolver.

Intuitively, one can recognize that communication and interpersonal skills are important skills for dealing with such complex issues as the interaction and relationship of parties to a conflict. Yet other programs did not provide this particular emphasis. The difference raises a question: Will individuals who are not given the opportunity to learn and practice these skills be less effective than they could be? Until the question is researched, the extent to which communication skills should be incorporated into training programs cannot be evaluated.

A related issue is that of communication competence. Researchers investigating the parameters of communication competence indicate that more attention will have to be given to the role of perception, for any situation may be variously interpreted by different participants and observers (Burton 1986). Wieman (1977) conceptualized five dimensions of communication competence: affiliation/support, social relations, empathy, behavioral flexibility, and interaction management. On this basis, it seems reasonable that training programs should also give more thought to the foundation of knowledge required for strong communicative skills, and that they should include more than the display of a few techniques. Indeed, since interpersonal competence and communication competence are inextricably linked, it would seem beneficial to provide trainees with theories of both.

On the other hand, because theoretical explanations did not play an important role in any of the actual training, the potential impact of theoretical explanation cannot be assessed without further research.

The Washington workshop exposed labor leaders to the benefits of widening their repertoires of useful skills, such as knowing how to make stylistic choices when participating in a conflict and assessing how others might perceive events. Since the trainees were more comfortable using an industrial model based on adversarial relations, an understanding of the roles and structure of negotiating teams was probably one of the greatest benefits they received. It would seem that an ability to analyze the possible ways that different people ask questions and process information would be an important addition to the knowledge base of conflict resolvers. Until such an assumption is examined, however, the benefit to trainees of the Washington approach cannot be ascertained.

The emphasis on enhancing such communication and diagnostic skills as learning reframing and fractionating issues was an important element of the Toronto workshop. This approach, comparable to a meta-communication process, would seem to be invaluable in a training model. Yet these skills were not substantial elements in other programs. Similarly, the strength of the training in Chicago was its use of simulations based on real and translatable problems. Although all programs relied on practice sessions, the Chicago program's use of economical, realistic simulations seemed to provide more practical ways of practicing and learning than did the longer, more complex role-plays of the other training programs. Testing the validity of employing economical versus complex role-plays would doubtless contribute to an understanding of what makes training effective.

No program investigated whether its particular methods constituted an effective way to train conflict resolvers. Neither comparative analyses of the effectiveness of its own training programs nor investigations of other approaches appears to inform the programs I observed. Several factors may account for this lack of comparative analysis: the investment that each training program has in its own development of material and methods, the satisfaction participants report with their training, the limited time for instruction, and the lack of opportunity to test and compare various training methods.

One implication of these data is the need for training programs to assess what knowledge, as well as what skills, should be imparted to their participants. For example, trainees exposed to the Fisher/Ury model would be familiar with the advice "focus on interests, not positions." But by going beyond the question of interests to inquire what else is at stake, conflict resolvers may gain more insight into possible remedies. Explorations of the broader issues of ethnicity and race, politics, and social class could also significantly enhance one's comprehension of the multiple forces affecting a willingness to change. Moreover, demonstrations of how one's use of language can foster greater trust and influence the choice of remedies might instill in trainees a greater understanding of the underlying principles of conflict resolution.

Conclusions

Just as mediators inform conflicting parties, "I have no magic wand, I can only deal with what you bring in here," this discussion of training programs can draw conclusions based only on the programs I examined. Drawing on the common themes as well as the unique emphases, it is possible to suggest the elements of a potentially effective training program. Such a program would emphasize the following:

1. Conflict resolution is a process that has discernible stages, each of which has different requirements and procedures.
2. Communicative skills, such as listening and assertiveness and the interpersonal skills of building trust and showing sensitivity are valuable personal attributes.
3. Choices in styles of managing conflict and styles of thinking are important for understanding the different perspectives of parties to a conflict.
4. Models indicating the structure and demands of problem solving aid the learning process. Dewey's "reflective thinking" model (awareness of a problem, defining it, proposing alternatives, choosing among alternatives, evaluating consequences) is a primary tool for teaching problem solving. Other diagnostic models, such as Fisher and Ury's "separate the people from the problem," "focus on interests, not positions," "invent options for mutual gain," and "insist on objective criteria," are also useful.
5. Strategies for agreement include developing options for settlement, examining issues, goals, and priorities, and managing the process of negotiation through all its stages.

In sum, within these four programs, one can discern a multitude of concepts and theories, derived from social psychology, psychology, and communication disciplines. The literature from which the principles and theories are extracted is vast, yet much of what is employed in training programs remains untested.

It is obvious that some of what is offered in training works, at least in the perceptions of the participants, and in view of subsequent evaluations and performance in the field. The opportunity to practice confronting conflict, and to receive feedback from those who have negotiated and mediated, sharpens one's skills. However, with so little attempt to evaluate how much of a mediator's effectiveness can be attributed to training or to discern what other knowledge would increase the competence of a trainee, the results of training

SCHULTZ

programs remain in the realm of the anecdotal.

These programs clearly demonstrate the significance of communication and interpersonal skills. What they identify as important—skill in using language, as in the ability to frame questions and issues, in knowing both when and how to offer "tradeoffs," and in recognizing both verbal and nonverbal cues—suggests that students need to learn communication theory. It is also evident that other theories impinging on conflict resolution—such as game theory, exchange theory, and decision theory—are not considered particularly influential.

This observation points to a need to determine which theories and methods would be essential to the development of a parsimonious yet effective model of training. It would be useful, for example, to explore the reasons for the omission of game theory from training programs, despite the emphasis in the literature for over twenty years (Pruitt and Kimmel 1977). Researchers could also evaluate which models would improve the quality of training. While some models are consistently employed in training, no current program evaluation informs us which ones are more effective in imparting the skills of conflict resolution.

Future research should investigate the factors that could lead to the development of a comprehensive model of training in conflict resolution. It could also enable us to determine the conditions under which each factor has greater or lesser influence on the process itself. Although much has been learned that is of value to instructors, more specific knowledge about what constitutes an effective curriculum or training program is still needed. Ultimately we must identify those theories and principles that are essential to conflict resolution so that the requisite skills can be taught to wider audiences.

References

Blake, R. R. and J. S. Mouton. 1964. *The managerial grid.* Houston: Gulf Publishing.

Burton, J. W. 1986. Generic theory: The basis of conflict resolution. *Negotiation Journal* 2: 333-344.

Colosi, T. 1983. Negotiation in the private sectors: A core model. *American Behavioral Scientist* 27: 229-253.

Coser, L. 1956. *The functions of social conflict.* New York: The Free Press.

Deutsch, M. 1973. *The resolution of conflict.* New Haven: Yale University Press.

Dewey, J. 1910. *How we think.* New York: Heath.

Filley, A. S. 1975. *Interpersonal conflict resolution.* Glenview, IL: Scott, Foresman.

Fisher, B. A. 1980. *Small group decision-making.* New York: McGraw-Hill.

Fisher, R. and W. L. Ury. 1981. *Getting to YES.* Boston: Houghton Mifflin.

Folger, J. R. and M. S. Poole. 1984. *Working through conflict: A communication perspective.* Glenview, IL: Scott, Foresman.

Hall, J. 1969. *Conflict management survey: A survey on one's characteristic reaction to and handling of conflicts between himself and others.* Conroe, Texas: Teleometrics International.

Harrison, A. F. and R. Branson. 1980. *INQ: Preferences in ways of asking questions and making decisions.* Berkeley: Bramson, Parlette, Harrison and Assoc.

Hocker, J. L. and W. W. Wilmot. 1985. *Interpersonal conflict.* 2d ed. Dubuque: Wm. C. Brown.

Kilmann, R. H. and K. W. Thomas. 1977. Developing a forced choice measure of conflict handling behavior. *Educational and Psychological Measurement* 37: 309-325.

Maier, N. R. F. 1963. *Problem-solving discussions and conferences.* New York: McGraw-Hill.

Poole, M.S. 1983. Decision development in small groups III: A multiple sequence model of group decision development. *Communication Monographs* 50: 321-341.

Pruitt, D. G. and K. Kressel. 1985. The mediation of social conflict: An introduction. *Journal of Social Issues.* 41: 1-10.

Pruitt, D. G. and M. J. Kimmel. 1977. Twenty years of experimental gaming: Critique, synthesis, and suggestions for the future. *Annual Review of Psychology* 28: 363-392.

Rubin, J. and B. R. Brown. 1975. *The social psychology of bargaining and negotiation.* New York: Academic.

Thomas, K. W. and R. H. Kilmann. 1974. *Thomas-Kilmann Conflict Mode Instrument.* New York: XICOM.

Sandole, D. J. D. and I. Sandole-Staroste, eds. 1987. *Conflict management and problem-solving: Interpersonal to international applications.* London: Frances Pinter.

Simon, H. A. 1976. *Administrative behavior.* 3rd ed. New York: Macmillan.

Watson, J. and R. Remer. 1984. The effects of interpersonal confrontation on females. *Personnel and Guidance Journal* 62: 607-611.

Wiemann, J. M. 1977. Explication and test of a model of communicative competence. *Human Communication Research* 3: 195-213.

The Art of Advising Negotiators

Jeswald W. Salacuse

Jeswald W. Salacuse
is Henry J. Braker
Professor of Law and
former Dean at The
Fletcher School of Law
and Diplomacy, Tufts
University. His latest book
*The Wise Advisor: What
Every Professional Should
Know About Consulting
and Counseling* (Praeger,
2000). He has been
awarded the Fulbright
Chair in Comparative
Law for Italy for the
Spring of 2000. His
negotiation interests
center on the area of
international business.

This article first
appeared in
Negotiation Journal,
October1995: Volume
11, Number 4, pages
391-401.

A declared goal of contemporary research and commentary on negotiation is prescription—providing advice and guidance to improve the performance of negotiators.[1] To be effective, advice not only requires good product in the form of sound theory and valid principles; it also demands good process in the form of a consciously guided method that enables negotiators to use the advice offered to resolve particular problems that they are facing.

The crucial link between good theory by scholars and improved performance by negotiators is a sound advising process. While negotiation scholars have profitably concentrated on developing the theories and principles that make up their product, they have devoted considerably less attention to the process of actually advising negotiators. Just as there are principles to guide the negotiating process, there are also principles to inform the advising process. The purpose of this article is to explore the advising process as it relates to negotiators and to suggest principles that should guide it.

The Nature of Advice and Advising

Advice to negotiators comes in many forms: background papers by consultants to government officials on negotiating with another nation over trade barriers; recommendations from corporate headquarters to executives in the field on strategies for completing a joint venture agreement; suggestions by a United Nations mediator to contending states on ways to resolve a long-standing border dispute. Despite differences in form, all advice is essentially a communication from one person (the advisor) to another (the client) for the purpose of helping the second person determine a course of action for solving a particular problem.

Advice and advising, however, are not the same thing. If the advice is actually to help the client, then the advisor must also be concerned with the advising process. For many persons, advising is essentially the delivery of information to another person. The better the information delivered, the better the advice. This view misconceives the nature of the process. Effective advisors recognize that advising is fundamentally a relationship between the advisor and the client, a two-way relationship in which both must participate. How well they manage that relationship determines the effectiveness of the advising process and, ultimately, the performance of the negotiator.

Relationships between advisors and clients demonstrate many variations but essentially tend to follow one of three basic models: the advisor as director; the advisor as servant; and the advisor as partner.

The Advisor as Director

In this model, the advisor tends to take control of the process, directing the client in the actions that ought to be taken to resolve the client's problem. In the advisor's mind (and sometimes the client's), the negotiator need only follow the advisor's directives in order to improve performance. Here the client is an empty vessel to be filled with the advisor's wisdom. Advisors to negotiators in this model often see themselves as conducting negotiations through their clients.

The Advisor as Servant

Rather than act as a director in the advising process, the advisor may play the role of a servant, responding to numerous demands of the client for help and guidance in a negotiation. Here the client remains fully in control of the negotiation and may limit the participation of the advisor to specific questions and issues. Often, the negotiator may have several advisors whose competition for the client's attention further underscores their roles as servants.

The Advisor as Partner

In certain situations, advisor and client may become partners. The essence of any partnership is co-ownership and joint participation. When advisor and client function as partners, they jointly manage the advising process and together take ownership of the problem to be solved. Here, as a result of mutual trust and confidence between the two, advisor and client draw on a common pool of knowledge and skills in order to resolve the negotiating problem at hand.

The precise nature of the advisor-client relationship depends on a variety of factors, including the experience and personalities of the advisor and the negotiator, the nature of the conflict to be resolved, and the organizational setting in which the advising takes place. The relationship between the two may also change over time. For instance, an advisor to corporate negotiators may begin in the servant role and then later, as the clients develop confidence in their advisor, attain the status of a partner. Similarly, clients of a high-powered, politically-connected advisor who arrives on the scene and assumes the role of a director may relegate the advisor to servant status if the advice or advising methods prove to be unhelpful.

Rules For the Art of Advice

Regardless of the role, the advisor must manage the advising relationship effectively in order to help the client. Managing that relationship is more a matter of art than science. Like music or painting, the art of advice is governed by basic principles. Based on the experiences of advisors in many different contexts, they are presented here in the form of seven simple rules addressed to advisors who seek to help negotiators.[2]

Rule 1: Know Your Client

Like the experienced actress who gauges her audience from the moment she steps onto a stage, an effective advisor seeks to know the client from the very start. Knowing the client is important for two reasons—one concerns what advice you give (substance) and the other affects how you give it (process).

Good advice must always meet the client's needs, circumstances, and values. The effective advisor, whether counseling a company in merger negotiations or a government in talks with rebels, must come to know the client first—before actually giving any advice.

The second reason for knowing the client concerns the way the advisor goes about giving advice. The effective advisor shapes the advising process to fit the client's abilities and background. Consequently, one might be blunt and direct in counseling American executives in a company with a tradition of assertiveness, but would need to be more gentle in advising Japanese managers because of their cultural aversion to confrontation and public criticism.

Although this first rule may seem obvious and few advisors would deny its importance, many experienced advisors fail to follow it. For example, in a case in which an established consulting firm was advising a small city in its negotiations with a federal agency to obtain funding for a project, the firm accepted assurances from the client that other cities in the region supported or at least did not oppose the project. In fact, a larger, nearby city believed that it should build the project in question, and was quietly opposing the smaller city's plans to federal officials and agencies. As a result, the advisor and the client were unprepared to deal with opposition when it surfaced in the formal negotiations. Had the consulting firm been less willing to accept the client's statements at face value and devoted more effort to understanding the client city's position within the region, it probably would have anticipated potential opponents in the negotiation and have developed plans to deal with them.

Getting to know a client is not easy. It requires time and effort by both advisor and client, and both may complicate the task by erecting barriers that inhibit knowledge of one another. These barriers include false assumptions and stereotypes made by the advisor about the client; the advisor's own desire for status and power within the relationship; and the limited amount of time that either advisor or client is willing to devote to the advising process.

Sometimes advisors face the problem of determining precisely who is the client. In many negotiating situations, the formal client is an organization, which may be fragmented into competing groups or factions. For example, in an international joint venture negotiation, the negotiating team may include senior officials of such departments as finance, manufacturing, and marketing, all of whom may have different goals and priorities. As a result, the team's advisor may be unsure of the client's identity. Indeed, in order to advance the negotiations, the advisor may have to assume the role of a mediator among the client's internal factions.

Rule 2: Help or at Least Do No Harm

Advising is helping. All clients, no matter how powerful or sophisticated, need help. They need help because in some way they are deficient (see Dror 1987:170). If they did not sense some deficiency in themselves with respect to a conflict or negotiation, they would not bother to seek the help of an advisor.

An important first step in helping is to understand precisely in what way the client is deficient. Often advisors like to assume that they have been selected by the client because of their superior knowledge and expertise. While that may be the case most of the time, there are other reasons why a client may seek the help of an advisor in a negotiation. In some cases, the client already has the necessary knowledge but is seeking confirmation from a third party. Here, the best help the advisor can offer is not to give learned opinions but rather to confirm the client's own ideas and strengthen the client's confidence in his or her own judgment. In other cases, the client lacks the time to do certain tasks in connection with the negotiation or does not have the will to take certain difficult or painful actions. Whatever the specific deficiency, if advising is to attain the basic goal of helping the client, the advisor must keep the process centered on the client (see Rogers 1951).

When Hippocrates advised Greek physicians "to help or at least to do no harm," he knew that the practice of medicine had the capacity for both helping and injuring. Advising has those same capacities. Unskilled advisors sometimes fail to appreciate the extent to which their advice can cause damage to their clients. It is, after all, the client, not the advisor, who pays the price for bad advice. U.S. President John F. Kennedy, who had received both bad and good advice in his political life, underscored this point when he remarked that an advisor, after giving advice, goes on to other advice, but the official whom he advises goes on to an election (Szanton 1981:140).

A client, of course, is always free to reject advice, but that fact does not relieve the advisor from the responsibility for the consequences of giving that advice in the first place. Advisors often fail to realize that, by virtue of their position as "experts," they have power over the client. The moment a client asks for advice, he or she is relying, at least to some extent, on the advisor. This reliance gives the advisor power over a part of the client's life. Both advisor and client should recognize that the advising relationship is also a power relationship, and that it is this power that enables the advisor to help or harm.

Rule 3: Agree on Your Role

Advisors are like actors in a film or musicians in a band: They have a definite role to play in the action. An advisor may be the director, servant, partner, or variations among these roles in the advising relationship. Both advisor and client need to understand and accept what role the advisor has. While some professional advisors believe that role definition is simply a matter of telling clients what they can expect, skilled advisors recognize that they can neither assume nor impose their roles. Instead, they know they must negotiate their roles with their clients, for misunderstandings can have disastrous results. Consider, for example, Hamlet delivering Ophelia's lines or a pianist playing the trumpeter's part of the score.

In a recent negotiation example, a corporate executive engaged in a difficult and much-publicized joint venture negotiation asked to meet with an advisor to discuss the project. It was a topic the advisor had followed with great interest and he prepared a long memorandum outlining alternative strategies. When their meeting began, he presented his list and proceeded to give a lengthy summary of his recommendations. Instead of being grateful for the presentation, the executive became cool and the meeting ended within a half hour, with no commitment for subsequent contacts. The advisor left puzzled, even annoyed, that the executive had not appreciated the time and effort he had spent on trying to help with the negotiation. The executive was also disappointed since she had hoped to use the advisor as a sounding board to react to her own ideas about how to conduct the negotiation. The executive wanted the advisor to play the role of a servant while the advisor assumed his role would be that of a director. The two differing conceptions of the advisor's role led to the meeting's failure.

Agreeing on one's role as an advisor is important for several reasons. First, it determines your strategy for giving advice. It decides your goal and guides you in focusing your energy, time, and talents in carrying out the task. If the agreed-upon role is to act as a sounding board for ideas developed by the client for a particular negotiation, then you obviously ought not to suggest new marketing strategies for the company. Second, a clear definition of the advisor's role gives the client an accurate idea of what the client must contribute to the advising relationship—how often the two should meet, what staff should be assigned to work with the advisor, and what resources must be devoted to the advising process. Finally, an accurate understanding of the advisor's role allows the client to evaluate the advisor's performance. For example, suppose an investment bank has defined its role as providing timely negotiating advice to a client in hostile takeovers but fails to do so when the client company is suddenly threatened with a takeover bid; the investment bank has failed to fulfill its promised role as advisor.

Rule 4: Never Give a Solo Performance

Some advisors think of themselves as "hired guns" while others see themselves as the "Lone Ranger." In either case, they like to project the image of the heroic team or individual who arrives on the scene and works to rescue clients from their troubles. The client is often just an object for the advisor's efforts—an object that contributes little or nothing to solving the problem. In such cases, advising, if it is an art, is a solo performance or a one-person show. Effective advising, however, is always a duet, at the very least. A truly artful advisor never gives a solo performance and never presents a one-person show. On the contrary, skilled advising requires the active participation of the client. One of the great challenges for any advisor is to secure from the client the maximum contribution to the advising process.

For many advisors, the idea that the client has something to contribute—other than fees, of course—is difficult to accept. After all, the very reason that the client has sought the service of an advisor is because the advisor has superior knowledge—knowledge that the client lacks.

As indicated earlier, clients do not always turn to advisors because of the advisor's superior knowledge. But even in cases were the advisor has specialized knowledge that the client lacks, the client still contributes to the advising process. Most problems—especially those relating to negotiations—have both technical and nontechnical dimensions. While the advisor may be the primary (or even the sole) source of knowledge on technical issues in a particular case, the client usually knows far more about the nontechnical aspects, such as those relating to the client's own interests, goals, values and culture, all of which are essential information in any negotiation.

A second reason for the advisor to involve the client in the advising process is that the problem to be solved is the client's, not the advisor's. It is the client, not the advisor, who ultimately must make the decision on what to do and bear the consequences of that decision.

In addition, clients are more likely to follow advice if they have participated in shaping it than if they have been isolated from the process. Clients not only want the "right" answer, they want an answer that meets their particular values, goals, and aspirations. If they have participated in finding that answer, they are usually more secure in the feeling that it meets their values than if they had nothing to do with arriving at the recommended course of action. By participating in the process, they will also often gain a better understanding of the proposed solution than if it were presented to them all at once as a finished product.

Rule 5: Make the Process Clear and Constructive
Advising is a process—a consciously-guided, progressive movement toward a desired goal. And, like any process, advising passes through a series of distinct steps:

- Get to know your client. As Rule 1 advocates, you really cannot be helpful unless you know the person you are trying to help.
- Define the problem. To understand the client's problem, you must look at it—at least initially—from the client's point of view. But that does not necessarily mean that you have to accept your client's explanation.
- Determine your client's objectives. What does the client want? What goals is the company pursuing in negotiating a joint venture? Why is the central bank thinking about renego-

276

tiating its debts to foreign creditors? The answer to these questions will determine how the advisor can best help the client. Often, clients are unsure of their objectives, so the advisor must devote considerable effort to helping with the task of defining them.

• Identify options. At this stage of the process, both advisor and client need to be at their most creative. Rather than evaluate an option as it is presented, advisor and client should first try to determine a whole range of options without deciding whether any of them is good or bad.

• Evaluate the options. Advisor and client next need to evaluate the jointly-generated options to determine their costs, benefits, consequences, and likelihood of allowing the client to achieve the desired objective. It is here that the advisor's experience and technical knowledge are particularly important. The advisor should be able to determine each option's impact on the client's situation—what will work and what won't, what each will cost, and what results can be expected.

• Your client decides on a course of action. Ultimately, the client must make a decision to adopt or refrain from a definite course of action. The decision is the client's.

• Assess the results. In developing an appropriate process, the skilled advisor should always seek to program a final phase where the two can review and evaluate the results of the client's decision. Often actions taken on one problem only lead to the necessity of making related decisions; assessment of the results of that first decision can help the client in making subsequent decisions.

In practice, of course, advising is never as straightforward as these seven process steps may suggest. Some may take place at different times in a particular case while others may not occur explicitly. Nevertheless, an understanding of these general phases will help advisor and client devise a process to meet the clientís needs.

Above all, the process should be clear and constructive. Clarity means that the client must understand the advice that is delivered. The basic test is not whether the advisor has presented a technically perfect opinion, but whether the client, as a result, is better able to deal with a problem. The proof of effective advising resides in the mind of the client, not the imagination of the advisor.

A skilled advisor also tries to be constructive throughout the advising process, particularly in understanding the client's problem and in recommending solutions. Being constructive does not mean being overly optimistic or telling your clients only what they want to hear. But it does mean avoiding unnecessary negative criticism of the client or his situation and always trying to offer preferable alternatives to deal with the problem.

Rule 6: Keep Your Advice Pure

Sir Francis Bacon remarked that the advantage of good advice is that it affords a "drier and purer light" for solving a problem than does the light that clients themselves can provide.[3] In theory, by virtue of their detachment and experience, advisors are able to give objective,

277

independent counsel that is unaffected by the client's own biases, fears, and blind spots. In practice, however, an advisor's light can sometimes also be impure.

Advisors give impure advice when they fail to fulfill either of two fundamental obligations to the client: their duty of loyalty and their duty of care. What clients expect—whether they are executives in a corporation or officials in a government agency—is first that their advisors will place clients' interests above their own; and second, that their advisors will look after those interests carefully.

The fact that a client is always free to reject advice does not relieve the advisor from the responsibility for the consequences of giving that advice in the first place. As noted earlier, advisors, by virtue of the reliance they foster, gain power over the client, and with this power comes the responsibility to use it loyally and carefully.

An initial test of loyalty comes in deciding whether or not to accept someone as a client. You are disloyal as an advisor if you accept a client for whom you know you have neither the knowledge nor experience to help. For example, an acquaintance is engaged in a complicated negotiation with the Internal Revenue Service over deductions taken in connection with oil and gas investments, and she asks you to advise her. You know nothing about this area of taxation but are flattered by the request. You would fail in your duty of loyalty to the client if your failed to advise her that other specialists might be able to provide her with the help she needs. Advisors display disloyalty when they use their position to profit at their clients' expense without their knowledge or consent.

The obligation of care is a complex notion that implies that advisors will devote serious attention, diligence, and skill to the task of advising. It does not mean that an advisor guarantees the results of the advice given, but neither does it imply a twist on caveat emptor: let the client beware.

Like disloyalty, carelessness can take many forms. It can mean, first of all, accepting an advising assignment without being reasonably sure you have the knowledge or skill to help the client. A second major form of carelessness occurs when the advisor does not devote the time and attention required to help the client. For example, a consultant who purports to advise an African central bank on renegotiating its foreign loans without studying the country's balance of payments situation would clearly be violating his duty of care to his client.

Rule 7: Have a Vision of the End and Know When To Stop
Determining the right time to stop in offering advice is always a matter of judgment and not subject to any fixed rules. Nevertheless, a basic rule of the art is: The client and the advisor should plan for the end of the relationship at its beginning. Often, conflicts and uncertainties surrounding the termination of the advising relationship arise because advisor and client do not have a common vision of the end, a clear mutual understanding of the goal they are trying to reach.

On the other hand, no amount of planning and discussion can anticipate all possible contingencies that might cause either the client or the advisor to want to end the relationship. Generally speaking, the advisor should stop advising when any of the following five conditions arises:

- Your client has reached the goal.
- You are in over your head. Consider, for example, the following scenario: A colleague in your organization asks for help in negotiating a land dispute with a neighbor. You agree but, as you study the problem, realize that you really do not have the knowledge to be helpful in this area. You have encountered a common advisor's problem: You agreed to work on what looked like an easy problem at the start, but later discover it is more complex than you realized. You are in over your head. In this predicament, your only course of action is to explain the situation frankly to your colleague and try to refer him to someone who has the knowledge and skill to help.
- You don't like your client's behavior. A client's actions may lead the advisor to end the relationship. The client may be hostile to the advisor or abusive to the advisor's staff, may be engaged in illegal or immoral activities, or may simply just be making unreasonable demands. Dropping a client before resolving a problem can have serious consequences. For a management consultant to abandon a client company in the midst of merger negotiations because the CEO is abusive under pressure may give the consultant personal satisfaction, but it may also cause the company financial loss. The reason it is so difficult to end the relationship in these situations is that the client has become dependent on the advisor—a situation that the advisor fostered and encouraged through assurance of help, competence, reliability, care and loyalty. Having helped to create the dependency, the advisor has an ethical obligation—and in some instances, a legal duty—not to withdraw from the relationship in a way that will injure the client.
- Your own situation changes. Sometimes your decision to stop is motivated not by your client's behavior but by your own situation: You are ill, you want to retire, you are busy with other matters, or perhaps you are just bored. Normally an advisor has an obligation to give the client ample notice of the impending end of the relationship and then, in many cases, to assist in finding another advisor.
- The client wants out. While the advisor must ordinarily take special steps to end the relationship, the client is usually free to end it for any reason whatsoever, subject to any financial commitments to the advisor or the provisions of any contract between them. The client is freer to end the relationship than the advisor is because it is the client who is dependent on the advisor, not the reverse.

Experienced advisors are aware of the various ways that the advising relationship may end, and they plan these eventualities at the beginning of the relationship. To paraphrase Euripides, "a good beginning is necessary for a good ending."

In Conclusion

The seven rules of the art of advice, in the abstract, are short and simple; their application in specific circumstances, however, is often complex and difficult. Nonetheless, these principles can serve as a useful guide to persons who are called upon to advise negotiators. Clients, on the other hand, may use them as standards of conduct to evaluate advisors seeking to help them in negotiations. For the client seeking negotiation advice, these seven rules translate into seven questions that should be asked to evaluate an advisor's performance:

1. How well does my advisor know me?
2. To what extent is my advisor committed to helping me and to protecting me from harm?
3. Have my advisor and I agreed on the precise role that the advisor is to play?
4. Is my advisor giving a solo performance? To what extent am I participating in the process?
5. Has my advisor made the advising process clear to me and is my advisor dealing with my problem in a constructive way?
6. Is my advisor's advice free of the impurities of disloyalty and carelessness?
7. Has my advisor given me an idea of how our advising relationship will end?

Positive answers to these seven questions are a strong indication that an effective relationship exists between advisor and negotiator

Notes

1. See, e.g., Stein (1988) and Pruitt (1986). One of the late Jeffrey Rubin's favorite questions in presenting a negotiating problem to students and executives was: "What wise advice would you give to the parties in the dispute?"

2. In addition to drawing on his own experience as an advisor over the last three decades to governments, businesses, universities, and international organizations, the author conducted a series of interviews with advisors in a wide range of professional fields, including law, medicine, management consulting, personal counselling, and financial management. These experiences are more fully treated in Salacuse (1994).

3. "And certain it is that the light a man receiveth by counsel from another is drier and purer, than that which cometh from his own understanding and judgment; which is ever infused and drenched, in his affectations and customs." From "Of Friendship," in Bacon's *Essays with Annotations*, edited by Richard Whately and Franklin F. Heard. Boston: Lee and Shepard, 1968 (p. 285).

References

Dror, Y. 1987. Conclusions. In *Advising the rulers*, edited by William Plowden. Oxford: Basil Blackwell Ltd.

Pruitt, D.G. 1986. Trends in the scientific study of negotiation and mediation. *Negotiation Journal* 2(3): 237-244.

Rogers. C. 1951. *Client-centered therapy*. Boston: Houghton Mifflin.

Salacuse, J.W. 1994. *The art of advice: How to give it and how to take it*. New York: Times Books.

Stein, J.G. 1988. International negotiation: A multidisciplinary perspective. *Negotiation Journal* 4(3): 221-231.

Szanton, P. 1981. *Not well advised*. New York: Russell Sage Foundation.

III. Tools and Techniques

Using Simulations to Teach Negotiation: Pedagogical Theory and Practice

Lawrence E. Susskind and Jason Corburn

Lawrence E. Susskind is Ford Professor of Urban and Environmental Planning at the Massachusetts Institute of Technology and Director of the MIT-Harvard Public Disputes Program.

Jason Corburn is a doctoral candidate at MIT's Department of Urban Studies and Planning.

The simulations discussed in this paper, HARBORCO, the *Oil Pricing Game*, *Win-as-Much-as-You-Can*, *Sally Soprano*, *Power Screen*, and *Hitana Bay*, are available from the PON Clearinghouse.

This paper first appeared as PON Paper 99-3 in 1999.

We believe that simulations are a valuable tool for teaching negotiation. There has been an enormous growth in the number of professional schools and corporations teaching negotiation, and most of these teaching efforts are built around simulations. Indeed, the professionals and academics who teach negotiation claim that well-designed simulations are the key to teaching graduate students and mid-career professionals. This claim is rooted in the idea that negotiation is best taught by "doing it." Yet, most of the research and writing on the use of simulations offer little evidence to back up this assertion. We will review the pedagogical theory behind the use of simulations and review what leading academics have to say about their importance as a teaching tool.

What is a Simulation?

Generally, simulations model a complex process or reality. They place participants in an assigned role in a specific situation and challenge them to find ways to address the circumstances and the consequences likely to follow from various courses of action. Simulations can be based on real-life situations or purely hypothetical premises. They can include computer-based packages of information or not, and they are usually carried out via face-to-face interaction, although asynchronous interaction involving computer-assisted communication is gaining in popularity. Simulations offer the learner a safe setting in which errors are not costly and experimentation is encouraged.

The differences between simulations, games and role-plays are significant. Each fits with a different set of teaching objectives. Games generally have an agreed upon set of rules that limit possible final solutions or agreement.

Success, or winning, in a game depends on adherence to a predetermined formula. Participants seek a solution that fits the rules of the game. Role-plays typically involve a set of

285

specifications or characteristics that are assigned to each participant. They are devised to impose specific restraints, pressures and influences on the participants similar to those they would experience in a parallel real-life situation. The shape of a final agreement, however, is generally not limited by the rules in a role-play. Simulations combine elements of games and role-plays. They typically consist of at least three parts: a written background piece that sets the stage, confidential instructions for each role player, and a teaching or debriefing note. The background introduces the rules of the game. The role-play, computer simulation, or related activity involves the players in a problem-solving situation. Typically, multiple groups or "tables" play the same game at the same time so that the results can be compared.

The debriefing of the results at multiple tables provides an opportunity for the full group to examine the differences in outcomes. Participants are encouraged to reflect, not only on their own results but on why the outcomes of the other groups playing the same game were different. Student reflections and simulation outcomes are generally discussed openly with everyone. The instructor must be able to highlight commonalities and differences that teach important lessons.

Debriefings require the instructor to link the group's outcomes to key negotiation concepts and theory. In our experience, debriefings are when most of the learning takes place. Thus, it is important that inexperienced instructors, especially, use a carefully prepared teaching note to guide their debriefing efforts.

It may be helpful to illustrate. We have selected a simulation, called HARBORCO, and highlighted: (1) what is conveyed in the background instructions to all players; (2) what is contained in the confidential instructions for each player; (3) the a range of typical results; and (4) the lessons usually raised during the debriefing.

A Sample Simulation: HARBORCO

General Instructions

HARBORCO is multiparty, muti-issue, scorable face-to-face negotiation. The simulation centers around a negotiation over a proposal by Harborco, a consortium of development, industrial, and shipping concerns, to build and operate a deep-water port in the city of Seaborne. The proposal is controversial because of its potential impacts on the environment, the direction in which industrial development will proceed, impacts on competing ports and the distribution of new jobs related to construction and operation. The participants must decide whether to grant Harborco a license for the port development and, if so, what the conditions are under which the license will be issued. The negotiation is organized by the Federal Licensing Agency (FLA). The participants include a representative of the environmental coalition, a spokesperson for the Federation of Labor unions, a representative of a consortium of other ports in the region, senior staff for the Federal Department of Coastal Resources (DCR) and the Governor of the host state.

Each of the parties to the negotiation views port development differently. Included in the background information that all participants receive, is general information about each parties' stated positions. The developers, Harborco, believe that the port will provide economic benefits for the region. The Environmental League is generally opposed to any coastal development because it threatens fragile ecosystems, will increase air and water pollution, and adversely affect health and safety in the region. The Federation of Labor Unions is pleased with the employment the port will generate and seeks guarantees that the new employers will hire only union workers. The neighboring ports are not supportive of the new port being built and are seeking significant compensation if the project goes ahead. The Federal Department of Coastal Resources (DCR), a cabinet-level agency with a mandate to encourage economic development along the coast while also protecting coastal areas, is supportive of new port development. Finally, the Governor of Seaborne is eager to promote development and considers the unions one of her political allies.

The parties negotiate over five controversial issues. The first is the type of industrial development that will be allowed. The options include: a dirty mix of oil refineries, petrochemical plants, steel productions plants and other similar facilities; a clean/dirty mix, and all-clean (i.e., high tech) industries. The second issue is the ecological impact that port construction is likely to have, including the impact on sensitive habitats in the tidelands. The parties must decide whether the project will be allowed to do some harm to the environment, should be required to maintain or repair the ecological balance, or should only be permitted if it improves the ecological setting. The third issue that must be decided concerns employment rules, including whether Harborco will be allowed to hire whoever it wants, or will be required to hire a certain proportion of unionized workers. The parties must also determine the size of the federal loan that the DCR will provide. The options include loans of $3, $2, or $1 billion at 15 percent interest over 20 years or no federal loan at all. Finally, the parties must decide on a compensation package for other ports. The options include Harborco paying $600, $450, $300 or $150 million or no compensation at all.

Confidential Instructions
In addition to the general instructions that everyone receives, each party is given confidential instructions that they are not allowed to show the other players. These outline a suggested negotiation strategy and rank each of the contested issues in importance. The confidential instructions specify the minimum amount of points each party must achieve in order to accept an agreement, the point total if no agreement is reached, and the maximum point total assumed possible. The confidential instructions are designed to create deliberate conflicts among the parties but still leave room for agreement. It is up to the negotiators to maximize their points while negotiating an agreement.

The Federal DCR is willing to make a loan to Harborco, but also seeks to extract some concessions. The Federal DCR wants to preserve the ecological integrity of the coast, but does not want to require unnecessary expenditures. The DCR prefers a $1 billion loan, the improvement of the ecology of the port, a maximum $300 million compensation to other ports, a development mix of clean and dirty industries, and has no preference with regard to employment rules.

The environmental league negotiator is primarily concerned about improving the ecology of the coastal region. She/he sees the port development as an opportunity to secure important environmental protections. However, the environmental league representative does not want to be excluded from the deal entirely, thereby risking no environmental controls at all. So, he/she desires an all-clean industrial mix and improvements to the environment, but does not feel strongly about any of the other issues.

The Governor's negotiator favors the project and insists on union preferences in hiring. The Governor's negotiator is also concerned with ensuring the maximum federal funding possible. His/her priorities also include a $3 billion loan, unlimited union hiring preference, a primarily dirty industry mix, the possibility of some harm to the environment, and no compensation to neighboring ports.

The Harborco negotiator would like to avoid additional costs especially those associated with environmental improvements, compensation to other ports, and union preference in hiring. However, he/she recognizes the enormous potential profit the port development can generate. Therefore, Harborco is willing to agree to some added costs as long as they are guaranteed by a $3 billion loan. They also want an industrial development that can be primarily dirty, allowing some harm to the environment. Harborco wants to avoid a costly lawsuit if no agreement is reached and thus seeks a consensual resolution of all the issues with all five parties.

The negotiator for other ports is concerned that his/her constituency will suffer if the Harborco proposal goes forward. He/she is instructed to do everything possible to derail the negotiations and to see that no agreement is reached. However, if a proposal has everyone else's support, the port representative is instructed to demand the highest possible level of compensation and to push to increase development costs for Harborco. The port negotiator supports unlimited union hiring preference, all-clean industries, and substantial environmental mitigation.

The union negotiator supports the project because of its job creation potential. The union negotiator also seeks guaranteed union preferences in all hiring and wants the maximum federal loan to ensure that the project is completed. The union supports a clean/dirty industrial mix, a small amount of compensation to other ports, but does not feel strongly about environmental impacts.

Typical Outcomes
The confidential instructions provide each "player" in the simulation with a desired set of outcomes. The negotiation includes periodic votes on the five issues. The parties score each issue based on the points assigned in their confidential instructions. At least five of the six parties must agree to a proposal for Harborco to get its license. Each party is instructed to seek its highest possible individual score.

The simulation is arranged so that a high-scoring issue for one party is a low-scoring issue for another. One objective in the simulation is to highlight the possibility that parties can work together to achieve a high score. In all, there are 55 possible agreements with only nine being six-way agreements. Generally, the Harborco negotiator will offer concessions to forge a winning coalition with at least four other players. Three typical results of the Harborco simulation include: (1) granting the loan with limited compensation to other ports and minimal environmental impact; (2) an agreement which leaves out the environmental league; or (3) no agreement at all.

When no agreement is reached, it usually means that the parties were holding out for more than their minimum scores or attempting to deprive others of what they presumed would be unduly large gains. When this is the outcome, no party leaves the negotiation better off then before it started.

Debriefing
The key negotiation lessons usually taught from this simulation are: (1) it is important to understand one's Best Alternative To Negotiated Agreement (BATNA); (2) there are opportunities to create value even in situations which are usually competitive; and (3) multi-party negotiations often hinge on the creation of winning or blocking coalitions.

The simulation illustrates how negotiators might best understand their BATNA by using a simple scoring system. By figuring the importance of each issue and its relative importance, parties can evaluate options more critically and be more clear about what others might need to be part of any agreement. In HARBORCO and other scorable simulations, a BATNA is assigned to each player. The lesson that can be explored in the debriefing asks simulation participants to articulate how they understood their BATNA; how it shaped the tradeoffs they were willing to accept.

A second important negotiation lesson from HARBORCO emphasizes that negotiations are rarely zero-sum. A key insight for participants to draw is that joint gains are possible because each player attaches a different level of importance to each issue being negotiated. In order for participants to fully grasp this, they must listen to the other parties' interests and communicate their true interests in a believable way. In order to create joint-gains, parties trade across issues they value differently while developing packages that allocate these joint gains.

A third lesson is the importance that coalition building plays in multi-party negotiations. Coalitions can form to both block agreement and to "expand" and "divide" the pie. Participants in HARBORCO needed to find other parties who share their interests and to assess the strength and stability of all possible coalitions. The simulation highlights how coalitions are often fragile because an outside party may lure a coalition member away by offering more than the coalition can provide. The stability of coalitions also depends on each party understanding the interests of the other parties and being creative about identifying shared interests. The simulation highlights the importance of building coalitions in the right way.

HARBORCO is an example of a scorable role-play simulation. It is conducted through face-to-face negotiations in which participants are assigned "roles." The entire simulation, including preparations, negotiations, and debriefing, typically takes about three hours to complete. HARBORCO, like many simulations, works best when there are two or more tables playing the same simulation so that outcomes can be compared. HARBORCO introduces students to many of the fundamental negotiation skills that comprise the mutual gains approach to negotiation.

Negotiation Skills
Teaching negotiation skills is different from teaching many other technical skills. Negotiation is not "one thing," nor even one set of techniques. Thus, learning negotiation is not like learning a scientific formula or a mathematical equation—which once mastered can be used again and again by following the same formula. Negotiation involves more art and science than that. While many authors have examined the bundle of skills involved in effective negotiation, or what we call "mutual-gains" negotiation, a short list of some of these skills is offered below:

Preparing for Negotiation
•Clarify your mandate and define your team;
•Estimate your Best Alternative to Negotiated Agreement (BATNA) and theirs;
•Improve your BATNA (if possible);
•Know your interests;
•Think about their interests;
•Prepare to suggest mutually beneficial options;

Creating Value
•Listening to and understanding the other parties' interests;
•Suspend criticism;
•Invent without committing;
•Generate options and packages that "make the pie larger";
•Use neutrals to improve communication;

Claiming Value
•Behave in ways that build trust;
•Discuss standards or criteria for "dividing the pie;"
•Use neutrals to suggest possible distributions;
•Design nearly self-enforcing agreements;

Follow Through
•Agree on monitoring arrangements;
•Make it easy to live up to commitments;
•Align organizational incentives and controls;
•Keep working to improve relationships;
•Agree to use neutrals to resolve disagreements.

Our emphasis is not so much on the particular skills on this list but on the fact that the range of skills requires mastery of concepts and methods from an enormously wide range of fields. Lewicki (1997) suggests that negotiation skills are "a complex collection of elements that entail aspects of strategizing, advocacy, communication, persuasion, and cognitive packaging and repackaging of information" (1997:265). Skills such as understanding, questioning, defining, framing and re-framing do not necessarily fit neatly into a recognizable discipline or pedagogy. This diversity of skills suggests that the best way to teach negotiation is by having students practice in actual conflict settings (or simulations). The next section briefly reviews the pedagogical assumptions behind this recommendation and how five teachers of negotiation view the usefulness of simulations from their teaching vantage.

Simulations and Pedagogical Assumptions
If negotiation is best taught through reflection on one's own practice, what does it mean to learn by doing? In other words, what are the pedagogical assumptions behind this approach to learning? Learning is often understood as a process whereby concepts, principles and ideas are internalized into the learner's cognitive processes thus leading to changed thought patterns and actions (Dewey 1938; Kolb 1984). Learning by doing implies that there is an experience, "the doing," that causes thought patterns and theory-practice connections to change.

This section will highlight three views about this process. The first, from Dewey (1938), stresses the interaction between the learner and his or her social environment. The second, from Lewin (1951), emphasizes the cyclical process of such experience (i.e., reflection allows abstract principles to form and these are tested in subsequent experiences). The third, drawn from cognitive psychology and epistemology, sees the learner "creating knowledge" by resolving "cognitive conflicts" which arise through challenging experiences. Taken together, these views provide a justification for experiential learning, or, more specifically, the use of simulations.

All three views postulate a process of confronting our existing ideas about how and why certain things happen, breaking them down and offering a new model or set of postulates to replace the old ones. This does not occur easily because we are often reluctant to give up what works for us or to see the world in a new way. As Argyris and Schön (1974) point out:

[T]he trouble people have in learning new theories may stem not so much from the inherent difficulty of the new theories as from the existing theories people have that already determine practices. We call their operational theories of action theories-in-use to distinguish them from the espoused theories that are used to describe and justify behavior. We wondered whether the difficulty in learning new theories of action is related to a disposition to protect the old theory-in-use (1974:viii).

Schön (1987) later suggested that a theory-in-use could give way to a "theory-in-action" through reflection. Addressing primarily how practitioners learn, Schön stated that we often see an unfamiliar situation as "both similar to and different from the familiar one, without at first being able to say similar or different with respect to what" (1987:67). What we may wind up doing in a learning situation is using the familiar situation as a metaphor for the unfamiliar.

Experiential learning theory suggests that we must open ourselves to what may seem a nonconventional view of the world. The process of challenging our existing "theories-in-use," is essential. Dewey's theory of experiential learning emerged in reaction to traditional educational strategy and asks the learner to embrace a new way of understanding or a new approach to practice.

Dewey and Experiential Theory
Dewey described learning as "intelligently directed development of the possibilities inherent in ordinary experience" (1938:69). He believed that learning through experience was the "progressive" alternative to more traditional education. Traditional education viewed information and skills as "givens" (formulated throughout history). The educational objective was to ensure that learners memorized and internalized this historical knowledge (i.e., what was "given to them"). In this model, students were viewed as passive spectators with empty minds waiting to be filled. The educator's role was to simply supply the learner with deposits of information.

Dewey's challenge to this model of pedagogy was his "progressive" model. His alternative was rooted in the belief that education should come through experience grounded in and relevant to one's social conditions. The goal for Dewey was to create genuine, positive and stimulating experiences. Dewey's educational theory had three major qualities: continuity; social awareness; and, "collateral learning."

For Dewey, learning entailed a continuity of experiences or, as he put it, "an experiential continuum." Each subsequent experience should be influenced by prior experiences. He claimed that every experience "modifies the one who undergoes it and this modification affects the quality of subsequent experience" (1938:36). Learning occurs when one experience opens the learner to other new experiences.

Dewey's theory was also built on a strong reaction to the social conditions through which experiences occur. One aspect of this view was that experiential learning could not occur to the person acting alone. Human contact and interpersonal communication were part of every meaningful learning experience.

Another feature of Dewey's theory were the "objective conditions," or the environment—both physical and social—within which experiences occurred and through which they were filtered. For Dewey, the objective conditions included everything from the physical conditions in the classroom to the learner's social and economic class. The learner's objective conditions often challenge internal, or individual, understanding. The result is a constant interplay between the learner's internal (individual) and objective (external) conditions—the sorting out of which contributes significantly to Dewey's idea of learning.

The third aspect of Dewey's theory of experiential learning includes "collateral learning." This is the process whereby a student learns a skill relevant to a particular experience and, at the same time, forms attitudes, likes and dislikes which he or she carries forward to apply in subsequent situations. Dewey stressed that experiential learning was not just about acquiring skills relevant to a single experience but also about understanding the relationships and meanings among many, seemingly divergent experiences. He wrote:

> What avail is it to win prescribed amounts of information
> about geography and history, to win ability to read and write,
> if in the process the individual loses his own soul: loses his
> appreciation of things worthwhile, of the values to which
> these things are relative; if he loses desire to apply what he has
> learned and, above all, loses the ability to extract meaning from
> his future experiences as they occur? (1938:49)

For Dewey, it was only in an experiential model of learning that these objectives could be met. Dewey viewed traditional education as teaching single skills in controlled laboratories where there was little or no room for creative relational idea making.

Dewey's Model

The focus of Dewey's learning model is the transformation of an impulse into purposeful action. It is built on a continuum of experiences in a social setting where collateral learning helps the participant make judgments. The model revolves around an initial impulse—an observation of "objective conditions"—and a knowledge of the experience which comes from the interplay between our internal and objective conditions. These all lead to a judgment about whether to or how to act. Dewey describes the cyclical process this way:

The formation of purpose is, then, a rather complex intellectual operation. It involves: (1) observation of surrounding
conditions; (2) knowledge of what has happened in similar
situations in the past, a knowledge obtained partly by recollec-
tion and partly from the information, advice, and warning of
those who have had a wider experience; and (3) judgment,
which puts together what is observed and what is recalled to
see what they signify. A purpose differs from an original
impulse and desire through its translation into a plan and
method of action based on foresight of the consequences of
action under given observed conditions in a certain way
1938:69).

Dewey's model is diagrammed in Figure 1. Postponement of action after the observaton
stage is crucial because a series, or continuum of impulses, observations, and judgments
should preced purposeful action.

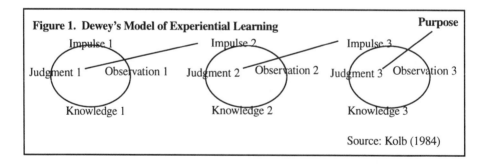

Figure 1. Dewey's Model of Experiential Learning

Source: Kolb (1984)

Lewin's Theory
The social psychologist Kurt Lewin offers a related model of experiential learning. Lewin's
experiential learning theory is rooted in dialectical tension between immediate concrete experience and anayltic detachment. Lewin developed his theory, often called T-groups ("T" for
training), by noticing that participants in training learned best when they were involved in
reflecting on and discussing their experience both with other participants and nonparticipant
psychologists. He brought together trainees with his staff of psychologists in open dialogue
where inputs from each could challenge and stimulate the others (Lewin 1951).

Like Dewey's cyclical model, Lewin also suggests cyclical experiential learning. Lewin
offeres a model with four stages; it differs slightly from Dewey's model, which has no real

beginning or end. The initial emphasis is on the present experience. By focusing on the immediate personal experience, this theory attempts to provide "personal meaning to abstract concepts while at the same time providing for a concrete, publicly shared reference point for testing the implications and validity of ideas created during the learning process" (Kolb 1984:21).

Lewin's theory also focuses on feedback. He viewed experiental learning as social learning and problem solving with feedback as a continual process of "goal-directed action." Experiential learning is optimized when observation on experience and action toward a desired goal are integrated and balanced. The four stages of Lewin's experiential learning model are outlined in Figure 2.

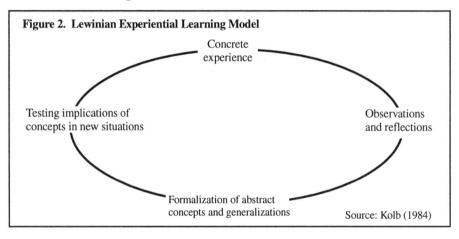

Figure 2. Lewinian Experiential Learning Model

Concrete experience

Testing implications of concepts in new situations

Observations and reflections

Formalization of abstract concepts and generalizations

Source: Kolb (1984)

Argyris and Schön (1996), expand on the idea of a "looped" learning process such as that offered by Lewin. They suggest that learning occurs whenever errors are detected and corrected, or when a match between intentions and consequences is produced for the first time. They found that in the learning process, individuals often design and implement a "theory-in-use" (actual behavior) that is significantly different from their espoused theory (what people say they do). They also found that individuals are unaware of the inconsistency when the theories they espoused and used were different. They are surprised to find out that there are often fundamental, systematic mismatches between individuals' espoused and in-use designs (1996:76). In addition, they found that individuals develop designs to keep them unaware of the mismatch. Argyris and Schön suggest that "single loop" learning involves changing behavior only to address the challenging situation at hand. This learning merely "satisfices" and does not change the underlying defensive routines that lead to the mismatch, implying that individuals are doomed to repeat the process never learning enough to understand the mismatch. In order for more meaningful learning to occur, Argyris and Schön offer a "double loop" learning process where the governing variables—the values and assumptions behind our understandings—are considered and questioned. Meaningful learning occurs in the "double loop" process because we do not merely solve problems but attempt to understand and challenge our governing variables behind our "theories-in-use" (Figure 3).

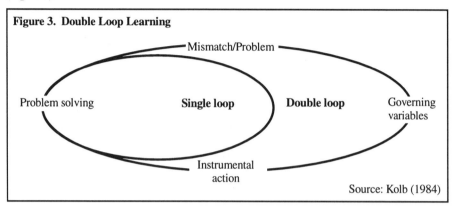

Figure 3. Double Loop Learning

Mismatch/Problem

Problem solving · **Single loop** · **Double loop** · Governing variables

Instrumental action

Source: Kolb (1984)

Cognitive Psychology Theories

Cognitive psychology offers a third model of experiential learning. One psychologist, Jean Piaget (1968), offers a model rooted in cognitive development. For Piaget, the learner constructs cognitive structures through two major processes: 1) assimilation—in which new information is integrated into existing structures; and, 2) accommodation—in which a learner's cognitive structure is altered to integrate new knowledge. Assimilation occurs when a new experience is consistent with one's existing cognitive structures and the knowledge from the experience is easily integrated. In Schön's terms, this is the role that metaphor plays.

Accommodation, on the other hand, challenges our established perceptions. In this process, our perception and understanding of experiences do not fit neatly within our existing cognitive structures. We find ourselves in a situation of "cognitive conflict," in which our established perceptions are challenged and we seek new ways to understand our experience. For Piaget, cognitive conflict stimulates a reorganization of our ways of thinking and seeing the world. Learning emerges through this reorganization of our cognitive structures.

Generally, cognitive psychology claims that our cognitive structures provide the framework through which experience is interpreted and through which we attempt to reorganize our understandings—leading to learning. Cognitive psychology suggests that we abstract principles from repeated experiences and also link the principles together through these same repeated experiences. The reorganization is a process of deducing from the abstractions actions which we have never previously performed (Furth 1969:71-75).

In the cognitive psychology view of experiential learning, our interpretive structures arise and evolve over time through repeated experiences. This interpretive process is similar to hermeneutics, which is the discipline (originally concerned with interpreting sacred texts) of interpretation (Palmer 1969). Hermeneutics is generally understood as a continuous cycle of interpretation and reinterpretation leading to new understandings. As such, it provides an important model for understanding experiential learning.

A classic example of a hermeneutic process leading to new learning and understanding is the interpretation of a written text as it is presented orally. The first reader gives meaning to the text not just through a reading of the written words, but also through the intonation in his or her voice. The meaning of the text for the listener can shift from their original understanding as the text is read aloud. Subsequent readers may present the same text differently as they read.

Hermeneutics suggests that only through this interpretive process does meaning emerge. Meaning of a text or an experience in the hermeneutic tradition comes about through an interplay between the parts of the experience and the whole experience. In the reading of the text example, the parts might be the meanings assigned to each word and the whole might be the entire text heard as an experience. As important in hermeneutics is reciprocity, where the meaning of the whole (e.g., the text) is dependent on the meaning of the parts (e.g., individual words). This process of parts and wholes taking on different meanings in each cycle in a continuous process of bringing understanding to an experience, is what is known as the hermeneutic circle (Palmer 1969).

The hermeneutic circle underlies all of the experiences through which we produce meaning. According to the hermeneutic perspective, meaning and meaningfulness are always contextual; they are part of the situation. There can be no understanding independent of a mutual set of experiences and interpretive practices. Learning occurs through the construction of common interpretive experiences. In this model, experiential learning is a cyclical process of interpretation and re-interpretation; assigning meaning to parts, to wholes, and back to parts again. The hermeneutic circle is similar to and consistent with the cyclical experiential learning models offered by Dewey, Lewin and Argyris and Schön.

Towards a Theory of Experiential Learning

The three theoretical approaches to experiential learning described above suggest that learning is a continual process of confronting and resolving conflicts between old "theories-in-use" and experiences (and interpretive frameworks). While the three have significant points of disagreement, their common embrace of dialectics and the multi-phased process of learning offer a basic pedagogical approach to experiential learning that justifies and explains the relevance of simulations for teaching negotiation. Similar to the hermeneutic process, experiential learning consists of ideas and concepts being formed, challenged and re-formed in multiple, often linked, experiences. Freire (1970) states that "knowledge emerges only through invention and reinvention, through restless, impatient, continuing, hopeful inquiry [people] pursue in the world, with the world, and with each other" (1970:58).

Lewin stated that the conflict between concrete experience and abstract reflection moves us to conceptualize abstract principles and then test these new abstractions in subsequent experiences. The axes of dialectic tension (Figure 4) however, in the experiential theories of learning still remain.

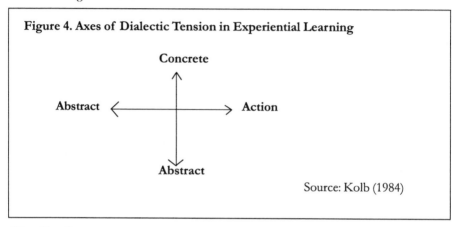

Figure 4. Axes of Dialectic Tension in Experiential Learning

Concrete

Abstract ⟵——————⟶ Action

Abstract

Source: Kolb (1984)

Views From Practice
In further developing how experiential learning is encouraged through the use of simulations, we spoke to five leading practitioners in the field: Professor Robert Mnookin, Harvard Law School; Professor Deborah Kolb, Simmons College; Professor Roger Fisher, Harvard Law School; Professor Michael Wheeler, Harvard Business School; and Professor Max Bazerman, Kellogg School of Management, Northwestern University. We sought to find out why they use simulations and how they use them to teach negotiation to both graduate students and mid-career professionals. These views are intended to document how experienced instructors handle the dialectic tensions in experiential learning. We asked each respondent to describe how simulations can be effective in helping students understand key negotiation dilemmas. We also asked them to describe the actual simulations they find most effective and why. Finally, each person was asked to talk about the debriefings that they do and how these can be most effectively coupled with simulation exercises to provide meaningful leaning opportunities.

What we found is that the practice of using simulations to teach negotiation is closely linked to the theory of experiential learning. Experiential learning, at a basic level, includes a structured experience, reflection on that experience, and a subsequent experience in which behavior may be altered based on the prior experience and reflection. We found that the instructors to whom we spoke use simulations to provide a carefully structured experience, encourage reflection through the debriefing and other techniques, and use different kinds of simulations to link experiences and reflections in different ways for different types of students.

Why Use Simulations?

According to Max Bazerman, "the most important thing simulations do is unfreeze people from past practice." Bazerman claims that simulations are used effectively to unfreeze past practice when the results of a simulation "are clearly lousy." Deborah Kolb agrees with Bazerman and adds that, "when you want to help people understand how they got a particular outcome—what they did—I think role-plays are great for that." Robert Mnookin claims that in his teaching, simulations help integrate negotiation theory and hard skills:

> In teaching I try to provide students with an intellectual
> framework for understanding negotiations and prescriptive
> advice on how to most effectively negotiate. Through
> simulations, students actually experience the negotiation
> process and as a teacher I can use these student's own
> experience in the simulation to both develop conceptual
> frameworks and get them thinking hard about what does
> work, what doesn't work, and why?

Roger Fisher agrees that simulations are a useful way to unfreeze past practice while also teaching new skills for dealing with people in difficult situations. Fisher notes:

> We use simulations because you can't tell someone how to
> deal with others and expect them to understand. They need to
> do it. There is clearly a difference between telling someone to
> put themselves in another's shoes and having them experience
> another's point of view in a role-reversal. Simulations are
> one way to do that.

In practice, the simulation of face-to-face interaction between parties offers the critical experience through which negotiation themes, concepts, and skills can be explicated. How negotiation themes, concepts and skills are raised using simulations varies from instructor to instructor.

Techniques and Types of Simulations Used

While a simulation offers an experience around which instructors can organize the lessons they want to teach, they often use different techniques to highlight both negotiation theory and skills. For example, Bazerman is "a big fan of scorable games." He believes that "the classroom is a great place to show you blew a million dollars." Michael Wheeler agrees with Bazerman, stating that despite some "misgivings," he is "still inclined to favor scorable games, ones in which it is possible to validate efficiency notions, for example, or coalition dynamics." However, other practitioners stress different concepts in their teaching and do not emphasize the use of scorable games.

299

Roger Fisher states that scorable games are often not the best way to introduce critical negotiation skills to students—whether they are graduate students or mid-career professionals. Fisher notes:

> I am less intrigued by scorable games because so much in life is scorable in terms of money. People really care about how they are treated, how they are respected, whether you acknowledge their interests. There are a whole set of concerns. While scores count in life, my view is that they tend to count too much. I don't want to emphasize more dollars and cents. My impression is that relationships are more important. You can't score relationships. I prefer a role reversal exercise or other simulations to scorable games.

Robert Mnookin best captures the advantages and disadvantages of scorable games when he states:

> The advantage [of scorable games] is that students can compare their outcomes. If you are trying to teach them that some outcomes are Pareto-superior to others, you can demonstrate it very effectively. The disadvantage of scorable games is that the creativity to think outside the box of things that can be scored counts for nothing. A lot of what I'm trying to teach is this type of thinking, so this is a disadvantage.

Practitioners also differ over how to most effectively use simulations to create a series of learning experiences that link reflection to concrete experience. Kolb noted that she uses a combination of games, cases, role-plays, and real-life applications in her teaching. Kolb finds games, such as the *Oil Pricing Exercise* and *Win-As-Much-As-You-Can*, to be extremely effective for their "ah-hah!" quality — the critical moment when a participant experiences a key lesson in the exercise, but finds role-plays useful for teaching specific skills. She notes:

> Games often don't look like the thing you're doing but have an "ah-hah!" to them. That is because they are an analogue to the thing you are trying to study. These are among the most powerful experiential exercises that there are. I combine these with role-plays, which help people create an experience where the data helps make specific kinds of points to teach specific kinds of tactics, techniques and ways of thinking.

Each practitioner's view on the usefulness of simulations drives, in part, the selection of the simulations they use in their teaching. Robert Mnookin said he tends to choose simulations to focus on negotiation themes he finds compelling:

> One of the basic themes of my teaching is that there are almost always opportunities to create value and there are almost always distributive issues. And, there is a tension between opportunities to create value and the problem of distribution. I want to choose situations not of pure distribution but where there are some value-creating opportunities, often ones that they may overlook. *Sally Soprano, Power Screen* and others, have this aspect. Not purely distributive, but there always is a distributive issue.

The faculty we spoke with stressed that teaching negotiation only with role-play simulations will deny students the opportunity to understand key negotiation lessons. They stated that role-plays may only capture certain skills needed to be effective in negotiation while missing others. Wheeler states:

> I'm troubled by so-called simulations that ask people to assume the role of the victim of sexual harassment or to be a rabid environmentalist or developer, for that matter. Such assignments trivialize the complexity of the issues and mask important questions of identity, relationship, and even ethics.

As to the second issue, our need to highlight certain issues (and to keep the exercises from becoming all-consuming), we typically squeeze out important aspects of negotiation preparation, discovery, and weighing our interests, for example, or pursuing nonagreement alternatives, including other negotiations. In order to get people to a point where they can actually come to "agreements," we often push them well down the negotiation road, saddling them with assumptions that are not their own and may be of dubious plausibility.

Kolb also expresses concern over the important negotiation skills that a teaching strategy that only uses role-plays might ignore:

> I have a number of issues with role-plays. One, the issue of complexity. In the world we don't get roles. The whole definition of how you decide what your preferences are, what your interests are, even what the issues are, is something that is

very interesting to me and role-plays don't do that. I use
different ways to get at these things. Role-plays are also not a
good vehicle to look at issues of gender, because they take
some of the things that might be gendered to the world out.
Because they tell people what to look for, role-plays are never,
by themselves, a sufficient reflection of reality.

Thus, when using simulations practitioners stress that instructors must be aware
of their limitations. All the instructors we spoke with agreed that to teach negotiation
effectively, whether to graduate students or mid-career professionals, requires a teaching
strategy which combines simulations with other games, cases, and readings. None of the
instructors relies heavily on computer-based simulations and all were skeptical that computer
simulations can replace the real-life dynamic that face-to-face simulations offer. They also
stressed that, no matter what the mix of simulations and teaching techniques in class,
reflections outside of class on the experience is crucial to teaching negotiation.

Debriefing in Practice
The debriefing of a simulation is crucial. Wheeler claims that "the debriefing is everything.
I can't imagine people getting much value from simply doing a series of negotiations." Kolb
states that "if you can't debrief it, there is not much to learn—the debrief is a way to make
the theory meaningful." Fisher concurs, stating, "reviewing what you did, either talking
about it or hearing other people talk about it, is crucial." However, techniques for using the
debriefing to convey lessons differ.

The success of a debriefing session depends on providing reflection "space" for
experiential learning. Mnookin states that his debriefing sessions have the added challenge
of providing meaningful space for reflection with a large group of students. Mnookin
describes his strategy as follows:

> I have them discuss in smaller groups first or themselves think
> about what some of the critical lessons are. When teaching a
> big group, only a few individuals get air time. The most
> critical aspect of the debrief is for the teacher to both be able
> to use and build on what students are saying on one hand and
> at the same time have an idea ahead of time what major
> messages you want to get across. The skill is to build on their
> own experience to get to your messages.

Wheeler finds that small group discussions often leave the students impatient with
the "he-said-then-she-said" type of reflections. Instead, Wheeler is more inclined to take an
active role in framing the discussion and stresses the importance of linking successive de-

briefing sessions. He states that in a debriefing, he might:

> Look at a data set and ask the group to construct a theory that ex-
> plains how, when dealt the same cards, people could arrive
> at such different outcomes. I reframe their observations, leave
> them with research results, and try to organize the discussion so that a
> coherent model of negotiation emerges, if not from one debriefing,
> then from the succession of them.

Bazerman stresses that instructors should be very clear before using a simulation what the lessons are that the students should walk way with after the exercise. He states that far too many times teachers pick an interesting game but students walk away after an ambiguous discussion not knowing what they've learned. To prevent this, Bazerman admits:

> If I have to be heavy-handed in the debrief I'll do that. I'll
> try to inductively get the point out from the students in the
> debrief, but if it isn't coming, I'll be heavy-handed. I tend
> to have very clear analytic punch-lines that I see coming out of
> cases I use. I always know going in the lessons I want the
> students to come away with. I usually use the last 20 minutes
> of class. Students should never be confused over why we did
> that case or what it is they were supposed to learn.

It is clear that the instructors with whom we spoke view debriefings as the setting within which learning takes place. Carefully structured debriefings with clear analytic lessons are crucial to the effective teaching of negotiation skills. Simulations, combined with other experiential learning techniques, create an environment through which negotiation skills can be learned, practiced and reflected upon.

A Typology: Teaching Negotiation Using Simulations
The pedagogical models and views offered by our respondents suggest five important considerations in teaching negotiation: students/participants; setting; the process used; views of conflict; interpretation of information; reflection; and, the role of the instructor. Using simulations effectively to teach negotiation requires instructors to actively engage students in the process of listening and questioning. This is how they will increase their understandings of their own interests and those of others. Simulations put students in conflict situations, within which they can redefine their understandings and use information to explore ways of creating and distributing value. The views we heard emphasize not only the importance of experience but also the need to create opportunity to reflect on that experience. Debriefing offers such a space. The instructor must become an active participant by encouraging reflec-

tion on specific negotiation skills and concepts. Each consideration might be carefully weighed in designing an appropriate teaching environment (Table 1).

All the instructors to whom we spoke agreed that since teaching negotiation involves building skills to get along better with others, there is no substitute for simulated experiences in which students can practice getting along with others. However, they differed on the choice of teaching strategies for creating experiential learning environments.

Teaching Strategies Using Simulations

The experiential learning model suggests taking part in a structured experience, reflecting on that experience, abstracting concepts from the reflection, and moving into subsequent experiences. Instructors describe a similar process using simulations as the primary vehicle for the "experience." However, our view is that there can not be a "one-size-fits-all" approach to using simulations to teach negotiation. Many factors ought to determine which teaching strategy works best including, but not limited to: teaching objectives; skill level of participants; comfort of instructor with simulations; size of the group; the technology available (e.g., computers); and, the extent and type of the debriefing sessions possible. Most importantly, instructors must be clear about their teaching objectives before introducing a simulation. Simulations work best when they are part of an overall teaching strategy, grounded in experiential learning, not simply as isolated exercises to supplement more traditional curricula. We offer four basic suggestions for using simulations to teach negotiation: start simple; rely on layering; encourage constant reflection; use mixed media.

When using simulations, we recommend starting with simple exercises that emphasize behavioral lessons. Simple games, such as *Sally Soprano*, *Power Screen*, and *Win-As-Much-As-You-Can*, introduce key negotiation concepts to students effectively. These games generally work best when they do not relate to the participants' real-life situations. That is, the more abstract or generalizeable the initial lessons, the better. Roger Fisher points out that if the introductory simulations are too familiar to participants they have a tendency to "argue and fight" with them. Simple games can be understood and played in a short time and highlight fundamental negotiation themes such as distinguishing interests from positions, creating value and distributing the value in a way that doesn't undermine relationships. The idea is to encourage students to re-think the way they might view a conflict-laden situation and to provide a framework for integrating additional negotiation skills later on. As many of the instructors we spoke to stated, getting the "ah-hah!" or the critical moment when the participant experiences a key lesson from the exercise, is often a crucial step before more complex simulations will work.

The second general suggestion for using simulations is to layer or add on complexity one step at a time. By this we mean that each simulation should build on the themes of the previous simulations. Layering can include starting with a two-party role-play that puts the participants in a situation with which they are not familiar. This challenges them to understand a negotiation from another party's point of view.

From two-party negotiations, students can move to multiparty negotiations where they must begin to understand the interests of several players. As the complexity increases, it is often useful to offer simulations that more closely (contextually) relate to the situations that students face in real life. This will enable students to apply what they have learned in simple simulations to more complex negotiations where they may be "stuck" in old ways of doing things. For example, in training public sector environmental officials, it is often useful to engage them in a simulation such as HARBORCO, where the parties include other governmental officials, private sector technicians, and environmental NGOs. Using this scenario, participants can begin to see how a range of concepts and skills might be applied in their

Table 1. Key Considerations in Teaching Negotiation

Characteristics	*Non-Experiential Learning*	*Experiential Learning*	*Teaching Negotiation*
Participants	Passive Spectators	Active; observant	Active
Setting	Laboratory-like	Social; interpersonal; real-life	Simulation, game, role-play
Procedure	Memorize and acquire skills	Cyclical; continuum of experiences	Questioning, listening
Conflict	Discouraged	Encouraged; occurs with internal pre-existing epistemology; cognitive conflict	Used to redefine understandings and create value
Interpretation	Information is given	Hermenutic circle; relationships stressed between experiences	Framing and reframing understandings of all parties' interests
Reflection	Not necessary	On each experience; on abstract principles derived from experience; assigns meaning	Debriefing
Instructor	Transmits information; not engaged in learning	Facilitates genuine, constructive experiences; active part of learning process	Active participant in debriefing

professional setting. They can also see how the mutual gains approach can work in a complex situation.

A third suggestion is to encourage constant reflection. The simulation itself is an important experience, but negotiation lessons must be "drawn out" from these experiences through critical, structured reflection. As we noted earlier, debriefings are crucial. During a debrief, instructors should build on student self-reflection as well as comparisons of the results achieved by different groups of negotiators playing the same "game." Simulations are effective only when they are accompanied by a carefully arranged review of the results by a skilled instructor. Students should be encouraged to reflect on how the simulation outcome relates to an experience in their real life and how they might have handled the real-life situation differently in light of what they learned from the simulation. We also recommend that reflection go beyond the debriefing. Students should keep daily journals as a written record of their reflections. Journals allow students to go back periodically throughout the course and review what they have learned.

A fourth suggestion is that simulations are often best combined with other teaching techniques. Many of the instructors we spoke with supplement simulations with case studies, videotapes, and even computer-based exercises. For example, one technique is to videotape all or part of a simulation and have participants watch themselves negotiate. This can enhance reflection. Another strategy is to use computer simulations outside of class to supplement in class exercises. Simulations in class are often limited because of time constraints. Computer-based exercises, where students review information and potential outcomes before negotiations begin, can supplement face-to-face role-plays.

These four suggestions do not capture all the possible advice regarding the use of simulations in teaching negotiation. There are additional questions an instructor should answer before choosing a simulation. For example, what negotiation lesson(s) is this simulation designed to teach? How does the simulation relate to other class exercises, readings and simulations? Can all students participate in the simulation? How much time will the role-play and debriefing take? Is there space for participants to "break away" and meet? Should the debriefing occur immediately after the exercise, the next day or during the following class session? Until questions such as these are answered, simulations should not be used.

Further Research
In reviewing the relevant literature and talking to our colleagues in the field, we found that simulations are in widespread use in negotiation courses in both graduate schools and in mid-career training. However, the theory behind how simulations ought to be used is relatively underdeveloped. Experiential learning theory provides a foundation upon which future research might build with respect to the effectiveness of simulations as a negotiation teaching tool. Three research gaps warrant further attention: the role of technology in simulation, using theory to develop new simulations, and systematic evaluation of simulation effectiveness.

Technology, specifically computer-based simulation aides, is influencing the way negotiation is taught. Negotiation skills can be taught using an interactive CD-ROM. Participants choose from a set of statements and the computer "acts" as the other negotiating party. Such simulations provide negotiation advice throughout the exchange and offer an evaluation at the end based on the negotiated outcome. According to Robert Mnookin, "computer-based negotiations can be very effective if you want to simulate how people are going to behave in a prisoner's dilemma. In terms of actual interaction in real world negotiations, I think it is very hard to do it through computers." Technology seems to be limited at present to transmitting information and not necessarily capturing important elements of negotiation. Most practitioners claim that there is no substitute for face-to-face interaction. Deborah Kolb thinks that there are important situations in teaching negotiation that computer simulations seem to miss. She states:

> The kinds of things I'm interested in are when someone says
> to a woman, "you're not a risk taker, you can't pick up this
> responsibility." That is an effort to put her in a down
> position and how can a person respond to this? Or, in a
> salary negotiation, the person says "you're being greedy."
> These are the kinds of things that disempower people when
> they negotiate. These are the things I'm interested in and
> I'm not sure how technology can help.

The most effective use of technology may be as a supplemental source of information that participants can use in a face-to-face negotiation. One simulation, Hitana Bay, uses a complex computer model to estimate the impacts of different development scenarios. Participants in that negotiation can better estimate their BATNA using this information than they otherwise could. Thus, computer-based information can often complement, but not substitute for, face-to-face negotiations.

The development and testing of new simulations is another area in which we feel more work needs to be done. Protocols for constructing simulations and systematically testing their effectiveness need to be refined. Roger Fisher states that in designing simulations the temptation is to make them complicated, rather than simple. He observes:

> [W]e can do better in making these exercises. I think a more
> clear understanding of why we are doing it and what makes
> it good is needed. We ought to have more theory of why
> simulation designs are good and apply it further. The tempta-
> tions is to make simulations complicated. I want the cases to
> be simple. It is much easier to learn things from simple cases.

Designers of simulations often start with a negotiation lesson(s) they want to convey. Next, they choose a conflictual situation and the parties to the conflict. A conflict is constructed where the negotiating parties confront the designer's key lessons. The designer often maps possible negotiated outcomes and then "tests" the simulation, using participants experienced in negotiation. In the testing stage, the designer and the "test" players determine whether the intended negotiation lessons are clear from the simulation. Often, the original design is altered after the "test-run." Designing an effective simulation is an iterative process. Simulation design is as much an experiential learning process as is simulation use in the classroom. More clearly articulating the theory behind the design of simulations is closely linked to the development of the theory itself. Thus, the two research agendas should proceed hand-in-hand—developing the theory behind the design while conceptualizing why and how the design will work in practice.

Finally, a noticeable gap in the field of simulation research is that there is no shared framework for evaluation. Most instructors rely on a range of tools to evaluate whether students have learned what is being taught—everything from journal entries to exams to course-ending evaluations. But, very little progress has been made in figuring out how to evaluate the success of specific simulations as tools for teaching particular negotiation lessons. Many instructors rely primarily on post-course/training feedback and word-of-mouth reaction. Student evaluations may not capture all the significant learning, however, because students may have difficulty articulating what they have learned in such a short period after a particular class. Indeed, they may not realize what they have learned until they face a challenging situation in their lives six or more months after the negotiation training.

We suggest that, in addition to "last-day-of-the-course" evaluations, instructors teaching negotiation with simulations should begin developing medium and long-term post-course evaluations. For example, Wheeler stated that scheduled "follow-up sessions, in which people are asked to identify situations in which they have tried to apply the ideas," might begin to structure more systematic evaluation. Deborah Kolb states that she is planning to incorporate long-term evaluation into her mid-career training by "asking people after the training to write down the one or two things they'd like to remember from the class. They give it to you [the instructor] and you mail it to them [participant] six months later." The idea is to develop some gauge of skill retention over time and develop a better sense of how simulations contribute to long-term skill retention.

Teaching Negotiation Using Simulations: Conclusions
Teaching students negotiation by having them participate in simulations builds on the experiential model of learning. We have shown that the models of experiential learning—in which an experience is followed by reflection leading to altered views of subsequent experience—helps to explain why simulations are an effective teaching tool. Simulations provide an important structured experience. When coupled with a well-managed debriefing session

and linked with subsequent simulations in an overall experiential teaching program, they can add enormously to the effectiveness of negotiation training.

While the instructors with whom we spoke differ on specific tactics and teaching strategies, they all agree that simulations help "unfreeze" past "theories-in-use" and provide space for reflection. Teaching negotiation through simulations is most likely to be effective when simulations are chosen with specific learning objectives in mind and when simulations are linked together to create a continuum of experiences and managed reflection in an experiential learning environment.

References

Argyris, C. and D. Schon. 1994. *Organizational learning II: Theory, method, and practice.* Reading MA: Addison Wesley.

_____. 1974. *Theory in practice: Increasing professional effectiveness.* San Francisco. Jossey-Bass.

Bailey, B.A. 1990. Developing self-awareness through simulation gaming. *Journal of Management Development,* 9(2):38-42.

Barkai, J. 1996. Teaching negotiation and ADR: The savvy Samurai meets the devil." *Nebraska Law Review* 75:704-751.

Boud, D., Keogh, R., and Wlaker, D. 1985. *Reflection: Turning experience into learning.* London: Kogan Page.

Dewey, J. 1938. *Experience and education.* New York: Macmillan.

Druckman, D. 1996. Bridging the gap between negotiating experience and analysis. *Negotiation Journal* 12:371-383.

Druckman, D. (ed). 1977. *Negotiations: Social-psychological perspectives.* Beverly Hills: Sage.

Faria, A.J. 1987. A survey of the use of business games in academia and business. *Simulation & Gaming,* 18(2), 207-224.

Fisher, R. and Ury, W. 1981. *Getting to YES: Negotiating agreement without giving in.* Boston: Houghton Mifflin.

Freire, P. 1970. *Pedagogy of the oppressed.* New York: Herder and Herder.

Furth, Hans G. 1969. *Piaget and knowledge: Theoretical foundations.* Englewood Cliffs, NJ: Prentice Hall.

Greenblat, C.S. 1988. *Designing games and simulations.* Newbury Park, CA: Sage.

Gredler, M. 1994. *Designing and evaluating games and simulations.* Houston: Gulf Publishing

Madigan, D., Weeks, T. and Susskind, L. 1984. *Harborco.* Cambridge, MA: Program on Negotiation at Harvard Law School.

Kolb, D. 1984. *Experiential learning; experience as the source of learning and development.* Englewood Cliffs, NJ: Prentice Hall.

Lane, D.C. 1995. On a resurgence of management simulations and games. *Journal of Operational Research Society* 46(5), 604-625.

Lederman, L. 1992. Debriefing: Toward a systematic assessment of theory and practice. *Simulation & Gaming*. 23(2) 145-160.

Lewicki, R. (1997). Teaching negotiation and dispute resolution in colleges of business; The State of the Practice. *Negotiation Journal* 13, 253-269.

_____. 1986. Challenges of teaching negotiation. *Negotiation Journal* 2:15-26.

Lewin, K. 1951. *Field Theory in Social Sciences*. New York: Harper & Row.

Laveault, D. and Corbeil, P. 1990. Assessing the impact of simulation games on learning; A step-by-step approach. *Simulation/Games for Learning* 20(1):42-54.

Neale, M and Bazerman, M. 1991. *Cognition and rationality in negotiation*. New York: Free Press.

Palmer, R. 1969. *Hermeneutics*. Evanston, Ill: Northwestern University Press.

Piaget, J. 1973. *To understand is to invent: The Future of Education*. New York: Grossman.

_____. 1968. *Structuralism*. New York: Harper.

Raiffa, H. 1982. *The art and science of negotiation*. Cambridge. UA:1 Harvard University Press.

Randel, J., Morris, B.A., Wetzel, C.D., & Whitehill, B.V. 1992. The effectiveness of games for educational purposes: A Review of Recent Research. *Simulation & Gaming*, 23:261-276.

Saunders, D. M., and Lewicki, R. J. 1995. Teaching negotiation with computer simulations: Pedagogical and practical considerations." *Negotiation Journal* 11:157-167.

Schultz, B 1989. Conflict resolution training programs: Implications for theory and research." *Negotiation Journal* 5:301-311.

Shubik, M. 1989. Gaming theory and practice, past and future. *Simulation & Games* 20(2):184-189.

Susskind, L. 1985. Scorable games: A better way to teach negotiation? *Negotiation Journal* 1: 205-209.

Susskind, L. and Cruikshank, J. 1987. *Breaking the impasse: Consensual approaches to resolving public disputes*. New York. Basic Books.

Thatcher, D.C. 1990. Promoting learning through games And simulations. *Simulations & Games* 21(3):262-273.

Lessons from Analogical Reasoning
in the Teaching of Negotiation

James J. Gillespie, Leigh L. Thompson,
Jeffrey Loewenstein, and Dedre Gentner

James J. Gillespie, a
Harvard Law School
graduate, is a doctoral
degree candidate in
organization behavior at
the Kellogg Graduate
School of Management,
Northwestern University,
Evanston, Ill. 60208.

Leigh L. Thompson is
the J.L. and Helen
Kellogg Distinguished
Professor of Organization
Behavior at the Kellogg
School.

Jeffrey Loewenstein is a
doctoral degree candi-
date in psychology at
Northwestern University.

Dedre Gentner is a
professor of psychology at
Northwestern University.

**This article first
appeared in**
Negotiation Journal,
October 1999:
Volume 15, Number 4,
pages 363-371.

A key goal of education is preparing students and managers to solve real-world problems. Given that most students
learn in a classroom setting that is different from their ultimate work environment, it is implicitly assumed that students' learning will transfer to that future environment. Yet
research on reminding (e.g., Gentner, Rattermann, and
Forbus 1993; Ross 1987, 1989) has shown that differences
between the contexts of learning and use decrease the likelihood of transfer. We believe that for a fundamental managerial skill like negotiation (Bazerman and Neale 1992; Lax
and Sebenius 1986), which is needed across a large variety of
business contexts and domains, we must question the implicit premise of transferability of knowledge.

Empirical evidence paints a rather gloomy picture of
people's ability to learn by example and to retrieve relevant
knowledge when solving a problem in a new context (see
Reeves and Weisberg 1994 for a review). People's ability to
solve problems in new contexts often depends on the accessibility of relevant knowledge, rather than a lack of information or a general capacity limitation. This is the "inert
knowledge" problem: information needed to solve problems is part of our cognitive repertoire, but fails to be ac-
cessed at the right time. In this report, we suggest that
negotiators' ability to access and use negotiation skills depends crucially upon how they are trained.

In the effort to learn more about learning, we have
conducted a series of intensive empirical investigations of
how undergraduates, MBA students, executives, and consultants learn and apply negotiation skills (Loewenstein,
Thompson, Gentner, in press; Thompson, Gentner, and
Loewenstein, in press). Based on this research, we report
the following propositions:

1. Transfer (or the application of concepts learned in one situation to a different, but relevant situation) is highly limited;
2. Making an analogical comparison among multiple, structurally-similar examples facilitates transfer; and
3. Recognizing when to make comparisons is not obvious.

Knowledge Transfer and the Limits of Learning

Transfer is the ability to apply a concept, schema, or strategy learned in one situation to solve a problem in a different, but relevant situation. It is important to distinguish surface-level versus deep (or relational) transfer. Surface-level transfer occurs when a learner attempts to transfer a solution from one context to a superficially similar context. However, in most situations it is desirable for learners to apply solutions and concepts that have deep, meaningful similarities, rather than superficial ones. Unfortunately, as we describe below, research has shown that this kind of transfer is difficult.

In typical negotiation training classes and seminars, people are exposed to cases and exercises that hopefully allow them to transfer principles to their own business situations. Yet, solving one problem barely improves the likelihood that one will solve a second problem in a different context (Reeves and Weisberg 1994). This is because people do not recognize the similarity between problems. Rather, people tend to access previous knowledge that bears surface, rather than structural similarity to the problem at hand.

Consider an example from Ross (1987). Participants studied examples containing principles of probability theory, and then attempted to solve problems requiring the use of those principles. If the study and test stories were from the same context, participants were more likely to be reminded of them than if the stories were from different contexts. However, just being reminded of the appropriate training example was not sufficient for participants to use the embedded principle to solve the test problem correctly. If the same underlying principle was carried out in the same way in the two problems, participants performed twice as well as participants who received stories in which the principle was carried out in different ways in the two problems. Surface similarity can play a large role in the reminding and use of prior problems.

Gentner, Rattermann, and Forbus (1993) directly tested people's ability to be reminded of stories with either surface or structural similarities. For example, participants first read a story about a hawk giving feathers to a hunter. Participants were then given one of four stories resulting from the crossing of surface and structural similarity (i.e., a story with similar characters and plot, different characters but same plot, similar characters but different plot, or different characters and different plot). Participants were over four times more likely to recall this story when later shown a story with similar characters than when shown a story with different characters. There was little difference in reminding performance based on plot, and participants were equally rarely reminded of stories with just matching plot or no match at all. In sharp contrast to these findings for remindings, when asked to give ratings of the quality of match between two stories, participants gave far higher ratings for stories that had matching plots than matching characters. Simply said, when people encounter a new situation or a problem, they do not tend to be reminded of prior examples with the same, underlying relations and causal structure which they themselves would value, but of examples with the same surface features (Gentner, Rattermann, and Forbus 1993; Ross 1987, 1989).

In total, the results of several research investigations point to a striking dissociation between what's most accessible in memory and what's most useful in reasoning: We often fail to recall what is ultimately most valuable for solving new problems (Forbus, Gentner, and Law 1995; Gentner, Rattermann, and Forbus 1993). Upon being informed of the "correct" approach to a negotiation simulation, students often express regret: "I knew that, I just didn't think to use it." Unfortunately, negotiators in the real world typically do not experience regret because they are not told when they have just made learning and application errors.

Making Comparisons Facilitates Transfer

An obvious question arises at this point for the learner as well as for the teacher: Are there ways to enhance people's ability to retrieve structurally similar, rather than superficially similar, instances? We think so. The key is to create a problem-solving schema or strategy that is decontextualized and uncluttered by irrelevant, surface-level information. This way, the negotiator's knowledge is more accessible and more portable. Indeed, experts in such domains as math and physics have been shown to develop problem-solving schemas that are abstract and not cluttered by irrelevant information.

We believe analogical reasoning offers an efficient mechanism to instigate the development of these problem-solving schemas. Comparing examples can lead to focusing on their key commonalities and abstracting out a productive problem-solving schema. According to Gentner's (1983; Gentner and Markman 1997) structure-mapping theory, the mental act of comparison entails a structural alignment and mapping process that highlights the similar aspects of the two examples. Simply by focusing on shared aspects between examples that have different surface features, learners naturally abstract a common relational structure that is uncluttered with irrelevant surface information. Thus, making comparisons can inform students and managers as to which aspects of experience are relevant and which are causally irrelevant. Analogical encoding refers specifically to deriving an abstraction based upon the commonalties resulting from the process of comparing two or more examples (Loewenstein, Thompson, and Gentner, in press). Evidence indicates that comparison naturally leads to schema abstraction, which in turn leads to transfer (Gick and Holyoak 1983; Loewenstein, Thompson, and Gentner, in press).

To test this theory of learning by comparison, we have conducted research investigations into how MBA students, executives, and consultants acquire negotiation skills (Loewenstein, Thompson, and Gentner, in press; Thompson, Gentner, and Loewenstein, in press). Thompson, Gentner, and Loewenstein (in press) found that studying by comparing examples, much more than studying by providing advice on a case-by-case basis, enabled

313

management students to abstract negotiation principles and later apply them to form agreements when actually negotiating. This effect was replicated and extended by Loewenstein, Thompson, and Gentner (in press), who found that the comparison effect remained even when all participants were asked to describe the solutions to the study cases (i.e., describing the common solution, or describing the solution to each case separately). Analogical encoding in these studies led to dramatic increases in transfer of a key negotiation principle—contingency contracts. The central conclusion from these studies is that analogical encoding, wherein people mentally compare and contrast cases to abstract a common principle, is a more effective means of learning than isolated case analysis, in which people analyze particular case situations independently of one another.

Recognizing When to Make Comparisons is Not Obvious

Based on the results of these experiments, we conclude that comparing cases is not automatic—even when the cases are physically and temporally juxtaposed. For example, in Thompson et al. (in press) and Loewenstein et al. (in press), less than a tenth of those studying cases individually mentioned the first example when discussing the second example, even when the two examples were on the same page. Thus, engaging the type of analogical reasoning process that we describe cannot be taken for granted in learners—even highly motivated ones. Reading more than one case is insufficient; it is comparing multiple cases that prompts knowledge transfer.

Issues for the Future

We think it is enlightening to structure our discussion and conclusions around the questions we find that those people both on the transmitting and receiving end of professional training and education ask most often. Sometimes their questions are similar; often they are different because they have different goals.

What Instructors and Trainers Like to Know about Learning and Analogy

Negative Transfer

By far, one of the most frequent questions we get concerns "negative transfer," or false mapping (Novick 1988). Negative transfer occurs when a learner transfers a concept or principle to an inappropriate situation as in the Ross (1987) study described above. Novick (1988) found that mismapping is particularly likely for novices. Our experiences accord with these findings; it is very common for new students to retrieve surface-similar incidents and apply those to the problem at hand. For example, students involved an "international negotiation" tend to retrieve international cases they've been exposed to and to try to apply them, even when there are (as far as we can tell) no real lessons to be learned through such transfer.

Perhaps the most widespread misapplication of principles students make is that they tend to fall back on what we term heuristic and biased thinking about negotiation (Bazerman and Neale 1992). For example, they assume a fixed pie, or they tend to compromise. We have substantial evidence that, in the absence of any training, students tend to compromise (Loewenstein, Thompson, and Gentner, in press; Thompson and Hastie 1990). Even after students and executives realize that compromise solutions tend to be suboptimal, they often want to know which "trick" to use. The challenge is knowing which principles apply to which domains and situations. The key is to discern perceptible, though nonsuperficial, features of a situation (e.g., differences in parties' future expectations can be an opportunity to form contingent contracts).

We have found that analogical reasoning is a powerful conceptual tool that helps people grasp critical features of a situation. Yet analogy is not a deductive method, but a psychologically powerful inference tool. Thus, there is no way to guarantee correct answers. One readily available practice for instructors is to provide good matches for students to compare. On the learners' side, it is helpful to "push" the conclusions of an analogy by thinking through the comparison explicitly; by doing so, one can often catch inappropriate matches (Gentner 1989).

Long-term transfer
Another question we frequently hear concerns the long-term transfer of knowledge. We have found short-term gains from comparison on later transfer, but are these temporary or lasting gains? The current literature suggests that learning experiences that incorporate analogy can show differences in performance months later (e.g., Chen and Klahr, in press). Still, an important question for future research is whether analogical encoding, specifically, persists in its benefits over time. We should also point out that we consider normal learning to consist of acquiring not simply one negotiation principle, but many. As negotiation principles rest on key aspects of a negotiation's structure, grasping these aspects is part of becoming an expert negotiator. Thus, learning negotiation principles should improve one's ability to parse negotiation situations. This kind of coherent system of knowledge in experts is related to durable and effective use of knowledge, i.e., long-term transfer.

Is the "case method" flawed?
Professional educators in law, management, and medicine extensively use the case method, which involves analysis of individual situations. The case method is founded on the belief that people can and will abstract higher-order relations from individual examples. We question the generality of this assumption, although clearly there are some cases with such enormous precedential value (e.g., in constitutional law, *Brown versus Board of Education*) that students should learn them in detail via the case method. Our concern is with using the case method to learn abstract principles. Our research shows that the case method can be improved by comparing examples and drawing out the common underlying principles. Separating causally relevant from irrelevant information appears far more challenging for learners without the use of multiple cases.

If abstraction of a principle is the key to analogical problem-solving, why not learn solely via abstracted principles?
This sounds reasonable. If principles are the key, why not simply give students abstract principles from which to learn (obviating the need for cases). However, this approach does not appear to be successful (Gick and Holyoak 1983; Ross and Kilbane 1997). For example, Gick and Holyoak (1983) found that providing learners with a principle was not as effective as comparing multiple examples. We suggest this is because it is critical for the learner to engage in the similarity mapping; principles presented alone may not be appropriately understood.

How does analogical reasoning compare to other learning techniques?
We know that asking people to make analogies can yield better learning than a completely didactic approach (from Gick and Holyoak). We have also examined this issue, pitting four types of learning against one another: feedback, repetition, observation and analogy (Nadler, Van Boven, and Thompson 1999). We found that analogy and observation were effective and efficient methods—at least for learning negotiation skills. Still, there are many other kinds of learning techniques whose relative efficacy is not known.

Questions Students and Managers have Asked Us

Is expertise a "shield" against the problems with transfer?
To some extent, yes. We define an experienced person as someone who has had some natural (i.e., real-world) experience but has not received formal training; we define an expert person as someone who has had many years of natural experience perhaps coupled with formal training. Although experts show somewhat more appropriate retrieval than novices do, they too retrieve many surface-similarity cases. For example, in Novick's (1988) study described above, experts showed greater transfer and less vulnerability to negative transfer than novices. Part of the reason for experts' greater performance was their ability to dismiss inappropriate cases quickly. Still, although experts performed better than novices did, they did not retrieve appropriate cases in all instances (Novick 1988).

The question concerning the optimal level of training is a difficult one and requires further research. It often takes ten or more years of experience to become expert in a particular domain, even for an obvious genius such as Mozart (Ericsson and Smith 1991). Training in analogical reasoning offers the prospect of shortening the length of time needed to achieve expert levels of performance.

Don't surface and structural similarity go together in the real business world?
Often, yes. Retrieving surface-similar cases is helpful to the extent that there are also structural similarities. It is true that many cases that share surface properties share structural properties as well, and experts pick up on these regularities (Blessing and Ross 1996). For example, if a manager is preparing an account statement, it is typical (and indeed optimal) to be reminded of last quarter's account statement. Such remindings have even been shown to be linked to some scientific discoveries and breakthroughs (Dunbar 1994). Finally, professionals often

express a strong preference for learning negotiation through in-depth, single-case study in domains that are highly similar to their own (e.g., finance executives like learning about negotiation cases that involve finance, etc.). If surface and structural similarity go together, then their request is valid.

Yet, surface and structural similarity do not always go hand-in-hand. As we argued at the outset, multiple principles of negotiation can be used in any given business context. There is evidence that if there are multiple possible structures in a given context, simply being reminded of the context will not directly lead to effective transfer (Ross 1984). That is, noticing surface similarities is not a guarantee of being able to notice and use a structural similarity. Surface similarities can lead people astray. For example, Gilovich (1981) found that sportswriters and football coaches gave high ratings to young players described as being from the same home town as a famous football player, or who had won an award with the name of a famous football player. The writers and coaches gave somewhat lower ratings to players from different hometowns or who had won an award with a different name. The bottom line is that negotiations occur in a wide variety of business settings. Thus, it is worth learning negotiation principles in ways that maximize the likelihood of their being used across contexts.

Is learning only about finding the right analogy?
Of course not. In many negotiation situations, the problem is not trying to figure out what principle or strategy is most optimal; rather, the challenge is to get parties to agree to apply a principle or strategy. For example, in the Middle East dispute between Israel and the Palestinians, both sides are well acquainted with the broad conceptual idea of integrative bargaining based upon differences in interests and priorities; to the extent that Israelis are more concerned about long-term safety/security and the Palestinians are concerned about land, the possibility exists for a mutually beneficial logrolling trade, as was done earlier in the Egyptian/Israeli dispute over the Sinai desert. In cases such as these, the difficulty is certainly not about finding the right analogy or accessing inert knowledge, but involves issues such as learning to trust the other party and learning how to set aside past animosities. In sum, our focus on analogy in this paper should not be taken as an indication that there are no further aspects to learning.

In Conclusion
Our central conclusion is that analogical reasoning, which involves comparing and contrasting cases, enables people to access what they learned from those examples when later confronted with a novel situation. This is because comparing examples makes explicit the relational structure explicit during the original encoding. Analogical encoding offers a cost-effective and conceptually simple technique for improving the negotiating skills of students and managers.

317

References

Bazerman, M. H. and M. A. Neale. 1992. *Negotiating rationally*. New York: Free Press.

Blessing, S. B. and B. H. Ross. 1996. Content effects in problem categorization and problem solving. Journal of Experimental Psychology: *Learning, Memory, and Cognition* 22(3):792-810.

Chen, Z. and D. Klahr. In press. All other things being equal: Acquisition and transfer of the control of variables strategy. *Child Development*.

Dunbar, K. 1994. Scientific discovery heuristics: How current-day scientists generate new hypotheses and make scientific discoveries. In *Proceedings of the 16th annual conference of the Cognitive Science Society*, edited by A. Ram and K. Eislet. Atlanta: Erlbaum.

Ericsson, K. A. and J. Smith, eds. 1991. *Toward a general theory of expertise: Prospects and limits*. New York: Cambridge University Press.

Forbus, K. D., D. Gentner, and K. Law. 1995. MAC/FAC: A model of similarity-based retrieval. *Cognitive Science* 19(2):141-205.

Gentner, D. 1983. Structure mapping: A theoretical framework for comparison. *Cognitive Science* 7:155-170.

———. 1989. The mechanism of analogical learning. In *Similarity and Analogical Reasoning*, edited by S. Vosniadou and A. Ortony. New York: Cambridge University Press.

Gentner, D., and A. B. Markman. 1997. Structure-mapping in analogy and similarity. *American Psychologist* 52(1):45-56.

Gentner, D., M. J. Rattermann, and K. D. Forbus. 1993. The roles of similarity in transfer: Separating retrievability and inferential soundness. *Cognitive Psychology* 25(4): 524-575.

Gick, M. L., and K. J. Holyoak. 1983. Schema induction and analogical transfer. *Cognitive Psychology* 15(1):1-38.

Gilovich, T. 1981. Seeing the past in the present: The effect of associations to familiar events on judgments and decisions. *Journal of Personality and Social Psychology* 40(5):797-808.

Lax, D. A., and J. K. Sebenius. 1986. *The manager as negotiator*. New York: Free Press.

Loewenstein, J., L. Thompson, and D. Gentner. In press. Analogical encoding facilitates knowledge transfer in negotiation. *Psychonomic Bulletin and Review*.

Nadler, J., L. Van Boven, and L. Thompson. 1999. *An examination of four common methods of training in negotiation*. Working paper, Kellogg School, Northwestern University.

Novick, L. 1988. Analogical transfer, problem similarity, and expertise. *Journal of Experimental Psychology: Learning, Memory and Cognition* 14(3):510-520.

Reeves, L. M. and R. W. Weisberg. 1994. The role of content and abstract information in analogical transfer. *Psychological Bulletin* 115(3):381-400.

Ross, B. H. 1984. Remindings and their effects in learning a cognitive skill. *Cognitive Psychology* 16(3): 371-416.

———. 1987. This is like that: The use of earlier problems and the separation of similarity effects. *Journal of Experimental Psychology: Learning, Memory and Cognition* 13(4):629-639.

———. 1989. Distinguishing types of superficial similarities: Different effects on the access and use of earlier problems. *Journal of Experimental Psychology: Learning, Memory and Cognition* 15:456-468.

Ross, B. H. and M. C. Kilbane. 1997. Effects of principle explanation and superficial similarity on analogical mapping and problem solving. *Journal of Experimental Psychology: Learning, Memory, and Cognition* 23(2):427-440.

Thompson, L., D. Gentner, and J. Loewenstein. In press. Avoiding missed opportunities in managerial life: Analogical training more powerful than case learning. *Organizational Behavior and Human Decision Processes: Special Issue.*

Thompson, L. and R. Hastie. 1990. Social perception in negotiation. *Organizational Behavior and Human Decision Processes* 47(1):98-123.

Scorable Games:
A Better Way to Teach Negotiation?

Lawrence E. Susskind

Lawrence E. Suskind
is Ford Professor of
Urban and Environ-
mental Planning at the
Massachusetts Institute
of Technology and
Director of the MIT-
Harvard Public
Disputes Program
based at PON, a
component research
project of the Program
on Negotiation at
Harvard Law School.
Professor Susskind has
served as a mediator
of public disputes at
the local, state, and
federal levels.

This article first
appeared in
Negotiation Journal,
July 1985: Volume 1,
Number 3, pages
205-209.

In duplicate contract bridge, several teams of players at different tables receive identical hands of cards, bid and then play. Possible outcomes of each game vary considerably since, even though the teams are playing the same hands, they may devise bidding strategies that are more or less effective than those developed by their counterparts at other tables.

The importance of strategy in duplicate bridge parallels the importance of negotiation strategy in scorable negotiation games, new teaching tools developed by the Program on Negotiation at Harvard Law School. Both can result in widely different outcomes and both use predetermined value systems to constrain how different sets of players work with the same information. The pedagogical objective of scorable negotiation games is to show disputants how they can secure win-win outcomes in conflict situations. To illustrate, I will briefly describe the characteristics and a typical "run" of one such game, HARBORCO, and comment on some of the advantages and disadvantages of using scorable games to teach negotiation.

Usually, three to ten groups of six persons play HARBORCO at the same time (sometimes in separate rooms, sometimes at separate tables in a large hall). Players can include participants in actual disputes, public officials, graduate students, or mid-career dispute resolution professionals. The players, or parties to this dispute, represent six different interests: HARBORCO, an industrial consortium that wants to build a major new deepwater port; a coalition of environmentalists opposed to the facility; union leaders worried that a modern, containerized facility will eliminate jobs; the federal agency responsible for both protecting and developing coastal resources; competing ports in the region who foresee a reduction in their business volume; and the governor of the state in which the new port would be located who is torn between the economic advantages of a new port and the possible loss of political support from unions and environmentalists.

An independent regulatory agency that must approve a license before any version of the project proceeds has called the six parties together in an effort to negotiate agreement. The agency has indicated that it will *only* grant licensing approval if at least five of the six parties agree on a "package" of policies, designs, and financial arrangements. They must do so before a deadline two hours away. And, within that two-hour period, the parties must reach agreement on five specific issues: 1. The industrial mix in the area adjoining the proposed port (all clean industry, a mix of clean and dirty industry, or mostly dirty industry); 2. the effort that will be made to mitigate adverse environmental impacts (the minimum required by law, maintenance of existing conditions, or enhancement of environmental quality); 3. Construction cost subsidies or loan guarantees provided to HARBORCO by the federal government; 4. Future hiring preference for existing unionized workers; and 5. Compensation, if any, paid to other ports.

Each player negotiator receives a package of general information spelling out the history of the proposed port, the results of detailed studies analyzing the choices facing the negotiators, and a summary of past positions taken by each of the parties. In addition, each receives a separate packet of confidential information, including arguments that each player can use to press his or her views, and score sheet. The score sheet indicates the player's minimum goal, or "walk-away" position, and the number of points that player will receive if each option under consideration becomes part of the final agreement. For instance, the environmental coalition learns it will receive 20 points if the negotiated agreement substantially improves environmental quality, 10 points if promises are made to mitigate some environmental damage, and a loss of 20 points if nothing is promised. Finally, each player is given an estimate of what no agreement represents in terms of a total number of points.

Negotiations then begin. Every half hour the convening agency asks if there is a package of options that HARBORCO would like to propose. If at least a five-way agreement is not reached, the agency indicates it will be back again in half an hour. The parties are free to caucus or take informal votes at any time before the deadline.

As soon as the negotiations conclude, a debriefing begins with the posting of scores from each table. It is not unusual for half the groups to reach no agreement, for several to reach five-way agreement, and for one to reach six-way agreement. For those at tables that reached no agreement, the value of each player's "walk-away" position is the score that each receives. For all others, each player's score ranges from the minimum needed for a yes vote to levels almost 20 percent higher (N.B., Don't tell anyone who hasn't yet played the game!).

The players at tables that reached no agreement then describe their negotiations. Usually HARBORCO, as instructed, had preempted discussion by proposing a package designed to ensure the greatest return on its investment. The other negotiators protested, and a series of caucuses began. HARBORCO, offering various concessions, tried to forge a winning coalition with at least four other players. Groups opposed to the port caucused simultaneously, seeking to block any pro-HARBORCO agreements. Few coalitions were stable. Each player was in something of a bind—not wanting to be left out of any settlement that might emerge, but also working to block packages that offered too few points. Sometimes agreement eludes the players even when the proposed package will allow five of the parties to vote yes (i.e., to do better than their required minimum scores). They were either holding out for still higher scores or blocking agreements in an attempt to deprive others of what they presumed would be unduly large gains. Often, the exchanges in the groups that fail to reach agreements become quite heated.

The debriefing continues with a description of the negotiations among groups that reached five-way agreement. Typically, there was very little activity away from the bargaining table. HARBORCO began by asking each group to express its concerns. It sought to build a package incrementally, attempting to pyramid proposals responsive to each group's concerns. Some players, usually the other ports, unions, and environmental coalitions, held out for no project at all since their assigned walk-away scores were high. The blocking coalition dissolved, however, in the face of increasingly attractive offers from HARBORCO to meet the demands of both the union and the environmentalists. The representative of other ports continued to vote no.

Some players are quite surprised to learn during the debriefing that a six-way agreement is possible. Of the 55 agreements that meet the minimum conditions for approval, only nine yield six-way agreement. Most of these produce relatively high scores for several players, although there are some five-way agreements that produce even better scores for individual players. Six-way agreements are reached only when the parties dedicate themselves to building consensus, working hard to respond to each other's concerns. While forbidden from revealing their confidential point allocations, they must find a way to communicate the contents in a manner that is believable to the others. In effect, the parties create joint gains by trading across issues they value differently and develop packages that allocate those joint gains.

The most significant moment in debriefing occurs when those who reached no agreement realize that they could have done better for themselves by working to help their adversaries do better. At first, there are cries of "foul." Those who reached no agreement claim that they have been tricked, that there is something inherently unrealistic about the scoring system. After further discussion they began to realize that they were not, in fact, in a zero-sum negotiating situation. Joint gains were possible because each player attached a different level of importance to the various issues being negotiated. Such gains could have been realized if they only had listened to each other more carefully. In addition, they discover that strategy and tactics made a difference.

Scorable games have several limitations. First, players must quickly read a great deal of material before negotiations begin so that everyone is working with the same set of facts. Improvisation is not allowed. For example, the environmental coalition in the HARBORCO game cannot propose alternative (i.e., out-of-state) locations for the port. The players are restricted to just the five items under discussion and location is not one of them. This limitation on the process of invention assures the scorability of the final package. It takes months of elaborate research to develop a realistic scoring system for each complex game. All the points and scores must be prefigured, so that there is an artificially small number of agreements that satisfy all six parties. Unless six-way agreement is difficult to achieve, it is not possible to make the primary pedagogical point: players will do better for themselves in a multi-issue negotiation when they try to help their adversaries do better.

Non-scorable games are usually followed by debriefings too, but in these the instructor asks the players to discuss their "feelings" about the outcomes. Objective evaluations are not possible. Since all possible agreements cannot be anticipated the parties can promise almost anything they want to achieve closure. The problem with this approach is that the players are not required to compare proposed packages with the precise value of walk-away positions or with results at other tables. They also cannot evaluate how well thy did relative to a highest possible score.

In the absence of such comparisons, there is no way for each player to evaluate the relative effectiveness of various tactics and strategies. While non-scorable games provide important pedagogical opportunities to stress the significance of creativity, they do not allow for rigorous cross-table comparisons or the analysis of best possible outcomes.

It takes months of full-time effort to develop realistic multi-issue, multi-party scorable games. The Program on Negotiation has developed several. Two were created for the U.S. Department of Energy to stimulate negotiations over the siting of low level radioactive waste disposal facilities. Another simulates a negotiation over the allocation of fishing rights in the face of competing pressures on a declining collective resource and substantial scientific uncertainty regarding the future of government planting policies. Still another involves a negotiation between an environmental regulatory agency and a company that is polluting a river.

All these games have been used for graduate level instruction as well as mid-career professional training. Some were designed to help the actual parties in real disputes come to grips with their differences. By working in a slightly fictionalized context, the disputants seem to have an easier time trying to resolve their conflicts. Because the stakes are much lower, they can try strategies different from those they might use in the actual dispute. In addition, the notion of maximizing joint gains take on greater meaning in relation to the details of an actual situation. In post-training interviews with the participants in one workshop, more than half of the players indicated that participating in a scorable game had changed their ideas regarding negotiation. They were now open to the idea that win-win options are most likely to be discovered when disputants try to present "yesable" propositions to their adversaries.

Two problems have emerged during some of the runs of the scorable games. Participants have complained about that they feel are unrealistic pressures to reach agreement, and the dominance of point-trading over matters of ideology or principle. As the negotiation deadline approaches, the group surges toward agreement, and holdouts find that they are under a great deal of pressure to submit to the will of the group. To the extent that such group pressure is nothing more than the result of one's table's desire to best the other tables (on the assumption that agreement will be rewarded), the criticism is justified. However, the criticism fails to recognize that the players become part of a "community" in which group norms often conflict with individual self-interest. Indeed, this is exactly what happens in a great many multi-party negotiations. Likewise, the imposition of deadline pressure in the game reflects a time factor that is often present in actual negotiations.

The second complaint is one that the makers of scorable games must heed carefully. In the games designed by the Program on Negotiation (since HARBORCO), the bottom line positions that the players must equal or beat have been defined not just quantitatively, but also in terms of key principles that must be protected. So, for example, the environmental coalition would not only have to negotiate a package that exceeded a certain total point score, but also one that did indeed enhance environmental quality. Points alone would not be enough. Such restrictions are required to ensure that negotiated outcomes are true-to-life.

While there is much more to learn about the design and pedagogy of scorable games, I would argue that they ought to be part of every negotiation training course. They complement traditional non-scorable games in important ways.

Some Techniques for Teaching Negotiation to Large Groups

Bruce M. Patton

Bruce Patton is Deputy Director and co-founder of the Harvard Negotiation Project and Associate Director of the Program on Negotiation at Harvard Law School. From 1985-1999, he was Thaddeus R. Beal Lecturer on Law at Harvard Law School. His most recent book (with Douglas Stone and Sheila Heen) is *Difficult Conversations: How to Discuss What Matters Most* (Viking/Penguin, 1999).

Patton's current work focuses on (1) how to create self-sustaining norms that help organizations internalize dealing competently with negotiation and conflict (whether with

This article first appeared in *Negotiation Journal,* October 1995: Volume 11, Number 4, pages 403-407

Teaching negotiation skills—whether in a university setting, corporate board room, or community mediation program—involves as much work on developing self-awareness, habits of mind, and communication as on developing analytical skills and understanding. Because of this complex mix of the interpersonal and the substantive, negotiation is most often taught in small groups with a low student-faculty ratio, such as 24 or fewer students to one teacher.

This presents a significant challenge if negotiation is to become part of the basic curriculum at professional schools, where class size for some required courses is often as large as 145 students. Is it possible to teach negotiation effectively to large numbers of students in one class?

Over the past ten years, my colleagues and I at the Harvard Negotiation Project[1] have developed a variety of techniques that address the particular challenges of teaching negotiation to large (100-plus) classes of students. My friend Jeff Rubin—himself no stranger to teaching large-sized classes—asked me to share some of the reasons why I believed our large classes were successful. In general, these classes are characterized by four structural elements: the use of teaching assistants who lead small group sessions; participatory questioning; task accomplishment and discussion in small groups; and the use of simple "in-place" negotiation simulations.

Working Groups Led by Student TAs

The fundamental structural technique we have used with large classes is smaller working groups led by student teaching assistants, or TAs. In a course of 144 students, we will have six working groups of 24 students. Each working group would be in the charge of two student teaching assistants chosen from among the best of former students for their combination of analytic and interpersonal skills.

Working groups are used to debrief exercises as well as provide students with an opportunity to explore their think-

customers, suppliers, or colleagues, in the boardroom or across the matrix), and (2) how to use effective difficult conversation skills to ensure successful implementation of vital initiatives such as strategic planning, TQM, becoming a learning organization, outsourcing, coopetition, alliances, mergers, joint ventures, and so on.

ing with colleagues in a setting that maximizes individual "air time." The working groups also provide convenient administrative units for logistical tasks, such as creating negotiating teams. The group identities and intergroup competition that develop also offer useful grist for discussion.

The role of the teaching assistants in these working groups is to foster a high-quality discussion that keeps the responsibility for learning from experience on the students. The teaching assistants are trained not to think of themselves as "deputy professors," but rather as learning facilitators; their role is explained to students in these same terms. Working from extensive notes prepared by the instructors for each session (but responsible for making their own choices about the ultimate conduct of the working group sessions), the TAs see to it that scarce time is well-spent and focused on important questions. They set the agenda (sometimes in consultation with students), manage time, and choose who is to speak and for how long (sometimes delegating these tasks to group members).

Perhaps most significantly, TAs monitor the quality of discussion in the working group and insist that it meet rigorous intellectual standards. (The TAs sometimes refer to their role as being "rigor police.") If a statement is abstract, they ask for an illustration. If a broad conclusion is stated, they ask for the data and reasoning that underlie it, then follow up by asking if others have different data or interpretations. If an argument boils up, they may interrupt and insist that each party first demonstrate their understanding of the other view to the other's satisfaction before offering a rebuttal.

Two TAs are used in each session to reinforce the notion that the TAs are not deputy professors, and to help separate the ideas presented and generated in the course from the personalities of the instructors. TAs often differ with each other and the instructor(s), reinforcing the notion that students need to think for themselves. This atmosphere is further reinforced by the fact that the TAs have no official grading responsibilities.

Over the years, the TAs have uniformly reported that they learned even more from this role than from their work as students in the course. (This will be no surprise to any teacher.) By having the TAs keep a journal and write a short paper on their experience, along with their regular group preparation and debriefing sessions prior to class, the entire experience can be treated as an advanced seminar, making the use of TAs highly economical. Alternatively, TAs can be paid, as is done in the case of many undergraduate courses.

Students generally have had positive things to say about their experiences in working groups. The same holds true even when the students are practicing lawyers participating in a professional development version of the course. All seem to enjoy the small-group setting as a change of pace, where many feel freer to think aloud without the presence of a professor grading their performance. Of course, TAs will not be possible in all settings, and may not be ideal for some purposes, particularly where the professor wants to explore difficult analytic concepts that TAs may not be prepared to handle. For such situations, other techniques are available to increase the efficacy and engagement of large classes.

Participatory Questions

Participants tend to feel that their engagement in an activity is proportional to their level of activity. One simple technique for exploiting this in a large class is to ask participatory questions. For example, a professor might say: "All of us have had the experience of asking for something and getting it, then realizing with a sinking feeling that it really wasn't what we wanted after all. Yes? How many of you have had that experience? Raise your hands."

Traditional open-ended Socratic questions also have some of this impact, if they are really open and crafted around an engaging puzzle. For example, after showing a short videotape or reading a case history, a professor might say: "How is it that two seemingly well-meaning people who work together so closely could have such radically different understandings of each other and of their responsibility for this situation?"

Talk It Over First in Small Groups

One way to increase individual participation greatly in a large-sized class is to pose a question for the group, then have students talk it over for several minutes with two or three others nearby before continuing with the large-group discussion. The energy this can generate in a usually staid classroom is quite remarkable. Many more students seem willing to talk after running their thoughts by a few colleagues, and the quality of the comments also tends to improve. I have also found this technique helpful in cultural settings where it is distasteful to "stand out" from the crowd by volunteering to speak. After a brief discussion with colleagues, people are much more willing to share the thinking of their group.

An efficient variation of this technique is to pose different questions to different small groups, allowing the large group to undertake several tasks without the transaction costs of moving to other rooms. Each group can then report back to the larger group. When the group is large enough, you can assign multiple small groups to report on each major question. The redundancy tends to increase the quality of the collective product.

The physics department at Harvard College is using a high-tech variation of this approach to great effect in its introductory physics course. Every 15 to 20 minutes during a class, the professor poses a problem that tests a student's conceptual understanding of the subject under discussion. Each student taps his or her individual answer into a computer terminal at their seat. (A sample problem: Is the strain on a rope tied between two identically pulling horses greater or less than the strain on a rope tied between one of the horses and a gate post?)

The professor receives instant feedback on how many of the class got the right answer. Usually, the professor then gives the students a few minutes to discuss the problem with one or two neighbors, before each again types in an answer. The percentage of right answers almost always increases dramatically after students have been able to talk it over. The professor can then decide whether to go on or spend more time on the topic at hand.[2]

Simple Exercises in Place

Another technique to increase participation is the use of simple exercises that can be done where people are sitting. One use of such exercises is to demonstrate a point by creating a memorable "ah-ha!" kind of experience. For example, the well-known ambiguous drawing of a woman who is perceived as either young or old can be flashed on an overhead projection screen while the group is asked to estimate her age to the nearest year and write down their estimate without any discussion with their neighbors. Results are collected, still without discussion. Groups can be formed around different age ranges and told to reach a group consensus. Then individuals or groups can be chosen to negotiate publicly with each other over the issue. The entire experience can then be analyzed.

A second example can be done with paper clips or M&Ms. After the rules are explained, a pile with one or two fewer items than twice the number of group members is placed at the center of each small group. Each person is then invited to take as many items as they want from the pile. At the end of each 30-second round, the pile is replenished by doubling the number of remaining items (if any), up to a maximum number. After several rounds, the results of different groups and individuals can be compared and discussed, exploring dynamics of cooperation and competition.[3]

In addition to demonstrations, this technique can be used to have participants practice a skill under discussion. For example, after a discussion of "framing" in negotiation, each participant can be asked to write down two ways of framing the situation in a negotiation exercise they have recently completed or will soon negotiate. One version should frame the situation as all or largely the other side's fault, the second should frame it in a way each thinks would be most likely to foster settlement. After a few minutes (and perhaps discussion with neighbors), examples can be collected, compared, and discussed.

When facilities permit, it is helpful for such exercises-in-place to seat participants in groups, such as at tables of six. This can also simplify the logistics of distributing materials, which can be sorted and distributed in labeled envelopes to each table in advance.[4]

Looking to the Future

Managing large negotiation classes is a challenging but not impossible task for an organized, articulate teacher who makes use of well-prepared teaching assistants and participatory exercises to motivate and illuminate key material. Even without teaching assistants, the task is manageable in shorter programs or by emphasizing analytic material and de-emphasizing communication skill-building. The Harvard Business School now has a required first-year negotiation course that takes this approach and also uses computers to simplify logistics and data collection. Assignments are distributed and results collected by electronic mail, allowing for rapid data analysis and reporting through the use of pre-prepared macros. This technique works best with scoreable exercises, but is also useful for data collection on less tangible issues.[5]

As more and more professional schools and undergraduate colleges offer negotiation as part of the "established" curriculum, it is likely that more will be learned about how the subject can be taught effectively to large groups. I hope this short report will stimulate others to share their experiences.

Notes

1. The Harvard Negotiation Project is one of the component research projects (as well as the precursor) of the Program on Negotiation at Harvard Law School, a consortium of scholars from several Boston-area universities and many different disciplines who are working together to improve the theory and practice of negotiation. Among the Program on Negotiation's initiatives is the publication, in cooperation with Plenum Publishing Corp., of *Negotiation Journal.*

2. More information on the physics department's use of computers can be found in the 6 April 1995 and 10 May 1991 issues of the *Harvard Gazette*. The 1995 article, by John Robinson, appears on page 9 under the headline "Explorers in a new frontier;" the 1991 article, by William Cromie, appears on page S3 of a supplement on teaching, under the headline "Pioneers in computer-assisted learning."

3. While a doctoral student at Harvard, Elaine Landry (now a management professor at Babson College) wrote a detailed teaching note on the "Paper Clip Exercise," which appears in Module One (pp. 5-7) of Landry, Kolb, and Rubin (1991).

4. This type of seating arrangement is used in a short (one and one-half day) negotiation training program that is offered seven times yearly by the Program on Negotiation at Harvard Law School. Between 150 and 175 persons attend each of these highly successful training sessions, the structural design of which also includes frequent use of participatory questioning and simple, "in-place" exercises.

5. For an excellent discussion of the use of computer simulations in negotiation classes, see Saunders and Lewicki (1995).

References

Landry, E.M., D.M. Kolb, and J.Z. Rubin, 1991. *Curriculum for negotiation and conflict management.* Cambridge, Mass.: PON Books (The Program on Negotiation at Harvard Law School).

Saunders, D.M. and R.J. Lewicki, 1995. Teaching negotiation with computer simulations: Pedagogical and practical considerations. *Negotiation Journal* 11(2):157-167.

Parker-Gibson: Teaching Plan for a Two-Party, Single Issue Exercise

Michael Wheeler

Michael Wheeler is a Professor of Management at the Harvard Business School, where he heads the required first-year negotiation course in the MBA program. He also teaches a second-year elective, Negotiating Complex Deals and Disputes, as well as various executive programs. His current research focuses on negotiation systems, that is, regimes to encourage, evaluate, and improve deal-making and dispute resolution on a recurring basis. He also continues to explore new techniques for teaching negotiation, including video and computer supported materials.

Parker-Gibson is widely used in the teaching of negotiation. It is available through the PON Clearinghouse.

As distributed to instructors, this simulation for teaching negotiation consists of a teaching note and confidential information for each of the parties. A set of overhead illustrations is also available. Use of such simulations, in varying complexity in terms of number of issues and players, typify the PON approach to teaching negotiation skills.

Teaching Note

Parker-Gibson is a two-party, single-issue negotiation for the purchase of a vacant lot. It is a refinement of an earlier simulation, Appleton-Baker.

Overview

The Parkers and Gibsons are neighbors. A vacant parcel of land, now owned by the Parkers, sits between their two house lots. The vacant parcel is smaller than the minimum required by zoning, but potentially has value to abutters for "accessory uses" or simply as a buffer. The Parkers bought the land some years ago for $12,000 thinking that they might build a tennis court on it, but never went ahead with this project. Very recently they sold their house, but the purchasers are not very interested in buying the extra land. As a result, the Parkers have approached the Gibsons to see if they would like to acquire the parcel.

As it happens, there is a large bargaining range in this case. The Parkers are moving out of state and will reluctantly sell the land for $15,000 to the purchaser of their home if the Gibsons aren't interested. Unbeknownst to the sellers, the Gibsons are very interested, having recently received an inheritance which they plan to use to expand their house.

The case was written to illustrate the dynamics of single-issue bargaining. To the extent possible, other issues have been suppressed. For example, the parties have a polite but distant relationship; with the Parkers departure, there is

Reflections

The Parker-Gibson note is a bit of an odd duck in this flock of articles on negotiation pedagogy. It is included particularly for readers who are interested in teaching in this field, but who have never used simulations. This exercise is simple in many respects—it involves the minimum number of parties (two) and just one apparent issue (price) —yet it supports rich exploration of eco-nomic, psychological, and ethical issues in negotiation.

Any author of such notes faces a di-lemma. If one writes about every nuance of interpretation or each twist and turn class discussion can take, he or she may intimidate prospective teachers, no matter how useful the information might be. The analysis in this note is thus quite spare. It was meant to give readers a point of departure, which they

no realistic prospect of future dealings. Likewise, the relatively small amount of money involved argues against elaborate deal structuring.

Mechanics

Two Parties: One person in each role

Materials: Confidential instructions for each party
                 (there is no separate general information).

Timing: Reading and strategizing: 10 minutes
                 Negotiation: 10-20 minutes
                 Debriefing: 45-75 minutes
                 Optional renegotiation: 15 minutes

Special Instructions

If you have an overhead projector, you can use attachment one to underscore the setting. The vacant lot is under discussion, not the Parkers' house lot.

Be sure also to emphasize that the parties should *not* exchange sheets during the negotiation. People can reveal as much or as little of their confidential information as they see fit, but must establish their credibility with their words or other actions. You may, as well, ask people not to swap sheets even after they have come to agreement, so you can reveal the key information during the debriefing.

Emphasize, also, that the negotiation is taking place under a tight deadline. (Ten minutes really will suffice.) By the same token, people should be encouraged to make good use of the time they have; tell them that they will get more out of the exercise if they do not rush to agreement in the first minutes.

Some instructors might be interested in adding an-other step in the game, namely by asking participants privately to record their goals *before* they negotiate. This will make it possible to explore the possible connection between aspirations and suc-cess. It will also demonstrate how for some people standards of success are relative not absolute. A seller may be very happy with a $20,000 deal, for example, until he or she learns that the buyer had much more to spend. To pursue this topic, hand out attach-ment two with the confidential information and give people an extra minute to complete the form.

could then embellish, depending on their own interests and the focus of their course.

Still it is interesting (and somewhat chastening) for me to return to the note after some years and see how my own approach to teaching such cases has changed. My ideas about negotiation have evolved, likewise my notions about teaching it. Most of those changes have come incrementally, having taught exercises like this one many times and having learned much from what my students have made of them.

If I were starting from scratch today, I would describe a rather different teaching plan, one that would make more of what appears as only a passing remark toward the end of the original note. Specifically, after tabulating the different deals that students reach and showing them the distribution, I would begin the actual

Debriefing

Before you record the results, ask people if everyone was able to come to agreement. Perhaps one in 20 pairs will have been stalemated; if there is a stalemate, make sure at the end of the debriefing to find out why the parties got stuck. Next ask people to raise their hands if they are satisfied with the agreements that they reached; almost everyone will do so.

Now it's time to record the results on an overhead or poster. You can have each pair submit a simple agreement (you only need the names of the parties and the agreed price) or you can simply put up a vertical scale (see attachment three) and ask people to report from the floor. If you use this latter method, make sure that you ask only the sellers to report so that you don't count the same agreement twice. To maintain suspense, you might ask first how many people settled in the $25,000 range (that is $25,000-$25,999), and then move up a bracket (20 threes) and down (20 ones), until you have included all the outcomes. The midway point between the two reservation levels is $28,000, but for reasons that are discussed below, the typical median is several thousand dollars less. If you are working with a small group, you might want to compare the results your group produces with attachment four which shows a distribution for 100 pairs.

As you record the results, you often will get gasps or laughter, particularly as you get toward either extreme. When the full distribution is displayed, the instructor might ask whether participants are still satisfied with their agreements. Some people will answer yes—because they sold high or bought low, or they are not relativists—but some others might admit to remorse.

You may choose at this point to explore the so-called "winner's curse." People should consider not only their own standards for satisfaction, but also how the person with whom they are dealing measures success. Negotiations are often stymied when people have unrealistic assumptions about what others can afford.

Early in the discussion, you might also step back from the problem and ask whether the wide range of results is realistic. One of the fundamental points of the exercise is that even when people have identical instructions, the differences in how they negotiate may produce very different outcomes. Whether

debriefing by asking them for theories that might explain the big range of outcomes. I want them to construct a conceptual framework. I want the students to draw on strategic and tactical insights, and then to organize them on their own. My hope is that this will help them learn at a deeper level, so that they can generalize from specific experiences, be they simulations or actual negotiations.

Also, I would push the ethical issues more. Students have always brought up questions of lying or concealing the truth, and sometimes also raise the matter of distributional fairness. Early in a course, it is important to acknowledge such issues and to provide a framework for analyzing them. Reference to the burgeoning research on the so-called "Ultimatum Game" can be very useful here.

the bargaining range is big or small (or exists at all) will depend on the situation. In a purely competitive market, there will be no range, though for many commodities—cars come to mind—there is some play in the numbers. The more unusual the subject matter and the smaller the number of available substitutes, the less certain the parties can be about the nature of the bargaining range.

One of the lessons in this particular exercise is that negotiators should be careful not to impose their assumptions and perceptions on the other side. The Parkers are desperate sellers and the Gibsons cannot walk away from this unique parcel of land as easily as they might leave a car dealer's showroom. If either focuses exclusively on their own needs, they will miss an opportunity to do much better than their respective BATNAs.

The variation in results invites rich discussion. If you don't mind going out on a limb, you have an 80 percent chance of being right by predicting that in the pair that reached the lowest price, the seller put the first serious number on the table (and conversely). Cover yourself, of course, by noting that your prediction is an educated guess. On occasion you will run into an extreme result that instead is explained by an even more extreme initial demand. In any event, the high and low outcomes should be juxtaposed.

If the prediction proves right, it demonstrates the risk of making the first offer, namely that one gives away part of the bargaining range. If, for example, the Gibsons start the conversation with a bid of $23,000, it is highly unlikely the property will be sold for less than that. What had been a range between ten and 25 instantly becomes truncated.

It is essential that you emphasize another aspect of such a bid: It fundamentally shifts the bargaining power of the parties. Going into the negotiation, each party is in a position of equal ignorance, knowing his or her own BATNA but in the dark as to the other's. (Indeed, neither can be sure that there is any range at all.) The moment the seller offers $23,000, however, the seller *knows* that a deal will be made. The only question is at what amount. He or she must determine if the $23,000 is a take-it-or-leave-it number or something the buyer is prepared to improve. The seller must also

Finally, I would make more of BATNA analysis. People do not seem to be very good at this, either in the classroom or in practice, so careful attention is important here. The exercise itself is short, so there is not much data to weigh, but it still is possible to show that one's BATNA and one's walk-away price are not necessarily the same thing.

Specifically, the seller here apparently has an offer of $10,000 on the property from someone else. Does that mean that the buyer must do better than that or, for that matter, that one dollar better will do? The answer depends on whether the seller factors any personal considerations into his or her equation. Do the Parkers like the Gibsons, or has their relationship been frosty? Considerations of risk come into play, as well. Does the seller believe that they

determine how much he or she can fairly extract (or whether fairness even comes into the question).

Many sellers in that situation will report that they rapidly recalculated their standards of success. Initially, a $23,000 deal might have seemed like a straight A outcome, but now their aspirations are higher. This is a very good time to explore the dynamic nature of success, specifically the connection between substance and process. You can make good reference to Neale and Bazerman's findings that negotiators often devalue concessions of the other side, once they are made. (See *Negotiator Cognition and Rationality*.)

Explore the interpersonal and communication dimensions of these exchanges, as well. Often the sellers will report being startled by the buyer's generous offer. Sometimes they have a too-good-too-be true reaction, which is surely not in the buyer's interest. Many of the buyers will be unaware that their number has triggered such thoughts and claim that their sellers had "poker faces." Perhaps this is so, but without videotape, you can't be sure: Some buyers may have been so absorbed in their own calculation, they did not look for a response.

Ask people to consider how this negotiation would have been different if it had been conducted by phone or fax. People usually will volunteer that they would have missed the nonverbal cues, but if you push hard, you'll probably discover that some people made much more of them did others.

Push hard on how people interpreted language, as well. If the buyer who initially offered $23,000 was eventually "talked up" to a higher figure, find out just how that happened. Did the seller say that number was "totally unacceptable?" If so, you have rich fodder for discussing the ethics of negotiation. (Ethics aside, it is also a risky strategy, as the buyer may be making a good faith offer.) If, as much more likely, he or she said something less explicit (such as "I really am looking for more"), ask the would-be buyer how he or she interpreted that. The experienced negotiator may well hear such a statement as not being a firm no.

It is important to stress that this is not a lesson in why you should never make the first offer. If people take that from the exercise, they can be sure of two things: first, they will

might get the other buyer to increase the current $10,000 offer? Other exercises offer richer options to weigh, but the basic principles can be introduced here.

Implicit in this note is the belief that simulations are powerful learning vehicles. A teacher could save time simply be presenting other people's data, a range of deals from low to high, and ask a class to analyze them. They might well uncover many of the same dynamics that they would if they had actually negotiated the case. But it is doubtful that they would internalize the lessons as successfully.

The best simulations offer "ah-ha!" experiences that allow people to understand why what they did may have worked or may have failed. Such exercises help establish the legitimacy and

never get burned; second, they will never make a deal. At some point, silence must be broken and someone has get serious about a reasonable price. People should be cautioned about throwing out a number before getting an impression of the other person's situation, but as noted below there can be advantage in talking from your own number. Psychological anchors come into play here.

In any case, people who put the first number on the table should be asked how they arrived at their numbers and what assumptions they were making. The Parkers don't know about the Gibsons' recent inheritance; the Gibsons are unaware of he Parkers' imminent move. Negotiators who glean that information before discussing dollars are in a much stronger position.

In the course of debriefing particular cases, the instructor should be explicitly establishing a vocabulary of negotiation analysis. Key concepts include bargaining range, BATNA, offer patterns, winner's curse, and the like. You might note that although the problem is necessarily fictitious and simplified, it does allow us to see what is seldom apparent in real life: namely the range of outcomes that might have been. In practice, we must negotiate with incomplete information and uncertainty. It behooves us to have a clear sense of our nonagreement alternatives, but we should be modest about what we really know about the other side. In debriefing the problem, we can see both ends of the bargaining range clearly, while in practice all but our end of it may be obscure.

It's also worth noting that persuasion is an important part of negotiation, so the bargaining range may move in the course of conversation. In ordinary sales situations, the seller will try to convince the buyer of the value of what he or she is offering; if this pitch is successful, the range is extended.

You can explain the coyness with which many people negotiate single issue cases in terms of each side's reluctance to make offers that are too generous or to reveal information that betrays the party's true need to make a deal. This reluctance can carry a big cost. At best, it wastes valuable time. At worst, parties who convincingly feign disinterest, each waiting for the other side to pounce, may miss profitable agreements.

If you have time, you might invite the buyer who paid the least and the seller who received the most to come forward and participate in a championship playoff. Having ex- relevance of negotiation plained all the dangers of the "dance of offers and counter- theory. At their core, offers," tell them that you have spared them that problem. they teach people to Each knows exactly what the other's situation is: Parker can see learn. $40,000 in cash bulging out of Gibson's pocket; Gibson knows that if there is no deal, Parker will turn around and sell the vacant lot for $15,000. You will stand by as a "truth officer" just in case either one starts bluffing or lying.

Give the two parties a couple of minutes to see if they can reach a deal, and have them talk loudly enough so that everyone can hear. Prod them to get past the pleasantries and into the heart of the negotiation quickly. You may have to count down the final seconds. About a third of the time, the parties will split the difference. In another third, one player will stand firm on a favorable number and the other will capitulate. In the other cases, the parties will be unable to come to agreement in spite of the fact that they both can see the large bargaining range.

Even when the parties agree, you usually will be able to illustrate the tug-and-pull of single issue cases. As the problem is written, it is hard to find joint gains. A dollar more for one party necessarily means a dollar less for the other. It is often clear that ego may be more important than dollars. The same people who did well in the first round may be disinclined to bend when up against one another. Splitting the difference is a convenient face-saving device, but there is nothing inherently "fair" about this approach. If Ross Perot is the seller and Mother Theresa is the buyer, the parties will have very differently utilities for the same dollar bill.

The result in this demonstration may give you a chance to comment on the distribution of results for the group as a whole. Typically the curve will be asymmetrical, with the median closer to the seller's end. Ask the group to propose explanations. One might be that sellers feel some sort of obligation to put a price on the thing that they are offering, and then will be more likely to give away part of the bargaining range. Some may suggest that the sellers feel more pressure to make a deal, given their undesirable alternative, and if people believe this is true, then it is. However, the buyer shouldn't be cavalier about missing the chance to buy a piece of property that is unique to them.

339

This last comment suggests a somewhat different way of starting the debriefing. Instead of predicting that the extreme cases are explained by first offers, you might instead ask people to suggest their own theories about the distribution. Possibilities might include the truncated bargaining range, psychological anchors, gleaned information, different aspirations, the interaction of particular pairings, differing notions of fairness, etc. You can then proceed to analyze the various transactions to see which of these factors were in place and how they worked against one another.

However you proceed, you should sum up by using attachments five and six. As noted earlier, the case was designed to be single-issue. Relatively few real life problems have this quality, but it is important to acknowledge their existence. There is a much larger set of multi-issue problems in which one issue dominates; often that issue is cash.

The problem nicely sets up a comparison with more complex cases. The Tendley case (also available from the PON Clearinghouse) presents a nice contrast, as its notes indicate. The same hard bargaining approach that sometimes prevails in single issue cases will be disastrous in others. There is, moreover, no bright line between those two kinds of cases. Indeed, an effective negotiator often succeeds by transforming zero-sum, win-lose transactions into ones in which there is possible joint gain.

If you do set up such a comparison, you should later revisit Parker and see if there is any realistic way of finding joint gains. Future dealings are assumed away, as noted earlier, and this really doesn't seem to be a case for seller-financing. There might well be advantage, however, in further subdividing the half-lot. The Gibsons' interest lies particularly in that portion of the land that will allow them to expand their house. Not every square foot of that parcel is of equal value to them. Faced with the choice of getting the entire property for $20,000 (let us say) or half of it for $15,000, they plausibly might prefer the latter; this would get them all the land they actually need and leave them with $5,000 more to spend on their expansion. The buyers of the Parker house, in turn, might be willing to pay more than half of their earlier offer of $15,000 for the remaining portion. If so, the Parkers will clear more than they could get from the Gibsons themselves. There are other approaches, as well; perhaps a variance or rezoning would create more value.

Attachments

Attachment One: Parcel Plan

M a p

T h e   M o o r e   E s t a t e

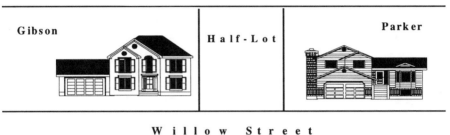

Gibson

Half-Lot

Parker

W i l l o w   S t r e e t

Attachment Two: Satisfaction questionnaire

Instructions
Please fill out Part 1 after you have read your confidential instructions and formulated your strategy but before you sit down to negotiate. Complete Part 2 after you have finished your negotiation but before you have had any follow-up discussion with your counterpart or in class.

Part 1 (prenegotiation)
A. Your Name
B. Your Role (circle one): PARKER/seller or GIBSON/buyer
C. Please fill the settlement amount which for you would result in the following levels of satisfaction (note: marginally satisfactory must equal the bottom line you've been given in your confidential information).

MARGINALLY SATISFACTORY	$
SATISFACTORY	$
VERY SATISFACTORY	$
OPTIMAL	$

D. Is there any amount which though seemingly even "better" for you than the OPTIMAL figure you just listed, you would reject as being unfair to the other side?

Circle One: YES   NO

E. Now that you have completed the inventory, you may begin to negotiate. Don't show this sheet to your counterpart.

Part 2 (postnegotiation/prediscussion)
A. Did you reach an agreement (circle one):   YES   NO
B. If YES, for what amount: $
C. How would you now describe the outcome (circle one):

MARGINALLY SATISFACTORY   VERY SATISFACTORY   SATISFACTORY   OPTIMAL

D. Did your standards for satisfaction (circle one): GO UP   GO DOWN   STAY THE SAME

Attachment Three: Results scale: Distribution of 100 pairs

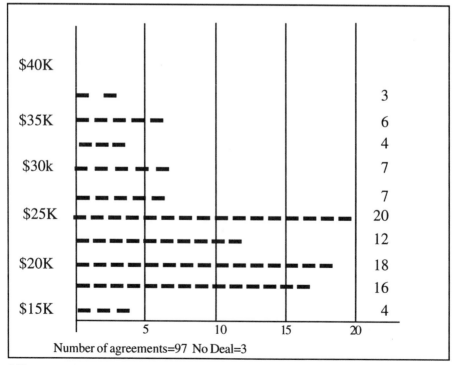

$40K	
	3
$35K	6
	4
$30k	7
	7
$25K	20
	12
$20K	18
	16
$15K	4

Number of agreements=97 No Deal=3

Attachment Four: Parker-Gibson Lessons

I. Preparation

    1. Assess your BATNA

    2. Analyze your BATNA

    3. Estimate their BATNA with utmost objectivity

    4. See what you have to learn

    5. Anticipate perceptiosn.

    6. Plan your process

    7. Be ready to adapt

II.Process

    1. Negotiate how you both will negotiate

    2. Communicate clearly

    3. Be prepared for surprises, pleasant and otherwise

    4. Avoid "anchoring' traps

    5. Be prepared to walk away

    6. Don't suffer the "winner's curse"

Attachment Five: Single-issue Bargaining

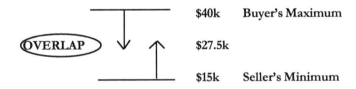

	$40k	Buyer's Maximum
OVERLAP	$27.5k	
	$15k	Seller's Minimum

1. Zero-Sum (or Win-Lose)
2. Positional (Bluffs)
3. Psychological Anchors
4. Split the Difference?
5. Risk of Lock-ins

Confidential Information for Parker

The Parkers own a house at 43 Willow Street. In 1985, they paid $20,000 for a 10,000-square-foot parcel that sits between their home and the home of the Gibsons, who live at 39 Willow Street. That specific parcel is less than 50 percent of the one-half-acre minimum building lot size required by the local zoning. The Parkers purchased the parcel thinking that they might someday use it for a tennis court, but they never got around to building one. They have used some of the land for a vegetable garden from time to time.

    Now the Parkers have decided to move out of state, having elected to take a generous early retirement package. They were lucky enough to find a private buyer for their house at 43 Willow. Because they got a good price and did not have to pay a broker fee, they are netting more than they expected. The only drawback is that the buyer is not very interested in purchasing the extra half-lot, seeing no real use for it. At the most, the buyer will be willing to pay an additional $15,000 (over and above the negotiating price for the house) for the parcel. This is less, of course, than the price the Parker themselves paid over a decade ago, but lacking other bidders, they would accept this $15,000 offer. It would make no sense to hang on to this land once they live thousands of miles away.

Before swallowing this loss, however, the Parkers have tried to see if they could do better by approaching other neighbors who abut the lot and who might have some use for it. Neither the people to the north or to the south have any interest, so their last hope are the Gibsons who live immediately to the west. As it happens, when the Parkers first acquired the half-lot, they had asked the Gibsons if they wanted to buy it jointly, but the Gibsons declined.

There are no bad feelings between the two families, but they have had little social or professional contact over the years. Bob is a teacher/coach at the local high school, and his wife, Jackie, is a part-time bookkeeper. They may not be any more interested in the land than they were in 1984, but the Parkers feel there is no harm in asking. Perhaps they might be persuaded of the value in adding yard space or getting a bit of a buffer between them and their new neighbors.

1. In this negotiation, you are to assume the role of one of the Parkers— or, if you are more comfortable, that of a representative fully authorized to act on their behalf.

2. Your goal is to sell the half-lot for as much as possible. Any deal you make with the Gibsons must be more than the $15,000 offer that the recent buyer of your home has already made. You should regard the $15,000 as an absolute minimum. Try hard to do much better. Remember that the Parkers paid more for it, and have had upkeep and taxes through the years.

3. It is true that real estate values fell generally in the latter part of the 1980s, but have rebounded somewhat in recent years. That fact provides little help here, however, as this is a unique piece of property. There really is no "fair market value."

4. You are only interested in a straight cash deal. Do not complicate matters by arranging seller financing, special easements, or introducing other issues or options.

5. A parcel plan, not to scale, is provided. (See attachment one.)

Confidential Information for Gibson

The Gibsons own a house at 39 Willow Street. They have been approached by their neighbors to the east— the Parkers—who have asked the Gibsons if they would be interested in buying the half-lot that sits between their two homes.

The parcel consists of 10,000 square feet, a bit less than 50 percent of the half-acre minimum building lot set by local zoning. The Parkers purchased this parcel in 1985 for something around $20,000. In fact, at that time the Parkers had asked the Gibsons if they would be interested in buying the land together and perhaps building a tennis court, but the Gibsons declined. The Parkers never got around to using the land for much. There are no hard feelings between the two families, but they have had little social or professional contact over the years.

Now things may change. Although the Gibsons are frugal people—Bob is a teacher/coach at the local high school and Jackie is a part-time bookkeeper—they recently came into a modest inheritance from a favorite aunt. They plan to use some of the money to expand their small house. They have already talked to an architect and contractor about alternative plans. Ideally, they would like to build a new kitchen/solarium to the east, but their house sits as close to the existing property line as the zoning allows. Acquiring the half-lot would completely solve this problem. Without the parcel, the Gibsons will have to expand in another direction. Doing so would be more costly and would not produce as attractive a house.

As a result, the Parkers' inquiry came as a pleasant surprise. (They live in a small town; perhaps the Parkers got wind of their building plans.) In any event, it's good news that the land may be available. The Gibsons don't want to be exploited on price, of course. In looking at their bank account and their construction alternatives, the Gibsons have set a firm maximum of $40,000 for the half-lot. If the Parkers insist on more, they will pass on the deal. They would naturally prefer to pay much less than the $40,000, if possible, as they have plenty of other good uses for the money.

A cousin who is a real estate broker advised them that there is really no "fair market value" for this parcel. It is unique and has value only to immediate abutters, therefore there are no comparable sales. It is true that real estate prices fell generally during the late 1980s, but have rebounded somewhat in recent years.

1. In this negotiation, you are to assume the role of one of the Gibsons— or, if you are more comfortable, that of a representative fully authorized to act on their behalf.

2. Your goal is to buy the half-lot for as little as possible. The $40,000 maximum they have stipulated is an absolute upper limit. Every dollar you can shave from this cap represents an improved result.

3. You are only interested in a straight cash deal. Do not complicate matters by arranging seller financing, reserving special easements, or introducing other issues or options.

4. A parcel plan, not to scale, is provided. (See attachment one.)

Thoughts on Facilitating
Discussion About Negotiation

Douglas Stone

Douglas Stone is a partner with Triad Consulting Group in Cambridge, MA, and co-author, with Bruce Patton and Sheila Heen, of *Difficult Conversations: How to Discuss What Matters Most* (1999 Penguin). For many years he was Associate Director of the Harvard Negotiation Project, and taught Harvard Law School's popular Negotiation Workshop. He may be reached at dstone@post.harvard.edu

Below are some thoughts on useful ways to facilitate a discussion or review of an exercise in a negotiation or communication workshop. Imagine that a group of participants has just returned from an exercise. You are the facilitator, or one of two co-facilitators. You have two goals: helping participants to learn, reflect on, and process their experience of the exercise, and helping the group to function effectively. This article focuses on the first goal.

Every review of an exercise should include (1) an introduction, (2) a "body" or the discussion proper, and (3) closure.

Introduction

One of the most common errors is to jump right into a discussion, without properly introducing the purpose of the segment. An introduction need be nothing more than saying: "For the next 30 minutes, I'd like to discuss the exercise you've just engaged in. I'm going to record comments on the flipchart so we can refer back to it...." Or perhaps the introduction will be more specific: "I'd like you each to take about a minute to simply reflect on the exercise. Write down two things you learned about conflict. After that reflection we'll take some 'I statements' about your experience with the exercise: 'I learned,' 'I was surprised by,' 'I wonder,' and then open up for more general discussion...."

Discussion

Two key skills come into play in the discussion phase: asking initial questions and following up. Initial questions get the discussion started and frame the direction. Following up involves responding to a participant's answer with either an acknowledgement, another question, or a comment. During the discussion phase, it is critical to listen carefully to *every* comment; to acknowledge *every* comment in some way; and to remain present and engaged. Keep eye contact and don't be afraid to show surprise (demonstrating that you too are learning).

This article was originally prepared for the Harvard Negotiation Project.

347

Reflections

Almost ten years ago, my HNP colleague Bruce Patton asked if I would be interested in providing feedback to student Teaching Assistants in Harvard Law School's Negotiation Workshop. I'd be required to sit in on the small "working group" sessions, where most of the course takes place, and observe and coach each TA. Somewhat reluctantly, I agreed.

I didn't realize at the time what a valuable experience this would turn out to be – for me. I had been facilitating for years, both in the Workshop and in more meditative contexts, but I learned at least as much about what works and what doesn't from the time I spent that winter *observing others* facilitate.

The TAs brought terrific skill and dedication to their task. And yet

Asking Initial Questions

The facilitator's main job is to ask good questions. By asking questions, and then providing a moment or two for the participants to reflect back on the exercise, you help focus the participants' thinking along productive lines. Broadly speaking, there are two kinds of questions you can ask: open-ended questions and focused questions.

Examples of *open-ended questions* are "What did you learn from the exercise?" "What worked well in your negotiation?" and "What surprised you during the negotiation?" These are open-ended because they do not focus on a particular topic, can be used with any exercise, and can not be answered with a mere yes or no. Almost any honest response that discusses something the participant learned is a good answer to these kinds of questions. The following is an illustrative range of responses to the question "What did you learn from the exercise?":

"Well, I learned that it seemed easy when I was planning what to say to the other side, but it was much more difficult to actually say certain things when the other person was sitting there."

"I was surprised at how differently they saw the situation."

"I'm not sure I learned anything. I didn't think the exercise was very realistic."

"I think I already knew this, but I was surprised by how powerful it was to simply sit and listen to the other side without interrupting or judging them."

Examples of *focused questions* are "What role did trust play in your negotiation?" and "What barriers to good brainstorming did you experience as you engaged in the exercise?" These questions are focused because they direct the participants' attention to a specific skill or area of concern.

As a general rule, we have found that it is best to start the discussion with open-ended questions. Each participant will come back with different thoughts about the exercise and open-ended questions allow each person to say what is on his or her mind. If a participant, for example, has learned something about listening, the question "What did you learn?" will allow the student to participate in the discussion. If, instead, you ask "Who thought of creative options?" the participant will be closed off from the discussion and might become frustrated. Open-ended questions allow each person to talk about what interested him or her most. A simple but extremely useful set of open-ended questions with which to structure a review are:

> What worked? (what did you or they do that moved the negotiation forward?)

> What would you do differently? (if you were doing it over again)

> What general negotiation guidelines emerge from this discussion?

Of course, depending on the specific exercise, where you are in the syllabus, and how much time you have for the review, you may make the pedagogical decision to begin with more focused questions.

Following Up

The second important facilitation tool is the follow up. As noted above, after every comment by a participant, some sort of acknowledgment is required. Sometimes, this will take the form of a follow-up question. Follow-up questions help the participant to clarify his or her own thinking, and help you and the class to find out more about what the participant is saying. Most follow-up questions are just variations on the questions "Why?" "Tell me more" and "What do other people in the class think?" Below are some examples of statements by participants and follow-up questions that might be useful:

even some of the more skilled were making "small" mistakes that were creating problems in the group. In an effort to capture what I'd learned, I wrote this short piece. It was intended as a simple, practical guide. So, for example, I include advice like "acknowledge every comment." Sounds easy, and yet a significant number of our TAs would on occasion fail to do so. The piece is now distributed to everyone who TAs for any of the negotiation courses offered at the law school, and I've been delighted at the impact it's had.

Participant: "The other side did a good job of listening to me."
Facilitator: "What was it that let you know they were listening?" or "Say more about what was good about it?"

Participant: "I thought I got a good agreement, but now that I hear everyone else's, I don't think mine was very good."
Facilitator: "How come?" or "What makes it more or less good?"

Participant: "I think I was talking too much during my negotiation."
Facilitator: [to the person the participant negotiated with]: "What's your reaction to hearing that?"

Participant: "How do you know where to start the negotiation? I never know what to say at the beginning."
Facilitator: [to the whole class] "Does anyone have any thoughts on that? How do you know where to start?"

Participant: "Our negotiation didn't go that well. We weren't really communicating."
Facilitator: "What would you do differently if you were going to try it again?"

More specifically, following up can include a range of responses. For example, Table 1 includes a range of responses to a participant who has just made the following statement: *"The most important thing during my preparation was realizing that what they really wanted was an apology."*

An effective facilitator can draw on all of these (and perhaps other) kinds of responses to participant comments.

Where Do Good Questions Come From?

Good questions can come from a number of sources, three of which are considered below:

Curiosity. Fundamentally, a good facilitator is a good *listener* who is naturally *curious*. If you are listening carefully and with genuine interest in what a participant is saying, questions of curiosity come easily to mind. If your goal is to understand and to help the participant "tell their story," then, like any good listener, you'll want to know more about what the participant is saying. If a participant says: "I learned how difficult it is to communicate effectively," questions that might occur to you are: "What makes it so difficult?" "What helped you to

---

Table 1. Possible responses to any statement (with an example)

Acknowledgment. "Umm hmm," or "that's interesting." A brief acknowledgment is often all that is needed. *Every* comment by a participant should be acknowledged.

Paraphrasing: "So knowing in advance that they wanted an apology was a key?" Not every comment needs to be paraphrased like this. It's useful to paraphrase in situations where you want to give particular acknowledgement to a participant (for example, to one who hasn't been participating much), or to provide the participant with a chance to clarify their statement where you feel you may not have it quite right.

Open-ended Inquiry: "That's interesting. Say a little more about that," or "Why do you think that knowledge was so powerful?"

Open-ended Inquiry to Others: "Does anyone else feel that way?" or [to their negotiation partner] "Did you think that affected the negotiation?"

Digging in: "Specifically, what did you do in preparing that helped you understand that they wanted an apology?" or "When you say `important' what do you mean? Important in what way?" These are questions intended to take a general statement and examine what's underneath. The goal is to help the participant go lower on the "ladder of inference" (see on following pages).

Challenging: "You say you realize what they really wanted was an apology. I wonder if that's true. I would have said they care most about money" It's important to be careful with tone of voice and phrasing when you challenge; it's easy for participants to feel attacked or to become defensive. Challenging should be used sparingly, and only when you have a clear purpose in mind.

Generalizing: "A bit more broadly, focusing on the other side's interests is an important element in preparing well." Essentially, you are helping the participant go from "what worked" to a more general guideline. Again, you would probably only want to do this after those comments from which useful generalizations can be derived (how's that for a tautological guideline).

Assertion: "I think the issue of apologizing is an interesting one in general. Apologies can be quite powerful and you can always apologize about something, even if it's just apologizing for how things turned out. I don't want to focus on it now, but it's an important issue and something you might want to keep thinking about...."

learn that?" "What do you mean by communicate—listen, talk, understand?" "Is there anything you can do to make it easier?" Each of these would be an effective follow-up question.

Learning Points. Good questions can also arise from the learning points you'd like to get across in a session. As noted earlier, you can't "tell" participants what they've gotten from an exercise; you can, however, stimulate their own processing of what they've learned in one direction or another depending on your questions. Keeping in mind the three or four major learning points you hope will emerge from a discussion helps you to generate purposeful questions. So, for example, if you have chosen an exercise in part because participants often learn about the role of trust in communication, you might focus in your follow-up question on that aspect of a participant's comment that relates to this topic. Consider the following exchange:

> *Participant:* I learned so many things. First, to be prepared. Second, just how difficult communication is with a stranger, and third, not to assume you know more than you really do.
>
> *Facilitator:* I want to look at a piece of what you've said a little more closely. You mentioned that you found it difficult to communicate effectively with someone you don't know. Say more about that.
>
> *Participant:* If you don't know someone, it's so easy to have a misunderstanding. And you can't be sure they're giving you the whole story."
>
> *Facilitator:* The whole story? So you aren't sure you can trust them?
>
> *Participant:* You have no way of knowing.
>
> *Facilitator:* And what effect does that have on how you communicate with them?

These questions were motivated by the facilitator's desire to explore certain areas rather than others. In so doing, the facilitator needs to be careful not to 'force,' or to attempt to take the conversation in a direction the participant does not want to go. The learning points inform the direction the questions take, but do not inform the participant's response. In the exchange above, the facilitator is careful to listen to the participant's response and to ask questions which make sense based on what the participant has said.

How We Learn. A third source of good questions comes from how people learn: We learn most from experience. Based on past experiences, we all have certain values, beliefs and assumptions about how the world works, what is right and wrong and what works well and what is less effective. In order to alter a belief or value, we must experience something unexpected or surprising, or process an experience in a new way or with a new question in mind. We reason from our new experience (or new perspective on an old experience) and reach a new conclusion about how something works or what is or isn't effective. This thinking process is captured in a diagram that Chris Argyris calls the *ladder of inference.* (See Chris Argyris, Robert Putnam and Diana Smith, *Action Science*, Jossey-Bass, 1985.) We reason upward from our experiences toward general conclusion, like this:

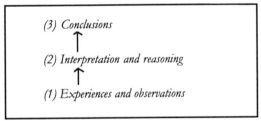

Usually this process is done unconsciously. We experience something, interpret it, and draw a conclusion about it without even noticing that we have done so. Because we all have different experiences, notice different things about these experiences, and bring our own values and beliefs to the interpretation of these experiences, different people develop different conclusions about what is true about the world.

Effective communication—particularly communication aimed at creating new learning—is based on slowing this process down. Rather than talking only about our conclusions, it is important to discuss the experiences and reasoning upon which our conclusions are based. Helping participants slow down the process of reaching conclusions provides an enormously rich source of questions from which a facilitator can draw. Behind the questions lies the facilitator's interest in helping the participant clearly understand the specific experiences upon which their conclusions are based, and the reasoning processes they used to reach such conclusions.

To achieve this, a facilitator should:

Locate a participant's comment on the ladder of inference: Is their response to my question at the level of conclusion or at the level of experience? Or have they shared their reasoning process? Once you have located their response on the ladder,

Ask questions that move them down the ladder, and then back up. In other words, if their answer is at the level of conclusion, ask them for more detail about what their actual experience was. Once you understand the data from which they are working, you can inquire into their reasoning, and then help them to check whether their reasoning makes sense and whether their conclusions are sound. In the following exchange, a facilitator helps a participant move down the ladder and then back up:

Participant: She agreed with what I said. And then she changed her mind.
> *[This is at the level of conclusion. No experience or data is given to support the conclusion, nor do we know what the reasoning process was. The facilitator, therefore, wants first to help the participant investigate the data.]*

Facilitator: When you say she agreed with what you said, how did you know?

Participant: I could just tell.

Facilitator: How? What specifically did she do or say that helped you to know it?

Participant: She just looked like she agreed.

Facilitator: What does that look like?

Participant: When I was talking she was nodding her head and not saying anything.
> *[Now we are beginning to hear what the direct experience was. We are at the bottom of the ladder, and now we want to move back up. The facilitator now wants to inquire about the reasoning process.]*

Facilitator: Say more about how you got from your observation of her nodding and not saying anything to your conclusion that she agreed with you.

Participant: It's obvious.

Facilitator: That what.

Participant: That when you nod yes it means you agree.

Facilitator: Why do you say it's obvious?

Participant: Because that's how most people I know are.

Facilitator: So your reasoning is that because most people you know are this way, then this other person you don't know is also likely to be this way.

Participant: That was my reasoning.
> *[Now we have a sense for the reasoning process the participant is using. The facilitator can now continue to move up and test the conclusion.]*

Facilitator: Can you think of alternative conclusions to be drawn that are also consistent with the data you observed?

Participant: I suppose she might have just been nodding in understanding and not necessarily agreement.

Facilitator: That's interesting. So that conclusion is also consistent with the data. And that's also consistent with your partner's claim that she didn't actually agree with you.

Participant: I'd never thought of it that way....

In this example, by going down the ladder to the directly observable data and then back up through the interpretation and conclusion, you have helped the participant to clarify the point at which a misunderstanding may have taken place, and helped the participant to question their assumption about what certain behaviors "always" mean. Of course, you can use any template this same way (e.g. the Circle Chart, the Tension between Creating and Claiming) by locating a comment against the template and moving the participant in a constructive direction through the template.

Closure

As with the introduction, closure acts as a signpost. Allow adequate time for closure (don't just say, "well, our time's up"). Closure can involve as little as saying, "Okay, we've been considering the role of trust in negotiation. Keep thinking about this as the workshop continues...." or it can be a more elaborate statement of your view of the subject, a summary of what you observed happening during the discussion, or a transition from where we've been to where we're going: "What we've been talking about—this distinction between being trustworthy and being trusting—seems really important. My view is that there are no situations in which failing to be trustworthy helps you, but people can test that proposition out as the workshop progresses. I think this question of trust will continue to arise and I'd like for people to consider how it plays out in our next unit, which will involve a more complex negotiation...."

Finally...Just Be Yourself

When all is said and done, the main rule to follow in facilitating is to just be yourself. You aren't always expected to ask the perfect question at the perfect time, nor to know the answers to all the questions that people might ask. In fact, you don't even need to know the answer to *any* questions. If someone asks a question you don't feel comfortable answering, you can say you don't know the answer, or you can ask the question to the class ("Good question. Does anyone have some ideas about that?")

Being yourself also means accepting the fact that not everything will go according to your plan. For example, you might ask a question that nobody wants to answer. Or you might forget to tell people when to come back from the exercise. Or you might try to answer a question and realize half way through that what you're saying is totally confusing. Or you might forget what you're supposed to do next. But this kind of thing happens to everybody who facilitates, even people who have been doing it for years. You'll be much more relaxed and confident if you remember that it's okay for things to go differently from how you planned, and that it's okay to make mistakes.

Teaching Negotiation
with Computer Simulations:
Pedagogical and Practical Considerations

David M. Saunders and Roy J. Lewicki

David M. Saunders is
Dean of the Faculty of
Management at the
University of Calgary
His most recent publica-
tions are three textbooks
all written with Roy
Lewicki and John
Minton, *Negotiation;*
Essentials of Negotia-
tion; and *Negotiation:*
Readings, exercises and
cases (all published by
Irwin/McGraw Hill).
Dean Saunders is
interested in all aspects
of negotiation, espe-
cially (1)negotiation
strategy; (2) global
negotiation; and (3)
individual differences
and negotiation.

Roy J. Lewicki is Dean's
Distinguished Teaching
Professor at the School

This article first
appeared in
Negotiation Journal,
April 1995: Volume 11,
Number 2, pages 157-
167.

The development of new media—computers, videotape, compact disks and laser disks—has begun to change the face of education in negotiation and dispute resolution. Complex simulations and interactive scenarios are available on these media, and create significant new opportunities for instructors. Yet, without proper consideration of the reasons for using these media and adequate preparation of the technical aspects of their use, the classroom experience can be an embarrassing flop.

A primary question for the teacher of negotiation considering the use of a computer simulation is: What is the purpose of using the simulation? Computer simulations are often quite engaging, providing a compelling world within which the participants can interact. However, without a sound pedagogic foundation for the integration of the simulation with other aspects of a negotiation course, using it may become a monument to lost opportunity. Computer simulations, like any other pedagogical tool (such as roleplays, films, case discussions, and guest speakers) must be integrated into the broader pedagogical foundation of the course. If not, there is a tendency for participants to perceive the teaching tool as an end in itself, rather than as an additional way to achieve some of the overall objectives of the course.

In our opinion, there are potential uses of computer simulations of negotiation: (1) acquiring new knowledge; (2) reinforcing and practicing the acquisition of knowledge previously acquired; and (3) evaluating and testing the acquisition of that knowledge. Each use is conceptually distinct, and they are not mutually exclusive in practice. The discussion that follows focuses on the advantages and disadvantages of each potential use of computer simulation.

Acquisition of New Knowledge

Computer simulations, particularly those that use multimedia applications such as full motion video, are compelling

357

of Management at Ohio State University. He maintains research and teaching interests in the fields of negotiation and dispute resolution, managerial leadership, organizational justice and ethical decision making. His recent research includes trust development in organizatons and the framing of environmental disputes. He is the author of *Negotiation* (Third Edition, Irwin/ McGraw Hill, 1999) and "Trust and Distrust: New Relationships and Realities" (*Academy of Management Review*, 1998).

teaching tools that capture and hold participants' attention. They provide an excellent opportunity to inform participants in an environment where the video component creates a high level of attention.

Consider a concrete example of a typical negotiation lesson: more preparation leads to better negotiation outcomes. This lesson is usually taught by lecturers and textbooks promoting the merits of preparation, by telling participants about how to prepare properly for negotiation, and by using examples that demonstrate the benefits (or costs) of good (or bad) preparation.

In a roleplay situation, because the instructor does not monitor the process directly, poor preparation may go unnoticed, both by the negotiator and the opponent. However, the consequences of this lesson can be made very clearly with a computer simulation. Participants can be told that the simulation will reward preparation, and that there will be penalties for mistakes made during the negotiation that are a result of poor preparation. For instance, the inability to answer questions posed by the other party, when the information is clearly available in background information contained in the computer simulation, may lead to negative consequences in the simulation.

It is not clear exactly which lessons may be best acquired through a computer simulation. We suspect that many lessons can be acquired more efficiently through more traditional pedagogic methods, such as books and lectures. Perhaps the best use of computer simulations is to emphasize those lessons that occur as the negotiation process evolves. In other words, if learning occurs over a period of time, and requires repeated practice to understand the lesson fully—such as the effects of different patterns of concession making on the other party's concessions—computer simulations would seem to be an especially useful tool to help learning. On the other hand, lessons that are basically one-time, "ah-hah" type experiences—such as understanding the effect of an inflation clause on the net present value of a contract—may be more efficiently learned with other pedagogic tools.

Reinforcing and Practicing Lessons
Perhaps the most compelling reason for a teacher to use computer simulations is that they reinforce and help students prac-

tice lessons learned with other pedagogic tools. Computer simulations provide a rich, complex environment for integrating lessons obtained with other pedagogic techniques. They allow participants to make strategic negotiation decisions and to practice new behaviors in an environment where the costs of making a mistake are low. Computer simulations can be created to reinforce numerous negotiation lessons; the bounds of the system designer's imagination are the only limits on the lessons that can be learned through simulation modeling.

Computer simulations also add a measure of control not possible with other active pedagogic tools such as roleplay exercises. One of the weaknesses of roleplays is that they provide a learning experience that is yoked to the other party participating in the exercise. If the other person takes the exercise seriously and is skilled and creative, then the roleplay can provide an excellent learning experience. On the other hand, when the other party in the exercise is unwilling or unable to adopt their assigned role, then the participant's learning can be severely restricted.[1]

Computer simulations overcome this weakness by providing a programmed response to the participants' strategic choices during the computer simulation. That is, all participants who behave in the same manner will receive equal treatment in the computer simulation. Of course, it is also possible to program some random responses into the computer simulation, to provide participants with a realistic experience of generally rational behavior with some of the additional randomness that occurs in daily life. Computer simulations, however, are only as good as their system designer. At best, they provide a simulation of how one person might behave as your counterpart in a given negotiation. Who decides how the computer simulation "behaves" is a particularly critical issue. For instance, system designers who model distributive (win-lose) negotiations are going to reinforce very different negotiation lessons than designers who seek to simulate integrative (win-win) negotiations.

This design question begs the more general question: Should computer simulations of negotiations be based on descriptive or prescriptive models? This is a difficult question to answer, if for no other reason than there are few absolutes in negotiation. For instance, research shows that more extreme opening offers usually lead to better outcomes for oneself in distributive negotiations (Chertkoff and Conley 1967; Weingart et al. 1990). This outcome does not always occur; in some cases, if the opening offer is too extreme, a deadlock is more likely to result. Thus, should the "descriptive" system designer model a situation which research findings suggest will occur the majority of the time, and ignore the other occasions? If so, then how should the system designer deal with the multitude of negotiation topics that are "common sense" but do not appear to have a strong research tradition to support them? For example, those who teach negotiation argue that a good negotiator is well prepared; yet one cannot point to any real research which has supported the importance of preparation vs. no preparation for a negotiation. Should the simulation designer simply assume preparation is necessary, and reward it accordingly in the simulation construction? And how should the "descriptive" system designer deal with the randomness that is present in many actual negotiations? Should "unpredictable' and "random" events and outcomes be written into a simulation? Does this alter or undermine the pedagogical value of the scenario?

The "prescriptive" system designer may be in an equally uncomfortable position. One can construct a model of negotiation "oughts" that can be reinforced by using a computer simulation. There is a major difference, however, between advocating something in a theory and building it into a computer simulation. For example, in a lecture about the concept of sharing one's interests with the other side, one can make explicit the assumptions underlying the recommendation, discuss the rationale underlying the advice, and weigh the advantages and disadvantages of the advice given. The reasons why interests should be shared with the other party can be discussed, the risks (if any) of this sharing can be highlighted, and the limits of the advice (if any) can be presented.

Compare this to the situation of modeling prescriptive advice in a computer simulation. Among the numerous other factors occurring during the simulation, participants receive feedback on a variety of different behaviors. For example, they may get positive reinforcement for sharing their interests with the other party, and this may lead to a more positive outcome than would be the case if they had not shared this information. If participants understand that sharing their interests with the other party helped achieve their outcomes, then what exactly is the lesson learned? Should they always share their interests? When is the best time to share interests—early or later in the negotiation? Are there any circumstances when interests should not be shared? While each of these factors could be built into the computer simulation (and one could construct a very complex simulation of how to handle just this issue) we know of no prescriptive model currently sophisticated enough to provide an adequate theory base for this model. In addition, even if the theory could answer such concerns, it would require an enormously complicated simulation to model such a reality.

Regardless of whether a descriptive or prescriptive approach is adopted, some other pedagogical concerns remain. For instance, in the complex world of the computer simulation, how likely are participants to identify the message intended by the system designer? Cause-effect relationships are difficult to determine in a computer simulation. For example, was a participant successful because of sharing their interests or because of numerous other choices that they made during the simulation? In other words, the participant may fail to see cause-effect relationships that account for the outcomes of simulated negotiations because more than one causal explanation is possible. While this reflects the reality of the multiple causes that also influence negotiations in real life, we are not sure that computer simulations can be created that are sophisticated enough to model the complexity of real negotiations, nor to be able to identify and separate the major causal factors in a multi-causal environment.

Thus, while computer simulations can be very powerful tools for reinforcing negotiation lessons obtained elsewhere, we do not believe that they can model the complexity of real-life negotiations. Rather, their strength appears to be in modeling a "piece of reality" in a very vivid and realistic manner. The questions that a teacher should keep in mind, however,

360

are: Whose piece of reality is being modeled? And what perspective does the simulation implicitly or explicitly promote?

Underlying the choice of which lessons to reinforce with a computer simulation is another philosophical issue: whether or not the lesson should be shared with the participant before engaging in the simulation. For instance, should participants be informed before starting the simulation that disclosing their interests will be rewarded? Or should participants be left on their own to discover the effects of sharing their interests? We have already discussed the problem of participants understanding the cause-effect relationships in a complex computer simulation; we suspect this problem is even more difficult when participants are not told about intended lessons in advance. On the other hand, identifying the lesson to be learned before the simulation begins may create an artificial environment that poorly models the self-discovery process that occurs during real-life negotiations.

Evaluation of Participants

The third use we see for computer-simulated negotiations is the evaluation of participants. Two types of evaluation are possible: (1) identifying whether or not participants have acquired knowledge about various negotiation topics; and (2) assessing the extent to which participants use or integrate new skills into their negotiation repertoire.

Identifying the extent to which participants have acquired knowledge does not require a computer simulation. This can be done by evaluating responses to questions typically found on course exams (e.g., "What is the difference between an interest and position?"). Of course, a computer simulation could contain a teaching module that contains a test and assesses participant learning. For instance, after learning about the difference between interests and positions, participants could be provided with a series of multiple choice questions to ensure that they have acquired understanding of the concept.

Computer simulations may be even more useful in assessing the extent to which participants integrate new negotiation skills into their behavioral repertoire and use these skills during the simulation. They can provide participants with an opportunity to use newly acquired skills and provide a check to see if they are used appropriately. For example, participants may have learned the value of asking questions as a way to understand the difference between the other's positions and interests. The computer simulation can provide the participant opportunities to ask appropriate and inappropriate questions, in order to evaluate the extent to which students have mastered that skill.

Another tempting use of computer simulations is for the evaluation of participant performance on the overall outcomes of their simulated negotiation. Students could be assigned a grade based on their overall negotiation skills, or attributions about participant negotiation abilities may be drawn as a function of their relative performance on the computer simulation. We advise caution in using computer simulations in this way. Any given outcome of a computer simulation is influenced by many factors, but each of these factors is framed by what the system developer considered to be a realistic simulation of an actual negotiation.

At the very least, instructors considering using computer simulations as evaluative tools need to understand the model that the system developer used in the simulation's development. At best, the outcome of a computer simulation provides one piece of information about the skill of the participant. Whether that information is a valid and reliable predictor of negotiator success needs to be demonstrated with research. In short, we advise caution in interpreting the results of computer-simulated negotiations as signs of negotiator effectiveness, and strongly suggest that at best they are simply another piece of information that can be used in the overall assessment of the participant. In addition, instructors should, before beginning the exercise, be clear—to themselves and to their students—about the extent to which they will use the results of computer-simulated negotiations to determine grades for negotiator effectiveness.

Pragmatic Concerns

The pragmatic issues involved in using computer-based technology can be divided into two groups: issues concerning technology, logistics, and setup; and an individual's teaching style.

Technology, Logistics, Hardware and Setup

As most instructors know, the technology of teaching is changing rapidly. It began with the introduction of the overhead projector and has moved rapidly into videotape, whiteboards, in-flight projectors, distance education using satellite uplinks, synchronized audio-visual slide presentations (including multiple projectors), overhead projection of computer images, and now interactive compact and laser disks. There are times when today's instructor wishes for "the good old days"—a simple blackboard and a piece of chalk that always works!

As anyone who has begun to experiment with this new technology knows, the first few iterations are often rocky. Numerous mistakes can be made, both with the setup and initial use of these contemporary technologies. Many instructors are afraid of the technology, others refuse to learn how to use it, and still others will not proceed without a licensed, uniformed technician at each elbow. If your institution has a computer or audio-visual staff person who can give you technical advice and setup assistance, much of what we say here will be for your information only, because you have someone else who can advise you on the technical issues. On the other hand, since problems with equipment often occur (usually when the technician is not available), it is most useful for the instructor to be informed and truly understand what is required to make the equipment work. We offer the following general guidelines for the novice; if you are already a trained expert, you can skim this section quickly!

In general, two forms of setup are required when using computers to teach negotiation. The first is to position the equipment in a library or computer laboratory where students may use it one at a time or in small groups. In these cases, the instructor may assign the students to experiment with the equipment before or after a particular class, in order to become familiar with it and absorb the pedagogical lessons that are built in. Once this equipment is properly assembled and located, it does not need to be moved or constantly adjusted. More commonly, however, instructors need to assemble the same equipment and transport it to the classroom. Classrooms differ in the degree to which they have some or all of the necessary hardware built in ("hard-wired"), or require all necessary equipment to be put on a portable cart and wheeled in when the equipment is to be used.

Most computer-assisted instruction requires, at the minimum, the following hardware:

- a personal computer with keyboard;
- a display system, such as a computer monitor, large television set or projector that will put the image on a flat screen;
- a "sound board" which interprets and transmits the audio signals from the computer program;
- an amplifier/speaker system which can project the audio signal into the classroom (this can be accomplished through portable "computer speakers" available in any computer or audio store, the amplifier and speakers of the large television monitor, or the permanent audio system installed in a newer "high tech" classroom);
- a compact or laser disk player. If the software has two or more videodisks, it is most helpful to have two players, so that one does not have to swap disks in the middle of the program.

It is critical that all of these elements be assembled, linked together and completely pretested by the instructor well before the class meets. There are no set "industry standards" for how some of these products communicate with each other, and thus each configuration may require different interface equipment. For example, certain laser disk players require different computer sound boards (and vice versa), and can interface effectively with different monitors or amplifiers. Each configuration requires different cables to link the parts together, often requiring multiple trips to the local electronics store for connector cables and plugs.[2] Also, if your institution does not now have this equipment in place, be prepared for two initial issues: (1) who understands the equipment and knows what configuration is needed; and (2) who has the budget money to purchase necessary computer boards, laser disk players, speakers, or even wires and plugs. Search out your institution for a technician who knows what he/she is talking about (to advise on what to purchase and whether it the parts are compatible),[3] and for a pool of funds to purchase hardware that may not be currently available. Many institutions often have small instructional development grants or pools of money available that may be used for these purposes.

Computer technology is best configured in a classroom that permits large-screen projection—either large television sets, or projection on a flat screen—so that images are large, clear and easily readable. Many of the programs are designed for the "small screen"—a computer monitor that one or two people can use—and require constant reading of information and responding to response options. Unless those screen images can be easily ac-cessed by a larger group of people, the potential usefulness of the simulation drops off rapidly. One of the authors of this paper recently used a computer-mediated simulation with a seminar of ten students. Because a large classroom was not available for a class that small, the equipment was all placed on a movable cart and ten students had to crowd around a 13-inch video monitor on the cart, to see the video presentation and read the decision choice options. Needless to say, even though class members were reading the monitor to others, some members of the class—those farther away from the monitor—could not read the choices well, and rapidly lost interest in the simulation and its pedagogical objectives.

Murphy's Law—whatever can go wrong, will go wrong—seems to prevail in using technology in the classroom for many instructors, with the corollary that the more critical it is to use this technology with a particular audience, the more likely it is that it will not work.

If an instructor really intends to rely on the technology for a particular class, and does not have a technician available to fix problems quickly "on the spot," we recommend having an alternative exercise or class activity to do that day. We always test out any new equipment (for example, a change of monitors) in advance, or when the setup has been taken down or moved and needs to be reassembled. There are not too many more frustrating or embarrassing teaching moments than to hold a class of students hostage while you helplessly try to cope with a short-circuited cable, two plugs that fail to fit into each other, a computer that won't boot the program effectively, or a monitor that provides sound but no picture![4]

Pedagogical Style

The second major practical concern is how to involve groups of students in the simulation during the class. As stated earlier, since most of these systems are designed to be used by one user at a time, they have not specifically been designed for groups or large class use. Small computer screens compound this problem because it is easy for students to disengage, become disruptive and miss the entire point of the material. As a result, the instructor must be resourceful in figuring out how to sustain involvement as the class works through the program. The following suggestions offer some ideas on how to meet such challenges:

1. Introductory background and briefing information. The instructor should probably require students to review the background or briefing information before the class, so that everyone has had a good chance to understand the basic information in the scenario. This may be accomplished by providing a transcript of the briefing information so that students may read it in advance or follow along with it as it is presented in class. Alternatively, if the equipment can be set up in a library or resource center, students can review it in small groups on their own time before class.

2. Small groups. When the simulation is presented to a class group, it is often useful to have the students broken into small groups to discuss and debate optional courses of action. These small groups can be used to discuss overall strategy, and then how they would respond to each alternative course of action. Differences of opinion or rationales for different action strategies should be explicitly identified for group discussion—both during the simulation and for later debriefing. Individuals frequently disagree as to how cooperative or competitive their strategy should be, and it is useful to identify and discuss these issues as they emerge, and later on when the group debriefs the process in light of the actual outcome of the simulation.

Small groups can be configured in a number of ways. It is recommended that teams not exceed four or five members, in order to permit adequate time for each group member to express their views. Preexisting teams in a class may be used, or ad hoc groupings may be available. We have often found that dividing groups by gender or nationality is often a useful idea. For example, representatives of different nationalities have clearly different cultural styles (Salacuse 1988; Hofstede 1989). In addition, in our experience, the process women use when negotiating in simulations is more cooperative then men (see Kolb and Coolidge 1991; Lewicki et al. 1994 for expanded discussions of gender differences).

3. Focus on group process. Because of the differences that individuals have on their preferred strategy and tactics, the group discussions create internal conflict which must be resolved. As in most group decisions, groups deal differently with this conflict and the way the decisions are represented to the instructor or the rest of the class. These group dynamics can be captured later by having groups focus on their internal deliberation and decision-making processes. Groups can be asked to complete a team assessment questionnaire and discuss it as a team. This often highlights important issues of leadership, decision making, conflict management over the selection of key group roles (e.g., spokesperson), etc. Alternatively, the simulation may be run in a "fishbowl" format, such that the inside group debates the simulation's choice alternatives while the external group observes the group's process and then provides feedback. Comparisons and analogies may also be made to the importance of intrateam dynamics in group decision making and intergroup conflict and negotiation (see Lewicki et. al. 1994).

4. Capturing learning. Finally, there are several ways that the learning principles of the simulation can be captured:

•Instructors can lead a general discussion after the simulation is completed. Topics of this discussion could include: how effectively individuals or teams performed; the "design assumptions" behind the simulation—i.e. what models of negotiation did the designers advocate; action choices that were effective and not effective; alternative forms of the simulation that might make it more interesting or effective; differences between groups or teams in their choice patterns, and the factors which appeared to drive those different choices; group dynamics within the teams as they debated action alternatives, and personal learning that can be derived from examining their process effectiveness.

•Small groups can debrief their own intrateam dynamics, perhaps assisted by an assessment questionnaire that is completed individually and then shared with others in the team.

•Individuals or groups can complete written papers on the simulation, focusing both on the nature of their strategy with the simulation, its effectiveness, or the interpersonal dynamics that emerged as their team worked together to make decisions.

In Conclusion

Two sets of issues—one set focused on teaching objectives, the other set on practical concerns—must be addressed if the instructor hopes to use computer-based teaching materials effectively in the classroom. If these issues are not addressed, the simulation may either be used in ways that do not forward the instructional objectives of the seminar or course, or the technology will not be managed and used in a manner that is most conducive to effective learning.

Notes

1. In addition, students' previous role-playing experience with other students allows "reputations" to emerge—that is, based on previous roleplays, students develop expectations about the other which can be an advantage or a disadvantage in enacting the current exercise. Many computer simulations do not create these expectations, although we expect that future simulations may well take this factor into account. Introducing this element will permit effective modeling of the type of negotiations that occur in ongoing, long-term relationships.

2. It took one of the authors of this article over six months to make a portable system work! It started with general unfamiliarity about how to put a sound board into a computer and hook a laser disk to it. Naturally, the instructions seemed like they were written for someone with a Ph.D. in computer engineering. The problem was then compounded by the discovery that the sound board was defective, out of stock at the manufacturer, and that the second sound board shipped was defective as well. This type of orientation to the technology does not leave a novice with a positive and optimistic sense that the technology is worth the effort.

3. It also does not hurt to periodically lavish this person with expensive gifts and take them out to lunch!

4. We have our own horror stories to prove it. One of us made five (!) trips to a local electronics store to obtain the correct configuration of plugs and wires to get the system to work. Another held a class of executives hostage while the audiovisual personnel brought in three different monitors, trying to find one that worked.

References

Chertkoff, J.M. and M. Conley. 1967. Opening offer and frequency of concessions as bargaining strategies. *Journal of Personality and Social Psychology* 7:181-185.

Hofstede, G. 1989. Cultural predictors of national negotiation styles. In *Processes of international negotiations*, edited by F. Mautner-Markhof. Boulder, Colo.: Westview.

Kolb, D. and G.G. Coolidge. 1991. Her place at the table: A consideration of gender issues in negotiation. In *Negotiation theory and practice*, edited by J.W. Breslin and J.Z. Rubin. Cambridge, Mass.: PON Books (Program on Negotiation at Harvard Law School).

Lewicki, R.J., J. Litterer, J. Minton and D. Saunders. 1994. *Negotiation.* 2nd ed. Burr Ridge, Ill.: Richard D Irwin.

Salacuse, J. 1988. Making deals in strange places: A beginner's guide to international business negotiations. *Negotiation Journal* 4:5-13.

Weingart, L.R., L. L. Thompson, M. H. Bazerman and S. J. Carroll. 1990. Tactical behaviors and negotiation outcomes. *The International Journal of Conflict Management* 1:7-31.

Negotiating with Your Professor:
An In-Class Simulation

Joseph F. Byrnes

Joseph F. Byrnes is
Dean of the Graduate
School and Professor
of Management at
Bentley College, 175
Forest St., Waltham,
Mass. 02154.

As I prepared to teach my second course on negotiating, this time with undergraduates, I began searching for a relevant, exciting and instructive first exercise. None of the published exercises and role plays seemed appropriate, particularly for students about 20 years of age with little business experience. I was specifically concerned about the natural fear and shyness that many undergraduates seem to possess.

After much thought, I devised a simulation/role play that proved to be ideal for such a young and inexperienced group. I call it, "Negotiating With Your Professor" and it is included as Appendix I of this article. (Please read it before proceeding.)

On the first day of class, I explained to the students that "Negotiating With Your Professor" would be our first simulation and that it would occur in the next scheduled class, one week later. After giving them five minutes to read the simulation, I made the following points:

(1) I would select one student from the class to negotiate with me about the final grade in front of the entire class. Each student should prepare as if he/she would be the one chosen. I would announce my choice for this role play during the next class, 10 minutes before the simulation would begin. Thus, each student would have to prepare as if he/she would be selected. That meant strategies and tactics needed to be considered before the next class by every student in the class.

(2) To be fair to the student chosen, he/she could say "time out" at any time during the actual role play. This would suspend the negotiations, and I would leave the room so that the student could consider the next steps to take. The student could confer with his/her group (the class was divided into four groups during the first class) during the first class. I would re-enter the room and continue the negotiations when I was called back. There was a ten-minute maximum on each time-out.

This article first
appeared in
Negotiation Journal,
April 1990: Volume 6,
Number 2, pages
189-196

(3) I distributed three actual application papers and a final exam paper from my previous class. The names of the authors were removed from the copies. These four papers would be the basis of the negotiations. How students decided to use these papers would be up to them. They could prepare to discuss one, some, or all of these papers with me.

(4) The student selected would not be graded on his/her performance. However, I assumed that the student would want to do the best job possible, particularly since the instructor and the entire class would be observing. I also reiterated that each student should assume he/she would be chosen, and that everyone should be totally prepared.

(5) If students wanted to investigate me and my style, they could ask other students or even other professors. This was permitted, and might be a good way to prepare for the negotiations.

At the beginning of the second class, we had a general discussion about negotiating styles and ethical issues, such as the acceptability of deception in negotiations.

As students volunteered their opinions and actual experience, I assessed the class, trying to find the student for the upcoming simulation. I zeroed in on a female student who was both articulate and seemingly sure of herself. She stressed the importance of "holding a few cards close to your chest" during negotiations and the need to "diffuse conflict with humor." I had also discovered through some background checks that she was an excellent student with an overall grade point average of 3.7 (A-). She blanched when I chose her, but then smiled and said, "I knew you would pick me." The other students laughed, mostly out of relief that they were not chosen.

I then divided the class into three groups: the first group would be her advisers, the second would concentrate on me during the negotiations, and the third would concentrate on the student. The forms used to record observations are included as Appendix 2 and 3.

The Negotiations and Students' Evaluations

After cautioning the entire class about the need to be silent during the negotiations (no laughing, talking, groaning, and so on), we began. I had no idea how it would go or what it would take to change my mind about the grade issue. I sat in a chair with a desk in front of me; she sat in front of my desk in another chair.

We began with small talk. ("Are you finished with all your finals? Are you going home for the holidays? Do you know w hat classes you are taking next semester?" etc.) I initiated the small talk and it seemed to put her at ease. After about three minutes of such talk, she brought up her disappointment with her final grade.

From that point on, we had a serious, complicated negotiation with three time-outs called for by the student and, finally, an agreement. (She would take an incomplete for the course, do another final paper with a different interviewee, with no guarantee that her new final exam paper would even be at the "B" level.) It was an exhausting but exhilarating experience for everyone.

I then handed out an after-exercise questionnaire for the class to fill out. The three questions were: (1) What did you like most about this exercise? (2) What did you like least? and (3) What did you learn about negotiating from this exercise? A selected sample of responses follows:

Liked Most
•Knowledge about grading policies; getting to know the instructor better.
•The opportunity to observe an actual negotiation as an objective bystander.
•The exercise was very true-to-life and relevant to students; I also liked the fact that both parties won.
•Both sides were attentive and understanding of the other's views, and they even repeated the other's ideas to show this understanding.
•It seemed very real. I think this is a very good start to the class.
•In all honesty, I was glad I didn't have to do it; it gave me a chance to see what negotiating is about without too much stress on me.
•I liked the professor getting so involved—too often role plays only involve the students. I was glad to see the professor, a knowledgeable person, interact and perform.
•It's reality—it was two people negotiating over a subject that interests everyone in the class.
•What I liked most was that both parties handled themselves in a professional and gracious manner. And, of course, the positive outcome.

Liked Least
•This was a situation where one person was in a position of authority and power and one was not. Most negotiating situations exist on a peer level.
•The negotiation was lopsided to the extent that the outcome affects one participant more than the other.
•It was difficult watching someone else do all the negotiating. I wanted to jump right in.
•I think the exercise felt very real, but I don't know if you would be able to take a time-out in a real negotiation.
•I felt the professor was impatient toward the end: he was drawing pictures on his note pad.

Learned About Negotiating
•That a negotiation can appear to be deadlocked, then suddenly a deal is struck.
•It takes a lot of staying power and believing in your stance. Also, everything is not always black-and-white—I expected it was either change your grade or not. A very different solution evolved through discussion and I thought that was surprising and quite interesting.

•That a breakthrough can happen suddenly and that things can get settled fast.

•Look hard enough and a solution that satisfies the needs of both parties can be found.

•Persistence works. Emotion plays a big part in negotiation. Preparation is the key to successful negotiation.

•Negotiating is not a black-or-white matter. Nothing is really set in stone and cannot be debated.

•It's easier to think of more options when you are not emotionally involved. Also, you can be more aware of body language, voice intonation, facial cues when you are watching, not actually negotiating.

•There are many different tactics you can take in negotiations. Deciding which one to use and when to switch tactics and other techniques are things we can learn.

•I learned you must be patient in negotiating. I also learned that you might have to give up something to get something.

•I learned it is important to be open and honest in negotiating.

•One should always show the other side that you are attentive and are really trying to understand the other's point of view. But, at the same time, you should not lose sight of your own views.

•Don't give up on your principles; be willing to compromise, but try not to lose sight of what you really need.

•Always know the least you will take to make an agreement.

•I learned that each party should not just come right out and tell the other party their final position.

•Concessions and compromises are keys to the negotiation process. What I learned from this exercise was that one can negotiate almost everything, if one is savvy, persistent, flexible, and creative.

Observations of the Teacher

I was quite pleased with the impact of this simulation on my undergraduate negotiating class. It involved them totally, introduced some important negotiating concepts and principles, and "broke the ice" in a naturally shy student group. There were a number of critical observations about negotiating theory and practice that emerged during the class discussion of this simulation. First, the students learned that a seemingly clear-cut distributive negotiating situation can be converted into an integrative opportunity. Most of the students believed that either the professor or the student would win—I would change the grade or I would not. What was amazing to everyone is how the role players transformed this simple distributive setting into a complex integrative negotiation. As the student and I discussed options during the role play, many imaginative slants on resolving the disagreement were developed, such as:

•giving the student an incomplete and allowing her to revise the final paper;
•re-evaluating the application papers;
•changing the weights of the various evaluation components;
•having another professor review the papers; and
•completing another final paper with a different interviewee with no guarantee that the new final paper would even attain the "B" grade.

The students also discovered that my needs were critical elements in the negotiating process. I kept referring to my desire to be fair to all students in my class. How could I provide one student with another chance, knowing that many more students would have liked the same additional chance? The jeopardy factor (the student could actually receive a lower grade on the substitute final paper) allowed me to maintain my own sense of fairness and obligation to other students. The realization that I had strong needs was quite surprising and revealing to the class, and underscored the importance of putting yourself in your counterpart's shoes in all negotiations.

It was also clear from our class discussion of the simulation that students were amazed that a seemingly powerless person (the student) could negotiate with a very powerful person (the professor) and not automatically lose. This realization expanded the usefulness of negotiating as a social process and as a substitute for power or hierarchy. Business students tend to over-emphasize the legitimacy of hierarchical decision making and this simulation revealed another alternative in a rather dramatic way.

Another interesting aspect of the simulation and of most effective negotiations was the value of establishing a personal relationship with the other side. I initiated the small talk, and this set a tone for the negotiations. It was not going to be all business. While this distracted the student in the beginning, it also led to a friendly back-and-forth banter. When I returned from a time-out with a cup of coffee, the student teasingly asked, "Where is my coffee?" This banter helped establish a good relationship and developed the social grease necessary for effective negotiations. I mentioned in the class discussion that many other cultures rely on personal relationships more than ours does, and that students should keep this in mind if they become involved in international negotiations.

A few closing observations for instructors contemplating using this simulation are necessary. Clearly, the careful selection of the student is the critical element in having this simulation work. From my experience, there is always at least one articulate, self-assured, and intelligent student in any class. You need that type of student to develop the complexity and drama of the exercise.

Finally, it is important for instructors to be positive role models for their students. In too many classes, professors force students into role plays and keep themselves unsullied and uninvolved. In the post-simulation discussion, the students noted that I appeared nervous and impatient at the end (the class was coming to an end and I wanted to conclude the exercise). I admitted that I felt the time pressure and commended them on their accurate observations of my growing impatience and tension. This admission opened up the class and resulted in many revealing comments by the students about themselves and their perceived strengths and weaknesses.

Based on my experience, I recommend that instructors of negotiating classes consider using this simulation as a potent and informative first exercise Coupling a highly relevant and realistic simulation with direct instructor involvement is a powerful way to capture the attention and interest of students in a first-level negotiating class.

Appendix 1:
Negotiating with your Professor

You have just completed the course on Negotiating taught by Professor Byrnes and now you are preparing to negotiate with the instructor himself! You don't believe you received a fair grade for the course and the only way you can change the grade is to convince Professor Byrnes to change his mind. In your hand are the three applications papers and the final exam paper. The grades are as follows:

Application Paper #1	B	(10% of course grade)
Application Paper #2	B+	(10% of course grade)
Application Paper #3	A-	(10% of course grade)
Final Exam Paper	B	(30% of course grade)

There were two other evaluations you received—a grade of B in your simulation paper (20% of course grade) and a grade of B+ in your class preparation/involvement/contribution (20% of course grade). You feel you were graded fairly on the simulation paper and the class preparation/involvement/contribution dimension and do not wish to discuss these grades with the instructor.

However. the application papers and the final exam paper are entirely different stories. On the course syllabus, Professor Byrnes stated the following:

Application Papers: (Three individual papers, each worth 10% of your course grade)
An application paper is useful in connecting the assigned text and readings to the real world. You should take the assigned reading material for a specified week and apply the concepts, theories, models and/or endings to the particular negotiating situations you encounter or observe at work, school, or home. The key task is to demonstrate the relevance, or lack of relevance of the specified concept, theory, model and/or finding to your particular experiences.

In order to further your understanding, you should discuss each application with your group and include some of their reactions and comments in your paper. Since each group will have at least one member writing an application paper each week, groups should schedule weekly meetings to consider the applications and to help each other with these assignments.

Application papers will be collected from the third week of class (September 25) to the last week (December 11). Please turn in a schedule of application paper assignments within your group by September 25.

Application papers should be no more than three typed, double-spaced pages. I am looking for quality, not quantity. The best papers will be tight, well-written, logical, and interesting.

Final Exam Paper: (30% of your course grade)
Your final exam will be a report of an interview with a negotiator. You must develop a series of questions, based on the material covered in this course, and arrange an interview with someone you consider a negotiator.

Your final exam paper will contain the questions, the responses to the questions, and an analysis of the type of negotiator the interviewer seems to be, using the material covered in the course. Finally, you will compare/contrast the interviewee with yourself. How similar/dissimilar are you and the interviewee as negotiators?

This final exam paper should be no longer than ten typed, double-spaced pages. As always, quality is essential. If you have taped the interview and have produced a transcript, you should include the transcript as an appendix to your paper. The appendix does not count in the ten-page limit requirement. The paper should be clear, well-written, well-reasoned, and interesting. The due date is 12 noon on December 20.

It is Thursday, December 21 and the secretary has just posted the course grades on the bulletin board. You received a course grade of 3.0 (B). The secretary also gave you your final exam paper, which had a disappointing grade of B on the cover page.

You have made an appointment to talk with Professor Byrnes in the morning the next day. In response to your question. the secretary informed you that Professor Byrnes would not be turning in the official grade reports to the Registrar's Office until the afternoon of Friday, December 22. He still had a few more final exam papers to grade. However, he was leaving town to visit his parents that Friday evening and would not return for a week.

You are really interested in negotiating and had hoped to receive a 3.7 (A-) in the course. However, as the course progressed and you started receiving your grades, you became convinced that a 3.3 (B+) was all that you could attain. But a 3.0 (B)! You never expected to receive a grade this low. After all, you are an excellent student, with an overall grade point average of 3.2 and 3.4 in your major, which is Management. The Negotiating course is an elective within the Management major.

As you begin to prepare for this discussion with Professor Byrnes, you jot down a few thoughts:

1. Professor Byrnes was a friendly instructor, but seemed to enjoy a good argument in class. He would frequently assume the "devil's advocate" role to get the class moving and students thinking. He would push students pretty hard, but would never belittle or embarrass them.

2 . I never talked to Professor Byrnes about any of my grades before, even though I was unhappy about the grades on my first two application papers. I always thought I would pull it out with a high grade on my final exam paper.

3. Professor Byrnes mentioned a number of times that he would reward improving grades by giving students the benefit of the doubt if their final grade was between two grade categories. So, if you had a high C + but had shown improvement over the course of the semester. he would probably give you a B-.

4. The College Bulletin lists the following grade scale:

GRADING DESIGNATIONS

Grades are recorded on a scale which is interpreted below

Grade in Quality Points	Alphabetical Equivalent	Numerical Equivalent
4.0	A	95-100
3.7	A-	90-94
3.3	B+	87-89
3.0	B	83-86
2	B-	80-82
2.3	C +	77-79
2.0	C	73-76
1.7	C-	70-72
1.3	D+	67-69
1.0	D	63-66
0.7	D-	60-62
0.0	F	below 60

5. Professor Byrnes only gives the students alphabetical equivalent grades (A, A-, B+...), but must record the final course grade as quality points (4.0, 3.7, 3.3 ...). He never discussed in class how he would translate letter grades into quality points. That's all you can jot down right now. But you had better be clear about your strategy and tactics before you walk into the Professor's office. Maybe you should discuss this with other students first. It's hard to say exactly what you should do. But there's not much time left. It's now 2 p.m. On Thursday, December 21 and your appointment with Professor Byrnes is at 9 a.m. on Friday, December 22.

Appendix 2: Negotiating With Your Professor:

Professor Observer

I . Concentrate on the professor during this simulation. Jot down your observations about the professor's behavior, emotions, use of words, tone of voice, approach toward the discussion, relationship with the student, attitude, and any other observable aspect of the professor's conduct

Appendix 3: Negotiating With Your Professor:

Student Observers

I . Concentrate on the student during this simulation. Jot down your observations about his/ her behavior, emotions, use of words, tone of voice, approach toward the discussion, relationship with the professor, attitude, and any other observable aspect of his/her conduct.

Groundhog Day:
Teach it Again...and Again...

Robert J. Robinson

Robert J. Robinson is
Associate Professor of
business administration
at the Harvard
Business School. His
mailing address is:
Morgan 143, Harvard
Business School,
Soldiers Field, Boston,
Mass. 02163.

The problem of teaching the same negotiation class again and
again, yet remaining fresh and spontaneous, is a dilemma familiar to academics. The situation is akin to that of characters in the
movie, *Groundhog Day*, living the same 24 hours over and over,
trying to get things "just right." This article reflects on this problem, and offers some advice.

There is a silly old joke about the fictitious but famous
Italian tenor Fabriccio, who, after many years on the recording and
commercial concert tour, returns to his roots to sing serious opera
in Rome. A little nervous about his technical skills in front of a
knowledgeable and critical audience, he goes on stage for his first
solo. He sings his heart out, and the audience responds by stomp-
ing their feet, whistling, and yelling, "Fabriccio, Fabriccio, sing it
again!" Touched by the sentiment, he glances over the orchestra
conductor, who nods, and Fabriccio launches into his solo again,
giving even more effort and emotion. Again the audience screams
out, "Fabriccio, Fabriccio, sing it again!" Spent, but inspired, Fabriccio
cues the orchestra, and launches into his number again. Singing
with every ounce of strength in his body, he ends triumphantly,
sinking to his knees, arms outstretched. Yet again, the audience
yells, "Fabriccio, Fabriccio, sing it again!" This time, however, being
closer to the front row, he hears the patrons there add, "you will
sing it again, and again—until you get it right!"

* * *

The other day I taught two sections of the same negotiation
class. Each class was comprised of about 80 executives, and the
two sessions were separated by 20 minutes.

The case for the day was the *Malta Story*, set in the
early 1970s, when the brilliant but erratic Maltese Prime Minister, Dom Mintoff, completely out-thought the British negotiators. Faced with a radical reduction in the rent paid for
the use of the dockyards in Malta, Mintoff, by adroitly playing
off Cold War tensions, actually triples the rent, gains a large
cash settlement, and in the process becomes the debutante of
the Mediterranean, courted by Libya, the Soviets, and NATO.

This article first
appeared in
Negotiation Journal,
January 1998:
Volume 14, Number
1, pages 87-91.

379

It is a wonderful story, and the discussion can be a dynamic one, exploring ethics, brinkmanship, and coalitional strategy.

In my first class, everything went according to plan—and then some. I had one of those days where I could see everyone, I could feel the emotions of the class, and I couldn't seem to make a wrong turn. The conversation flowed effortlessly. My questions seemed to extract the exact information I wanted, my jokes were received uproariously, comments were insightful and deep, and the class was completely engrossed. At the end of 80 minutes, the model I was working to describe had appeared, almost as if by magic, on the blackboards; the faces of virtually every student seemed to show expressions of deep insight (well, at least to me). Like Fabriccio, I concluded triumphantly, and the class roared in approval. There was warm applause, and at least a half-dozen students rushed down to express their enjoyment of the class, and to excitedly discuss points which they had not managed to get into during the class.

It was a transcendent moment for me as a teacher. One of my very best classes ever, and one of those moments when a case teacher knows they will seldom do better. Flushed with confidence, I extracted myself from my happy students, and strolled over to the next class. This should be simple, I reasoned: I would just do it again.

A Different Story

It would be too easy to say that the second class was a disaster. On a ten-point scale, it was probably a comfortable seven out of ten. Yet compared to the perfect "10" I had just experienced, it was a complete let-down. My timing was half a beat off, my jokes evoked smiles rather than raucous laughter, and my questions drew a smattering of hands, rather than the forest of urgently waving digits I had seen previously.

As the class progressed, the labor of trying to get things back to that giddy plateau became too much for me, and energy drained from my legs. I actually sat on the edge of the desk, something I had not done in the first class. I doggedly tried to recreate the conversation, and appealed in vain for the timely delivery of points that would allow me to construct my model on the board.

Rather than giving me what I wanted, the students kept raising annoying new points, forcing me from my perfect template. Pulling things together at the end, I noted to myself that my summary actually included a number of points we had not really discussed. My conclusion was met with polite applause, and far from being mobbed, I was left free to wander back to my office, shaking my head in disappointment, thinking about what had just happened.

In the movie *Groundhog Day*, the lead character, played by comedian Bill Murray, is a vain television weatherman, who inexplicably finds himself reliving the same day—over and over again. Worse yet, he is the only one who seems to notice what is happening. Eventually he decides that, as a shallow and uncaring man, the gods are punishing him; in order to get out of this situation, he has to get the friendly and vivacious new producer (played by Andie McDowell) to genuinely fall in love with him. Like a new teacher trying to learn how to deliver a new subject, his early attempts are ineffective, sometimes disastrous. But every day is a new day, and he slowly gets better.

One day, Murray decides to stop trying and just enjoy himself. The day goes surprisingly well. He is genuine, spontaneous, funny, and touching. McDowell finds new depth in the man, and they have a wonderful day together. At the end of the day, he tries for a goodnight kiss, and due to a minor misunderstanding, doesn't quite make it. Disappointed, yet encouraged by the otherwise perfect day, he reasons: No problem, I know what to fix at the end of the day, and otherwise I'll do everything else the same way tomorrow.

The next day is a disaster. Murray is artificial, posed, and tries to hurry events along to the things that "worked" the previous day. McDowell is repelled by the premeditated nature of his approach, and finds nothing of the man who so charmed her the previous day. Things predictably end disastrously.

Using the Same Script

Sitting somberly in my office after the two classes, the image of Bill Murray's bemused face popped into my head, and I realized what I had done. Inadvertently I had repeated his mistake. After somehow finding that magic and elusive formula for a great class, I had ignored what it was that made it successful. Instead of understanding that it was my spontaneity, willingness to go with the mood of the class, to wait for the right comment, and to simply channel the conversation, I had instead seized upon the content of what had transpired in the previous discussion. I had tried to turn my students into willing reciters of the exact same comments, in the exact same order that had come up in the first class. Instead of letting my own sense of humor guide the occasional joke, I mechanically told jokes that had "worked" at the same point in the previous class. In all, I was like Bill Murray on the second day: posed, artificial, and trying with grim determination to turn this occasion into the previous one.

How simple this insight seems to me now, yet how perpetual this problem.

In addition to teaching the same class twice on the same day, I teach the same class several times a year, year after year. In many ways, I and all those who teach for a living, are trapped in *Groundhog Day*. We try again, and again, for that perfect class, that day which lets us escape from the endless trying, and admits us, briefly, into pedagogical nirvana. Yet if we ever achieve that perfect class, we seldom repeat it; like Bill Murray, we confuse the style and substance of the thing, and pay attention to everything that does not matter.

While this problem probably faces all who teach the same material more than once, it seems to me that the difficulty is much more of a constant in the case of teaching in the area of negotiations. This is because in teaching negotiations we rely on the experiences of the students to guide the learning in the classroom. We have them do simulations and exercises, and then attempt to extract order from their chaotic and impressionistic experiences. We always want to be able to conclude the same things, and have a preferred way of getting there, and yet every time the experiences of the students are different.

Even in the case of the Malta discussion—a case, rather than an exercise—each new class reads the account with fresh eyes, and in a way which is unique from any group which has ever done so before. It is the job of the teacher to rediscover the insight in the case with the class, rather than to try, as I did the second time around, to herd them down a trail previously blazed.

The Secret of Professor X

When I was in graduate school, I worked one year as a teaching assistant for a famous teacher (called Professor X here), who is one of the greatest introductory psychology instructors who ever lived. Students wait their entire undergraduate academic career to be able to take his course, and the wait is well worth it. He is a brilliant pedagogue, capable of turning huge lecture theaters of 250 students into intimate discussion groups, and each class is a one-man play, replete with special effects, costume changes, and audience participation.

The year I served as Professor X's teaching assistant, and about three weeks before classes began, he casually mentioned during a meeting that he was "in a bit of a panic" because he had lost his notes for the course. Now, understand that these were not normal notes. These were more like the detailed schematics for a Broadway production, together with slides and other aids. You could have written a book from these notes. In fact, Professor X has written an introductory psychology text based on these notes, a textbook which has made him rich and famous, since it was (and is) the best-selling introductory psychology textbook in the world. So losing the notes which ran the elaborate productions which brought the textbook to life was no small matter.

"Gee," I said, "that's terrible!"

"Yes, lost my notes. Completely gone," said Professor X happily, and we went on. The course, three weeks later, was as brilliant as ever.

The next year, I was almost run over by Professor X as he rushed down the corridor.

"What's up?" I asked one of his harried-looking teaching assistants who were following him down the hall.

"Oh, it's just terrible," she replied, pale of face. "Professor X has lost all his intro psych notes."

At this point my brain went "Hmm..."But it wasn't until the following year, when Professor X lost his notes again three weeks before classes started, that I realized what was happening: The class was always fresh and vibrant because it was new every year. In order to find the challenge and joy in a course he had taught dozens of times, every year Professor X would throw his brilliant, wonderful notes away after the last class—and start from scratch again the next year.

I had never really understood what Professor X was doing (other than marveling at his commitment, and obvious masochism) until I started to reflect on the *Groundhog Day* phenomenon. While perhaps a little extreme, Professor X's strategy is perhaps the key to teaching the same class again, and again. Rather than trying to get it "just right," it is, of course the process of learning and discovery which contains the thrill to be found in the classroom.

To do this, we have to ask ourselves every time we teach: "If I had never taught this class before, what would I find most exciting about this case or lesson? How would I like to teach this? What is important here?" Our answers to these questions, if we are indeed growing and changing, could well be different from one occasion to the next.

And when we get into the classroom, we have to ask ourselves, "What is the class feeling today? What is unique about this group, here, now?" All too often, we use a cookbook approach, trying to get that balance of ingredients which has worked, sometimes better, sometimes worse, in the past.

And so we do it again, and again—always trying to get it right. Poor Fabriccio.